After obtaining his doctorate at Oxford, Christopher Duffy divided his time between researching history and teaching officer cadets and student officers at the Royal Military Academy Sandhust and the Army Staff College. From 1996 to 2001 he was Research Professor in the History of War at De Montfort University, and he now devotes himself entirely to travel and writing. He is the author of some twenty books, including The *Army of Frederick the Great* and *Siege Warfare*, and his work on European military history of the eighteenth century has won him international renown.

THROUGH GERMAN EYES

THE BRITISH AND THE SOMME 1916

Christopher Duffy

PHOENIX

A PHŒNIX PAPERBACK

First published in Great Britain in 2006
by Weidenfeld & Nicolson
This paperback edition published in 2007
by Phoenix,
an imprint of Orion Books Ltd,
Orion House, 5 Upper St Martin's Lane,
London WC2H 9EA

1 3 5 7 9 10 8 6 4 2

A CIP catalogue record for this book
is available from the British Library.

ISBN 978-0-7538-2202-9

Printed and bound in Great Britain by
Mackays of Chatham plc, Chatham, Kent

The Orion Publishing Group's policy is to use papers that
are natural, renewable and recyclable products and
made from wood grown in sustainable forests. The logging
and manufacturing processes are expected to conform to
the environmental regulations of the country of origin.

www.orionbooks.co.uk

IN MEMORY OF MY FATHER,

William Noel Duffy,

IRISH GUARDSMAN OF THE GREAT WAR

Contents

List of maps

List of illustrations

1. British prisoners under guard in a German train.

2. Nurse Cavell. The coup de grâce.

3. Four portrait studies by Otto Stiehl: English, Irish, Scottish and Canadian prisoners.

4. A support company of the Tyneside Irish Brigade advancing from the Tara-Usna Line, opposite La Boisselle, 1 July 1916.

5. British troops advancing to the attack.

6. British troops in gas masks.

7. The Fokker monoplane, the De Havilland DH-2 and the Nieuport.

8. Oswald Boelke.

9. A German anti-aircraft gun.

10. A British tank against unprotected German infantry.

11. British 9.2-inch howitzers.

Acknowledgements

I owe a great deal in the first place to Mrs Pam Bendall, as Librarian of the former Army Staff College in Camberley, who pointed me in the direction that led me to embark on the present enterprise. The foundation of the study was then formed by the holdings of the Bavarian War Archives (*Kriegsarchiv*) in Munich, which were made so cheerfully available by Dr Achim Fuchs and his staff; the documentation is both massive and easily accessible. The Bavarian Archive staff also gave me access to their rich stores of secondary German literature, as did the libraries of the Vienna War Archives (with the Max Paulsen collection of regimental histories), the London Library, the British Library and the library of the Imperial War Museum (London).

My former place of work, the Department of War Studies at the Royal Military Academy, Sandhurst, remains my spiritual home, and I profited much from conversations with Duncan Anderson, Lloyd Clark, David Hazel, Paul Harris, Paul Latawski, Michael Orr, Chris Pugsley and Klaus Schmider, and also with Jim Beach, Ian Fotheringham, Tony Heathcote, Nick Perry, Ian Passingham and others of the company of the *Tafelrund* of the Sandhurst WARDIG (War Studies Discussion Group). Andrew Orgill and his staff of the RMAS Library rendered assistance throughout.

Chris McCarthy (Imperial War Museum) put me much in his debt by reading the draft and correcting many an error. The remaining mistakes are to be laid to the account of my ignorance and obduracy.

Introduction

The Wider Setting

The troops were making their way to the new front. The grumbling of artillery, so familiar from Ypres, had lost none of its disturbing power, but surely here it would be different?

> What a welcome contrast! In place of the low plains of Flanders we had before us a countryside of gentle and appealing hills, with deeply sunken roads, broad hollows, and patches and wider spreads of woodland.[1] The Somme ... always a beautiful river, now excelled itself by dividing into a number of arms – they looked like lakes among the fresh green of the meadows and thickets. The little waves sparkled in the sun, and its light intensified the cheerful colours of the cows and horses as they grazed along the banks. The whole of nature breathed freshness and beauty.[2]

Only the sight of a distant clutch of a dozen captive balloons indicated 'where hell must be reigning on earth'.[3] Another two hours and the thunder was all too near, and invisible squadrons of aircraft were cruising somewhere among the clouds. The muddy road was narrowed by masses of rubble, and not a single one of the local people was to be seen, just more and more soldiers, cars and convoys, and in the background the artillery was muttering and bellowing ... Troops were pressing through, along with sick and wounded, and columns of vehicles laden with equipment, ammunition, entrenching tools and timber frames. Men were coming back in an extremity of exhaustion, clad in rags and tatters, and wearing the vacant expressions of cattle.[4]

A little further, and it became evident that something terrible had happened here.

Fresh and half-decomposed corpses had been ploughed into the torn-up earth. Staring eyes, open mouths and grinning teeth showed in hideous, blackened skulls. The slope leading up to the hill was covered with gas masks, contorted limbs, British and German rifles, lengths of barbed wire, bottles of wine, pots of jam, boots with human bones, wooden knife-rests, ammunition and fragments of countless thousands of shells. A narrow path indicated the way that was being followed night and day by the men as they hastened along in their terror and apprehension ... Then it was our great moment, when we had to enter our assigned positions.[5]

More and more shells were bursting around and above us, and we quickened our steps as we moved forward. I bustled along a side trench where the wounded were pressing against the sides to make room for us along the narrow passage ... I was startled by a piercing scream, which echoes in my ears even today. My bayonet scabbard had caught in the bandage of one of the wounded men. I was overcome with shock and remorse. I could only blurt out, 'Sorry, mate!'[6]

A glance over the parapet, and streaks of white across the opposite hillside revealed the presence of the unseen enemy, the British.

THIS BOOK IS WRITTEN from a particular perspective. It is not a comprehensive history of the Battle of the Somme, for that would demand, amongst other things, giving proper consideration to the involvement of the French. It is not, directly, the story of the Germans on the Somme. Its purpose is to set out the German view of, and interest in, the British performance and mentality as they were experienced in the course of that long struggle. The evidence is both copious and unfamiliar, and is to be found in official papers, histories, memoirs and letters, and most revealingly of all in the results of the interrogation of British prisoners of war.

The questioning by the German intelligence officers was more systematic and detailed than that employed by their British counterparts. It was also more open-ended, and encouraged the captured officers and men to speak freely and at length when they were still in shock from combat and capture. Their recollections are of unique interest because they were immediate, separated from the event by a matter of hours or a few days at the most, rather than being contaminated by the passage of time. Charles Carrington noted that the process was in full train by the 1930s, under 'the influence of later writers who invented the public image of "disenchantment" or "disillusion"'. He rightly set greater store by 'an earlier stage in the history of ideas'.[7] By the end of the twentieth century some of the last survivors had become 'Veterans General Issue, neatly packed with what we wanted to hear, exploding at the touch of a tape-recorder button or the snap of a TV documentarist's clapperboard. Up to my neck in muck and bullets; rats as big as footballs; the sergeant major was a right bastard; all my mates were killed.'[8]

If the present study is to have any value it must hold its focus, except where some kind of scene setting is called for. The place and the time were chosen for two reasons. The first is that 1916 was the year in which we find represented most comprehensively all the elements that made up the British Army in the Great War – the pre-war Regulars, the Territorials, the Kitchener volunteers and the first of the conscripts. It was also the year when the British Army first took a front-ranking role in the continental war (as the British officers and soldiers were ready to declare to the Germans), and in which army and public alike first came to know the nature and penalties of a full-scale confrontation with an extremely formidable enemy.

Conflict of this order (if not of this magnitude) was a matter of living memory on the European mainland, and we shall encounter two German commanders whose formative experiences actually came from the war of

1870–71, namely General von Gallwitz as a young officer of artillery, and General Sixt von Armin as a volunteer in the *Garde*, who was wounded at Saint-Privat. Geography, diplomacy and even language had combined to shield the British from reality. The French *bataille* and the German *Schlacht* signified 'slaughter' in a way that had been lost in the mundane British 'battle'. Likewise an obscure but most revealing connection linked *guerre* with one of the roots of the German *Verwirrung*, denoting 'confusion'.

Bloody turmoil is therefore inherent in combat, and the point is worth stressing when we come to look at the conduct of the Great War. Why were the British fighting at all? The origins of the war and the burden of 'war guilt' still divide the historians, but it is likely that an allied defeat would have established the Germans as masters of Belgium, and converted Antwerp and the northern Channel ports into German naval bases. German annexation of areas rich in coal and iron would have relegated France further down the ranks of industrial powers, and much of western Russia would have become a German economic colony, as actually happened for a time in 1918. German gains and the expansion of German influence in Africa, the Middle East and the Pacific would have fragmented the British Empire, and put the survival of British Australia and New Zealand in some doubt. In the German view the Irish and some at least of the Indians were gifted but oppressed peoples, ripe for liberation.

Having sent the British to war, we have to ask why they and their French allies were impelled to mount offensives so many times over and at such a cost. In part it was because almost any gain of ground was desirable if it held the Germans away from the remaining northern Channel ports, from the nodal point of Amiens, and not least from Paris, which represented so much to the allies in both symbolic and practical terms. If Berlin as an objective was impossibly distant, it was not unrealistic for the allies to think of gaining the Belgian ports, or of recovering the area of north-eastern France that lay under German occupation, which made up only 6 per cent of the national area but had accounted for 64 per cent of France's pre-war production of pig iron, 58 per cent of the steel and 40 per cent of the coal.[9] Worthwhile targets might lie closer to hand in the shape of a dominating ridge line, a nodal point of communication like Cambrai, or the prospect of cutting a transverse route like the road (the present N 17) that ran by way of Bapaume to Péronne, and helped the Germans to maintain a coherent defence of the Somme front.

In essence, unless the Germans were pushed off their ground they would be able to keep the military advantage and ultimately gain favourable terms of peace. The problem for the allies was how to undertake successful offensive action at a period when the balance in warfare had swung so heavily in favour of the defence. Napoleon had been able to exploit gaps and flanks, but that had been more than a hundred years before, and since then populations had expanded mightily, and generation upon generation of conscripts had been fed through the continental armies. By the end of 1914 the Western Front was packed with troops all the way from the Channel to the Swiss border, the gaps and the open flanks had disappeared, and a breakthrough could now be attained only by a frontal assault of one kind or another.

Commanders were being forced to come to terms with a major technological mismatch, which also told in favour of the defence. The simple device of barbed wire now made it possible to set up a cheap, speedy and effective barrier in front of positions. From the 1860s, moreover, firepower of every kind had gained immensely in range, volume and accuracy, and the losers were the troops who had to leave protection to advance across open ground. It was a relatively easy matter to lay down a curtain of defensive fire in front of one's own lines, but it took a colossal weight of accurate fire, amounting to the order of 400 pounds of shell per yard of trench, to destroy or suppress the defenders, and then at the cost of sacrificing surprise, and ploughing up the ground over which the infantry would have to attack.

It was not just a question of counting off the yards of front, for a German defensive position of 1916 usually consisted of an outlying improvised *Trichterstellung* (shell-hole position), a main position of multiple fighting and communication trenches, and further positions in existence or active preparation behind. Most attacks broke up in no man's land or the *Trichterstellung*, and even if a wide breach were effected in the main position, the attacker would then have to bring up his artillery and make other preparations to deal a completely new blow against the rearward position. These 'shock-absorbing' defences were to acquire still greater depth and resilience in the following year.

Advances in signals and transport – telegraphs, the telephone, the railway and motor vehicles – favoured communication and movement behind the fighting line, and helped the defender to move up reserves to the threatened points, but little useful technology was yet available to assist attacking troops across the battlefield. The men still had to struggle forward on foot, just as at the time of Napoleon, but now with considerably greater difficulty, for command and control were in a technical void. In the conditions of warfare at that time it was impossible to direct more than a tiny number of troops by voice alone, and the first generation of field radios made its appearance only towards the end of the war. Most senior commanders (contrary to myth) did what they could to keep in contact with the progress of the fighting, but news of success or failure usually came too late to enable them to do anything about it. Infantry reserves were rarely at hand to exploit an opening, and logistics dictated that cavalry – a potentially valuable means of exploiting in depth – was held further still to the rear. The outcome of even a 'successful' attack was more often than not to produce a 'salient', a saucer-shaped bulge in the enemy defences, which might leave the attacker worse off than before, as he would now be coming under fire from the flanks as well as from the front.

The British commanders of 1916 reached no consensus as to how to overcome the daunting obstacles that they faced. The Fourth Army became the chief instrument of the offensive on the Somme, and its commander, General Sir Henry Rawlinson, preferred not to test the boundaries of what was possible, but rather to achieve objectives that lay within the capacity of the troops and technology available to him. What he called his 'bite and hold' or 'step by step' form of attack was actually designed to reclaim the advantages of the defensive from the enemy, and he explained to Haig in a much-quoted letter that 'our objective ... seems to me to kill as many Germans as possible with the least loss to ourselves, and the best way to do this appears to me to be to seize points of tactical importance which will provide us with good observation and which we may feel quite certain the Germans will counter attack'.[10]

In his *Final Dispatch* of 1919 Field Marshal Sir Douglas Haig, as overall commander of the British Expeditionary Force, claimed that the British offensives between 1915 and 1918 formed in effect one battle, which ultimately wore down the German forces. That might have been the outcome, but it is doubtful whether he had that in mind when he opened his offensive on the Somme. General Sir Hubert Gough, who commanded on the northern wing from 2 July, gave the lie when he wrote some time after the war that 'we always thought that the capture of the front line, or at most the second line, would ensure a complete victory and the retreat of the whole hostile army, however narrow was the front of the attack ... We were always looking for the GAP, and trying to make it, hoping that we would pour through it in a glorious, exciting rush, and so put an end to any more heavy fighting.'[11]

Organisation and Terminology

The investigation of military structures is not calculated to grip the imagination of readers, except those of a certain mentality, but a general acquaintance with formations and units does help us to make sense of what happened on the Somme in 1916. The information is particularly relevant when we try to draw any comparison between the British and German forces, because the same designations can cover quite different entities.

THE BRITISH

HIGH COMMAND

In 1916 Sir Douglas Haig held the rank of full general, and from his headquarters in Montreuil he commanded the sixty or so divisions of the British Expeditionary Force. He was answerable to the coalition government in London, which was headed until early December by the Liberal prime minister Herbert Henry Asquith. The Cabinet's War Committee took its military advice from the shrewd ex-ranker General Sir William ('Wully') Robertson, as Chief of an enhanced Imperial General Staff. There was a consequent diminution in the power of the successive Secretaries of State for War, the charismatic Lord Kitchener (died 5 June) and David Lloyd George (succeeded as prime minister on 7 December).

ARMIES

An army was a large formation of no fixed size, and numbered between 200,000 and 300,000 men. It was normally commanded by a full general, and consisted of three or so corps. Three such British armies were engaged on the Somme:

- Third Army (General Sir Edmund 'Bull' Allenby) only marginally, on the left flank;

- Reserve Army (General Sir Hubert Gough), formed out of divisions on the left wing on 2 July, and redesignated the Fifth Army on 29 October;

- Fourth Army (General Sir Henry Rawlinson) on the right wing.

The style of command could differ fundamentally from one army to the next. Gough was an impatient and abrasive individual, who could interfere directly in the affairs of the divisions, as when he stampeded the 32nd Division into the attack on 2 July, or the 2nd Australian Division into assaulting Pozières on the 29th of that month. Rawlinson was more inclined to stand back from the detailed business of command.

CORPS

The corps level of command had originated in continental Europe at the time of the Napoleonic Wars, when it brought together the divisions (and their component formations and units) into manageable groupings. In the Grande Armée the corps had been commanded by marshals, many of whom were household names, which emphasises the point that one of the great advantages of the system was seen as giving a large body of men a distinctive character and a literal *esprit de corps*. For the British the corps was an unfamiliar concept, having been introduced for active service only in 1914. By the time of the Battle of the Somme the British corps was evolving fast, having acquired greater responsibility for artillery support, traffic management and planning, but it sacrificed one of its potentials by remaining little more than a headquarters or holding bag for two or more shifting divisions. The corps commander therefore had little incentive to train up any particular division, for he knew that he must lose it sooner or later to somebody else. The Canadian Corps (Lieutenant General Sir Julian Byng) and the antipodean Anzac Corps (Lieutenant General Sir William 'Birdy' Birdwood) were much closer to the original inspiration of the corps, for they had the advantage of being stable formations, which made training and development much more worthwhile over the long term. They enjoyed, moreover, a direct line of political authority to their home governments.

DIVISIONS

The division was commanded by a major general, and comprised at full strength some 12,000 infantry, together with artillery and other supporting arms and services, which brought the total to about 19,000 troops. On the Somme the division occupied a frontage of 2,000 yards or even less, and in such a way the first three days of the battle could cost Tom Bridge's 19th (Western) Division 3,500 men in an area 'not much larger than Trafalgar Square'.[12] According to Australian Major General John Monash, by one account 'the ablest soldier of the war',[13] the division was 'the nearest point to the front where co-ordination of all arms took place, where reserves could be committed, where plans could be significantly modified. It was also the key point for the collection and transmission of information to corps, army and GHQ.'[14] The division was a stable fighting entity, which could be imbued with the character of the commander and the material of its recruiting area, though few divisions could be counted as consistently 'good' or 'bad', regardless of a great deal of myth-making during and after the war.

- Most of the Regular Army divisions on the Somme bore numbers that came early in the scale (1–8, 29). The Guards Division (formed in 1915) stood apart, as claiming precedence but being altogether too grand to consent to be numbered;

- The numbers of the Territorial Force divisions on the Somme fell mostly in the forties and the fifties (46–51, 55, 56);

- The New Army divisions on the Somme had two runs of numbers, one mostly in the teens and early twenties (9, 11, 12, 14–15), and the other mostly in the thirties (30–41, 63).

BRIGADES

The three brigades of a division were usually deployed as two in the front line and one in close reserve. The individual brigade was commanded by a brigadier general, and comprised four battalions, which gave the division as a whole a total of twelve such battalions, with a further battalion designated (sometimes against its will) as Pioneers. A brigade at full complement numbered nearly 4,000 infantry, though combat strengths stood at nearer 3,000.

REGIMENTS

For all the talk of 'regimental spirit', the regiment as such did not appear in the order of battle, since the component battalions of British regiments might well be split between totally different theatres of war. However, there was no set limit to the number of battalions in a regiment, and a concentration of battalions from a single regiment could give a Territorial or New Army division a strongly tribal character, such as the presence of the multi-battalion London Regiment in the 47th and 56th Divisions of Territorials, or that of nine battalions of the Northumberland Fusiliers in the New Army 34th Division.

BATTALIONS

The battalion of four companies was commanded by a lieutenant colonel, and at its rarely attained full strength numbered 997 officers and men. The battalion was a focus of loyalty which compared with that of the division at the higher level. Indeed the fate of the Pals battalions has become almost synonymous with the first day of the Somme, though there were many others that were just as worthy of record, even within the New Army. The battalion was identified by a number and a slash, thus the 15/West Yorkshire Regiment denoted the 15th Battalion of the West Yorkshire Regiment, better known by its unofficial designation as the battalion of the Leeds Pals.

COMPANIES

The company of four platoons was commanded by a major or captain, and had a typical combat strength of about two hundred of all ranks.

PLATOONS

The platoon of some fifty men was a lieutenant's or second lieutenant's command. As a fighting sub-unit, equipped with a spread of weapons, the platoon became the basis of British tactics as they developed from January 1917.

SECTIONS

The section, the most basic sub-unit, was a force of up to a dozen men commanded by a corporal.

THE GERMANS

HIGH COMMAND

Supreme command was invested nominally in Kaiser Wilhelm II and his Supreme Headquarters (*Oberste Heeresleitung*), and under him in the Great General Staff, headed at the opening of the Battle of the Somme by General Erich von Falkenhayn. In 1916 the credit of both Kaiser and Falkenhayn was waning, and on 29 August far-reaching power was invested in Field Marshal Paul von Hindenburg as the new Chief of the General Staff, and his close associate General Erich von Ludendorff as First Quartermaster-General. At the same time a period of prolonged organisational instability on the Western Front was brought to an end when Crown Prince Rupprecht of Bavaria assumed command of a new army group which was responsible for the effort against the British and French on the Somme. The Kaiser's son Crown Prince Wilhelm ('Little Willy') commanded the companion *Heeresgruppe Deutscher Kronprinz* on the declining Verdun front.

ARMY CORPS

The classic continental model of the corps served the Germans very well until its admirable stability was overset by losses and piecemeal reinforcements in the first days of the Battle of the Somme. From the middle of July and under the pressure of circumstances the Germans were forced to adopt something closer to the British pattern, with its population of shifting divisions. Thus the old XIV Army Corps was transmuted into the *Gruppe Stein*, and the IV Army Corps into the *Gruppe*

Sixt von Armin. The shift of emphasis from the structure to the name of the commander was significant, and a *Gruppe* of this kind might contain between two and six divisions, though three or four at a time were more common.

DIVISIONS

The German division of about 17,600 men corresponded closely with its British counterpart, and was likewise made up of twelve battalions, and about the same complement of artillery – seventy-two barrels as opposed to the British seventy-six.

REGIMENTS AND BATTALIONS

In 1915 the Germans had abolished the brigade level of field command as an unnecessary complication. The standard regiment of about 4,400 troops was in any case a large body that equated almost exactly with the British brigade in both size and deployment. It comprised twelve consecutively numbered companies, grouped four at a time in three battalions, numbered I, II and III. The first and second battalions were usually placed in the front of the battle line, and the third in close support. The battalions in turn were made up of four companies each.

DESIGNATIONS AND ETHOS

The titles of German formations, units and personnel appear at first sight to be as complicated as German wine labels, but were organised on identifiable principles. *Reserve* in German usage does not signify a reserve in the operational or tactical sense, but formations and units made up of personnel who had most recently completed their two years of conscript service. *Landwehr* and *Landsturm* designated successively older age groups. *Ersatz* formations and units were made up of men who were physically fit, but who for one reason or another had not been called up for the normal conscript service. The terms *Garde*, *Grenadier* or *Füsilier* related to elite status or historical origins, and did not betoken any essential difference in organisation.

After 1871, as a sign of newly found national unity, the regiments of the German army were given a common sequence of numbers, which reached well into the hundreds, only the Bavarians standing aloof with their separate numbering system. However, the German Empire had a federal structure, made up of the states of Prussia, Württemberg and Saxony as well as Bavaria, and the federal states themselves incorporated many smaller entities that had lost their sovereign independence. As a relic of olden times the full titles of the regiments therefore retained their historic regional numberings in addition to the common sequence. Thus the 88th Infantry Regiment was also the Royal Prussian 2nd Nassau Infantry Regiment, the full title being *Das König. Preuss. 2. Nassauische Infanterie Regiment Nr. 88*. Some regiments added the name of an historical figure, or that of a living colonel-in-chief, usually of a royal or ducal house.

Something of a truly German national army emerged only in the 1930s. A veteran remarked that 'our proud 12th Grenadier Regiment Prince Carl of Prussia has ceased to exist – and it will never be called back to life. For the whole of the period of our youth we had every reason to believe that the Empire, under whose protection we lived, by which I mean the Second German Empire of 18 January 1871, had represented the final political evolution of the German people. But now we know it was only a step towards final German unification. Its accomplishment we owe to our Führer, Adolf Hitler.'[15] It had been otherwise in the Great War, when 'mighty differences stood out when it was a question of who was to be relieved by whom, who might be your neighbours in combat, or when you might be applying for billets – and then the legendary "fellow feeling" might vanish altogether, for the experience of going into quarters depended enormously on whether the town major was a Bavarian, a Saxon or a Prussian'.[16]

Germans and British alike regarded the Prussians as the least biddable element in the German army, and other Germans often got word to the enemy trenches that they themselves did not come from that part of the world, or when they were going to be relieved by those people, so that the British would give them a bad time. They were 'damned Prussian pigs' according to the Württembergers,[17] and a prisoner told the British that he 'saw many troops passing through Bapaume, but could not tell what troops they were, because the State badge is being covered up to avoid quarrels between various states, particularly between Prussians and Bavarians'.[18]

The Württembergers were renowned among the Germans as serious and hard-working people, and their pride was engaged heavily in holding the Thiepval sector in the Battle of the Somme. The 'dark-haired Bavarian types' were not particularly aggressive, but proved to be cohesive and obstinate in the defence, and capable of launching some determined counterattacks. The Saxons as a whole were the 'most decent of the bunch',[19] but still showed considerable local variations, with the rural-based 40th Division remaining solid, while the 24th hailed from the western industrial areas and was being undermined in morale by socialism. Poles and Alsace-Lorrainers were a source of potential instability in whatever unit or formation they might be found.

In 1916 the German Army was still remote from disaffection on any significant scale, and one of its great strengths, deriving from the old Prussian tradition, was its philosophy of command. Ever since the Napoleonic Wars the formations were directed by a commander-in-chief and a chief of staff who worked almost as co-equals in a military marriage – the first supplying leadership and energy, or at least the prestige of high birth, and the chief of staff the element of rational calculation. Orders throughout the army were issued in the expectation that subordinates would seize on the essential points of what was to be achieved, but think for themselves when it came to the execution; one of the results was that authority was devolved down the chain of command, with German NCOs exercising many of the functions that would have been carried out in the British Army by lieutenants or even captains. The German units were therefore much more lightly officered than their British counterparts.

SOME USAGES

In former times the word 'English' was used on the Continent in a much wider sense than now. In translating from German sources I have therefore felt free to substitute the word 'British' where this seems more appropriate. The Germans, as defenders, naturally write of dugout 'exits' (*Ausgänge*) where the British encountered 'entrances'.

In conformity with the standard military usage 'shrapnel' denotes balls discharged from an air-burst shell, and 'splinters' the fragments from the casing of a shell or mortar bomb. Again, 'barrage' is used not to signify a generalised bombardment, but a wall of artillery fire, as is much clearer in the German *Sperrfeuer* or the original French *barrage*, which preserve the direct connection with 'barrier' or 'dam'. I was tempted to invent the term 'barrier fire', to make the meaning clear, but hesitated to enrage the purists. They will be offended in any case by the way I employ 'grenade' interchangeably with 'bomb', the latter being the official British usage from early 1916, for the Grenadier Guards had insisted that they alone were entitled to use the word 'grenade'.

As regards defences, 'trench' signifies an individual trench, whereas 'line' or 'position' applies to a coherent system made up of two or more fighting trenches and the necessary communication trenches. A 'redoubt' is a strongpoint with all-round defence, set in such a position.

Some German words have been left untranslated, to avoid clumsy circumlocutions. A *Trichterstellung*, as already indicated, was an ad hoc position established in shell-holes in front of the proper defences. An *Engländernest* signifies an improvised but strong position dug by infiltrating British troops. *Trommelfeuer* (lit. 'drum fire') was artillery fire of such intensity that the sound of the individual explosions merged into a continuous roar.

Sir Launcelot Kiggel, Haig's chief of staff, pronounced his name as 'Kidgell'.

PART ONE

THE MEN AND THE NATIONS

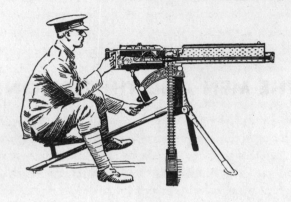

CHAPTER ONE

Knowing the Enemy

When we look into the cultural and military interchange of Germany and Britain in the early twentieth century we are brought face to face with a series of paradoxes. The overt manifestations of hostility among the British ranged from the populist and crude (the anti-German riots in October 1914 and May 1915, the pages of *John Bull* and the like) to the pseudo-intellectual. The Germans on their side were being told about 'the almost incomparable bravery of the French army and the sacrifice of the Russian soldiers', but were asked to believe that the Germans were fighting above all 'English gold, English tenacity and the imperturbability of English political methods'.[1] The British were condemned as the instigators of the war. They had joined with the French and Russians to exert a continental stranglehold, and their navy and their global empire stood directly in the way of a young Germany that was striving for its place in the sun.

The British character was supposed to be a denial of German values. The Anglo-Saxon race had been corrupted by Celtic and Jewish

influences, and by a selfishly mercantile outlook (*Manchestertum*) origi-
nating in the sixteenth and seventeenth centuries, which elevated private
profit above the good of the community. As the Germans could see in
the trenches, it was the mentality of 'got mittens' as opposed to *Gott mit
uns*! [God with us]. The beefy British ignoramuses – unresponsive to
religion, scholarship and heroic ideals – found their fulfilment in a
demeaning *Sportsidiotismus*. Some of the first British taken prisoner in
1914 tried to shake hands with their German captors, just as if it had
been at the close of a football match, and 'they were shocked when they
received the appropriate response: namely, a kick in a certain part of the
body'.[2] The German accounts indicate that their troops viewed the
prospect of facing the British with a heightened interest. A gun detach-
ment cheered when it sent its first round on its way on the Ancre on
5 November 1916, for 'this was the first time that we were facing the
British, and we had a particular score to settle with them. Was it not the
politics of the British which had encircled us with enemies?'[3]

These antagonisms had been generated artificially, for in other respects
the relations between British and Germans had been extraordinarily
close, and indeed had shown signs of developing into an Anglo-German
culture. German social elites were aping what they took to be the
yachting, fox-hunting and country-house style of the British landed
aristocracy, to the extent that Crown Prince Wilhelm built a replica
Tudor mansion, the Cecilienhof, amid the lakes and pinewoods of
Potsdam. The stone above the entrance bears the date '1916'. Four years
earlier, in an exchange of views with the former prime minister A. J.
Balfour, Karl Max Prince Lichnowski wrote only half-jestingly 'now
that British customs, fashions, sport and play have conquered the world
… there is no ground why the English example should not hold with
regard to the fleet'.[4]

The British royal family was related many times over to German
counterparts, and not least to those minor Protestant houses of central
Germany that were the most immediate victims of Prussian aggrandis-
ement. However, it was not easy for the uninformed British public to
distinguish between various kinds of Germans, and the most prominent
victim of popular outcry was Louis Alexander Prince of Battenberg,
who was forced to resign as First Sea Lord in October 1914. Relative

obscurity spared the career of Major General Albert Edward Count Gleichen, son of Victor Prince of Hohenlohe-Langenburg, who was another British admiral and a nephew of Queen Victoria. Count Gleichen commanded the British 37th Division from 1915 to 1916, and then organised and directed the Intelligence Bureau in the Department of Information. He once took a sentry to task for failing to shoot a German who had been in plain view. 'Shoot him? Why, Lor' bless you sir, 'e's never done me no harm.'[5] (Among his gifted sisters the Lady Feodora was a monumental sculptress – and pig breeder – and the Lady Helena a painter who received the Italian Medal of Valour for her medical services on the Alpine front.)

Sir Edward Elgar, so easily dismissed as a bewhiskered epitome of Edwardian and Georgian patriotism, was steeped in the musical life of Central Europe rather than in the 'cowpat' idiom cultivated by Ralph Vaughan Williams and George Butterworth, and his circle in London was populated heavily with men and women of German extraction or nationality. Indeed, the form in which much of his music has come down to us is through the agency of August Johannes Jaeger, his editor at the publisher, Novello. A comparable milieu formed around the Bavarian-born Sir Hubert von Herkomer (1849–1914), whose art school at Bushey gained worldwide renown.

Just as British universities had been inspired by their admiration for German *Wisssenschaft* to embrace the alien German concept of the research doctorate, so German students by the hundred took to studying at Oxford, and the names of some of them are listed on the memorial to the war dead in New College. There was German blood in the families of Siegfried Sassoon, Ford Madox Ford and Robert Graves, the last being related on his mother's side to the line of Saxon country pastors that gave rise to the historian 'von' Ranke, who was Robert's great-uncle.

Graves had an uncle who was a middle-aged lieutenant in the Bavarian artillery, and a cousin, Conrad, a Bavarian major who was awarded the *Pour le Mérite*. Graves writes that 'in the trenches ... I happened to belong to a company mess in which four of us young officers out of five had, by a coincidence, either German mothers or naturalised German fathers'.[6] German names, in fact, occur frequently among all ranks in the British services in the Great War. A cursory glance at the technical branches in 1916 alone shows Major General Sir Stanley von Donop as Master General of the Ordnance, Brigadier General Acton Lemuel Schreiber as commanding the engineers of the III Corps, and Lieutenant Colonel Frederick Gordon Guggisberg working under his authority as chief engineer to its 8th Division.

Survivals like these testify to generations of connections between the two peoples, dating from the time of medieval merchants, and augmented since by clients of the House of Hanover, by religious and political refugees, and by commercial links at every level. Colonel Richard Meinertzhagen, descended from a merchant family of Bremen, is renowned in the history of the Great War as one of the most deadly and ingenious of the British intelligence officers, and he was an even more enthusiastic German-killer than Count Gleichen. Members of the banking houses of Rothschild, Kleinwort and Schröder might aspire to the ways of the British gentry, while the fast-industrialising aspect of Germany was represented by the British branch of the electrical engineers Siemens-Halske, and by the giant chemical concern of Brunner, Mond & Co (founded 1873, and the ancestor of ICI). British ladies and gentlemen inflated the tyres of their bicycles with Bluemel (i.e. Blümel) pumps, and the first British tanks were powered by Daimler engines. When the British looked for a source of liquid chlorine in 1915, the only British firm capable of producing the toxin proved to be the Castner-Kellner Alkali Company. Lesser German folk came in great quantities, often in search of temporary employment, and the 35th (Bantam) Division found that in each batch of its prisoners 'there were fellows who spoke perfect English, having lived in England as waiters and hairdressers, or clerks, or merchants'.[7]

These manifold connections are central to our story, for they encouraged the German intelligence service in its ambition to build a comprehensive picture of the life and mentality of the British as enemies. Poor, blinded Captain Gilbert Nobbs halted at Aachen on his way to repatriation by way of Holland. The German senior medical officer told him that his sergeant major was eager to visit him, and would like to bring along a friend and a bottle of wine. Nobbs' first doubts were put to rest. 'They were Germans who lived in England and worked in the Deutsche Bank in George Yard, Lombard Street.' They turned the conversation to British public opinion, the military contribution of the Dominions, the state of affairs in Ireland, and the British government's tolerance of strikes (all subjects of lively interest to German intelligence). 'I soon found that they were not bad fellows at all.'[8] Nobbs relates the story in all innocence, not grasping how completely he had been taken in.

The British intelligence was less well served – either because fewer British bothered to learn German in the first place, or because German-speakers were wasted by having enlisted in the fighting arms. Brigadier General John Charteris complained on 15 November 1916 how 'somebody at home tried to saddle us with a man for intelligence work who was said to be an excellent German scholar. He translated *mit Rücksicht darauf* ['in relation to'] as "in marching order", probably with some idea in his mind about rucksacks; and better still, that *bei Aufstellung der Colonnen* ['in forming the columns'], as "by order of the colonel".'[9]

As for the battlefield, great armies of British and Germans were in close confrontation on the Somme, 'but enemy were invisible. Our sleepy sentries heard him cough from the far side of the craters. He patrolled, and we patrolled. But patrols had a sensible habit of avoiding personal contacts with one another.'[10] When it came to taking or sparing life the behaviour of the troops was governed as much by ancient usages of war as by the current antagonisms. In a much-quoted passage Robert Graves wrote that 'the troops with the worst reputation for violence against prisoners were the Canadians (and later the Australians)'.[11] The grudges of the Canadians dated in part from an episode at Ypres in 1915, when Germans were reported to have crucified a Canadian prisoner on a door with bayonets.[12] In fact German prisoners made their way back unscathed from Courcelette on 15 September through wave after wave of advancing Canadians, and German accounts also make specific mention of the good treatment of the men taken by the Canadians at Mouquet Farm on the 26th of the same month. Likewise the 'merciless' Australians were happy to participate in the 'give and take' which reigned towards the end of the campaign along the Ancre, and in front of the Butte de Warlencourt where 'both sides apparently left the killing to be done by the artillery unless an attack was launched'.[13]

There exists, on the other hand, trustworthy evidence as to the British 18th Division's authorised mass killing of surrendered Germans at Thiepval on 26 September, and the Lewis-gunning of German prisoners by the 51st (Highland) Division at Y Ravine on 13 November.[14] The 36th (Ulster) Division and the Grenadier Guards were as tough on the enemy as they were on themselves, and Lieutenant Brian Lawrence of the latter regiment writes casually of an episode in front of le Transloy when he 'noticed a party of Boches walking ... towards our lines, probably to surrender, as our men did not shoot. I told the Lewis gunners to fire, which they did, and I don't think many of the Boches returned to tell the tale.'[15]

Graves is probably sounder when he refers to the wide range of reasons or pretexts that could be evoked to justify atrocities. In some cases a specific order might have gone out in advance, like the one which baffled a German soldier in August: 'We have real English in front of us, and have orders to take no prisoners but to despatch them all with the bayonet; not a bad idea, but they always get prisoners from us too, and what do they do with them?'[16] Prisoners might well be too inconvenient to be allowed to live. On 18 July a counterattack by the German 26th Regiment carried halfway up the length of Longueval, where the Germans found that a large number of British had taken refuge in deep dugouts. 'But they were quick to show themselves. They could easily have put up a fight, for we made up just a handful of little fellows, but they instead stood on the upper steps and hastened to raise their hands. We could not escort them back, and so we made short work of them with hand grenades.'[17]

Survival of individuals or small groups often hung upon a notion of some kind of fair exchange. Taken by surprise in one of the Somme woods, a small party of British wisely threw aside their rifles without hesitation and put themselves at the mercy of Lieutenant Störel and his patrol of the 72nd Regiment. The British took out small treasures and offered them to the Germans, though 'to judge by a pair of shilling pieces which an extremely young lad tried to press into my hand, the poor devils did not put too high a price on their lives. "Look here," said one of my men, "what do I want with money? I'm after cigarettes!" It was not long before we all had fags sprouting from our lips.'[18]

Bargaining was scarcely possible when the captured troops were specialists who might have been responsible for killing hundreds of your comrades. Gallwitz writes that German prisoners had seen how 'two of our *Minenwerfer* [trench mortar] officers were shot or beaten to death with rifle butts. In general our pioneers, *Minenwerfer* operators and machine-gunners were treated more badly than infantrymen. Chivalry diminished according to a kind of graduated scale.'[19] At the Butte de Warlencourt on 5 November a Durham Light Infantryman laid a grenade on the chest of a wounded German machine-gunner and blew him to bits.[20]

On the other hand the high command on both sides strove in vain to 'combat the inclination of the troops not to provoke the enemy'.[21] Captured Bavarians were received kindly by the Catholic Irish of the 16th Division at Ginchy on 9 September, while the testimony of Private Giles Eyre shows that the 2/King's Royal Rifle Corps got on well with a variety of north-west Germans in the opposite trenches. A regiment of Holsteiners was able to throw across cigars and bottles of schnapps in return for bully beef and jam, and a certain 'Johann' entertained the British with light classical airs on his violin until the recital was ended by British mortar bombs, which in turn brought on a full-scale exchange of fire by the artillery.[22] Eyre was later captured by a Hanoverian regiment which bore the battle honour *Gibraltar* on a blue band on its sleeves, and he was treated well.

To have a prisoner in one's hands deprived the enemy of his services as effectively as if he had been killed, and, unlike a corpse, he might be able to tell you something of value. It is therefore important to look more closely at the circumstances in which a soldier might pass from the disposal of one army to the other. One of this kind manifested itself before the German 84th Reserve Regiment near Martinpuich early on the foggy morning of 20 July.

'Halt! Who goes there?' A huge lad appeared like a vision about fifty metres in front of our trench. He appeared to be a good ten metres tall and another two wide … and his round helmet looked like a huge parasol. Some of our men released their safety catches, but we gave the order not to fire as we wanted to see what kind of enemy this might be. We called out several times in English that he could approach, for we would not open fire, and finally he dared to come nearer, his hands still raised. He was a nineteen-year-old deserter. On his shoulder he carried the name *Duke of Wellington's* [49th (West Riding) Division (Territorial Force)]. He was a survivor of the attack which had just failed, and during the retreat he and others remained flat on the ground, intending to desert this morning. Another ten men duly appeared one by one.[23]

Deserters typically told the Germans that they had been reduced to a state of desperation by the conditions in the trenches, and by being driven into hopeless attacks.

There were signs of some calculation in cases like that of the Royal Fusilier Joseph Lippmann, who volunteered for a patrol just because it would give him a chance to come over to the Germans,[24] or the sergeant of the 13/Durham Light Infantry who deserted west of le Sars on 7 October. 'The prisoner is an old soldier, who had already fought at Gallipoli and been wounded there ... The prisoner had been lying along with twelve others in a stretch of trench with nobody else to their right or left. He tried to persuade his comrades to desert, for they were all weary of the fighting, but they would not follow him because they feared they would be shot by the Germans.'[25] He told the Germans about impending attacks by the 23rd and 47th Divisions, and in the course of two interviews he gave them details of what he had seen of a tank at close quarters.

Much of what the Germans learned of the life of the British soldier behind the front line came from a corporal of the 7/Cameron Highlanders, who deserted from the same location. He was an Englishman, a clerk in a big firm of accountants, who had chosen to join a Highland regiment out of misplaced feelings of romance (see p. 72).[26] It was rare to find a man of such education among the deserters. More representative was an obvious inadequate like the King's Own Scottish Borderer who abandoned the 2nd Battalion early in September. 'He is forty-eight years old. He has been a soldier for more than twenty-two years, but he is a drunkard and has never been promoted. Not long ago he was withdrawn from front-line service and did duty as an officer's servant and the battalion barber. On account of a drunken bout he was awarded fourteen days' Field Punishment, after which he was returned to the front line as a further penalty. He was so angry that he decided to desert.'[27]

The German officers, as upholders of military virtue, regarded the deserters with suspicion and distaste. They prized honest prisoners of war more highly in every respect. According to the chief of German military intelligence, Colonel Nicolai, 'the secret service behind the enemy lines was ... so restricted that, alone, it could not satisfy the needs of the army commands and of the supreme command. Our greatest and most valuable source of news in the western theatre of war – and at the front line the only one – was furnished by prisoners of war.'[28]

On the presumption that they were to take prisoners, the German troops near la Boisselle in July were told to learn a number of expressions by heart:

1. When Englishmen are met in the trenches, shout 'Hands up, you fool', to be pronounced *Hands opp ju fohl*, 'Arms away', *Arms ewa*.

2. At the entrance of a dugout, cry 'Is anybody inside?' *Is anibodi inseid?*

3. After throwing in a hand grenade, shout out, 'Come all out quick, quick'. *Kom ohl aut, quick, quick.*

4. If the Englishmen come out, shout at them, 'Hands up, come on Tommy'. *Honds opp, kom on Tomy.*

5. If the fellows want hurrying cry out, 'Go on, go on'.[29]

Altogether 192,319 British were taken prisoner by the Germans in the Great War. The really large hauls (75,000) were made at the start of the German spring offensive in 1918, but the Germans believed that by earlier standards the numbers they had captured on the Somme in 1916 were still significant, namely:

July, August, September	2,669
October	390
November	1,232
TOTAL	4,291[30]

By the middle of October it was reckoned that 'most of them were taken in the course of major attacks, others on patrol. We rarely have the impression that we are dealing with deserters.'[31]

By the harvest of 'major attacks' the Germans signified the human wreckage which was found after failed British assaults in no man's land, in the German trenches and, in surprisingly large numbers, among parties cut off behind German lines. Many other troops were taken by German counterattacks, and many again were captured when they were trying to find their way back to their own positions. The most celebrated example of a loser-of-his-way was that of William Smith, who had put in many years of service with the Gordon Highlanders, but who had the post of RSM in the 14/London Scottish when he was taken near Morval on 7 September. 'He relates that at eight this morning he decided to go for a stroll. Before long he reached a village [Combles], and after leaving by the north-west corner he stopped in front of a German bookstall. When asked how he had come through the enemy positions, Smith declares that he had seen no sign of wire or trenches, and that there were no Germans to be seen in the village itself. From there he continued on his way in a northerly direction until he was taken prisoner south-east of Morval by two pioneers who were engaged in digging.'[32] The German corps commander Kirchbach was scandalised by the lack of German vigilance.

Lieutenant Ernst Jünger writes that it was all to easy to lose orientation in the wasteland of shell-holes, and that the British could also be stranded among the German trenches in the course of trench raids. In June the British failed in an assault on the trenches of his 73rd Fusiliers in front of Combles. Only one of the enemy got through the wire, and this 'single exception Brecht – who, before the war, had been a plantation owner in America – now seized by the throat, and greeted with the words, "Come here, you son of a bitch!" The captive was presently being treated to a glass of wine ... He was a tall fellow, very young, fresh-faced, with fair hair.'[33]

Unusually detailed and matching evidence from both sides has recorded the career and capture of Lieutenant F. W. Harvey of the 2/5 Gloucesters. He was a solicitor in civilian life, who had volunteered on 8 August 1914, and was eventually commissioned on the record of his success in trench raids. Sheer bravado impelled him to go out on a one-man reconnaissance on 16 August 1916, and 'he made his way without being noticed through the wire and entered our first [German] trench, which was unoccupied along that sector. But then he heard footsteps to his left, and retired a short stretch along the trench to the right. When he turned a corner he was captured by some soldiers who were sitting in front of a dugout. He explains that he had failed to notice it because he was looking for a place where he could climb out of the rearward side of the trench and hide behind the parados. From there he thought he would be in a good position to ascertain the numbers of our machine guns and the strength of the defenders, for they were all still looking towards the enemy. He was armed with a revolver.'[34] This corresponds almost exactly with Harvey's own account, and he adds that one of the German soldiers 'looked so ridiculously like a certain labourer I had left working on my father's farm in England that I simply burst out laughing – which possibly saved my life'.[35]

The German standing orders laid down that the British prisoners were to be forwarded as soon as possible to the relevant army headquarters, whether in Saint-Quentin, Lille, Douai or other places, for 'in the conditions of trench warfare prisoners and objects of every description are ... almost the only reliable evidence on which we can build a picture of the enemy deployment'.[36]

The troops who took prisoners were forbidden to 'win' personal property, let alone objects of military value, but the letter of the law was not upheld with total exactitude, and the 'high rubber boots of the English troops, though the cause of lasting foot-troubles, often found fanciers among the German front-line soldiers at an earlier moment than the prisoners thought convenient'.[37] Prisoners were allowed to retain passes and pay books, money and personal items, but maps, official documents and objects of particular interest were to be forwarded to army headquarters. 'This applies especially to the British cap and shoulder badges.' The covering reports were to detail the numbers and units of the prisoners, the time and place of the capture, the German troops responsible and the circumstances of the event.[38] These procedures were designed to channel every source of information to the intelligence officer (usually a captain) of the relevant army. He conducted interrogations and examined material of every kind, and kept a constant liaison with the intelligence branch of the high command.

The Germans themselves termed their line of communication troops the *Etappenschweine*, and those heroes were inclined to treat the British prisoners very badly on the journey to the *Reich*. Worse was likely to await the prisoners in camps or locations of enforced labour, with other ranks suffering worst of all, and the Australian officers captured at Fromelles were rightly 'most concerned about the fate of their men. They say that the American ambassador had established that the British prisoners in Germany were starving, and that the matter had been raised in Parliament.'[39]

The experience in the first days was likely to be different. The British might steel themselves to face death or wounds in combat, but 'it is a strange thing, to be a prisoner is undoubtedly the most surprising thing that can happen to a soldier'.[40] Then again, German military intelligence was aware that the British had been told to expect beatings and other ordeals, and so 'prisoners who, still feeling the violent emotions of battle, found themselves humanely treated ... spoke more willingly even than the deserters'.[41]

It is not easy to establish the degrees of pressure that are suggested by the usual German words for 'interrogation', namely *Verhör* and *Vernehmung*. But among the terms also employed were *Besprechung*, which means 'conversation', and *Unterhaltung,* which signifies more of a chat. In any event Crown Prince Rupprecht could tell his troops confidently enough that they had nothing to fear if they remained silent after they were captured by the British, for both sides had renounced the use of force to extract information.[42]

As a general rule the Germans found that the British 'don't say much when taken prisoner. They are stubborn and sulky and know little in any case.'[43] Colonel Nicolai, as head of the German military intelligence, testifies that the British officer was 'a model of silence, though sometimes English NCOs and men of long service excelled him ... An iron discipline, maintained by a severe code of punishments, is in their blood.'[44] The Germans were ready to be impressed by martial values wherever they might find them, as they were by the Connaught Ranger captured by Delville Wood on 1 September. Englishmen were being drafted into his regiment, 'but the prisoner himself is an Irishman. He makes an excellent military impression. He gives terse and grudging answers to the questions that are put to him.'[45]

Limitations were also imposed by the show of ignorance and indifference displayed by the British when it came to military affairs. We are reminded of the descriptions of the battles in Napoleonic times, when the redcoats were waiting in stolid lines, while the French troops were speculating about the likely course of events. Pay books along with documentation of all kinds might be taken from the Tommies before an operation, and 'infantrymen are hauled before a court martial if they ask gunners about the positions of their batteries … The British soldiers appear to be left in deliberate ignorance about the make-up of their formations, the names of their leaders and military affairs in general. In this respect the British themselves term it the "deaf and dumb army".'[46]

It still has to be explained how almost every prisoner ended up by revealing something of worth. A number of the captives would still be in a state of shock, and beyond putting up any kind of defence. 'Gassed men were often very talkative and so were men in a high fever, the latter appeared to use the last ounces of their strength in order to give minute descriptions of their final impressions. Some prisoners made statements which were models of their kind. One of the first tank crews gave very accurate details while still shaken by the explosion from which he had escaped.'[47]

Few prisoners of any kind had it in them to resist the German request to fill in a card to be dispatched to their families at home. It had the appearance of an act of totally unexpected kindness, and at the same time established a sense of obligation, however trivial, to the captors. 'Great care was taken in the transmission of these cards. This permission often caused silent prisoners to find their tongues.'[48]

The rest is explained by the form and purposes of the German system of interrogation. The German intelligence officers were at pains to obtain their information from a bigger and more representative body of prisoners than were their British counterparts. Large numbers of prisoners, if captured together, might be processed in groups of up to fifteen in rapid succession, but more commonly in groups of an NCO and two or three men at a time. Individual interrogations of selected prisoners were, however, longer and more productive. Whereas the British intelligence officers concentrated on malcontents such as were to be found among the Russians, Poles, Saxons and Alsace-Lorrainers, the ideal target for the German style of interrogation was an officer or man of education and worldly experience who had set himself against telling the Germans anything that might be of use to them. Such an individual was a wounded and unnamed 32-year-old first lieutenant of the 9/West

Yorkshire Regiment. He was in the textile business in civilian life, but he made 'an intelligent and military impression', and was 'most reticent and circumspect in his answers. For that reason the interrogation was extraordinarily detailed.'[49]

The opening questions of the interview were designed to supply the basic details for the standard report, whereby the Germans hoped to learn of the prisoner's identity and unit, the circumstance of his capture, the location and composition of neighbouring units and formations, along with their histories and losses. None of the prisoners grasped that the Germans were interested in a great deal more, for they wished to learn of British life in all its aspects, embracing the relations between the ranks of the army, between the categories of the troops – Regulars, Territorials and so on – and between the British, the troops of the Empire and the French, and all of this in every possible combination. Conditions inside Britain were also of great interest to the Germans, as were the political tensions in Ireland and India, and prisoners' opinions as to the possibilities of breakthrough on the Western Front, and the causes, conduct and outcome of the war.

The German intelligence officers set no limit on the duration of their investigations, or the length of their reports, and it is evident that very few British prisoners grasped when their interrogation in all its forms began or ended. There were many well-tried techniques for setting the necessary mood. We may imagine how an inclination of the head or a concerned expression might be enough to persuade a soldier that he could at last pour out his miseries into a sympathetic ear, and there was an engaging simplicity about many of the pilots and observers of the Royal Flying Corps. 'We have found from experience that the enemy aviators, and the British in particular, are most inclined to chat and give answers to their German counterparts. That is why the interrogation of the enemy flyers should be conducted only by the airmen who are attached to the intelligence officer.'[50] According to Nicolai 'the airmen on both sides were bound together by technical interests, and a certain sporting spirit. In addition, many were quite young and the English and French airmen were often recruited from inferior material ... and their news was all the more valuable because airmen often had exact information regarding strategic conditions.'[51]

The British memoirs indicate that the Germans had a particular method for putting men of affairs at their ease, so that it almost appeared to them that they had 'dropped in to see a lot of rather eccentric strangers'.[52] Instead of a bullet-headed Junker in a spiked helmet they were more likely to encounter a perfect English-speaker, who could talk of mutual acquaintances in the City of London, or 'a distinguished old gentleman' who offered his guests cigars and wine, and had been educated at Eton.[53] These agreeable people would supply their prisoners with astonishingly accurate details about their parent units, as if to persuade them that anything else they cared to tell their hosts would be of merely conversational interest.

The British accounts suggest that these devices were recognised for what they were, but the German records make it clear that the captives had no inkling of the range of German interests, and that their tongues were loosened once they believed that they had held their silence on matters of military importance. Lieutenant Harvey, already mentioned, was convinced that he had never given away anything of value, yet from him the Germans learned of the reinforcements for the 48th (South Midland) Division, the heavy losses among the Australians at Pozières, and the officers' estimates of the British losses in the opening phase of the Battle of the Somme.[54]

Lieutenant Trevor Colin Hambling, a company commander of the 2/Worcesters, talked freely about political affairs in Ireland and India,[55] and the Germans knew that they had a particularly valuable catch in Lieutenant Godfrey Walter Phillimore of the Highland Light Infantry, on attachment with the 2/South Wales Borderers, taken south of Beaumont Hamel on 4 April. He was the son of the Lord Justice of Appeal Sir Walter George Frank Phillimore (one of the fathers of the League of Nations), and himself a barrister, though no longer practising. He was aged only thirty-six, but recently widowed, and lived on his estate at Henley-on-Thames. 'He refuses to say anything about military affairs', which did not prevent him from speaking at length on matters of more general interest. 'Lieutenant Phillimore himself has a wide education, but his thinking about the war, its causes, its present state and its likely outcome is typically English in its insularity.'[56]

When, finally, what the prisoners had to say had ceased to be of military or political relevance, they remained of academic interest to bands of German anthropologists, musicologists, philologists and the like, who for years had been investigating the world's cultures before they were extinguished by the machine age. The professors now found that the world had been brought to them in the shape of allied prisoners of war, and between 1915 and 1918 they took the opportunity to tour the camps in the name of the Royal Prussian Phonographic Commission. Thus the British prisoners were encouraged to sing popular songs (including a genuinely moving 'Tipperary' with solo and chorus), and read out the passage concerning the Prodigal Son from the Bible, thus identifying, for example, the differences between the Lancashire and Yorkshire accents. The sounds were preserved on shellac discs or wax cylinders, and the aural record was reinforced by portrait studies by First Lieutenant Otto Stiehl, who was a gifted photographer as well as being the deputy commandant of one of the camps.

CHAPTER TWO

The Imperial Troops

THE EMPIRE GOES TO WAR

In the years before the Great War the German General Staff became
convinced that Australia, New Zealand, Canada and the South African
Union would all be ready to assist Britain in the event of a European
war. An Imperial General Staff was now in being, and the Germans had
little doubt that the necessary understandings had been reached in a
series of secret conferences. The Germans also noted that the Dominions
had passed roughly similar laws, which provided for a basis of service
in a home-defence militia and the projection of force overseas by
formations of volunteers.

On 4 August 1914 Britain declared war on Germany, a measure that
automatically brought the whole of the British Empire into the conflict.
Eight days later Prime Minister Asquith sent a three-word telegram to
the Imperial governments: 'War. Germany. Act.' A few measurements
can be applied to the degree to which the Empire responded. Britain
introduced conscription in 1916, New Zealand in May the same year

and Canada in August 1917, but no conscription for foreign service existed in Australia or South Africa. In the course of the war more than 20 per cent of the British male population enlisted for military service, and the figure would have been higher still if conscription had been extended to Ireland. Comparable contributions from the other states of the Empire stood at more than 19 per cent from New Zealand, and nearly 13½ per cent each from Australia and Canada. In 1916 the units of cavalry were the only remnant of the Indian Army still deployed on the Western Front, but contingents from the Empire grew to four divisions and one cavalry brigade of Canadians, five Australian infantry divisions and a division of New Zealand infantry, and a South African infantry brigade. In the cultural history of Canada, Australia and New Zealand the experience was a matter of groping a way 'down a parallel path in responding to the demands of war on an unprecedented scale'.[1] The notion of natural-born soldiers, the sons of the open air, as typified in the Australian 'larrikin', became a treasured part of the cultural myth, sometimes at the expense of the hard training which was, eventually, to make them the fine troops that most of them became.

THE SOUTH AFRICANS

The South African Union was in several ways unique among the Dominions. The white population was a minority, and was not only divided by race and language (which was also the case with Canada), but a substantial proportion of the Dutch-descended element had been engaged in armed conflict against the British and other Imperial forces only a dozen years before the outbreak of the Great War. In the first weeks of the new conflict the Union was moreover threatened by a rising among the Boers, and engaged in hostilities against an immediate neighbour, the German colony of South-West Africa (later Namibia).

What was again remarkable was that there was no popular South African hostility to the Germans as such. 'They are good citizens, and are reckoned to be excellent farmers. The war counts for nothing in the relationships with them, and there is no question of an eventual boycott of German goods.'[2] Many Germans had 'lived among the Boers so long that they were happy to converse in the Afrikaner-Dutch *Taal* (a word which just means language). This *Taal* is ideally suited to the slow, comfort-loving, not to say lazy mentality of the Boers. It does not have a settled written style, and only the most basic grammar. Many expressions have been borrowed from the English, and some also from the blacks and the Portugese.'[3]

German sympathisers were discovered among the Boers taken prisoner from the South African Brigade,[4] though

> the Boers seem to be quite indifferent as to who their rulers might be, as long as their personal lives are not affected. For that reason there is no antagonism towards the British, even though they have deprived the Burghers of their political freedom, from which we may deduce that the Boers too have fallen under the influence of British colonialism. The obstinate Transvaalers are the only exception, for they will never forget the violation of their land by the British, and want to have nothing to do with them. But we must bear in mind that the Transvaalers in general are ponderous and pig-headed people, who have the reputation of being mistrustful and withdrawn even among the other Boers.[5]

Tensions among the Boers were exacerbated when, almost immediately after the outbreak of war, the Germans encouraged Salomon Maritz and Christiaan De Wet to raise a revolt in north-west Cape Province, upon which German troops crossed the border from German South-West Africa on 21 August. 'According to the general belief in South Africa, the war was caused by the German invasion of South African territory. It was thought that Germany had embroiled Britain in a war in South Africa to hinder reinforcements being sent to Europe.'[6] ' … General Botha, who was personally friendly towards the Germans, was thereby so enraged that he took the field against them.'[7] In fact the British had urged the Union government to eliminate 'German South-West' from the war for strategic reasons, for the ports of Lüderitz and Swakopmund together with the radio station at Windhoek could have supported a German cruiser squadron, which might have played havoc with the British communications around the Cape.

Maritz and De Wet commanded little support in South Africa, and their rebellion was put down speedily by another pair of Boer veterans, General Jan Smuts and Prime Minister Louis Botha just mentioned.

Early in 1915 Botha opened a full-scale campaign against German South-West Africa, and to this end he employed large numbers of men who had been enlisted since 1912 for home service in the Union Defence Force. The fighting in this theatre ended on 9 July 1915 with an unconditional German surrender, amid lively debates as to the propriety of having used the men of the Defence Force beyond the borders.

It was hoped that the new campaign against German East Africa (later Tanganyika, then Tanzania) would prove less controversial, for it involved volunteers only, who were paid at the high rate of three shillings a day. By the time of the Battle of the Somme, however, the operations there had lasted far longer than the campaign in South-West Africa, and the prisoners told the Germans that they would rather have endured a winter in France than face the disease and hardships of campaigning in 'German East'.

In July 1915 the London government accepted an offer on the part of the Union government to send an Imperial Service contingent to the war in Europe. The British stipulated that they would require infantry only, which lessened the appeal to the Boers, who prided themselves on their horsemanship, and they therefore made up only 15 per cent of the first troops to go out. Otherwise 'the South Africans, like the colonial troops in general, were not averse to being deployed in Europe, for it was something attractively novel and would give them a chance of seeing that part of the world. They were as yet unacquainted with the dark side of war.'[8] That kind of enthusiasm was now difficult to detect in the British homeland.

The South African Brigade in France was commanded by Brigadier General Lukin and comprised four regiments:

1. Cape Province Regiment;
2. Natal and Orange Free State Regiment;
3. Transvaal and Rhodesia Regiment;
4. The Scottish Regiment ('The men of this battalion wear the kilt, but those of the first, second and third battalions the Kitchener uniform').[9]

All ranks were volunteers, and the discipline and the turnout were reckoned to be of a high order.

The South Africans were shipped from Cape Town in September 1915, and disembarked in Britain in the middle of October. They missed the worst of the European winter by being transported in January to Egypt, where the second and third battalions in particular suffered heavily in operations against the Senussi. The brigade landed at Marseilles on 8 April 1916, and moved first to Armentières, then to a tented camp at Bray, and was finally deployed as the 3rd or reserve Brigade of the 9th (Scottish) Division, which had been depleted very heavily at Loos in 1915.

From 14 to 20 July the South African Brigade was engaged in exceptionally intense fighting in Delville Wood. The losses on both sides were very heavy, and on the 19th the Germans rounded up 200 prisoners, 'part of English, part of Dutch descent; all were magnificent men. Some of them carried our men on makeshift stretchers, men who had all been wounded in the great action yesterday – they were Storm Troops. The Englishmen treated our wounded in an excellent manner while in their short captivity. Their medical welfare, food, drink, smoking materials were all offered in a friendly manner … It confirmed again that in general the Englishman was a decent adversary, and that against them, if the expression may be allowed, it was a pleasure to conduct war. It was very different from their allies, the French, who acted with a distinct spite at every opportunity and who were responded to with honesty by our side!'[10]

Brought up to strength, and with an increasing representation by the Boers, the brigade was deployed at High Wood on 9 October, and attacked the Butte de Warlencourt on the 12th of that month. These were severe engagements, but after the war a veteran told the German general Grauthoff that '18 July in Delville Wood and Longueval stood out as the worst single day of action faced by the South African Brigade in the course of the entire war. It was almost wiped out by the destructive German artillery fire, followed by the counterattacks by the German infantry which arrived with irresistible force. Even now the day of "Delville Wood" represents South Africa's day of mourning and commemoration.'[11]

THE CANADIANS

Canada had been the first among the Dominions to send a full and independently supported contingent to the Boer War. In 1911 the Canadian government proceeded to form a mobilisation scheme, based on an expansion of the volunteer militia. When, however, the war broke out, the war minister Sam Hughes overset the carefully thought-through timetables by a headlong expansion of the forces, and not least because he wished to outdo the Australians and Canadians, who were in the process of forming full army corps.

The resulting 1st Canadian Division made up part of the British V Corps at Ypres in April 1915; the 2nd Division arrived in September, and two more divisions came in the course of 1916. The Canadian government had hoped that the putting-together of a large Canadian contingent would serve as a nation-building exercise, though in the event disproportionately few of the troops hailed from the 1.7 million people of the French-speaking province of Quebec. According to the Germans, 'it is difficult to define the Canadians as such. From what they know of our prisoners, the French Canadians have taken little or no part in the war. Otherwise the various British races as represented among the Canadian prisoners are fundamentally very similar to the British in the homeland, the only difference being that the blinkered mental uniformity of the British has been moderated by the wide open spaces of Canada, which allow more of the natural man to appear.'[12]

The Canadians were the first of the troops of the Empire to arrive on the Western Front. They were quick to learn from their experiences, and proved willing to pass on their hard-won lessons to the Australians and New Zealanders. They enjoyed, moreover, first-class leadership in the person of Lieutenant General Sir Julian Byng, who commanded the Canadian Corps from May 1916, and the gifted Major General Arthur Currie (commander of the 1st Canadian Division), who had been on attachment with the French at Verdun, and who in 1917 became a tactical pioneer among the British forces in general.

In late August 1916 the German General Staff rated the Canadians highly, placing the 1st and 2nd Divisions among the top eight available to the British for use on the Somme, and the 3rd Division among the five divisions of medium combat-worthiness. The Germans had paid particular attention to what they were told by an officer of the 7th (1st British Columbia) Battalion who was captured in the fighting at Mouquet Farm on 7 and 8 September. He was a 'tall, imposing man, much praised on account of his courage and circumspection by the prisoners of the 14th Battalion, among whom he spent the night'.[13]

In detail the Germans became aware of certain ill-feeling and resentments among these people. Voluntary recruiting was flagging in a way that suggested conscription could not long be delayed (it was introduced in 1917), and most of the recruits had obviously been drawn from the disposable elements of society. 'A typical case was that of the tramway worker from Vancouver who received a slip with his pay: "Your country needs you, we don't want you any more." He could not find any other employment, and so he joined up.'[14]

If the officer already mentioned had won the regard of the men of the 14th Battalion, the same did not apply in reverse. The troops were French-Canadians of the Royal Montreal Regiment, which was an alien element in the otherwise Scottish-Canadian 3rd Brigade, 'and he speaks most dismissively of the 14th Battalion, even though they are supposed to be excellent troops. He maintains that the discipline among his own men [of the 7th Battalion] is excellent, in contrast to the discipline among the Australians, where the officers let the men do what they like.'[15]

On a particular point the Canadians were in full agreement with one another and even with the Australians and New Zealanders. The French Canadians captured on 8 September 'all assert that they had already heard from the Australians that they would have to put up with a great deal. They find it demeaning that the British always commit the colonial troops on the worst sectors of the front.'[16] The officer taken with them 'remarked in the course of conversation that the British set the colonial troops the most unpleasant tasks. To begin with they regarded it as a great honour, but now they have come to the conclusion that they are just being exploited. He says that the mood among the Canadians is not of the best.'[17]

ANZAC

In August 1914, in response to London's appeal, the Australian brigadier general William Throsby Bridges offered to send 12,000 Australian and 12,000 New Zealand troops to 'any destination desired by the home government'. By the end of the year 52,561 volunteers had enlisted, and Bridges was able to form the Australian Imperial Force (AIF). The men did not materialise from thin air, for the Australians had been building up from a base that consisted of the 4,000 personnel of the long-standing Regular Service, and the men who had been trained in the militia-like Citizen Force, service with which had been made compulsory in 1911.

The Germans had already looked into the motivation of the men of the South African Brigade, and discovered that 'conditions are similar among the Australians, who enlisted just to take part in the campaign against the Turks, which they imagined to be some kind of game and adventure'.[13] By 1916 the young men had experienced more than enough adventure, but the pay of the Australian private soldier continued to exercise an attraction in its own right, being set at the monstrously high rate of six shillings a day.

The white population of Australia and New Zealand was of over-whelmingly British stock, much of which had arrived recently, which had not been the case in Canada, and still less in South Africa, and the powerful ties of blood together with the very remoteness of the Antipodes reinforced the links with the British homeland. It was a coming-together of sentiment and (although the term would not have been understood) of geopolitics. When the Germans questioned the prisoners they had taken at Fromelles they were told that 'Australia stands in the same relationship to the British Empire as do the federal states of Germany to the German *Reich*. By playing their part in the greater cause they wish to show their loyalty to the motherland.'[19]

America was disliked and despised, and did not come into the reckoning as an alternative protecting power. Germany had established a presence in the Pacific before the war, but 'the feeling in Australia against Germany has sharpened only in the course of the war. At the beginning there was no pronounced hostility towards Germany. Australia just wanted to help the threatened motherland, which most of them still call "home", and Australia would have helped Britain against any other country with which it was engaged in war ... In the course of time, however, the mighty power of the German Army changed this feeling into fears for the security of the Australians' own land. It would appear that this fear has been encouraged assiduously by the press. When the men are asked why they are fighting, they almost invariably reply "to prevent Germany conquering the world, and Australia in particular".'[20]

It was significant that New Zealand's first active intervention in the war was in the shape of an expeditionary force which seized German Samoa on 29 August 1914.

Japan, too, had been expanding in the Pacific, and especially at the expense of Russia after the war of 1904–5, and 'the economic rise of Japan has been followed with some anxiety in the large towns of Australia's east coast, and not least because many ships bearing the Japanese flag have taken to calling in recently'.[21] In the present war the Japanese, as allies of the British, had seized German harbours and islands in the Pacific, but this had been of no comfort at all. 'One of the prisoners said "we Australians are fed up with the war, but what can we do? We have just four million people, and we have to stick with the British, so that they can protect us against the Japanese".'[22] 'In general the Australians regard Japan as their natural enemy. As long as the Anglo-Japanese compact endures the danger does not arise, but it has only been put off, and one day it will certainly pose a threat to Australia. The apprehension concerning the Japanese danger to Australian national interests was undoubtedly an unspoken but powerful factor bringing about the introduction of compulsory service with the Citizen Force on 1 July 1911. The captured officers are firm believers in the "Yellow Peril", and are of the opinion that one day all the white races will have to band together against the coloureds.'[23]

The experience of the Great War is now seen as decisive in the discovery of an Australian identity independent of Britain, with the blighted landscapes of Gallipoli and the Western Front standing as an alternative 'Outback'. Even at the time the Germans became aware that the commitment of the Australians to the British was not unreserved. New Zealand introduced conscription in May 1916, and most of the Australian prisoners feared that the decline in voluntary enlistment would bring conscription to Australia as well. The principle was distasteful to them, and at the time of the first referendum on the subject, in October 1916, one of their number noted that 'most of our men seemed resolved to vote "no". The main reason was the reluctance of the men (all volunteers, and still willing to fight for the cause that brought them overseas) to vote in favour of forcing their countrymen to join up and help in the fight.'[24]

In the event the referendum rejected conscription, but there were suspicions that a second vote was in the offing, and the Germans were told of an interesting effect in the 19th (New South Wales) Battalion of the 2nd Australian Division at the beginning of December 1916, when a draft of more than two hundred replacements turned out to be of remarkably good quality, for many of the troops bore the South African ribbon. The reason was that the veterans wished to volunteer before they could be re-enlisted by force. The informant was one of their younger comrades, 'a strong man of twenty-three years, who makes a good impression. He is much disgruntled with the British, for Australia and the Australian workers get nothing out of the war, and the British high command always puts the Australian divisions in the most dangerous sectors.'[25] A second referendum was held in December 1917, and rejected conscription still more emphatically.

More of the Australians' resentments came to light when the Germans examined the fighting record of the Anzac Corps. The travails of the Gallipoli campaign were lodged in the collective memory of that formation, and the notion of a shared, non-British experience was already taking root. 'The conversations of Australian officers and other ranks demonstrate strikingly the prevailing ill-will against Britain. As an example we may cite the events of the first attacks at Gallipoli, when troops could not be disembarked in time to help the men already landed before they were wiped out. They claim that the British arrived a good two days too late, which is something for which the Australians will never forgive the British. They complain that they are always being set missions which will result in heavy losses, as recently when they were committed time and time again on the Somme.'[26]

The Germans were at some pains to identify the percentages of the veteran *Gallipolikämpfer* in the Australian formations on the Western Front. Very few, for example, were to be found in the unfortunate 5th Division, which was a composite affair, put together in Egypt at the close of the campaign, and mauled at Fromelles on 19 and 20 July 1916. 'The proportions of the tried and tested troops from Gallipoli to the inexperienced men differ in the individual brigades of this ... division. In the 8th Brigade [Victoria, New South Wales, Queensland, South and West Australia battalions] it stands at one in eight; in the 14th Brigade

[New South Wales only] at one in four. The relationship in the 15th Brigade [Victoria only] is unknown, as we took just one prisoner from that brigade and it remains an unknown quantity.'[27]

Among the curiosities noted by the Germans were a number of the Australian Light Horse, frustrated at having been relegated to rear-area service in Egypt, guarding railway lines, bringing up ammunition on mules, and the like. 'But the men who were sent to France came with their horses. According to a number of prisoners these people had mastered the art of horsemanship from their early youth, and wait eagerly on the chance of a cavalry charge in the service of their motherland. They are "Bushmen" through and through, and ride only the finest horses.'[28]

In August 1916 the Germans calculated that 265,000 men had enlisted in Australia, and 50,000 in New Zealand, making a total of 315,000 troops. The Australians had lost about 58,000 from all causes, and the New Zealanders about 12,000, 'and so at the present time the Australian and New Zealand forces amount to about 245,000 men, of whom 185,000 have been sent overseas and 60,000 remain in the homelands'.[29] Altogether some 130,000 Australians and New Zealanders were believed to be now serving in France. The current establishment of the Anzac Corps was now put confidently enough at five divisions of Australians and one of New Zealanders, though it was difficult to pin down the whereabouts of the various formations, and on 31 July the Germans had admitted that they had lost track of the 3rd Division (which was training in England).

No doubts were attached to the presence of the 5th Australian Division, which had been sacrificed in the 'operationally and tactically senseless attack at Fromelles on 20 July'.[30] On 2 August a survivor of the 53rd (New South Wales) Battalion entered in his diary:

Today we have the usual six hours of drill. But we don't want drill, we want organisation. Colonel Beevers, Brigadier General Glasgow and General Cox may say that they don't want to get personal glory or something of a name from the demands they put on their men, but it's not at all to their credit that the organisation of this battalion is so dismal. B Company can field only three officers instead of six, and it's

just the same with the NCOs. The men who have had some training
with grenades are now stuck away in the machine gun platoon, and our
bombers are mostly men who have never thrown a grenade in their lives
... 2 August: General Birdwood was here yesterday. He first read out a
whole lot of material, and then made a little speech in which he told us
that we ought to use our spare time to write letters to our nearest and
dearest, even though he knows perfectly well that it is very difficult for
us to get our letters sent off once we have written them. But his encouraging words will look good in the Australian press.[31]

The kind of bloodletting the 5th Division had experienced at
Fromelles was repeated on a larger scale and over a longer span of time
at the expense of the 1st, 2nd and 3rd Divisions at Pozières in the weeks
that followed. It was the product of ignorance and inexperience among
the Australians as well as impetuosity on the part of General Gough.
By 26 August the German General Staff reckoned that only the 3rd and
5th Divisions would be available for action, albeit at the lowest category
of combat effectiveness.

Some of the British were already inclined to regard the Australians as
elite attacking troops,[32] but Australians wondered whether their reputation was being bought at too high a price. 'Most of the Australians do
not have a great deal of time for the "Tommies" or the "big pots" ...
They feel that they are much neglected in the matter of supplies, for
while the Tommies get the best, the Anzacs end up with the left-overs.
Whenever the Australians complain they are told "yes, but they pay you
six shillings a day".'[33] (The British private only got one.) Towards the
end of the year the Germans persuaded themselves that with the troops
like the Australians, 'who have virtually no military discipline, their
expressions of ill-will and discontent against the British army command
could have sinister implications. We have recent confirmation through the
stories which are circulating in the trenches about peace moves, reliefs and
winter quarters in France.'[34] The Germans were reading altogether too
much into the grumbling, and they could see for themselves that the
Australians were fitted out in a magnificent way.[35]

The Germans were unaware that large numbers of their Australian
captives were British-born, for the sun of Australia and the Middle East

endowed them collectively with an appearance of bronzed strength. Canadians as well as British were nevertheless appalled by the indiscipline that prevailed among these magnificent physical specimens, and the Germans could not find among them the slightest interest in soldiering as it was understood in Europe.[36]

No particularly good example was set by their leaders, who appeared to the Germans to be grotesque buffoons.

> The Australian officers are inferior in every respect to the British. As might have been expected from their training, they have not the slightest idea of what is, and what is not militarily important. We may cite those officers who have told us repeatedly that to reveal military secrets would be against their honour as officers, and yet without the slightest hesitation they gave chapter and verse as to the whole plan and execution of the attack [at Fromelles] and the deployment of the troops concerned. The only information which they recognised as being important was the identity of the forces beside or behind their division, as the details – fragmentary at that – could be extracted from them only by subterfuge. But perhaps their whole military training was so defective that they genuinely did not know any more.[37]

New Zealand's contribution to Anzac consisted of Major General Andrew Hamilton Russell's New Zealand Division of three brigades of four battalions each. The Germans could as yet construct no clear picture of a separate New Zealand identify, for their information was obtained from only a small number of New Zealanders, and from what they were told at second hand by the Australians. The recent history of the division was put together from the evidence of a single soldier of the 2nd (Wellington) Battalion of the 2nd Brigade, who had lost his way on the Albert–Bapaume road on the night of 1/2 October. He told them that the division had come to France from Egypt in the middle of April, and that from the beginning of May until the middle of August it had been in or behind the line in the 'nursery' sector at Armentières. The New Zealanders arrived on the Somme at Fricourt on 9 September, and were committed with the British XV Corps in the grand offensive on the 15th.

By the prisoner's account

the division lost 3,500 men in the capture of Flers and in other attacks. His company was down to 75 per cent of its strength, or scarcely fifty men. Apart from small parties of recovered convalescents from Armentières the division had received no replacements ... The prisoner gives every impression of high intelligence. He signed up as a soldier in 1914, and for no other reason than a love of adventure. He maintains that he and all his comrades were very angry at they way they were being exploited by the British. They had worn the same clothes on their backs for three weeks on end, and were struck by the fact that the New Zealanders were being left in the front line while the British divisions to either side were rotated much more often. He did not know the reason why. All the same every New Zealander will do his duty, and we were extremely unlikely to receive any deserters from them.[38]

Almost the only authenticated deserter was Private William Powell Nimot (Nimodt), who abandoned his comrades of the 1/Wellington Regiment. This treachery was followed by a crude and demoralising purge of the men bearing German or even remotely suspicious family names. For unknown reasons the winnowing spared the nineteen-year old private Howard Karl Kippenberger of the 1/Canterbury Regiment, whose family had emigrated from the Palatinate in 1862. He became a highly regarded brigade commander in the Second World War. His superior in that war was Lieutenant General Bernard Cyril Freyberg, VC, DSO, who commanded the New Zealand Expeditionary Force throughout. He was altogether immune from the purge in 1916, being commander and acting lieutenant colonel of the Hood Battalion of the Royal Naval Brigade, with whom he gained his VC in the action at Beaucourt on 13 May. Freyberg was born in Britain in 1889, and although little is known of his family origins, it almost certainly derived its name from the trading town of Freiberg in the Erzgebirge of Saxony.

The Germans already knew something of the appearance of the newcomers. 'The uniform of the New Zealanders is similar to that of the Australians, apart from having a rather smaller slouch-hat, with a red band instead of one of khaki.' One of the Australians had seen up to two hundred of the Maoris at Laventie. 'They are attached to the New

Zealand Division [as its Pioneer battalion], and the Australian troops regard them as being completely civilised and fully up to standard. The prisoner estimates that there are 2,000 Maoris in France, including many officers, some of whom the prisoner himself had seen at Laventie. They are strongly built fellows, in colour rather like half-castes. Their hair is curly but cut short.'[39]

THE INDIANS

On 14 July 1916, in the battle of the Bazentin Ridge, the right flank of the attacking British 7th Division was screened by one squadron each of the British 7th Dragoon Guards and the 20th Deccan Horse. Together they belonged to the Secunderabad Cavalry Brigade, which was a part of the forces of Indian cavalry that remained on the Western Front after the last infantry divisions of the Indian Corps were withdrawn for service in the Middle East towards the end of 1915.

The Indian Corps had been mobilised on 8 August 1914, as the only reserve of trained troops available to the British Empire at the outset of the war. The greater part of the Secunderabad Brigade landed at Marseilles on 12 October, and the Poona Horse and two squadrons of the 7th Dragoon Guards were in dismounted action on 2 November. The infantry element of the corps was a large body of twenty-three divisions, and spent altogether fourteen months in France, suffering heavy losses at Neuve Chapelle. It was difficult to find replacements when the Indians were fighting so far from home, and the urgent need for manpower was now also being met by the Canadians and the first troops of the British New Army divisions. The infantry left the front line between 4 and 10 November 1915 before they had to face a second winter in France.

By the time of the great battles in July 1916 the Germans therefore had had ample opportunity to take stock of these, the most exotic of the British forces they had to face on the Western Front. The troops had been drawn from some of the least politically aware populations of the sub-continent, and 'when they were asked about their attitude to the World War, the Indians declared that they had been told nothing about it, and were conscious only that they had been transported first to Calcutta, then put aboard ship and landed in France. Even in the battle in which they were taken prisoner they were not aware against whom they were fighting, or why.'[40]

The prisoners found to their surprise that the Germans not only did not line them up and shoot them, but were willing to attend to their dietary requirements. The Muslims were easy to accommodate, as they shunned only pork. The Hindus were awkward people, since all beef products were abhorrent, as also any utensils which might have been contaminated by them. 'They rejected even a kettle which was almost new, and in which coffee had been made only a couple of times. The reason was that it could have been stirred by spoons which might have been in contact with beef.'[41] The Hindus were at last placated when the Germans distributed flour, rice and potatoes and left the troops to prepare the food for themselves.

The 'small, active Gurkhas' appeared to be peoples of varied stock, some resembling Mongols, others Malays, and the rest a mixture. The Germans were much amused by a Gurkha NCO who knew a little English and used this advantage to assert his authority over the others. The Sikhs from the Punjab were objects of fascination. 'Their complexion of dark bronze, their tall stature and proud bearing made them remarkable figures, corresponding very much to us Northerners' vision of the Mysterious Orient. They are greatly given to cultivating their appearance, as manifest in their artistically curled beards and their carefully wound-about turbans. Like all the Indians, these people too keep within their caste and maintain strict discipline, so that punishment is hardly an issue. But every now and then you become aware of a sudden flash in the eyes or a tightening in the expression which indicate that a tigerish and volcanic-hot passion lurks behind the rigid dignity of their manner.'[42]

The Germans were at pains to cultivate the Muslims in general, and for this purpose concentrated more than 10,000 Muslim prisoners in a camp at Zossen-Wünsdorf south of Berlin. Among the prisoners taken from the British the Germans invested particular hopes in the Pathans and the other semi-mercenary types who hailed from Afghanistan and thereabouts. Many of the Afghans had the appearance of 'pure Indo-Germans. Their sturdy and upright build, their complexions burnt lightly by the sun, and the open, candid look in their eyes would belong just as well in a peasant farm of north Germany as in the huts of their native land.'[43] The great majority of the Indian deserters and turncoats indeed came from this source, influenced less by the Germans invoking Muslim brotherhood and the alliance with Turkey than by 'the natural Pathan propensity for seeking personal advantage'.[44]

The Germans also became aware of tensions which it might be possible to exploit over the longer term. British prisoners were eager to tell them that the Indians and other coloureds were 'good for warfare in the bush, where they attacked bravely enough, but they failed under artillery fire or when it came to holding a piece of ground which had been won. They were also inclined to surrender too easily. The Hindu cavalry had sworn to charge home whatever the odds, but that just made them ridiculous.'[45]

The British held back from commissioning Indians as officers, and 'many of the British officers with the Indian regiments had fallen at the beginning of the campaign [of 1915]. They are difficult to replace, since only Indian-speaking officers come under consideration.' On a related point 'most people regard the employment of the Indians in France as a mistake, which should never have been allowed to happen. The present difficulties in India have arisen because the old British troops who knew the country have been withdrawn, and their place taken by Territorials. The self-confidence of the Indians has grown mightily in this war, from the experience of having fought shoulder-to-shoulder with the British against other whites.'[46]

Lieutenant Hambling of the 2/Worcesters had travelled much in Africa and India, and believed that the troubles in India were of a still more serious order than the disturbances in Ireland. 'The restless elements come mostly from influential Indian families, and have returned home after an education in British universities. They will exploit the great embarrassment which has been occasioned to the British by the failure of their Gallipoli expedition and the defeat at Kut-el-Amara.' It was true that the countless millions of the sub-continent were sunk in ignorance, and that the British were accomplished rulers, 'but the loss of prestige will make it very difficult to resolve the Indian problem, that is to say, the future relationship between India and Britain'.[47]

CHAPTER THREE

The British Army

THE FORCES IN OVERVIEW

The British Expeditionary Force went to war in 1914 largely as a projection of a full-time Regular force of about 250,000 men. In contrast, the British Army of the victorious Hundred Days in 1918 was overwhelmingly a body of conscripts, wearing cap badges that rarely related to place of birth or local loyalties. Between these two experiences, the one and a half million British troops who saw service on the Somme were the most representative of all the types of troops who took the field in the Great War, comprising as they did four elements:

1. The Regular Army
2. The Territorial Force
3. The New Army of Service battalions ('Kitchener Men')
4. The 'Derby Men' and the first conscripts

The German military intelligence went to considerable lengths to establish who these people were, and what respective contributions they were making during the institutional turbulence of 1916. By February, long before the conscripts were making their presence felt, 'a considerable mixing up of the formations has taken place. Among the old divisions, whole brigades, or individual battalions from the brigades, have been extracted and replaced by new Kitchener brigades. This blending of regular units with the younger ones is probably the result of bad experiences with the Kitchener divisions.'[1]

The Germans learned by the end of August that in the 13/Middlesex 'there exists no longer any cohesion ... about two-thirds of the men have reached the battalion over the last few days as various batches of replacements.'[2] Other prisoners were telling the Germans at the same time that the system of regional replacements was collapsing under the weight of the losses, and that all the 'Kitchener' reserve battalions were being thrown into a common 'Training Reserve', from which recruits would be forwarded to the various battalions according to need.[3]

In the middle of October the Germans analysed the age groupings of 2,700 prisoners taken by the First Army since the opening of the Battle of the Somme:

	17–24	25–35	over 35
July	57.3 per cent	33.5 per cent	9.2 per cent
August	56.8 per cent	36.5 per cent	6.6 per cent
September	52.0 per cent	33.3 per cent	14.7 per cent

'This means that after two years of war Britain is still able to put into the field a very high proportion of young and vigorous men. The figures hardly vary, for at both the beginning and end of this quarter of a year, which has been so costly to the British, the men are still at the height of their physical capacities.'[4]

The Germans repeated the same exercise in the middle of December, and found that 'there has been little variation in the categories of British by age':

	17–24	25–35	over 35
October	50.0 per cent	43.0 per cent	7.0 per cent
November	53.0 per cent	36.0 per cent	11.0 per cent

'The proportion of the captured Regulars has fallen from 17 per cent in

July to 9 per cent in October, and to 10 per cent in November. The number of Kitchener Men and volunteers has fallen from 71 per cent in June to 51 per cent in November, while there has been little difference in the percentage of the Territorials (12 per cent July; 10 per cent in October; 14 per cent in November). The difference has been made up by the Derby Men, who made up 27 per cent of the prisoners in October and November, whereas they had not yet been committed in July.'[5]

The impression was that the British Army was an institution undergoing significant changes in character, and this in itself makes it difficult to identify consistently 'good' or 'bad' divisions as they existed in 1916. It would not be realistic, for example, to expect the 90th Brigade (39th Division) to be unaffected by the influx of replacements, mostly returning convalescents from other regiments, who arrived between 12 and 19 July. So it was that 'the battalions which went into action before Guillemont [8–9 October] bore little resemblance to those fine battalions which began the push on July 1st. The South Country reinforcements did not mix well with the men from the North and many officers and men were complete strangers to one another.'[6]

If we are tempted to think otherwise, it is probably on account of one of those bold generalities ventured by Robert Graves, and repeated in one form or another many times since. Graves refers vaguely to a German document which listed the British divisions in terms of quality. If such a paper ever existed, it probably resembled the one produced by the intelligence branch of the supreme command (*OHL*) on 26 August 1916, which assessed the combat-worthiness of the divisions that the British might be able to bring against the First Army:

Good: 47th [Territorial], 6th [Regular], 20th [New Army], 50th [Territorial], 18th [New Army], 1st Canadian, 2nd Canadian

Medium: 11th [New Army], 39th [New Army], 41st [New Army], 3rd Canadian, New Zealand

Poor: 61st [New Army], 40th [New Army], 60th [New Army], 63rd [Royal Naval], 3rd and 5th Australian, 4th Canadian.[7]

These categories were not intended to indicate absolute worth, but the effectiveness of the formations at a given time, as influenced by permutations of training, freshness, experience and battle losses.

THE OFFICERS

By 1916 the German impressions of the British officer, in so far as they were obtained from the specimens at first hand, were most commonly derived from intelligent and talkative lieutenants, with a sprinkling of captains. People like these had been commissioned in the course of the war, and their civilian lives had been those of the bank clerk, accountant, solicitor and the like.

Lieutenant F. W. Harvey of the Gloucesters provided the Germans with a typical career pattern. Although a lawyer, he enlisted as a private soldier in 1914, went to France with his battalion, and was promoted to corporal in the same year. He gained his commission in October 1915 – a rapid promotion, which he said had become more difficult by 1916. He returned to England to qualify at the schools of musketry and bombing, then helped to train recruits at the reserve battalion before coming back to active service in France.[8]

An officer of the 6/Shropshire Light Infantry had yet to take up a civilian career, and 'when war broke out he was an undergraduate at Oxford. Like many of his friends he went through an officers' training course because he believed it was his duty to enter the army.'[9] Patriotism was, however, difficult to distinguish from the prevailing beefy obsession with sport, and Lieutenant W. Black, shot down on 20 October 1916, was 'sorry to have been taken prisoner, for he says he had had "much fun" in the war. War is a good school for young Englishmen who like to be out and about.'[10]

Intellectuals, as the Germans would have understood the term, were thin on the ground. In the summer of 1916 the Germans completed a *Deutsches Theater* in Lille, and 'lately they had a Shakespeare festival there'.[11] If there was a Lessing or Schiller season staged by the British in Rouen or le Havre it has still to be discovered. With few exceptions, therefore, 'the captured British officers are typical examples of the young subalterns of Britain's new army. They lack a sound education, and furnished only with what, from the English point of view, is considered a healthy dose of the English arrogance.'[12]

The veteran NCOs were the element in the army most critical of the shortcomings of the new officers. Typical was the experience of an NCO of the Gordons who had been sent to reconnoitre an unoccupied trench in broad daylight. 'The prisoner, a long-serving NCO, said that only a young, inexperienced officer could have given a crazy order like that ... He was at once detected by the enemy, as was inevitable, and his retreat was cut off by a bombing party.'[13]

The lack of professionalism was evident to the other ranks as well, and prisoners complained to the Germans that 'the officers who owed their rapid promotion to money or the favouritism of some "big pot" had almost no idea of what war is about. They were devoid of experience. They advanced according to plan, certainly, and they were brave to the point of rashness – but only to conceal just how ignorant they were. These "golfing officers" had no grasp of the wider picture, or how important it was to set about exploiting a newly captured position without any loss of time.'[14] ' ... Most of them are simply a blank page.'[15]

In some of the battalions the officers were viewed by the men as remote figures, indifferent to the welfare of their men, as emphasised by prisoners from the 2/Border Regiment (22 February), the 6/Gloucesters (18 March) and most forcefully among eighty-five men of the 1/South Staffordshire Regiment captured in Delville Wood on 31 August. 'A number of the prisoners complain strongly about the conduct of the young officers, some of whom crouch in the dugouts and are not to be seen at their places of duty. They remark bitterly how convenient it is for the officers to report sick or make constant excuses of "shell-shock" in order to quit the trenches.'[16]

It was not difficult to find soldiers who argued the contrary. Two men of the 8/Rifle Brigade who were captured in March made 'an extremely good impression, while being at the same time totally unmilitary. They are very fond of their officers and praise them as "good lads". They had no hesitation about volunteering for trench raids and the like under their command.'[17] Similar testimonies were offered by men of the 4/Rifle Brigade, the 15/West Yorkshires (Leeds Pals) and the 2/Lancashire Fusiliers.

The accusations of the lack of tactical sense are too strong and too consistent to be ignored. However, the British Army was asking a great deal of its officers, who were expected to be sub-unit leaders as well as military managers after the German style. Thus the British battalion was commanded by twenty-five officers, many of them doing the work that in the German battalion would have fallen to NCOs. A prisoner taken from the 17th Bavarian Reserve Regiment was 'very much astounded by our officers going on patrol'.[18] The large German battalion was commanded by just eight or nine officers, and the more senior of them would not have left their dugout during an action.

The complaints of personal failings among the British officers were largely confined to specific units. Crown Prince Rupprecht found that accusations of poor leadership were much more current in the German regiments, which contrasted with what was heard from the British prisoners. 'I'll just mention a long-serving NCO who said, "fair enough, the younger officers know very little about the trade of soldiering; all the same they are brave lads and real gentlemen". You hear the same praise from the other ranks. They find it entirely in order that there is better food in the officers' messes. But envy is the besetting sin of the Germans. They don't like it when anybody is in any respect better off than themselves.'[19]

THE MEN

THE REGULARS

At the outbreak of war the Regular Army existed on a small (by continental standards) base of 247,432 personnel, 145,798 time-expired troops of the Army Reserve, and the separately recruited 63,933 of the Special Reserve, who had undergone six months of full-time training, then two-week annual refreshers.

In November 1916 the Germans found that 'in the bases, and probably also in the combat units, the long-serving Regulars still form the backbone of the army. They are the only ones who are habituated to strict discipline, and who are esteemed and trusted by their officers and comrades on account of their fighting experience in the Boer War, India and Egypt.'[20] The Germans traced a representative career in a corporal of the 3/Worcesters, captured at Thiepval on 3 September. He had joined the regiment in 1910, served in central India in 1911, and returned to Aldershot in March 1913. In April the same year he sailed to Egypt, coming back to England in November 1914. He joined the 3rd Battalion in April 1915. 'On account of drunkenness he was demoted to private soldier in May 1916. In July 1916 he was made up again to corporal. In his company and in the battalion as a whole there are still comparatively few Derby Men, and he talks about them very dismissively.'[21] The men of the Army Reserve and Special Reserve were not different in type from the full-time Regulars, to judge from eight of them on the strength of the 2/Lancashires who were captured on 19 February 1916.

Idealism was less in evidence among the Regulars than were professional pride and a high sensitivity to conditions and entitlements. They were unwilling to sign on for new engagements, unless in return for specific rewards, like a generous leave,[22] and yet the Regulars provided the only NCOs and private soldiers who consistently regretted that their service in the trenches had been cut short by captivity.

THE TERRITORIALS

In the years before 1914 the German General Staff monitored closely the steps by which the British government was coming to grips with the implications of intervening in a likely war on the mainland of Europe. It seemed to the Germans that the Territorial Force, which was created on 1 April 1908, was no more than a stop-gap. It was on an establishment of fourteen infantry divisions and fourteen mounted brigades, with a total of 316,094 officers and men, but after a promising start to recruiting the Germans knew that in 1912 it was short by some 70,000. The Territorial Force had been raised for home defence only, but the Germans could not believe that the restriction would be allowed to stand in the event of war, and they were convinced that the Territorial Force itself was an expedient that was designed to postpone the inevitable introduction of conscription.[23]

At the outbreak of war the Territorial Force stood at about 268,777 officers and men, or more than 47,000 below establishment. Afterwards Major C. H. Dudley Ward painted an idealised picture, in which he represented that 'what England owes to the Territorial is beyond computation. As the descendant of the old Volunteer he was enrolled to serve in England alone. But when war with the Central Powers was declared he did not hesitate – his response was immediate and unanimous.'[24] Many of the Territorials in fact held back from being 'volunteered' for service overseas, and in 1916 the recalcitrants were finally coerced by law. The

Germans were fully aware of the state of affairs. Corporal Stead of the 6/Gloucesters, 'a motor-boat builder from Clifton', taken prisoner at Serre on 18 March, told his captors that 'the men have a fundamental source of grievance, in that, having volunteered for "Home Service" only, they were sent to France regardless'.[25]

The Germans also knew how difficult it was to generalise about a body that was recruited from such a diversity of backgrounds. They were genuinely impressed by what they discovered of the 4/Royal Berkshire Regiment, as related by one sergeant, three corporals and seventeen men of 'B' Company, taken at Hébuterne on 16 May 1916. There was one professional man (a pharmacist) among them, the rest being artisans or agricultural labourers.

> The men make a favourable military impression, and are physically remarkably fresh. Most of them are still young, some less than eighteen years of age, and they are not as rigid in their bearing as the men of the Kitchener battalions, where the discipline is anyway much more strict. The men from any given battalion hail from the same locality, and are mostly friends. This means that when one or the other is promoted to NCO, he is unable to command the requisite authority. The same applies to some of the Territorial officers. The consequences may still be seen, even though the Territorial battalions in the field have been built up with a large number of men who have enlisted since the beginning of the war, and have been brought to a higher state of military discipline by Regular officers and NCOs.[26]

Already by February 1916 the Germans conceded that the Territorial divisions were beginning to bear comparison in efficiency with the divisions of the former Regular Army.[27]

THE NEW ARMIES ('KITCHENER MEN')
On 7 August 1914 Field Marshal Kitchener, as the newly appointed Secretary of State for War, issued his celebrated call for volunteers. The resulting New Armies were 'new' in every respect, for most of the resulting battalions lacked the most basic clothing and equipment, and some did not even have a skeleton cadre of experienced officers and NCOs. Less than two years later, transformed in every respect, the New

Army 'Service' battalions were in action on the Somme, and in the enduring British public imagination they have come to stand for the national voluntary spirit, the British experience on the Somme, and indeed for the British experience of the Great War as a whole. The celebrated Pals battalions were not necessarily typical of the New Armies, but they represented local communities and ways of life with an immediacy that did not survive the Battle of the Somme, or even in the most tragic cases its first day.

The New Armies were also 'new' in that a phenomenon of this kind had not entered remotely into the calculations of the German General Staff before the war. The Germans now found it convenient to term all the New Army troops 'Kitchener Men', and in 1916 they registered a steady increase in proficiency. Towards the end of February Captain Hugh Stewart Walker of the Camerons claimed that 'the training of the Kitchener Men, which has been going on seriously and for more than a year, is now so good that they can be reckoned alongside the men of the old regiments'.[28] That was something of an exaggeration, but a month later the Germans were told that 'the training of the Kitchener Men is said to be considerably more thorough than before. It has improved steadily, and the men who are now arriving as replacements are seen as good soldiers.'[29]

The Germans failed to identify the peculiar culture of the Pals battalions. They knew, for example, the Leeds Pals only as the 15/West Yorkshires, but they could see for themselves that the three men they captured on the night of 20/21 May near Serre were of exceptional quality, namely the 24-year-old businessman Rawnsley, the twenty-year-old pharmacist Hargreaves and the tailor Hewson, who was thirty. They were all Kitchener Men, and, most unusually for British soldiers, they knew the names of all the senior officers of their regiment. 'The prisoners come across extremely well, from both the physical and military point of view. Two of them have a good general education, and they judge the war and its consequences in a logical way.'[30]

A lieutenant of the 9th Battalion of the same regiment impressed the Germans equally.[31] Conversely it transpired that many of the men of his battalion had enlisted simply 'because there was no work for them'.[32]

Another reality of British life presented itself to the Germans in the shape of thirty-five men who were captured at Ypres on 12 February 1916, belonging to 'the lowest and the most venal stratum in England's population ... crooked legs, rickety, alcoholic, degenerate, ill-bred, and poor to the last degree ... There is an immense and significant difference between this crowd and the first regular troops we fought against in 1914. The equipment is very good, as usual.'[33] In physique, at least, this is paralleled by British descriptions of the men of the 25th and the 24th (Bantam) Divisions, 'being the dwarfed children of Industrial England and its mid-Victorian cruelties ... poor little men of a diseased civilisation'.[34]

A curious case, which interested the Germans, was that of a corporal who deserted to them at le Sars on 25 May 1916. 'The prisoner is an educated man (clerk with a large firm of accountants) and makes a very good impression. He joined up on 18 January 1916. He was so taken with the Scottish kilt that he enlisted with the Cameron Highlanders (see p. 37). He has no hesitation in telling us that he came over with his weapons because he has had enough of the war.' Among his discontents he cited 'the uniform of the kilt, puttees and laced boots, inadequate and indeed impossible for trench warfare in the winter'.[35]

THE 'DERBY MEN' AND THE CONSCRIPTS

In the German military shorthand the 'Derby Men' signified all the recruits who joined under a degree of compulsion, though strictly speaking the term ought to have been applied only to the men caught up in the Derby Scheme during its existence from 23 October to 15 December 1915, which was just one stage in a process of creeping conscription. The Germans tracked its progress from its inception in the National Registration Act of 15 July 1915, which was little more than a survey of all British men and women between the ages of fifteen and twenty-five. Those who were considered economically vital to the war effort were designated as working in 'starred' trades, while the 'unstarred' able-bodied men of military age were thereby put under increasing pressure to enlist.

The German General Staff had long expected something of the kind. Doubts had been expressed in the German press as to where the British could possibly find leaders for a mass army, but the soldier-poet Rudolf Binding commented that 'what the British do they do well; they will make good soldiers. Perhaps not so many as people think, but good ones. If England were to introduce conscription it would be more dangerous for us than anything she has ever done.' The officers and NCOs would come from 'the rowing blues, the leading lights of cricket and football teams, the athletic trainers, runners and many more'. He called to mind the mentality of the Berlin police, drawn mainly from Prussian ex-NCOs, who were not aware of the difference between influence and brutality, but 'the English policemen know how to deal with crowds; they handle them perfectly'.[36]

Binding had hit upon a significant contrast. In Germany (by a Prussian tradition dating back to the eighteenth century) discharged NCOs had become figures of local civilian authority – schoolmasters, postmasters and the like – as well as policemen, whereas in Britain in the Great War it was the leaders of civilian social life who naturally took on military authority.

The process began to acquire teeth in the actual Derby Scheme of October 1915, which 'rested on the knowledge that the former system of voluntary enlistment was no longer up to maintaining the divisions in the field at full combat strength'.[37] The 'unstarred' males (excluding Ireland) were given the option of enlisting without further ado, or attesting that they would be available for military service at a later date. The Derby Scheme was wound up in December, by when it was clear that 650,000 men neither joined up nor attested. Curiously enough the feeling in the Coldstream Guards was that those people had at least had the courage of their convictions, whereas the Derby Men in the narrower sense had given way to moral pressure. 'To be called or even thought a "Derby Man" is, in fact, an insult.'[38]

Through the Military Service Act of 27 January 1916 all 'unstarred' single men (again excluding Ireland) were made subject to outright conscription, and by the German reading of the British figures 316,464 men would be available for service after the unfit had been eliminated, and 'in such a way that the stock of unmarried men between eighteen and forty would have been exhausted'. If conscription were extended to married men (as it was on 25 May), it would produce another 280,000 bodies. The total yield from conscription, together with the volunteers from Ireland (who were unlikely to exceed 30,000) was thought to give the British 1,702,961 men, after which the reserves of manpower would be exhausted until more men came of military age.[39] These figures were of interest to the Germans, as indicating the likely effect of attrition, though the large number of prisoners in their early twenties indicated that the British still had a considerable stock of men in the physical prime of life.

The Germans also explored what the British had to say about the worth and impact of conscription. Captain Walker of the Cameron Highlanders told them in February 1916 that 'the Derby Scheme was a failure, and he does not expect much from the new conscription law, as it is alien to the British people. Nearly 50 per cent of the fit men would be able to evade military service, by one excuse or another. The best and most serviceable elements had already joined of their own free will.'[40] He was right, at least in the short term, for by July 1916 conscription had raised only 43,000 men. Unlike the Kitchener Men, who had come to France as formed bodies, the Derby Men were trickled into existing units as replacements, and in the course of July prisoners told the Germans that numbers had already arrived in the front line. 'In one of the divisions it is said that they had undergone only five or six weeks' training in England and then a further six weeks in France.'[41]

From that time until the end of the battle almost every source of information indicated that the Derby Men and the outright conscripts were wretched creatures of little value. Their shortcomings were revealed most starkly when they arrived to fill out battalions that had just suffered heavy losses in action. No less than 450 replacements, mostly Derby Men, were with the 8/Royal Warwicks when they attacked to the west of Mouquet Farm on 17 August, 'and when the leadership failed they had not the slightest idea what to do. They ran in all directions and crouched as best they could in shell-holes, where most of them were shot to bits by their own artillery. The present prisoners tried to escape from the shell-holes when night was falling, but they lost their way and were captured ... The prisoners made a thoroughly unmilitary impression, though there are some intelligent men among them. They are all completely weary of the war, and glad to have been captured.'[42]

The story was repeated in the 1/Essex Regiment, which had been depleted heavily in its first tour on the Somme. In the late autumn, in its second tour, many men were killed or wounded when they were still marching up through the communication trenches, and the survivors were thinned out when they attacked north of Gueudecourt on 12 October. The informant was a Derby Man, one of many in the battalion. 'The prisoner looks totally unmilitary, and is happy to say what he knows.' All that he could tell of the action itself was that he was aware that the men around him were being cut down by machine-gun fire.[43]

Something of the old spirit could even now be detected in those men who took advantage of a provision whereby they could anticipate conscription by offering themselves to a unit of their choice, rather than being thrown into a common pool. 'In Britain, now that Lord Derby has pronounced the words "you must", a completely different atmosphere reigns. They hasten to enlist as volunteers while there is still time.'[44]

The 'completely different atmosphere' also brought a new awareness of inequalities. From the prisoners taken in October and November the Germans deduced that 'there is much dissatisfaction in the British Army, and the prisoners are particularly aggrieved at the unfairness in the conscription. Most of the countrymen are spared because they are reckoned to be specialised labour, while great numbers of unmarried men work in the ammunition factories, sport the medal *On War Service* and earn a great deal of money. At the same time many married men are in the field, and claim that their families receive an inadequate subvention.'[45]

Sheer curiosity made the Germans take an interest in a man who had declared himself a conscientious objector. He was an earnest individual, who was keen on sport and earned his living as a lecturer in theology. He had at first welcomed the war, being an idealist, but then a personal crisis coincided with his revulsion at the slaughter. His reasoning must have failed to convince the relevant tribunal, for he was captured in the ranks of the 13/Middlesex.

It is comic when he describes how he was thrown among other soldiers in small, stinking rooms, where he had to clean his uniform and learn how to use 'weapons of murder' like rifles and hand grenades. He found it below his dignity when he was loaded with others like a herd of cattle on a ship for transportation for France ... On the march he was loaded down like a mule, and it would make you laugh to hear him complain indignantly how he sat on a packing case in streaming rain and in a state of desperation while the other soldiers were setting up tents, where they would have to spend the night on the muddy ground 'like herrings in a box'.[46]

FLYING MEN

One of the consequences of Brigadier General Trenchard's aggressive strategy of air war was that large numbers of aviators crashed or force-landed behind the German lines. Among the many informants, Second Lieutenant William Charles Mortimer-Phelan and his observer, Second Lieutenant W. A. Scott Brown, had been photographing the notorious anti-aircraft battery at Fampoux when they were abandoned by their escort and had the distinction of being shot down by Lieutenant Immelmann and another pilot.[47] Scott Brown told the Germans that he had been doing his three months' duty as an observer as one stage towards qualifying as a pilot,[48] which confirmed to the Germans that the selection process was severe. To weigh more than eleven stone (154 pounds) was to be excluded from the start, and most of the observers were told after only fourteen days that they would never have the makings of a pilot. Training was carried out at fields like Brooklands, Blackbushe, Farnborough, Hendon, Salisbury and Montrose. The initial course lasted for up to twelve weeks, though it provided only about seventy-five hours' flying time, and the Germans concluded early in 1916 that 'this gives substance to the complaints that the basic training is too short. The final stages take place over or behind the front, which is a bad idea, and helps to explain why there have been so many crashes in recent times.'[49]

The survivors were in various states of disarray when they fell into German hands, but they conveyed a comprehensive picture of the background and character of the British flyers. They had all come from other branches of the army, but most of them fell into identifiable types. Lieutenant W. Black was born in Sunderland and worked in his father's salvage business in continental harbours. 'In addition to his native tongue he speaks German and French and comes across as an intelligent and well-educated man.'[50]

Black's spirit was representative of the entrepreneurs and colonisers

THE BRITISH ARMY

(the Germans identified farmers from Canada and South Africa, a cattle trader from Argentina, an official of the Royal Mail Steam Packet Company in Montevideo, and the son of a businessman resident in Japan). Others were budding bankers or lawyers, or well set-up young men like Lieutenant W. Baxter Ellis of Newcastle (the son of a mill-owner of substance). Two had learned to fly at civilian schools at their own expense.

It was the social style expressed after the war at the Brooklands motor racing track, where the devotees of the daring young men were certain to find the 'right crowd' without being too crowded. Thus the leadership of the Royal Flying Corps preferred to recruit in the Dominions rather than commission former drivers or engineers who did not command an acceptable accent. The talkative P. J. Shaw therefore belonged to a small but distinct minority. He had been a mechanic in civilian life, and had continued to work as such in the Royal Flying Corps. 'This employment finally became too boring for him, and he volunteered as an observer in the hope of qualifying as pilot before too long, and gaining rapid promotion after further training in England.'[51] He had yet to be commissioned by the time he was shot down.

THE BRITISH MILITARY EXPERIENCE AND MENTALITY

The British were well provided with the things that mattered most in their limited order of priorities. 'The British show in general more interest in good food and accommodation than in the make-up of their formations, the identity of their neighbouring forces or the names of their commanders.'[52]

By all the German accounts the British equipment and material were of the highest quality, and the verdict was confirmed after the war by an American major general who compared the forces of occupation in the Rhineland. 'In set-up and personal appearance, it is hard to equal the British soldiers. As to horses, equipment and wagons, the British are easily ahead of any troops of the allies.'[53] Even on campaign the clothing of the Tommies compared well with 'the sloppy, ill-fitting grey uniforms of the German Army. The German field service uniforms always seemed … to be most depressing and convict-like. The British and French uniforms were much smarter, even in the worst conditions, and much more conducive to good morale.'[54]

77

By February 1916 the British front-line troops were wearing a mixture of cloth peaked caps and the new steel helmets. In the spring the steel helmets were clearly the norm in the forward positions, which put the British well ahead of the Germans, who caught up with their coal-scuttle helmets only in the course of the summer. George Coppard and his friends once amused themselves by battering away with pick-axes at a selection of British and German helmets. Some of the British helmets were merely dented, others pierced; which was put down to different qualities supplied by different contractors. In this rigorously scientific experiment all the German helmets were holed without exception.[55]

The differences between the G98 Mauser and the Short Magazine Lee-Enfield (SMLE) Mark III were so marginal that they rarely aroused comment, though most favoured the British rifle. The SMLE was at a slight disadvantage in terms of accuracy and muzzle velocity (2,440 feet per second as opposed to 2,850), but it was lighter (SMLE 8.2 lb; G98 8.9 lb), shorter, held ten rounds at a time instead of five, and its downturned bolt came easier to hand than the straight bolt of the Mauser. It seemed to the Germans that the SMLE gave the louder report, and that the Mark VII cartridge was a dum-dum in all but name, for the brittle point was liable to split on impact and allow the soft core to fragment.

The Germans were in a bad way when the weather closed down in October 1916, but 'in this respect the British were much better off'. They had the advantage of leather jerkins or fur outer coats, and so were 'much better able to withstand whatever the weather could throw at them, and all the more because they enjoyed good and regular food and frequent reliefs'.[56]

It was typical of the British to complain about the very measures that were being provided for their benefit. They suspected that the supplementary clothing was just a device to make them undergo longer spells on working parties. The goatskin outer coats were smelly, and the long rubber gumboots were unpopular 'as once they got wet inside they were difficult to dry, uncomfortable to wear and did nothing to keep out the cold'.[57]

The routine of daily life was equally demanding on both sides, and it was the standard drill for all the troops in the forward trenches to 'stand to' with clean and loaded weapons in the hours of dawn and dusk, and for longer still in special states of alert. For the rest of the time the men were set to work on fatigues or allowed to rest, apart from the lookouts who were posted at regular intervals along the fire-steps. Even in the front line it was usual to rotate the companies between tours of duty in the forward and rearward trenches. Thus for the 2nd (Natal and Orange Free State) Battalion of the South African Brigade in September 'the normal course of reliefs was four days in the first trench, four in the second and eight in rest'.[58] These alleviations were of more benefit to the British than to the Germans, who were on the whole exposed to a much heavier harassing fire of artillery and even machine guns deep into their defences.

There were occasions when the British soldiers were reduced to subsisting on their hard ration 'dog biscuits', but each company normally owned a cook who had his steamy abode behind the second trench, and kept the troops well supplied with containers of hot food and tea. When that failed, dixies and tins could be heated in forward positions on spirit stoves or improvised burners. Prisoners assured the Germans that in all normal conditions the food was both plentiful and of excellent quality.[59] The tins of bully beef and Maconochie beef or pork stew were sometimes so plentiful that they were thrown away or traded with the Germans. However, the British water arrived as a chlorine-flavoured liquid in a variety of containers, whereas the Germans were supplied with bottled mineral water which was manufactured in villages behind their lines.

Two soldiers in every British company were designated as stretcher bearers, who carried the injured men to the casualty stations of the Royal Army Medical Corps. There were notorious locations where the communication trenches were non-existent or had collapsed, which forced the bearers to strike across open ground and put themselves at the mercy of the enemy. In the fighting around Mouquet Farm in August the Australians were grateful to the Germans 'that they did not fire on their stretcher bearers, who carried little white flags'.[60] German commanders warned that the British might be exploiting their forbearance, but this two-hour morning *Sanitätspause* became the norm along the Ancre from the late autumn, and was honoured by both sides.

The lightly wounded were patched up at the casualty clearing stations, while the walking wounded and the bad cases were dispatched to the brigade dressing station. The base hospitals were altogether bigger affairs, which were established in the deep rear and tended the badly wounded and the long-term sick. A corporal in the Cameron Highlanders said that 'he had been at the hospitals in Boulogne and Rouen, and seen that the conditions there were very good. Beds, food and treatment were all first class. He had seen a separate hospital for the German wounded in Rouen, where the food and accommodation were excellent. Every British soldier released from hospital was given a week's light duties before being returned to his unit.'[61]

The Germans deduced that by the late summer of 1916 the French still showed evidence of a much longer and harder war than the British, but that the difference was narrowing. 'It is worth drawing attention to the fact ... that of the British captured between July and October only 17 per cent had been wounded already, as opposed to 36.5 per cent of the French. In November the comparable figures stood at 27.68 per cent of the British and 41.73 of the French. Of these:

	French per cent	British per cent
Wounded once	30.25	23.78
Twice	9.26	2.17
Three times	1.96	0.57
Four times	0.26	0.16

These figures do not include the enemy wounded who were delivered to the field hospitals only [i.e. the lightly wounded].'[62]

Almost everyone was affected by some kind of intestinal upset at one time or another, but in 1916 the most frequent cause of disability was trench foot. In reasonably dry weather, and among well-disciplined troops, the disorder could be minimised by frequent foot inspections and airings. These conditions did not obtain among the 23rd Battalion of the Victoria Brigade of the 2nd Australian Division towards the end of the year. One of its officers, captured on 21 November, informed the Germans that he had lost about fifty men of his company from this cause over the last seventeen days. He blamed the notorious rubber waders. 'Even when the boots gave protection against the wet, it was his experience that the feet became icy cold and swollen over a period of time. If the men were not at once sent to the rear their feet became black, and the worst cases were amputated. The symptoms were the same as with frost bite.'[63]

British officers were entitled to a relatively generous leave allowance of seven days every quarter, not including the outward and return journeys. Soldiers usually qualified for leave after nine months in France, though their release could be delayed for a multitude of reasons. By the same token the private's miserable pay of one shilling per day could run well into arrears.

For the troops in bulk, service in the line was ameliorated by rotations on the theatre of war. Among the Germans fourteen days was reckoned to be the normal limit of front-line service, and from the memoirs and histories it is evident that many units were pushed beyond their endurance. For the 30th Reserve Regiment the thirteen days under artillery and gas attack from 15 to 27 September 1916 cost the Germans 1,176 of all ranks killed, wounded and missing.[64] When the troops were taken out of one sector it signified all too often that they were merely flung in somewhere else, or put to exhausting work like digging new lines of defence.

The British managed affairs better, even though the length of their spells in the line could vary greatly. When units were taken to the rear

the rest days are spent in something like the following order: Breakfast about eight in the morning (tea, bacon, bread, butter, marmalade). The food is brought up by two men from each platoon. Lunch is at one in the afternoon (soup, fresh meat, and frequently raisins and dates as well). The evening meal is at four or five (tea, bread, cheese, marmalade). From the third day onwards the time between the meals is spent on various duties, but on the first two days after leaving the trenches the men are free to do as they please. The duties in question are the cleaning of weapons, roll-call, tidying up the quarters, and sessions devoted to marching, musketry and tactics. There are instructional classes in topography, map-reading and so on (for the officers in separate groups). Otherwise the men are at liberty. They enjoy football, and picture shows are also available.[65]

British troops were accommodated in empty or partly ruined houses, schools or factories, or, least desirable of all, in bug-ridden barns. The larger tented camps were usually to be found in the distant base areas, as along the coast at Etaples. Hutted camps were a convenient way of concentrating troops behind the front line in preparation for a 'push', as in the forty-man huts established in June in two large woods behind Bray and Morlancourt. Most welcome of all were the semi-circular Nissen huts, fashioned from lengths of corrugated iron, with the two ends closed off by wooden walls.[66]

Whole British divisions could be moved to genuinely quieter sections of the line (like the 7th Division after its mauling in August), or taken out of the line altogether and placed in reserve. The Germans were long exasperated and puzzled by having to face what seemed to be fresh formations, and finally concluded towards the end of 1916 that 'one of the main reasons why the British infantry become relatively good troops, in spite of a short period of training, is probably that the British high command knows how to bring them into action with their nerves unstressed. From the evidence of prisoners it has been verified beyond doubt that individual divisions have been brought into the relevant sector on the night before an attack; they then deliver the attack during darkness and are relieved the following night. In such a way the troops are exposed for only a short time to the destructive power of modern artillery, and remain more combat-worthy than if they had been exposed to *Trommelfeuer* in shot-up trenches for days on end.'[67]

The periods in rest or reserve gave the British soldiers their first opportunity to learn something of France and the French. As recorded by the British the relationship was good, and sometimes led to lifelong friendships and marriages. The evidence collected by the Germans suggested the contrary. The British military administration is described as treating the French population with draconian severity, while French prisoners complained that the Royal Flying Corps and the Royal Artillery reached far behind German lines to smash villages and towns.[68] German propaganda played on the French resentments, and claimed that the British would stop at nothing to drive the Germans from northern France and Belgium. Dwellings, factories and monuments like the cathedral at Saint-Quentin were all sacrificed 'in the interests of British policy'.[69]

To some of the French it seemed that the British regarded themselves as the saviours of France. 'For a long time the British officers and soldiers simply did not pay their bills in coffee houses or for their tram tickets. They would just give an inclination of the head and say *souvenir pour vous!* as if in payment for what they owed. The British authorities had to institute orders and punishments to convince them that such conduct was unacceptable.'[70]

The French repaid with interest the real or imagined slights to their pride. In the experience of the 8/East Surreys 'the relations between the French civilian population and the British soldiers are just about as bad as they can be. It often happens that when the troops are marching through villages they find that the water pipes have been stopped, the pump handles removed, and so on, just to prevent them from drinking. In most cases this arises not to safeguard the facilities but out of sheer malice on the part of the population.'[71] Some Royal Munster Fusiliers added that 'they did not allow us to take even the smallest piece of wood without payment, and they put in immediate complaints if we did so. One man of our company was fined fifteen francs because he picked up a decayed bit of a garden fence from the road as firewood.'[72] There were many testimonies of the same kind.

The British troops grumbled at the work they had to put into cleaning up positions they had taken over from the French, as before the Battle of the Somme. Their opinion of the French military was, however, positive, albeit based on hearsay rather than first-hand contact.[73] Only now and then did the British catch sight of French infantry 'with their quick lurching step, leaning forward under heavy packs and in long sky-blue greatcoats'.[74]

The fine inflicted on the Munster Fusilier was indicative of what was being enforced throughout the British Army. Colonel Nicolai, the chief of the German military intelligence, testifies that by international standards 'an iron discipline, maintained by a severe code of punishments, was in their blood'.[75] On 2 April 1916 a German investigation set out the full range of such measures available to the authorities. Field Punishment No. 2, the mildest of the formal penalties, typically involved fatigues, fines and (out of the line) confinement to quarters. Field Punishment No. 1 was a primitive and degrading sentence, which in addition tied a man to a fixed object for two hours a day. The more fearsome penalties at the disposal of a General Field Court Martial extended to death or an extended imprisonment with hard labour.[76]

The code, though severe in itself, was subject to wide interpretations. Three Kitchener Men of the Leeds Pals testified that 'the discipline is not really harsh, but you have to remember that the battalion consists mainly of volunteers from the better middle class, who have the necessary self-discipline. Punishments are therefore rare.'[77] In the view of twenty-one men of the 4/Royal Berkshire Regiment, all of them neighbours, 'there is not a great deal of punishment', and they considered Field Punishment No. 2 a reasonable penalty for having a dirty rifle.[78] Elsewhere, as in the unhappy 2/Border Regiment, 'the discipline is extraordinarily strict, even by the standards of Regular units. The punishments are frequent and severe, evidently to bring the young recruits up to the military mark as soon as possible.'[79]

When the Germans assessed British morale as a whole in the middle of October 1916 they discovered that 'the younger NCOs, who have gained their promotions through good conduct, are disliked by their men as they have too high an opinion of themselves and are fond of finding fault. The old Territorials complain of the excessively harsh discipline, which seems to be more severe than even among the Germans.'[80]

The full force of the code was felt in the cases of the 346 British who were executed by firing squad in the course of the war, forty-eight of them on the Somme. Although the comparable figures among the continental armies are dificult to establish, the Italian army shot many more of its own men than did the British, while the German army (which respected its men as 'citizens in uniform') shot far fewer. The best framework of reference is however among the British soldiers of the time, who were aware of the issues in all their complexity. According to a sergeant and two soldiers of the 2/Lancashire Fusiliers

discipline is upheld severely. A man of the battalion was shot by sentence of court martial in May [1915] because he ran away in two gas attacks. He was a nineteen-year-old volunteer, and the troops could not understand why he was punished so harshly, for he evidently acted only when things got too much for him. A second man of the same battalion

was shot for being absent from his post and for drunkenness (at Armentières). One of the present prisoners was sentenced to death for
cowardice in the face of the enemy. The sentence was commuted to
fifteen years' imprisonment, and this in turn to five years in jail in
consideration of good conduct. He began to serve his sentence in
Rouen, but was sent back to his company after one month.[81]

The Germans uncovered something of both the causes and consequences of this code of discipline when they examined the behaviour
of the enemy under stress. They were unimpressed by some of what
they saw, and totally baffled by much of the rest. Careful observations
were made of the 160 or so NCOs and men of the 48th (South Midland)
and neighbouring divisions who had been wounded and captured
between 1 and 3 July on the sector from Gommecourt south to Fricourt,
and were now being treated in the German hospital at Caudry. They
were in the first shock of the disaster, and the cohesion of the units had
broken down.

Most of the wounds were very severe, and some of the men have
already died. But many others are only very slightly wounded, and from
what we have seen in the hospital it is clear that our German soldiers
endure their pains much more stoically than do the British, who are
much given to bewailing their lot. It is also worth alluding to the lack of
comradeship which is evident among these men. The lightly wounded
soldiers, who are not confined to bed and can walk about, show not the
slightest concern for their badly wounded comrades, even though they
could alleviate their condition – and indeed their deaths – through a
little attention. The devoted personnel of our hospital do all they
possibly can, but in view of the numbers of British and German
wounded who crowded in, and the great number of operations which
had to be performed, it was not always possible for our people to attend
at once to all the wishes of the patients. These lightly wounded British
heard their comrades call out for water but did not bestir themselves in
the slightest, and yet they came rushing up when the food was being
given out. We had to take pretty severe measures to make them fulfil
this simple human duty to their own countrymen.[82]

Such behaviour seemed to run counter to the cult of the 'iron will' which was current among the Germans at that time,[83] but it probably had less to do with a lack of fortitude than with the passivity engendered by a style of leadership which was dedicated and paternal at its best, but rarely engaged the intellect. A well-educated Saxon *Vizefeldwebel* told his British captors that 'both our [i.e. British] officers and men are admirably brave, and incomparably better soldiers than ... the German and Austrian troops. However they suffer from a lack of enlightened and intelligent training ... as is shown by the stupid dispositions which our staff make for the attack. In the German army an intelligent appreciation of operations is maintained by popular lectures behind the lines, illustrated by slides and moving films. Also, pamphlets and booklets are issued to all ranks. Prisoners had such booklets concerning the battle of the Aisne, the French offensives, our attacks at Festhubert and Loos, the fighting at Vimy and the big German advance in Russia.'[84]

The Germans were confirmed in their opinion by what they saw of the British in captivity. '"Fed up with it", is the usual answer they give when they are asked what they think of the war.'[85] ... 'With these prisoners we also note their surprising lack of interest in military affairs and the indifference with which they regard the war.'[86] Some were unaware of what was meant by terms like 'platoon' or 'company', and some did not even know in what country they were fighting.

Once a few 'misunderstandings' had been sorted out, the British prisoners accustomed themselves well to camp routine, and they made the best working parties out of all the nations in German captivity. They were provided with parcels of food and clothing from home, but they displayed none of the cheerful willingness of the French to make the best of a bad situation, and refused to join in competitions to prettify the surroundings of their huts by laying out gardens. 'It goes without saying that they were much taken with the cult of football, but even this enthusiasm died the death when they found that they were being beaten by the French ... Most of the time Tommy Atkins was sunk in a state of apathetic, sullen indifference.'[87] The Germans were willing to make distinctions between the English proper and the other peoples of the British Isles, who were more positive in their outlook. The Welsh, like the Irish, were quick-witted and lively and retained a sense of their own nationhood. 'The Scots form a further sub-group, some of them of Celtic origin, but the majority probably of Scandinavian. The most typical of them wear just as hard an expression as do the English, but there is a reflective look in their eyes which indicates a fundamentally different mentality.'[88]

To the Germans the heart of the British identity appeared to be an unimpressionability and a lack of commitment. In March 1917 Rudolf Binding read Haig's official report on the Battle of the Somme, and found it vague, tedious and devoid of imagination. 'Therein he is typical of the whole British policy in its attitude towards the war. It began as an expedition; its troops were called "expeditionary forces", Britain has never waged wars in such a way that the soul of the population entered into them ... she fights without enthusiasm, as one fights against mice or other vermin.'[89]

The German analysis is convincing to a certain point, but it fails to explain how the same people could be consistently on the attack, and in a way which constantly evoked the word *zäh*, meaning 'dogged', 'persistent' or 'obstinate'. Some of the Germans addressed the paradox by persuading themselves that the fatalistic, phlegmatic British had first to be got drunk, then driven forward by officers on horseback. It was a formulaic fantasy, which was repeated in the official reports and memoranda and found its way into the regimental histories.

In fact the instincts of the seemingly ignorant and unresponsive British *Frontsoldaten* about the nature and outcome of the war were better informed than those of many statesmen and senior commanders on both sides. The high hopes which had been invested in the great offensive on the Somme were for some of the survivors dashed totally at the outset. 'A captain, whose company was committed only on the second day, estimates the overall losses of the British front on the first day at 80–100,000 men, if they corresponded to those sustained on the sector of his brigade.'[90] By September it was noted that the 'high confidence in being able to "drive the Huns out of France" is by no means as great as at the start of the offensive on the Somme. The planned "walk-over" had become a "steeplechase" with an endless succession of obstacles, and before the "finish" many of the morale-raising leading articles in the Northcliffe press would fall flat, and still more of the prophecies in

Bottomley's would bite the dust.'[91] Neither the British nor the Dominion troops could see any prospect of a breakthrough.[92]

For all their disillusion, officers and men like those of the 2/East Lancashires 'still retained enough of a sense of duty to do their best if ordered into an attack'.[93] There were many expressions of the same kind. 'They are … personally "sick of the war", even the "sportsmen" among the flying officers, and yet they are convinced that the reserves of men and gold are still so great that final victory is assured. They know very well the cost of the offensive since the beginning of July … but leaders and men alike are full of confidence.'[94]

If there were a phrase which summed up the mood of the British officers and soldiers in 1916 it would be 'morose optimism'. They looked to their financial strength, the depth of manpower in the Empire, the achievements of their war industry (in which they took great pride) and the effects of the naval blockade. 'It's true that the ground they intend to win is not great, but the main consideration is to wear down the stock of the German manpower.'[95] The process would therefore be one of attrition, and when the British were asked how long it would take to bring down Germany, there was one reply which summed up most of the others: 'Not before two years have passed. Britain is determined, as you know, and it will wait out that time patiently.'[96]

THINK!

ARE YOU CONTENT FOR
HIM TO FIGHT FOR **YOU** ?

WON'T YOU DO YOUR BIT ?

WE SHALL WIN
BUT **YOU** MUST HELP

JOIN TO-DAY

CHAPTER FOUR

The Home Fires

THE RIVAL DOMESTIC FRONTS

The Germans were rightly proud of the transformations that had overtaken their country, so recently come together from separate states. Between 1870 and the outbreak of the Great War the population had grown by 60 per cent, and the production of steel fifteen times over – which was just one of the pointers indicating that Germany was now the foremost industrial power of Europe. Germany enjoyed basic social welfare, and the nation was at the forefront of chemical, mechanical and electrical engineering and the study of the Classics and history. The British competitors were duly impressed. 'One of them, a businessman from Leeds, told us how difficult it had been for British firms before the war to match the imported German goods, which were far superior in quality as well as being about only half the price.'[1]

By 1916 this exemplary society was nevertheless under heavy strain. There was lack of enthusiasm for the war effort among the soldiers from the industrial areas of the west, and from Upper Silesia, Saxony and

Alsace-Lorraine. The component states of Germany were competing for dwindling resources, and there arose fears that Germany would not be equal to the strains of the new *Materialschlacht*. 'In our homeland the people had to face the consequences of a bad potato harvest, and a dismal winter loomed ahead. There was a shortage of coal, and this, together with the lack of other raw materials, appeared to be leading our war industry to an inexorable catastrophe. Shortfalls of ammunition were experienced on every front, which was felt most painfully by our armies just when they were so heavily engaged with the enemy.'[2] So little ammunition was coming up from Germany in the first week of the Battle of the Somme that there was scarcely enough for defensive barrages and the most immediate needs of infantry support.

Salvation appeared to arrive in the bulky shapes of Hindenburg and Ludendorff, who in the late summer of 1916 stamped their joint authority on military and political affairs. On 31 August Hindenburg wrote a letter to the war minister, which became known as the 'Hindenburg Programme'. He set the tone when he urged that 'the exertions of men, and horses as well, must be increasingly replaced by those of machines. This will be all the more difficult because the enemy have grasped this principle as well ... All other branches of industry must take second place to war industry. If necessary we must resort to measures of compulsion.'[3] This last phrase was a reference to the example set by the British Ministry of Munitions. Before the year was out both the state and private industries in Germany were being co-ordinated by military-appointed War Offices (*Kriegs-Ämter*) in the component states, and all men between the ages of seventeen and sixty were conscripted to work in the war economy if they were not already doing military service.

Some of the gains of the Hindenburg Programme were illusory, but the German soldiers and civilians were persuaded that 'in this our state of need ... two men were called to the head of the army – men whose superhuman strength was equal to the immense task of guiding army and people through the unimaginable dangers and obstacles which pressed in from every side ... We at once sensed a change in the leadership.'[4] Artillery ammunition became available in greater quantity, and the fine new aircraft that reached the front in September and October were also credited to the Hindenburg Programme, though it is unlikely that there was any direct connection.

Britain as well as Germany was engaged in total war, and it was important for the Germans to take stock of economic and social conditions in the British homeland. In this respect the prisoners taken from the British on the Somme were a prime source of information, and in their innocence they were willing to talk to the Germans on such matters without reserve. The insights were registered and collated by the intelligence officers at the headquarters of the various armies. The final destination for this information even now remains unknown, although Holger Herwig suggests that it may have ended up with the committee of civilian experts – economists, businessmen and the like – which the German Admiralty set up to investigate how vulnerable Britain might be to a renewed all-out campaign of U-boat warfare.

As Hindenburg admitted, Britain had set an example in the directing of the economy and the labour force to military ends. The 'shell scandal' (a shortage of ammunition for the attack on Aubers Ridge) had con-tributed to the foundation of a coalition government in May 1915, with the charismatic David Lloyd George as the head of a new Ministry of Munitions. On 6 July 1916 he was appointed Secretary of State for War, a post that had been vacant since the death of Kitchener. He became increasingly dissatisfied with Haig's conduct of the Battle of the Somme and with the lack of energy on the part of the other branches of the coalition government and, in a political crisis, on 5 December both he and Prime Minister Asquith tendered their resignations. Two days later Lloyd George emerged as prime minister, and on the 9th he formed a new War Cabinet.

The Germans found that their British prisoners were divided in their responses to the rise of Lloyd George, and that the differences corre-sponded to rank. The officers shared the public perception that Lloyd George would bring an admirable vigour to the conduct of the war, and that he would confront and defeat the U-boat threat in the same style as he had overcome the shortage of ammunition. 'But the troops have an altogether different opinion concerning the "Dictator". The prisoners say that all the Tommies without exception would like to see him on a spell of duty in the trenches, an experience which would incline him to peace soon enough. The soldiers believe that he alone is to blame for the fact that the war has lasted such a long time and that it is still going on.'[5]

The British Foreign Office received a German peace note on 17 December 1916, and the news reached the British trenches over the following days. Many soldiers allowed themselves to hope that they would be rescued from their miserable state. However, the government did not take the offer seriously, and 'the officers, and some of the men as well, were of the opinion that the peace offer was a sign of weakness on the part of the Germans. Germany is at the end of its resources, short of men and material, and Germany must make peace! This way of thinking is very pronounced in Britain, though it is said that their strong inclinations towards peace are already in evidence there as well.'[6]

Officers and men nevertheless agreed on other issues. They admired the endurance that was being shown by Germany and the German forces, and they deplored the volatility of opinion back home. In the period from 11 to 21 September alone the Germans recorded three totally contradictory indications of the popular mood. To the well-educated second Lieutenant Phillimore this lack of moral steel was not at all 'the spirit of the England which withstood Napoleon over the course of thirteen years'.[7]

The prisoners believed that opinion was being manipulated unscrupulously by publications such as Lord Northcliffe's *Times, Daily Mail* ('*Daily Liar*'), *Evening News* and *Weekly Dispatch*, and Horatio Bottomley's notorious *John Bull*. The British troops were not taken in by stories that extolled wonder weapons like the tank and super-heavy guns, 'and they more than once made the point that it would be wrong to judge public opinion by the reports in the newspapers'.[8] The officers nevertheless gave the Northcliffe press the credit for urging on the public to ever greater efforts, and 'without this propaganda it would have been scarcely possible for the British government to put the whole of Britain in the frame of mind to make the necessary sacrifices, or to implement conscription'.[9]

The Germans did not help their cause by continuing to provide material for atrocity stories, after their misdeeds during the invasion of Belgium and France in 1914. In 1915 they shot Nurse Edith Cavell, and in 1916 the execution of Captain Fryatt awakened new hatred against Germany.[10] Charles Fryatt was the captain of a packet that had been plying to Holland, and on 28 March 1915 he had made at full speed for the U-33 and compelled the submarine to break off an attack. He was later captured by the Germans, and after a brief spell in the internment camp at Ruhleben he was hauled out and shot for piracy at Bruges on 27 July 1916. The Battle of the Somme was now in full swing, which was bad timing on the part of the Germans, and the Tommies took to chalking Fryatt's name on extra-large shells which were destined for his executioners.

The documentary film *The Battle of the Somme* received its premiere before an invited audience at the Scala Theatre in Clapham on 10 August 1916, and went on general release on the 21st. On 5 September it was being shown to troops on a screen that had been set up in a muddy field at Morlancourt on the Somme; it was judged 'a wonderful and most realistic production',[11] and although the sound of rifle and machine-gun fire was lacking, the noise of the artillery was being provided by real guns firing in the background.

The film had been shot between 26 June and 7 or 9 July by Geoffrey Malins (29th Division of VIII Corps) and J. B. McDowell (7th Division of XV Corps), and in spite of heavy cuts and censorship it still ran for a sizeable seventy-seven minutes. Both the thinking behind the film and its reception were of great interest to the Germans. An article in the *Berliner Tageblatt*, by a neutral reporter in London, explained that the British cinema was now taking a more serious turn, and 'the government has helped to bring about this change by arranging the production of real war films, and that pictures of *The Battle of the Somme* attract large crowds. I must admit that we can see nothing more absorbing and exciting.'[12] The Germans found a letter from an ardent filmgoer who had seen the documentary on 26 August, and written straight away to a soldier at the front that 'I must cross my heart and say that once you have seen this film you will never forget it ... I really must tell you something about it. Before the showing every filmgoer is given a leaflet which states that what we are about to see in a few minutes is not intended for our entertainment. In other words that we are being shown an official film of the actual battle, and I can imagine that the production must have cost a lot of money. It will certainly succeed in opening the eyes of the audience in a way that would not have been possible before.'[13]

The Germans naturally made a close and prolonged examination of the living conditions in Britain. They found that the evidence pointed on the one hand to strain, and on the other to the underlying strength of the British economy and its access to resources. The greatest single pressure on the poor and on people living on fixed incomes undoubtedly came from the rise in the cost of provisions. The Germans estimated that by May 1916 the price of bread had increased by up to 50 per cent since the beginning of the war, meat by 70 per cent, fish by 90 per cent, tea by 50 per cent and sugar by 130 per cent. Rationing had still to come and there was no regulation of prices. Butter was being priced out of the reach of many families, though margarine, peas and beans remained relatively cheap. The German intelligence service thought it worthy of note that, in spite of such hardships and inequalities, 'the economy is carrying on just as in peacetime, even though many men are no longer available. Women are busy in the munition factories and the war-related industries.'[14] They were 'working alongside old and young men who are disqualified for military service on account of their age. The working hours are regulated by law, with special provision for women and minors.'[15] The regulations extended to 'the enhanced wages, the wider opportunities for employment and the state subventions, which means that many people are at least not worse off than they were before the war. None of the prisoners doubt that Britain has the financial strength to last the war, in spite of heavy subsidies for the allies.'[16]

The Germans were alert for any signs of social unrest, but if we exclude Ireland the undoubted discontents fell short of anything with revolutionary potential. If Britain in 1916 lost 2.5 million working days in strikes, as opposed to only 245,000 in Germany,[17] it is fair to mention that the rate of strikes in Britain had been far higher before the war, attaining a peak of 41 million working days in 1912. Strikes were officially forbidden in both countries, but whereas in Britain they were treated with sage tolerance, in Germany they could be put down by military force. The Socialist deputy Philipp Scheidemann contrasted the British way to its advantage with the German methods, which were evidence of a lack of social cohesion. There were 'Englishmen and Frenchmen who fire on Germans because they have to. But on the other hand there are Germans who dance with joy at the idea of Germans firing on Germans.'[18] Lloyd George, in contrast, reasoned in person with striking Welsh miners, and Haig had been happy to be photographed alongside Ben Tillett, the founder and leader of the Dockers' Union.

There was general resentment among the British soldiers at the high wages being earned by the munitions workers, and at the backwardness of welfare provision in Britain, where a state old age pension had been introduced only in 1908, in other words twenty-eight years after Bismarck's Germany. 'Parliament had debated for months on end about the cost, which came to about 6 million pounds, and the great war-mongers were the very ones who were most opposed to giving the pro-letariat some kind of security in their declining years. The soldiers commented bitterly that sum, which Britain was ... supposedly not rich enough to afford at that time, was now being spent day in and day out for the purposes of a war which, they believe, can only result in years of poverty for working people.'[19]

In the summer of 1916 the Battle of Jutland came second only to the opening of the Battle of the Somme as a shock to the prestige of British arms. However, the German High Seas Fleet still shrank from sallying forth to threaten Britain's sea lifelines, and the only weapon available to the Germans for that purpose was the U-boat. A powerful body of opinion in the German armed services therefore argued, like Falken-hayn and Ludendorff, that Germany had a duty to make use of this potentially decisive instrument by resuming unrestricted U-boat attacks (discontinued in 1915). Crown Prince Rupprecht of Bavaria was not against U-boat warfare as such, but he was aware of the consequences of sinking neutral as well as British shipping without restriction or warning. 'Ludendorff ... should really steer clear of political questions, bearing in mind the maxim of Clausewitz that war is a continuation of politics with other means. Ludendorff is a distinguished soldier, certainly, but he understands nothing of politics.'[20]

The evidence of the German Admiralty's committee of experts proved decisive. It formed the basis of a paper which the Chief of the

Admiralty Staff von Holtzendorff put before the Great General Staff and Chancellor Bethmann Hollweg on 22 December 1916. The Chancellor abandoned his objections on 9 January the next year, and the campaign was initiated on 1 February. For America the consequent sinkings added to the evidence of hostile intentions, and the United States declared war on Germany on 9 April. For a time the campaign inflicted very heavy losses on British, allied and neutral shipping, but it proved to be an ultimate failure on its own terms, as well as being a gross and predictable political blunder.

The German Admiralty's committee had failed to allow for the increase in British arable farming, and the number of U-boats on patrol (though much increased) rarely exceeded forty at a time, which was inadequate to deter the shipping of grain and meat to British ports from the Americas and Australia. The British prisoners had told the Germans in 1916 that the steep rise in the price of food in Britain was linked with the U-boat campaign then being waged, 'but the higher freight rates, together with the highly developed trade with allies and neutrals have made up for the losses. So much British treasure had had to be expended in America for munitions and provisions that Britain has been forced to look for a loan there on unfavourable terms. But now the money will be retained in the country through the increase and expansion of the ammunition factories, and an intensive programme of putting pasture and landed estates under the plough. "Britain is cultivated", to use their own words.'[21]

The British officers doubted whether the numbers of U-boats and the technical resources available to the Germans would ever have a decisive effect, and they said that Lloyd George was conducting anti-submarine warfare in an energetic way. 'Also there was an officer who claimed to have seen a great quantity of U-boats in the Firth of Forth (though he cannot give the exact number), all of which had been caught in nets which had been spread for the purpose.'[22] This must have been a tall story, designed to discourage the Germans. The British officers were unanimous as to the ability of their country to survive the worst that the U-boats could do, and their opinions must either have been unknown to the German Admiralty's civilian committee, or were discounted completely.

There remained the possibility of direct attack on the British homeland. On the night of 15/16 December 1914 German cruisers had staged a hit-and-run bombardment of the east coastal towns of Hartlepool, Scarborough and Whitby. The German Admiralty soon abandoned the strategy, and turned instead to its force of Zeppelins, which opened their attacks in 1915. The raids in the course of 1916 amounted to thirty-eight, and accounted for 311 fatalities. When they were questioned on the subject the British officers said that the material damage was of no military consequence, and that the casualties were counter-productive, in that they encouraged men to volunteer for the army. These detached perspectives were not shared by the civilians, and the Germans were able to read a letter that had been posted from London on 24 September: 'Last night we had to endure a frightful raid by the Zeppelins. It's reported that four Zeppelins took part and bombed various parts of London, by which I mean Stepney, Lea Bridge and Essex Road. A whole lot of people were killed or injured [forty killed, 140 wounded], and they say that this raid was the worst of all.'[23]

The Zeppelins flew at high altitudes at night, which posed considerable challenges to the air defence of Britain. From the testimony of Lieutenant A. Cairnduff, captured on 31 May, 'the British are currently testing an incendiary bomb in the form of a dart, and have already employed it against Zeppelins. The bombs are suspended from the lower wing, and released by the operation of a handle. The aircraft descends at a dive to aim the bomb at the target, and a device triggers the explosion in the interior of the balloon ... Lieutenant Cairnduff worked for some time in the War Office and had the anti-Zeppelin operations under his direction, after which he himself flew for a month with a squadron designated to chase the Zeppelins. He reckons that sorties of that kind at night are totally useless. They give rise to many crashes with consequently heavy fatalities.'[24]

With the longer nights later in the year the Germans renewed their offensive, but now the British scored a number of successes with their incendiary ammunitions. They shot down two of the airships engaged in the raid described in the civilian letter just quoted, and the Germans sustained further losses in the course of October and November, culminating in the shooting-down of two Zeppelins over the east coast on 17 November.

Something like the true cost of total war was therefore becoming evident to the British public in 1916, but a hardening of opinion was evident towards the end of that year, just when the Germans chose to make their peace overture. The British saw the Battle of the Somme as no more than a first act, and they looked forward to a spring offensive that was intended to drive the Germans from France and force them to peace on the allies' terms. The form of the attack, according to an officer just returned from home, would be offensives against the two German flanks – by the French in Alsace and by the British in Flanders. The officers and the soldiers did not share the optimism of the public, 'but they say with one voice that an offensive can be opened as early as spring – an offensive which will put the Battle of the Somme in the shade'.[25]

THE IRISH

1916 was a year of some interest in the relations between the Irish and the English, and the Germans went to some trouble to establish whether the frictions could be turned to some use. The Germans knew their Catholic Irish prisoners were men of a different mentality from the English, being more lively and more alert to their surroundings. The German doctors found that many of them were in poor physical shape, which probably derived from heavy recruiting among the poor of the Irish towns but which the Germans attributed to generations of malnourishment and oppression. The English had represented the Irish to the world as 'an uncultured, intellectually inferior people. But those of us with a knowledge of history will be aware of the spiritual, scholarly and artistic achievements which distinguished the Irish above all other peoples in the early Middle Ages.' It was the Irish who had preserved Classical culture through the chaos of the Dark Ages, and who had brought Christianity to Central Europe and thus promoted the flowering of the Middle Ages.[26]

At this stage of the war Irishmen of atypically good physique were to be identified among the Irish-Australians who were captured at Fromelles on 19 and 20 July 1916, and in the 'large rural Irishmen of farming stock' who were recruited into the Irish Guards.[27] More representative were the troops of the 16th (Irish) Division, which was an expression of the soon-to-be-defunct form of Irish nationalism as represented by John Redmond and his National Party.

It is one of the true truisms that the outbreak of the Great War averted civil war in Ireland, a war between the predominantly Catholic Irish nationalists and the intransigent Protestants of Ulster. After decades of constitutional struggle Redmond and his nationalists had just wrung from the London government the promise of internal self-rule for Ireland as a whole, and the British Army and the Royal Navy could well have found themselves under orders to implement London's will by force if Europe had not been overtaken by the reality of a far greater struggle in August 1914.

At the outset of the Battle of the Somme the Germans were intrigued to have captured an Irish captain who was a Member of Parliament of the National party and pro-German in sentiment. 'Asked why he had voted for war in the sitting on 3 August, he replied that it was for the same reasons that the German Chancellor found an absolutely unanimous Reichstag on the same day. Otherwise he did not concern himself with "high politics".' He was aware of the difficulties in his own position. 'He had dedicated himself to war as to the knife in the separatist Irish nationalist cause. He seemed to be something of a fanatic on that point. He did not believe in the possibility of a compromise between Catholic Ireland and the Protestant minority in the province of Ulster. At the moment the contradictions were being plastered over, but they would emerge all the more strongly after the war unless the situation were handled with the greatest tact.'[28]

The biggest exercise in 'plastering over' was made on 18 September 1914, when the Home Rule Bill received the royal assent, but the execution was simultaneously suspended for twelve months or the duration of the war. Two days later John Redmond issued an appeal for volunteers to join the new Irish formations to fight for the British Crown. The core of his support came from his military wing, the National Volunteers, who furnished 22,000 of the 54,000 Catholic Irish who had volunteered by the spring of 1916. But for the international crisis of 1914 these were the same men who would have been fighting against the Protestant Ulster Unionist Volunteers, who in their turn made up 25,000 of the more than 43,000 Irish Protestants who had come forward to serve over the same period. To Colonel Nicolai, the chief of German military intelligence, 'it was remarkable that the Irish ... sided with Great

Britain in the war against Germany … All the colonial troops were like the Irish, united in their feelings for Britain and the view that England had never entered a war which she had not won.'[29]

Redmond hoped that his show of good faith would reconcile the Unionists, and that the British government, grateful as well as victorious, would bestow Home Rule on a truly united Ireland after the war. However, a Kilkenny labourer was careful to explain to the Germans that the show of loyalty was strictly conditional. 'The Irish are fighting for England only to have their services recognised by the introduction of Home Rule after the war.'[30] In the view of the English battalion commander of the 6/Connaught Rangers the Irish were 'difficult to drive … but easy to lead'.[31]

Of the two predominantly nationalist divisions, the 10th fought at Gallipoli, while the more politically orientated 16th left for France at the end of 1915. The 16th was commanded by Major General W. B. Hickie, who was a Catholic Irish nationalist, and its officer corps included the activist Stephen Gwynne and John Redmond's younger brother Willie. They came first under the command of Sir Hubert Gough's I Corps on the Loos salient. Gough was a classic representative of the Anglo-Irish Protestant Ascendancy, and admits that 'brought up, as I had been, in an atmosphere of hostility to Home Rule, and all who supported it, I found in these two – and many Irishmen of this division, Home-Rulers though they might be – a loyalty, a devoted sense of duty, and a gallant spirit, which won my esteem and affection.'[32]

After a prolonged and taxing tour at Hulluch the division passed on 31 August 1916 to the XIV Corps of Rawlinson's Fourth Army, and on 9 September the Irish captured and held Ginchy in a distinguished but little-known action which became one of the foundations of the imminent battle of Flers-Courcelette. By then Irish constitutional nationalism was under severe pressure. Voluntary recruiting in Britain as a whole had fallen away sharply, but the collapse in Ireland was unusually significant, for Redmond had obtained a significant exemption for Ireland from the conscription that was being enforced over the rest of the realm, and volunteers offered the only means by which the Irish divisions could be made up from the homeland. The 16th Division had lost 3,491 men on the Loos sector between January and the end of May

1916, and another 4,330 (out of 10,845) between 1 and 10 September, and bloodletting of this order was fatal to the division's character, for it had to be made good by drafts from England.

What did the Germans learn of these developments? They were aware of the decline in Irish recruiting in January, and on 22 March they captured four men of the 4/Royal Munster Fusiliers at Hulluch, 'Kitchener Men, who had joined up respectively eight, twelve and fifteen months ago, having been "volunteered" by their employers under a greater or lesser degree of compulsion. Only one of them enlisted out of genuine free will. He is a lad of sixteen years, who pretended to be older in order to be signed on. His parents meanwhile reclaimed him, and it appears that he would have been released over the course of the next few weeks.'[33] By September, according to a soldier of the 6/Connaught Rangers, 'the battalion had not received replacements for a long time. On account of the poor recruiting in Ireland the battalion now contains many English.'[34] His words carried all the more weight because he was Irish, he had a fine military bearing, and he was speaking only unwillingly.

The root of the problem was that the war was proving unexpectedly long, which was postponing Home Rule into the indefinite future, and the Ulster Unionists and the London government showed no sign of being impressed by Redmond's stance. The dramatic events in Ireland in the spring of 1916 put the loyalties of the Irish troops to a severe test, but were not in themselves decisive.

On 24 April, while the 16th Division was being bombarded and gassed at Hulluch, the Easter Rising broke out in Dublin. Before long Patrick Pearse and Joseph Plunkett were beleaguered in the Post Office. Pearse had just proclaimed an Irish Republic in terms which can be repeated accurately enough by many Irish schoolchildren, but he did not rule out the welcome possibility of a German victory, which might result in the installation of a German prince as head of the new state, the most suitable being Prince Joachim (1890–1920), the sixth and youngest son of the Kaiser.[35]

On 30 April, the day of the first surrenders, another German prince, Rupprecht of Bavaria, noted in his diary that 'there were a large number of street battles in Dublin, but from what I know of the Irish character I cannot promise myself much from the disturbances over there'.[36] This corresponded with the experience of the German agent Captain Franz von Rintelen in the United States, who found that the Irish dockworkers were fanatical but well-nigh uncontrollable assistants. 'They swarmed about the ports with detonators in their pockets and lost no opportunity of having a smack at an English ship.'[37]

When they summed up the mood of their Irish prisoners on 8 May the Germans found that 'the recent Irish uprising was actually misconceived from the Irish point of view, for only the extreme radical wing of the Irish nationalist party was involved, and not the party as a whole'. The Irish could not bring themselves to believe that the English would ever allow an independent Ireland to come into being just two hours from their western coasts, or that Ireland could survive economically once divorced from the rest of Britain. 'There will always be rebellions in Ireland, for that comes from the Irish character, which flares up easily but cannot carry through anything serious over the long term.'[38]

The Irish–Australians captured at Fromelles on 19 July dismissed the Dublin affair as being of no account in itself, but symptomatic of a major problem that would face the British once the war was over. Sir Roger Casement had tried in vain to raise an 'Irish Brigade' from among the prisoners being held at Limburg in January, and he had been captured after being landed by a U-boat on the Irish coast. He was now under sentence of death, but here again the Germans were disappointed by the response. The Australians believed that the penalty was just, for he had been employed by the Crown and honoured by the King. The Royal Munster Fusiliers' Patrick Sharkey did not disagree in principle, 'though he was of the opinion that he could have been pardoned, like the Boers'.[39]

The only unease concerning the recent troubles was identified by an intelligence summary of 11 September, which reported a number of conversations with the 8/Royal Irish Fusiliers. 'They complain bitterly about the heavy-handed censorship of both the incoming and outgoing mail. When the "Dublin affair" broke out many of them agreed to desert at the first opportunity, but at the last moment they were deterred by the implications. They were unable to obtain any information concerning the Sinn Feiners from either Ireland or their relations, and the newspapers were just as uninformative as to the fate of their countrymen.'[40]

Otherwise, for all their sympathies with the cause the rebels represented, the Catholic Irish were kept to their allegiance by loyalty or affection towards their officers, or the kind of fatalism that was found among the ranks of the Royal Munster Fusiliers. Patrick McMahon, a cabinet maker from Limerick, and now a private in the 8th Battalion, told the Germans that regardless of what had happened in Ireland, 'they had no alternative but to keep on fighting'.[41] Four other men made it clear that 'in spite of all their dissatisfaction, the Irish will ... fight bravely. It is in their blood, and they can do no other.'[42]

PART TWO

TO THE SOMME

CHAPTER FIVE

The British in France, 1914–15

If we accept the evidence of the German General Staff, the German military and political planning went hand in hand in the years that led up to the Great War. One of the considerations that weighed most heavily in the gloomy mind of General Helmuth von Moltke, Chief of the General Staff at that time, was that Germany might be snuffed out within the foreseeable future by the encircling powers of France and Russia. There was every reason to believe that Britain could be counted as a *de facto* member of the hostile league. The Germans took due and suspicious note of King Edward VII's visit to Paris in 1903, and how the British and French patched up their differences in Africa in 1904 and 1905. Moreover, the Germans were alerted to the possibility of the British lending direct military assistance to France by a series of articles that were published in *Le Matin* in October 1905, and were attributed to the former French foreign minister Delcassé.

Between 1906 and 1911 the suspicions hardened into near certainty, for the Germans attached great importance to the interchange of British and French officers at manoeuvres, and not least the frequent visits to France on the part of Sir John French, who would be the most likely commander of a British Expeditionary Force to the Continent. A programme of reconstruction in the ports on the French side of the Channel indicated that the French were making ready to receive support from Britain, and in 1909 the Germans learned that the British staff was studying the Belgian roads, bridges, rivers and canals, which indicated a likely area of British deployment on the Continent. By that time also Britain was acquiring the attributes of a formidable modern military power, with the establishment of an Imperial General Staff and Territorial support for the Regular Army, and the German General Staff took care to circulate the details in memoranda and more widely in its quarterly publication *Vierteljahrsheft*. It was true that no political alliance or written military agreements subsisted between Britain and France, but a feature in the *Journal de Genève* in 1911 confirmed what the Germans surmised, that the two powers maintained verbal understandings. In that year and the next memoranda from the hand of von Moltke showed that the General Staff fully expected to find the British among the ranks of Germany's enemies.[1]

In 1914 von Moltke let slip some derogatory remarks to Grand Admiral Tirpitz about the British land forces, but these words ran counter to the judgement of the body of the German General Staff, which in no respects regarded a potential British Expeditionary Force as the 'contemptible' or 'contemptibly' little army of legend. The Germans were aware that the British had managed the transition from what had been a colonial police force writ large to a body capable of projecting to the Continent an initial six divisions of infantry, one of cavalry, and two mounted brigades, making up 132,000 active Regulars and Regular Reservists. 'A glorious history shows, and battlefields throughout the world confirm that he [the British Regular soldier] is ready to die at any time for the honour of his arms … his long period of service gives him a high degree of individual training. Most of the men serve for seven years with the colours and five more in the Regular Reserve. The discipline is good, even if it does not correspond exactly with our notions on the subject. The men of the Regular Reserve can be counted as being of almost the same worth as the serving troops.'[2]

The Germans had followed closely the work of Lord Haldane as Secretary of State for War in building up a Territorial Force of fourteen divisions of infantry and fourteen mounted brigades. The Germans suspected rightly that the Territorials, although enlisted for home service only, would be made available for the war in Europe. Even so the number of the Territorials was running about 47,000 short of establishment (see p. 69), and the German General Staff concluded that the British would resort to drastic measures to win a war in which their status in the world was at stake. 'We believed that the British would encounter unavoidable difficulties if they introduced a general conscription on the German model. But the principle came as no surprise to us.'[3] At no time, however, did the Germans reckon with the possibility of a stop-gap arising in the form of Kitchener's army of wartime volunteers.

A system of Imperial defence was implicit in the creation of Britain's Imperial General Staff in 1908, and the Germans had no doubt that a number of the details were discussed in the colonial and imperial conferences of 1907, 1909 and 1911. Militia-type conscript service was being introduced in the Dominions, and the Germans believed that those parts of the world would not only see to their own security but also contribute to the defence of the motherland. In 1911 the *Vierteljahrsheft* had to recognise that Canada and Australia were 'lands of endless opportunities'.[4]

In matters of detail the German General Staff acknowledged that among the British Regulars 'the training of the individual infantryman and his units up to battalion level is good. It would be difficult to improve on their marching and musketry, and they make good use of the ground.' The weapons and equipment were likewise admirable. The officer corps was 'recruited from the best classes. The British officer is physically fit, he has a practical turn of mind, and he shows great personal dash. Less good are his general education and his grounding in military particulars.'[5]

The British as yet lacked skill and experience in mobile warfare, and the senior officers were unacquainted with the command of larger formations. However, there was every reason to expect an improvement. An article in 1908 drew attention to the fact that 'British officers have studied the battlefields of Manchuria [in the Russo-Japanese War of

1904–5], and you find them at the manoeuvres of the great military powers, busy observing, comparing and learning. And what they learn is processed in the General Staff which has just now been set up by Haldane, and put at the disposal of the army.'[6] From this mass of evidence the German General Staff concluded in 1912 that 'the British field army is small, certainly, but an enemy to be reckoned with'.[7]

On 28 June 1914 a Serbian fanatic assassinated the Austrian Archduke Franz Ferdinand at Sarajevo. This precipitated war between Austria and Serbia, and before long the conflict extended far beyond the Balkans, for Austria was linked closely with Germany, and Serbia with Russia, and Russia in turn was an ally of France. Mobilisation and contingency plans now came into effect, and powerful German forces swept into Belgium as the first stage in a grand manoeuvre to get behind the left flank of the French army. The artillery general (and later war minister) Hermann von Stein was enraged to hear two passengers in a railway carriage talking as if the declaration of war and the attack through Belgium had been a mistake. 'It never entered their heads that it would have been suicidal for us to wait until all our enemies had completed their mobilisation and opened hostilities.'[8]

In 1916 we find German intelligence officers curious to learn what the reactions in Britain had been. The consensus among the better-considered answers was that Britain was committed to Belgium by specific treaty obligations (which was not the case with Britain's relations with France), but that the legal case for Britain's going to war had been less important than the need to confront an enemy who had shown his true colours at last. A businessman from Leeds, one of the city Pals, was of the opinion that Britain was fighting to do away with the evil of war itself, and that Germany 'must be deprived of the means of falling upon a neighbour in such a brutal manner ever again. That is Britain's war aim. Economic rivalry played no part whatsoever.'[9]

More disconcerting for the Germans was what they were told by a very rare bird, an unnamed but 'well-educated officer, a lawyer from Cambridge University, who is well travelled, speaks German, and has a detailed knowledge of German literature. He has lived for years in the German intellectual world, and has maintained a constant interchange of ideas with some of the leading thinkers of Germany. He says that it is through his very familiarity with the German mentality, the German ways and the German record that he knows better than any of his countrymen what a grievous threat Germany presents to his [British] homeland.'[10]

The prisoners had assumed that war of some kind was bound to come sooner or later, and they now said that Germany had played into Britain's hands by taking the initiative in August 1914. British public opinion had then been stirred by the appeal of the king of the Belgians and the reports of German atrocities, and the reaction had spurred men to volunteer for military service by the thousands.[11] The high state of feeling was sustained by further outrages. On 12 October 1915 Nurse Edith Cavell was shot in Brussels for having aided the escape of stranded British soldiers. The killing was justified by the strict letter of military law, but it revolted British and neutral opinion, and the naval captain Franz von Rintelen testifies as a prisoner of the British that 'the news of the shall I call it grotesque, execution of Nurse Cavell seemed most revolting to the vast majority of the inmates of Donington Hall [prison camp]. Many ... officers openly expressed themselves that they would have flatly refused, had they been called upon, to order a firing squad to shoot a woman; others, like myself, were grieved as well on the gross miscalculation of the British Spirit.'[12]

The German General Staff, at least, had long assumed that Britain would intervene on behalf of France. In recent years the French had been developing their Channel ports, doubtless to facilitate a swift and secure passage for the British, as already noted, and the German General Staff reckoned that the British could begin to embark their troops on the twelfth day of mobilisation, and land all but the two divisions from Ireland at Dunkirk, Calais or Boulogne by the evening of the fifteenth day. 'Thereafter the employment of the British troops on the Continent would inevitably have been influenced by the need to maintain the communications all the way back to the points of embarkation.'[13]

The German forecasts were only slightly astray. Between 13 and 15 August 1914 the British shipped to France four divisions of infantry and one of cavalry, and the last of the remaining two divisions of infantry on 10 September. The follow-up divisions therefore arrived later than had been foreseen, and the British disembarked at a wider spread of ports than had been expected (le Havre and Saint-Nazaire as well as the closest Channel ports), and they made a more extensive use of the railways within France than had seemed likely. The Germans were, however, right to believe that the command of the British Expeditionary Force (BEF) would fall to Field Marshal Sir John French.

The BEF first saw action on 23 August 1914 when von Kluck's First Army attacked General Sir Horace Smith-Dorrien's II Corps along the Mons–Condé Canal. The subsequent British retreat to the Marne was marked by a costly rearguard action at le Cateau on 16 August, but the British were able to consolidate on the French and made a small contribution to the counter-offensive, which removed the immediate threat to Paris. The German General Staff had anticipated the excellent tactical performance of the British Regulars, and, as had been expected, British concerns for the security of their communications led to the BEF being re-inserted on the northern flank of the allied array, in this case around the little Belgian town of Ypres, and in time to beat off mass German attacks between 19 and 31 October. These episodes closed the 'race to the sea'. The Western Front was now filling up from end to end, and the fighting congealed into a trench deadlock.

One of the prisoners taken later by the Germans was the well-connected Godfrey Walter Phillimore. He told the Germans that in retrospect it had been a mistake to throw the first seven divisions so speedily into France, for they had been 'the cream of the British Army, and sacrificed in the face of overwhelming numbers ... Only in the course of time did the British recognise that it would have been better to hold back the standing army, and use it as the framework for the mass army that was to be called into being.'[14]

The British forces built up impressively. The first-line Territorial divisions completed their training and arrived in France in the spring of 1915, which corresponded to the span of time anticipated by the Germans. To the surprise of the Germans, however, 'the greatest of the new formations to appear during the war was represented by the Kitchener Armies. They took shape in the autumn of 1914, according to a grand scheme devised by Field Marshal Kitchener, who was the minister of war at that time. Thirty divisions were created altogether, and the first of the Kitchener divisions arrived on the various theatres of war in the summer of 1915 ... In addition new divisions were put at the disposal of the motherland through the goodwill of the Dominions, namely four Canadian divisions, five of Australians, a New Zealand division and a number of South African brigades.'[15]

The Germans established that about 200,000 British troops were present in France and Belgium by the middle of October 1914, about 100,000 more by May 1915, and a total of about 900,000 by February the next year. The numbers would have been greater still if so many British and Australians had not been committed to the Gallipoli peninsula in the attempt to open up the Dardanelles Straits of Turkey (25 April 1915 – 10 January 1916). Lieutenant Phillimore was highly critical of 'certain operations during the Gallipoli campaign which were devised by politicians who set themselves up as "amateur" soldiers, and were carried out by generals who showed themselves to be totally incompetent. More than anything else the failures at Gallipoli enraged Phillimore because they struck at Britain's international prestige.'[16]

On the Western Front the Germans launched the world's first-ever poison gas attack, against the French at Ypres on 22 April 1915. The 1st Canadian Division, fighting alongside the French, was engaged on the following day, and heavy fighting on this sector continued until the end of May, with the Germans being checked just short of Ypres town. Otherwise the allies were mainly on the offensive. The British attack at Neuve Chapelle (10–12 March 1915) was a well-planned operation, achieving an initial success which the British were unable to convert into a breakthrough. The pattern was repeated on a larger scale at Loos, on 14–16 September, a major 'push' designed to support a French offensive in Champagne. The failure was again one of exploitation. Captain Hugh Stewart Walker of the Cameron Highlanders told the Germans that 'the British attack at Loos ... would have broken through the German line, if only the 15th and 28th Divisions had been supported properly by the following divisions. The offensive had begun so well, but the lack of genuine reserves meant it ended so badly.'[17] The British would be certain to renew their efforts with greater resources the following year.

CHAPTER SIX

Designs and Preparations

Between 6 and 8 December 1915 the representatives of the allies – British, French, Russians and the newly joined Italians – met at the French head-quarters at Chantilly, and agreed to open simultaneous offensives in the following year, thereby putting the enemy under the greatest possible pressure. After their chastening experiences in 1915 the British would have preferred to hold back until 1917, but gave way in the general interest. This grand strategy was inherited by General Sir Douglas Haig, who assumed command of the BEF on 19 December 1915. The new chief was a highly professional and much-travelled commander, sustained alike by his religious convictions, his family's whisky fortune and his wife's connections at the royal court.

Early in 1916 the British took over the sector from Arras south to the Somme valley. The Germans were alerted to the presence of these newcomers by the white puffs of their high-bursting shrapnel, the British and American stampings on the munitions, and 'the unwelcome increase in the numbers of the enemy machine guns. The leisurely tick-tack of the French machine guns, which ceased after every twenty-five rounds to allow a new strip to be inserted, was replaced by the headlong and endless chatter of the new weapons, which sprayed the landscape with bullets and endangered our approach routes by night.'[1]

The calculations of both sides were now upset by the obsession of the German chief of staff, General Erich von Falkenhayn, who was determined to bring the French to breaking point by staging a deliberate battle of attrition for the fortress-complex at Verdun. The Germans attacked on 22 February 1916, but after a brilliant start they found that they were locked into their battle under unexpectedly adverse conditions. Their effort slackened in midsummer, for they had to send reinforcements to the Eastern Front to counter the Russian 'Brusilov Offensive', which opened on 4 June. The allies attacked on the Somme less than a month later, which caused a further diversion of German effort from Verdun. The Germans had to close down their offensive operations, and in October the French counterattacks forced them onto the defensive. The fighting at Verdun continued until 20 December, at great cost to both sides, but with the French holding firm.

Some of the German generals had been appalled by the whole Verdun affair. The attack was the business of the Fifth Army, and its commander, the Kaiser's son Crown Prince Wilhelm, had lost faith in the outcome of the offensive and indeed of the war. 'Little Willy's' opinions were shared by Crown Prince Rupprecht of Bavaria, who commanded the Sixth Army further north along the Western Front. Rupprecht was far from being the figurehead that his princely title might have suggested, but, according to Ludendorff, 'he became a soldier only out of a sense of duty, and not from any soldierly inclinations. He nevertheless approached his position and its responsibilities with the utmost seriousness, and, supported by his superb chiefs of staff – the Bavarian general Krafft von Dellmensingen and now General von Kuhl – he proved equal to the great demands which are made on every senior commander. Like the German Crown Prince, so also the Bavarian would have liked to have seen the war ended without any gain to Germany, but like everyone else he had no idea whether the enemy alliance would be so inclined.'[2] (By a quirk of genealogy Rupprecht was in the senior line of descent from James II, the last crowned Stuart king of Britain, though he never pursued the Jacobite claim.)

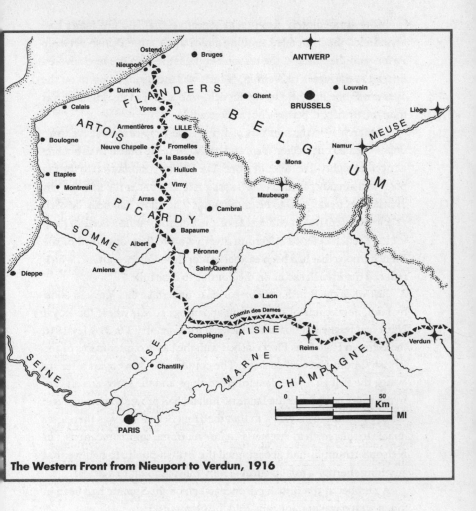

The Western Front from Nieuport to Verdun, 1916

More immediately Rupprecht regretted that the Germans had abandoned their intended spoiling attack against the British between Artois and the Somme, the reason being that resources were devoted instead to the attack on Verdun, 'which was the strongest point on the Western Front, and held by the French, who are far more skilled at war than the British, if perhaps not as dogged'.[3]

In March 1916 the numbers of British and Empire forces rose to an unprecedented one million men, and by that time the British were holding altogether eighty-five miles of front. The British contribution to the big push was already planned to be substantial, and under the force of circumstances it was now to be dominating. The effort had been devised as a joint offensive on either side of the Somme, but the need to prop up the French defence at Verdun diverted more than one-third of the French troops that had been earmarked for the combined attack, which reduced the French sector on the Somme to nine miles.

Just when the British were preparing to undertake their greatest effort by land, news came of unsettling happenings at sea, where the Royal Navy had reigned almost unchallenged for a century. On 31 May 1916 the German High Seas Fleet clashed with the battle cruiser forces of the British Grand Fleet off Jutland. The combatants drew apart after six hours, the British having lost fourteen ships and the Germans eleven. In the wider perspective the Battle of Jutland had proved to be a strategic victory for the Royal Navy, in that the High Seas Fleet was thereafter unable to sally forth to threaten Britain's maritime communications, but Nelson's triumphs had accustomed the British public to believe that anything short of a total tactical victory must amount to a defeat.

A number of the British prisoners taken on the Somme had been in touch with naval opinion, and told the Germans that

> when the British fleet steamed back to harbour a couple of days after the battle, the naval officers were greatly disconcerted to learn that in Britain the outcome of the battle was regarded as a reverse, and that everyone was sunk in the deepest gloom. 'It was no defeat,' they declared. 'We won't hold with that at all!' Influenced by the government, public opinion swung in the opposite direction, and a few days later the battle was being hailed as a brilliant British success, almost in

the same league as Trafalgar. This too seemed to the naval officers to be an exaggeration. 'It wasn't a defeat, but it wasn't a victory either.' But they were glad that the public opinion was pleased with the result, and they were content to leave it at that.[4]

This was an accurate description of the swings in public mood, influenced by the Admiralty's first unvarnished communiqué, and then by the more reassuring gloss that was put on the event by Winston Churchill, as the former First Lord of the Admiralty.

The British were still struggling to come to terms with the implications of Jutland when they learned that Lord Kitchener was lost on HMS *Hampshire* when she hit a mine on her way to Russia on 5 June. Private Triggs of the 2/Border Regiment testified that the report 'had the impact of an exploding shell. None of the setbacks we British have experienced has made anything like such an impression. The officers and men alike are stunned.'[5] The effect bears comparison with that of the death of President Roosevelt on the Americans in 1945.

When the news reached the German trenches the intellectual Rudolf Binding recalled Kitchener as the man who had had the Mahdi's body dug up and decapitated, and 'who destroyed a white population, descended from the Dutch, by the murder of women and children'.[6] More typically Kitchener appeared to the Germans as a big man in the style of Bismarck or Hindenburg, 'the great organiser and creator of the British Army', in the words of Crown Prince Rupprecht.[7] The former German consul general at Cape Town remembered him as a brilliant administrator and a man who kept his word,[8] and to Captain von Rintelen at Donington Hall it appeared inappropriate that such a great warrior should have been extinguished without a chance to fight back.[9]

On 1 February 1916 General Sir Henry Rawlinson had been appointed to command a new Fourth Army, formed partly from corps already in France and partly of reinforcements from England. On the 14th of that month Haig and the French commander-in-chief Joseph Joffre had agreed on the outline of a joint British and French offensive astride the Somme. After considerable modifications and postponements, not least on account of the happenings at Verdun, the final plan committed the British to attack on a frontage of eighteen miles.

On the British left (northern) wing two divisions of Territorials, the 46th and the 56th, were borrowed from Allenby's Third Army to carry out a diversionary attack on Gommecourt. The main burden of the assault fell, however, on the twelve front-line divisions of Rawlinson's Fourth Army. It was made up principally of Kitchener volunteers, with a stiffening of Regulars, and was to advance on a frontage of 18,000 yards between Serre and the French left at Maricourt. Two divisions of infantry and three of cavalry were to be held in reserve as an exploitation force under the command of Lieutenant General Sir Hubert Gough, an Anglo-Irish landowner who had the reputation of being a 'thruster'. To the right of the British array stood the two divisions of the excellent XX Corps, the nearest formations of the French Sixth Army under General Emile Fayolle.

Haig was almost certainly aiming to achieve a convincing breakthrough, which would bring the British an initial six or seven miles to a general line between Bapaume and Guillemont, in step with a French advance to the N 17 along the line Sailly-Saillisel, Rancourt and Péronne. The exploitation would then be in a general north-easterly direction, and carry the allies to the communications centre at Cambrai.

The chosen ground was a rolling chalk plain, overlain with spreads of what the French call *limon*, which is a layer of sand, silt and clayey loam. The overall hue of this earth is a light reddish-brown, but when wet and compacted it turns into a clinging yellowish mud. Because of this, the British wounded being carried back from in front of Mametz Wood on 8 July were 'all covered from head to foot ... all slimy and glistening like seals'.[10] The *limon* was thickest on the higher ground and along the valley bottoms, but it was not particularly deep at any point, and picks and shovels sooner or later penetrated to the underlying chalk. This rock made for excellent dugouts, and it was just as good in its way for the digging of trenches and tunnels, though the spoil could show a blinding white in the sunshine.

Nowhere rising to more than 150 feet, the ridges and swellings of the ground came to assume great importance in the conditions of static warfare, and in this country of 'long views'[11] they could open up wide fields of fire and observation. In such a way Pozières became the focus of a miniature campaign, for 'an elevation extended from its much

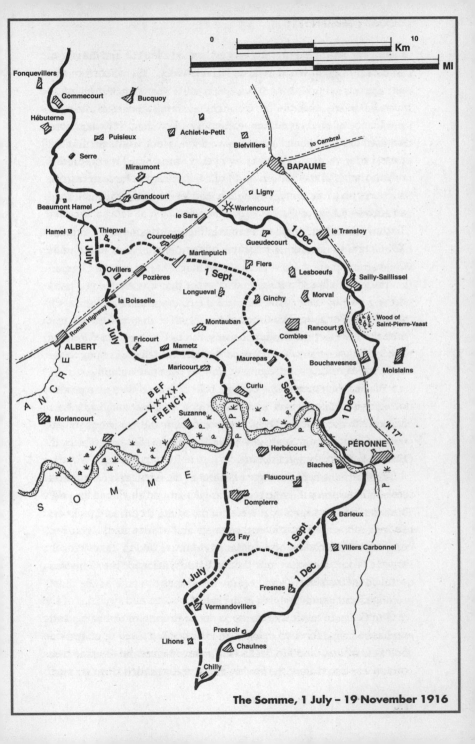

The Somme, 1 July – 19 November 1916

fought-over windmill hill ... by way of Bazentin-le-Petit and the north-east corner of High Wood as far as Delville Wood. The whole extent of this ridge was in our [German] possession at the beginning of the battle.'[12] It was inherently easier for the Germans, as sitting tenants, to grasp the significance of an unassuming feature like the Butte de Warlencourt, dismissed in a British intelligence appreciation as 'only a Roman tumulus at most fifty yards in diameter by twenty yards high. It commands nothing, being at the bottom of a hollow and cannot be seen from le Sars owing to a row of trees along the road leading from the main road to Eaucourt l'Abbaye.'[13]

With so much of northern France in their possession, the Germans had the luxury of making whatever adjustments in their position as would secure them the best tactical advantage. In essence the German first position followed a long, snaking ridge that was intersected in its northern part by the marshy valley of the Ancre stream, a tributary of the Somme. For about two-thirds of the length of their battlefront as it faced the British, from Gommecourt south to Fricourt, the Germans were looking generally west. Beyond Fricourt the defences swung to the east, before curving south again in front of Montauban and so to the sector facing the French. One or more belts of barbed wire gave protection against infantry assault, and a number of villages, which had cellars cut deep into the chalk, had been incorporated into the first line as strong-points – Gommecourt, Serre, Beaumont Hamel, the high-lying Thiepval, Ovillers, la Boisselle and Fricourt.

The Germans held the higher ground in the north and centre, and they could see down the Ancre valley as far south as Albert and beyond. The situation was generally reversed in the south, for British observers overlooked the area of Fricourt, Mametz and Montauban, though in compensation a cluster of woodlands (Mametz Wood, High Wood, Delville Wood, Bernafay and Trônes Woods) afforded the Germans useful cover from view, and became the scenes of some of the most prolonged and bloody fighting in the battle.

The German tactical doctrine at the beginning of the battle still emphasised rigid forward defence and the need to give the infantry a good field of view and fire, and so the greater part of the German first position was traced along the forward slopes and was packed with troops.

In the course of the British bombardments many of these unfortunates chose to abandon the prepared defences and disperse in the improvised *Trichterstellungen* in no man's land.

The Germans had built a second position two miles behind the first, which was enough to put the trenches beyond the effective range of the British wire-cutting artillery. The line corresponded roughly with the villages of Beaucourt, Contalmaison, Bazentin-le-Grand and Longueval. Work on a third position had scarcely begun, but the zone was to be fought over heavily in the last stages of the battle, when it threw into prominence le Sars, the Butte de Warlencourt, the farm complex of Eaucourt l'Abbaye and the villages of Ligny-Thilloy, Lesboeufs and le Transloy, which were reckoned by British intelligence to be 'among the worst and poorest in the district. They are situated on top of an arid plateau, in the centre of a district where the only industry except agriculture is sugar refining. They are inhabited by the typical Picard peasant, who never spends more than he can help on his house, and as the country itself is not calculated to enrich him or to attract the rich to live there, these particular villages are poorer than the surrounding districts.'[14]

The senior German officer most directly concerned with reading the signs of the coming offensive was General Fritz von Below, as commander of the Second Army, which held a sector of twenty-three miles from Monchy-aux-Bois south to the Somme. He was a 'true Prussian', according to his admirers, but became sensitive and difficult when he was upset by the inevitable changes in the German command system that occured during the battle.

Below was on good enough terms with his right-hand neighbour, Crown Prince Rupprecht, as commander of the Sixth Army, but each was concentrating on the threat he thought was building up against his own forces, and neither was able to bring his concerns home to the chief of staff, Falkenhayn. Still alert and sprightly in his early seventies, Falkenhayn was nevertheless a man of *idées fixes*, among which was the need to keep hammering away at the French at Verdun.

In January Rupprecht noted that 'the British infantry have become a great deal more active since Lord French was replaced as supreme commander by Sir Douglas Haig'.[15] He was referring to Haig's emphasis on trench raids, of which the British launched 106 in the six months before the battle opened. Fritz von Below was on the alert as well, and in February he believed that he could detect a danger to the right (northern) wing of his army, taking as a clue the hutments that the British were building for large numbers of troops on both sides of the Ancre. A little later and 'there was a distinct feeling in the air when the spring of 1916 arrived. The flower of the German army was bleeding at Verdun. Along the Ancre the British were showing signs of distinctly suspicious activity. Swarms of British aircraft were romping undisturbed over our lines. Messenger pigeons were flying from east to west. Spies were active in our rearward areas. British trenches were creeping nearer our positions to the north of the Beaumont Hamel sector. New batteries were making an appearance, and fresh British divisions were being inserted in the front.'[16] At the end of April a German spy reported that French journalists were writing about a big enterprise planned for the end of June or the beginning of July, though the German army commanders were still divided as to where the blow might fall, with the Fourth Army in the north believing that the offensive would arrive in Flanders, as indeed had been Haig's preference.

At great risk German pilots overflew the British lines, and their sightings of new roads and railways convinced Below by 14 May that his Second Army was the target of the attack. He was confirmed in his belief by the deliberately showy preparations against Gommecourt, as 'the most westerly point of our [German] Western Front, projecting like a beaky nose into the enemy positions'.[17] On 12 May Below accordingly extracted the 2nd *Garde* Reserve Division from his *Garde* Corps and entrusted it with the defence of Gommecourt and Serre. This was a significant alleviation to the six front-line divisions of his XIV Reserve Corps, whose frontage was thereby reduced from 30,000 yards to the 18,000 between Serre and Maricourt. Below was in general weighting his deployment heavily in favour of his right wing, north of the Albert–Bapaume highway, where his average divisional frontage amounted to six kilometres (three and three-quarter miles) as opposed to the seven and a half kilometres (four and a half miles) on his left wing. All of this was going to have profound effects on 1 July, and indeed until the battle ended in November.

By the beginning of June there were indications that the offensive was going to be a joint affair of the British and French, in spite of the emergency still prevailing at Verdun. 'Two French divisions made their appearance immediately north of the Somme, on a sector hitherto occupied by the British. At first we were under the impression that they were just there for defensive purposes, to give deep support to the attack going in further north. We changed our minds as soon as trench raids established that they belonged to the French XX Corps, which is recognised as an excellent offensive formation.'[18]

Below had seen two of his divisions replaced by a battered division from Verdun, and some of his most modern heavy artillery whisked away and replaced by captured enemy pieces of dubious provenance. On 16 June Falkenhayn and the Kaiser in person came to his sector of the Western Front, and Below found that Falkenhayn now talked about withholding the promised 11th Division, which was much needed to keep the Second Army up to strength. Below protested, and the Kaiser asked Falkenhayn '"What do you mean by that?" Falkenhayn drew himself up: "I trust the Prussian grenadier to be the kind of man to stand his ground." Below retorted "I don't doubt that for a moment. But we are duty-bound to take precautions."'[19] The division was retained for the Second Army.

Falkenhayn was perfectly well aware that the allies were going to attack on the Somme, and that the British would take the leading role, but he believed that the British, with their high proportion of New Army divisions, would flag and fail, and that in their sorry state they would be vulnerable to a great counterattack further north. He reinforced Below's Second Army with altogether four divisions, but left eight in the supreme command's reserve, probably to bolster Rupprecht's Sixth Army for the impending blow.

As regards the British designs on the Somme, the matter ought to have been put beyond doubt on 24 June, when the Germans discovered a wounded soldier of the British 4th Division crawling about in front of their wire. He told his captors that they were going to come under attack on a frontage of thirty miles, and that the offensive would open in two days' time.[20] Both statements were exaggerated, but they put the Germans on their guard.

For two days now the British artillery had been showing greater activity, and was registering 'skilfully and inconspicuously. The guns proved accurate: the effect of the shells was good, but the percentage of blinds [duds] was high. On many occasions the enemy purposely refrained from shelling batteries and observation posts the positions of which were obviously known to him before the offensive began.'[21] The one mistake made by the British gunners was to confine the bombardment of the 2nd *Garde* Division at Gommecourt within the boundaries of what was clearly an impending attack. The Germans were therefore able to withdraw their batteries out of harm's side to either side.

The German artillery made no attempt to answer in kind, and the German observation balloons came under attack by the aircraft of the Royal Flying Corps, which sent these defenceless objects collapsing to earth amid clouds of dense black smoke. In contrast the fall of the Royal Artillery's shot was being observed by British balloons which 'hung in the sky like yellow dragons'.[22] The German infantrymen felt that they had been left entirely in the lurch.

On 24 June the British opened a *Trommelfeuer* with their light artillery, and 'the blue sky was speckled densely with the white clouds of their shrapnel. The hail of leaden balls whistled through the air and the leaves of the trees, and flogged into what was left of the village of Beaumont Hamel.'[23] The casualties and the material damage on this sector were light, but the fire became more intense and more accurate in the afternoon, and the British heavy guns began to pound the villages in the German rear. At Longueval 'the very first shell showed its destructive power when it brought down the whole masonry on one side of a tall house. The walls were totally gone, and the stairways, rooms, furniture, stoves – in fact everything stood as if in the open air.'[24] Thiepval, Ovillers, Fricourt and Mametz came under fire as well, and the little town of Combles, which had pretensions to elegance and might have been considered safe in its hollow, was hit by 3,000 heavy shells on the night of 24/25 June alone. On the next day an ammunition train was hit in Combles station, and the sound of the exploding rounds gave the impression of a great infantry combat in the German rear. The wreckage of the train remained throughout the battle, presenting the very image of desolation.

The headquarters of the German regiments, up to now located in the various villages, became untenable, and the order went out to evacuate the French populations. In some places the Germans jeered at the villagers, who were now facing the reality of their long-wished-for liberation (foreshadowing Normandy in 1944). In Martinpuich, however, the town major was acknowledged to be 'a very excellent person and protected the civilians in every possible way'.[25] In Longueval the German 'king' (town major) noted that the pretty daughter of a prosperous family had a cart to herself. He made her come down, ignoring her tears, and replaced her by old folk and children.[26]

On 26 and 27 June banks of yellowish-brown smoke and chlorine gas rolled over the German positions. The British were launching one of their most ambitious gas attacks to date, and they later questioned German prisoners as to the effect:

1. The enemy suffered gas casualties all along the line. The casualties do not appear to be due to permeation of the anti-gas masks, which seem to have been effective, but rather to men not putting on their masks in time or taking them off while gas was passing. There is no evidence that the fit was anything but good, and casualties due to bad fitting must have been few in number. Men found gassed with their masks on, or showing signs of having worn them, were possibly first affected before adjusting their masks.

2. In many cases, the enemy soldiers wore their masks for one and a half hours at a stretch without serious inconvenience.

3. Of the troops in the first position, probably about 5 per cent were gassed. From our knowledge of the effects of the gas, it is probable that a high proportion of these cases proved to be serious, including many regarded as light at the time.

4. The effect of the gas was felt at least nine miles back (Bapaume), and casualties have been reported 4,000 yards behind the front line.

5. There does not seem to have been any serious moral [i.e. psychological] effect produced by the gas.

6. There is no information concerning the effects of the gas on weapons or on animals.[27]

The 26th had been the first of three days of low cloud and poor visibility, and the British artillery programme was now falling into serious arrears. On 28 June Haig forced the French to agree to put back the opening of the great offensive from the 29th, the date originally scheduled, until 1 July. Among the contradictory reports reaching the German commanders one had arrived on the 26th, which was based on false information from one of their spies and from their military attaché in Madrid, and had the attack falling on 1 July anyway.

The British were meanwhile intensifying their trench raids in an attempt to gauge the impact of the continuing bombardment. One such enterprise was launched by up to fifty troops against the 108th Regiment on 26 June. The Germans detected the attack in time, and for once their red signal flares managed to bring down an effective barrage from their artillery. Corporal Fetzer was able to shoot down one of the three men who were coming at him, 'but the other two British tried to haul him out of the trench with a pitchfork, the tines of which had been bent into an angle. Fetzer put up a tremendous fight, and so the British let him fall back and disappeared into the darkness, taking their wounded comrades with them.' A German patrol found two abandoned rifles, five steel helmets, three of those pitchforks, and a barbaric-looking knife that was probably a memento of Britain's colonial wars.[28] On the night of 30 June another failed British raid, this time against the 119th Reserve Regiment, helped to convince the Germans that they were going to come under attack on the Beaumont Hamel sector the next morning.

The trench raids were surprisingly unproductive of prisoners, and Haig was unaware that the results of the bombardment did not measure up to the efforts that had gone into it. From 24 June until the opening of the attack the British fired about one and a half million shells, and the Fourth Army alone devoted 1,010 field pieces and 427 heavy guns and howitzers to this work. However, the accuracy of the bombardment fell away as a result of mechanical wear and tear on the pieces, and many shells, particularly those of the heavier calibres, failed to explode at all, on account of faulty fuzes or defective fillings. Even of the shells that did explode, about two-thirds were of shrapnel, which had little direct effect on troops under any kind of cover. All of this, together with patchy aerial reconnaissance, left many German batteries and key positions undetected or otherwise untouched.

The bombardment was over-stretched in more than one dimension.

Haig had extended the depth of the objectives of the first infantry attack from the original 1,250 yards to an average of 2,500, which took in the German second position, and doubled the tasks of the Fourth Army's artillery preparation. The bombardment was also teased out in time, for the postponement of the attack gave the gunners two days of extra work with no increase in resources. Historians have still to investigate the targeting by the British artillery in detail, but it is fair to suppose that it suffered a diminution in the intensity of its fire, and therefore in its power of 'suppression', by which is meant the disorientation and shock that ought to complement the physical destruction.

Calculations like this were remote from the experience of the German *Frontsoldaten*, to whom the culmulative effects seemed devastating: 'After the fire had lasted four or five days it seemed as if our end had come. The clay subsoil of the battlefield had been ploughed up like fresh graves in a churchyard. Woods had been beaten into splinters, and the trunks lay across one another as if in some phantasmagoric tropical forest. Ponds had been turned into bogs, hilltops swept away, and hollows transformed into craters.'[29] ' ... our positions were horrible to behold. The belts of wire, however deep they might have been, had been cut into rags by the storm of shrapnel, or torn aside by the toffee-apple mortar bombs. The trenches had been filled to such an extent that they were reduced to shallow hollows. Half-blocked holes indicated the exits of dugouts.'[30]

PART THREE

THE CAMPAIGN

CHAPTER SEVEN

The Catastrophe of 1 July

As the high summer of 1916 came to the Somme, there could not have
been a single British, French or German soldier who was unaware that
a great allied offensive was about to break on the two sides of the river.
As the Germans learned afterwards, the British had been busy in the
rear areas for weeks, familiarising themselves with the drills of exiting
trenches, moving across open ground and bayonet fighting. Many of
the troops had assembled in the trenches on the night of 28/29 June,
ready to go over the top the next morning. They stayed there in the rain,
for the attack was being put off. There was talk that the British artillery
was taking casualties from defective ammunition and the German
counter-battery fire, but the Tommies themselves were almost unscathed,
which helped to convince them that the prolonged British preparatory
bombardment must have wrought near-total destruction. They could
see for themselves how 'the bursts of our shells resembled the smoke
from an endless row of factory chimneys, and through the fountains of
smoke one could see sods of earth and fragments of timber leaping

upwards'.[1] Their food was excellent, which helped to make up for the discomfort in the waterlogged trenches, and the men were waiting eagerly on the words of their officers. Early in the morning of 1 July Rawlinson's headquarters telephoned an encouraging message to all ranks. The notification to the 34th Division was intercepted by a German 'Moritz' (Arendt) listening station just south of la Boisselle. It was passed up the German chain of command, and the German troops were put on notice to meet a general offensive.

The British company commanders were now telling their own men that the time of waiting was over, and warned them to curb their enthusiasm, in case the enemy should hear the tumult. 'Both recruits and veterans were entirely confident that the assault would be carried through to a successful end … and the officers confirmed them in this belief by saying that the thing would be easy. As they described it, the first stage would be just a matter of taking the first two German trenches, which would be occupied only by dead bodies, as the preceding artillery fire would surely have been annihilating. It was fair to assume that the only survivors would be found in the third trench, but that the resistance would be so feeble that the British assault would overrun it in the same style. It is hardly surprising that the troops – most of them young – looked forward to the hour of attack with confidence and exultation.' However, the optimism seemed to diminish with increasing rank, 'and as an example we may take the case of Major General de Lisle, commander of the 29th Division, which had already suffered heavily at Gallipoli. By one account he said that "I am afraid after this affair, I may have to take my division back to England in a taxi-cab."'[2]

Zero hour for the great offensive was 7.30 in the morning of 1 July. The whistles of the company commanders gave the signal for the attack, and the leading assault troops obeyed without hesitation. The attack opened almost simultaneously along the whole front, but for the sake of clarity the scenes of action on this day (and over the whole course of the offensive) will be taken in sequence from north to south, or from left to right as the British saw it.

The Somme. British Deployments and Gains 1 July, and successive German positions 1 July – 19 November

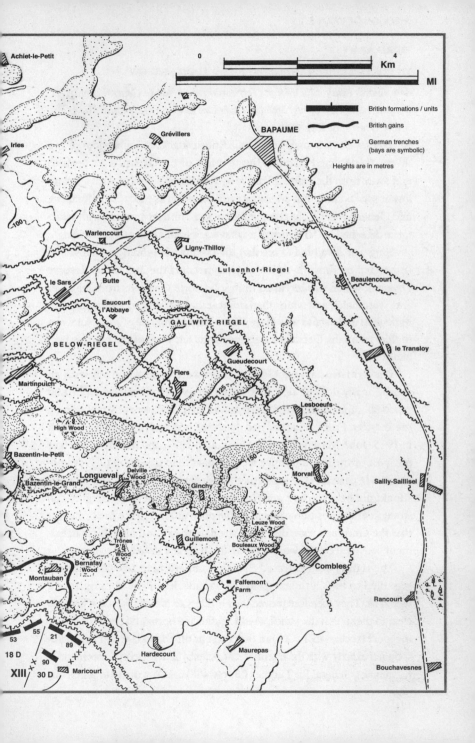

THIRD ARMY

VII CORPS, LIEUTENANT GENERAL SIR THOMAS SNOW

46th (North Midland) Division (Territorial Force), Major General Hon. E. J. Montagu-Stuart-Wortley; 56th (1/1 London) Division (Territorial Force), Major General C. P. A. Hull

In Haig's wider scheme of things the British attack at Gommecourt was a diversion, designed to attract the attention of the Germans northwards and away from the grand offensive by Rawlinson's Fourth Army further towards the Somme. But diversions can be every bit as costly as 'real' attacks, and General Allenby, as commander of the Third Army, only with reluctance detached his VII Corps for what was essentially a sacrificial role.

Haig was delighted to see that the German commander Below had responded by drawing down to Gommecourt the 2nd *Garde* Reserve Division, which was recruited from solid north Germans from Hanover and Westphalia, and which then stood at the height of its reputation. It is difficult to understand why Haig was so pleased, for one of the results was to thicken up the German forces facing the left wing of the main British attack.

The British attacking Gommecourt were meanwhile left with an exceptionally difficult task. The salient here was of both symbolic and practical importance to the Germans as their most westerly position on the Western Front, and they had defended it as such against the French in 1915. John Masefield saw the ground in 1917, and doubted 'whether any part of the line in France was stronger than this point of Gommecourt'. He describes the projecting wooded park as 'a big spur',[3] but this should not be taken as signifying any kind of dominating height. The strength of the position came from the open ground to the front, the fact that the Germans were dug in so strongly there, and also the concealment provided by the wood even in its shattered state.

The tightly concentrated British bombardment had unwittingly signalled to the Germans what the boundaries of the coming attack would be. They therefore moved their artillery to the flanks, and it became clear to them 'that the attack would be directed north and south of Gommecourt (sectors G.1. G.5) in order to cut off the village'.[4] This corresponded exactly with the intentions of Allenby and the corps commander Lieutenant General Sir Thomas ('Snowball') Snow, namely to pinch out the salient by converging attacks on the part of two Territorial forma-tions, the 46th Division coming from the north-west, and the 56th Division from the south-west.

The Germans nevertheless had to concede afterwards that 'the equipment and the preparation of the English were excellent. The assault-ing troops were amply provided with numerous machine guns, Lewis guns, trench mortars and storming-ladders. The officers were provided with excellent maps which showed every German trench systematically named and gave every detail of our positions. The sketches had been brought up to date with all our latest work, and the sectors of attack were shown on a very large scale.'[5]

The north Midlanders of the 46th Division had some experience of combat at Hooge and Loos in 1915, most of it bad, and nothing better awaited them at Gommecourt on 1 July 1916. There were 400–500 yards of no man's land to cross, and the barrage of smoke mortar bombs, which was designed to impede the German observation, now worked with the muddy ground to confuse and delay the Midlanders' advance. When, finally, they approached the German positions they found that much of the wire was intact, and they began to bunch together vulnerably in the gaps.

To the north of the salient the German 91st Reserve Regiment was caught up marginally in the combat, and 'in the dense clouds of smoke … it was difficult to make out objects of any kind, and that must surely be the reason why the British were able to break into our position … in spite of our heavy rifle'.[6] The burden of defending the salient itself fell on the German 55th Reserve Regiment, which had two of its battalions in line and the third three miles back in reserve at Bucquoy. Here as elsewhere the outcome of the fight depended largely on their timing. If they left the shelter of their dugouts and shell-holes too early they would be exposed to the British artillery fire; if they lurked too long they would find the British infantry on top of them. If they waited longer still they had a good chance of emerging in the rear of the leading assault troops and being able to hit them from the back.

Along the northern face of the salient the fate of the defence rested on the vigilance of First Lieutenant Count von Matuschka, who judged his moment very well. He summoned the troops from shelter just in time to meet the British with showers of stick grenades. The attacking troops were being held up at the wire, and by British accounts they were at a further disadvantage because the men bringing up fresh supplies of grenades were cut down by artillery and machine-gun fire in the wide no man's land.[7] After half an hour the effort of the 46th Division was spent, and the fragmented British survivors began to pick their way back to the lines. In the afternoon the divisional commander Major General Montagu-Stuart-Wortley rightly refused to renew the attack, in spite of pressure from Lieutenant General Snow.

The London Territorials of the 56th Division represented the right-hand jaw of the pincers. Their attack had been preceded by an unusually effective bombardment, which had taken the defences in enfilade and succeeded in cutting wire, levelling trenches and blocking the exits of dugouts. The gas, dust and smoke were actually thicker than on the other side of Gommecourt, and by a German account 'the sunlight became grey and feeble … our eyes searched to the west but encountered nothing but a single bank of smoke and fog, twitching here and there with flashes'.[8] The Londoners held together remarkably well, and with the help of bangalore torpedoes (metal tubes packed with explosives that were otherwise a little-used device) they broke intact stretches of wire and reached the first trench before they were seen by the Germans.

The attack was led by the 169th Brigade, on the left, and each of its four battalions formed one of the successive waves. Survivors told the Germans that 'the two left-hand battalions advanced without resistance and with minimal casualties as far as the third trench, and they dug themselves in there'. They had actually penetrated the wood and reached the Kern Redoubt, which was the core of the defence of the salient, but 'communication with the rear was lacking, and the reinforcements and the replenishments of ammunition could not get through. Germans reappeared in the first trench, and cut off most of the [British] defenders.' The 168th Brigade was over to the right. 'The two right-hand battalions got as far as the second trench without heavy casualties, but they too lost all touch with the rear … they suffered heavily in the course of the morning, and some of the men tried to get back to the British trenches. The two remaining battalions of this right-hand brigade were meanwhile waiting in their dugouts on the order to advance.'[9] It came only at four in the afternoon. They also attacked in four waves, but the Germans were now in possession of their first trench and cut them down.

In the murk and confusion the British had been unaware of what had been happening around them. The German *Sperrfeuer* had been falling to deadly effect in their rear. In front they were being assailed by the III (reserve) Battalion of the 55th Reserve Regiment, which Major Tauscher brought up from Bucquoy and threw into action early in the afternoon. In addition the Germans were able to exploit the gap that separated the British Third Army from the Fourth Army to the south, which left the Londoners exposed to counterattacks by the German 52nd Division from the south-east, and the fire of two artillery pieces, which were taking them in the flank from the direction of Puisieux.

By the late afternoon the British abandoned all the ground they had gained. The Germans found 1,400 enemy dead lying about, and identified prisoners from thirteen battalions. The 56th Division had lost 3,295 out of its attacking complement of about 5,000 men, and the 46th Division had lost 1,352. Looking back from the 1960s Charles Carrington reckoned that on the German side the 55th Reserve Regiment had put up the best demonstration of minor tactics that he had encountered in two world wars.[10] It was also to the Germans' credit that they let the Londoners retrieve their wounded, and even helped some of the stricken men back to the British positions.

FOURTH ARMY

VIII CORPS, LIEUTENANT GENERAL SIR AYLMER HUNTER-WESTON

The British were to attack in four waves, from their first and third trenches. The second [British] *trench was only weakly occupied, on account of the artillery fire which was expected from the Germans. A heavy German barrage arrived at the beginning of the assault, which occasioned great disorder, and the attack collapsed in front of the second German trench. A few men got into the third trench and were captured there.* (Bavarian War Archives, KA 10 ID, Bd 46, 'Preliminary Findings [*Vorläufiges Ergebnis*] of the Interrogation of nine Officers and 301 NCOs and Men (British) who were taken in the Actions on 1 July 1916', Army HQ, 5 July 1916)

VIII Corps was the left-hand formation of Rawlinson's Fourth Army, and was therefore dedicated to the 'real' attack. Its target was the ridge of chalk heights to the north of the Ancre, where the German defences had been developed in great strength against the French. The first line extended over the forward slopes, while the powerful rearward position ('Munich Trench') stretched over the summit. Two heavily fortified villages, with deep cellars, were embedded in the defences – Serre in the second position, and Beaumont Hamel just behind the first.

Out of all the formations in the great attack, VIII Corps occasioned Haig the greatest doubts. Its commander, Hunter-Weston ('Hunter-Bunter'), had probably not yet recovered from the sunstroke that had incapacitated him at Gallipoli in 1915. Young officers found him 'a figure of fun, the very image of a brass-hat as represented by the caricaturists, with features, voice, and manner, all in character'.[11] His troops had little experience of combat in France, and had yet to carry out a single successful trench raid.

In outline, the 48th Division on the far left was to be brought up from reserve only after the other divisions had opened the attack. The 31st Division, next in line, was to take Serre, then swing north to form a protective flank for the rest of the corps, and thus for the whole of the rest of the Fourth Army. The 4th Division was directed against the heights north of Beaumont Hamel, where the kernel of the defence was thought to be the Heidenkopf strongpoint. Lastly the objectives of the 29th Division on the right were Beaumont Hamel village and the outlying Hawthorn Ridge, together with the deeply cut Y Ravine. The German positions were held by the 52nd Division, formed predominantly of troops from the Grand Duchy of Baden in south-west Germany, and by their Württemberg neighbours in the 26th Reserve Division. Both divisions were of high quality, and therefore typical of the formations holding the right wing of the German battle line.

A number of sectors of VIII Corps' frontage came to occupy a unique place in British memory and commemoration. The 31st Division was made up of 'Kitchener Men' from the industrial towns of North England on both sides of the Pennines, and the fate of its component units – the Accrington Pals (11/East Lancashires) and the battalions from Leeds, Bradford, Sheffield and Durham – has become the symbol of the Pals battalions in general (the Hull Pals were in reserve, but were wiped out in the same location on 13 November). The 29th Division's objectives are nowadays among the most heavily visited sites on the battlefield, and

Geoffrey Malins' film of the mine explosion under the Hawthorn Redoubt features in almost every television survey of the Battle of the Somme, and most of those on the Great War itself.

48th (South Midland) Division (Territorial Force), Major General R. Fanshawe

There is little to record concerning the 48th Division, out on the far left, for it was brought up from its position in reserve too late to take part in the first day's fighting. Its presence on the Somme had long been known to the Germans, and prisoners told them that 'the supporting artillery had been with the 48th Division from the beginning, but had a pretty poor reputation. The infantry thought it was useless at giving them any back-up, and they never stopped complaining about it in the most bitter terms.'[12]

31st Division (New Army), Major General R. Wanless O'Gowan

The tasks of the 31st Division – to capture Serre, then wheel to the north – would have taxed the capabilities of troops who were better trained and more experienced than these Pals from the North Country. Serre was another fortress-village in the style of Gommecourt. It had deep-cut cellars, and formed an integral part of the German support line. The high-lying village commanded immense views on all sides, and multiple lines descended to the west as far as a row of tiny woods along a lip of ground that marked the outer defence.

The British were attacking on the usual frontage of two brigades, in this case the 94th on their left and the 93rd on their right. The 94th was the northernmost brigade of the whole Fourth Army, and was separated from the nearest troops of the Third Army, who had troubles of their own at Gommecourt to the north. It would have been possible for Hunter-Weston to have advanced his 48th Division to fill the gap, but he was holding it back, as we have seen.

All of this relieved the pressure on the Magdeburgers of the 66th Regiment, who were holding the German positions north of Serre. By their account an intense bombardment was followed by reddish-yellow clouds of gas. When the British opened their attack on the southern wing of the regiment it was 'enveloped completely in clouds of artificial fog, smoke and dust, while the northern half remained under shelling. We were under an extraordinarily heavy fire, and suffered accordingly, but the troops holding the sectors of trench under attack stood along the fire-steps of the parapet and awaited the enemy with rifles and machine guns. The waves of assaulting troops came under the concerted fire of all our weapons, and only isolated parties got as far as our wire.'[13]

The Germans were firing into the exposed northern flank of the 94th Brigade. Handfuls of both the Sheffield City Battalion (12/York and Lancaster) and its right-hand neighbours the Accrington Pals (11/East Lancashires) actually climbed as far as Serre, where they met the German 169th Regiment head on. According to the Germans 'the British succeeded in making their way through a zone of wrecked wire and trenches and a number of dugouts which had collapsed under the impact of heavy mortar bombs, and they broke into our position where flanks of our 4th and 3rd Companies adjoined. Major Berthold ordered a counter-attack on the part of our I Battalion, and such British as had penetrated our position were driven out again.'[14] The remains of soldiers bearing the brass shoulder insignia 'East Lancashire' were found after the Germans abandoned Serre in 1917.

The 31st Division's right-hand brigade, the 93rd, was lashed by machine-gun fire and an almost undisturbed German barrage even before it went over the top, though one party of the County Durham Pals (18/Durham Light Infantry) broke clear through the first German position south of Serre and reached the distant Pendant Copse before the men were wiped out. The Leeds Pals (15/West Yorkshires) were checked in front of a little rise, and the men taken prisoner by the Germans here turned out to be unusually intelligent and well-motivated individuals.

4th Division (Regular Army), Major General W. Lambton

The first four of the assaulting waves reached the first and second German trenches without sustaining heavy casualties. The reserves came up behind and suffered heavily under the German barrage and the fire of our machine guns. The British claim that some of the defenders of the first and second trenches deserted to them after the first attacking wave reached the third trench.

('Preliminary Findings')

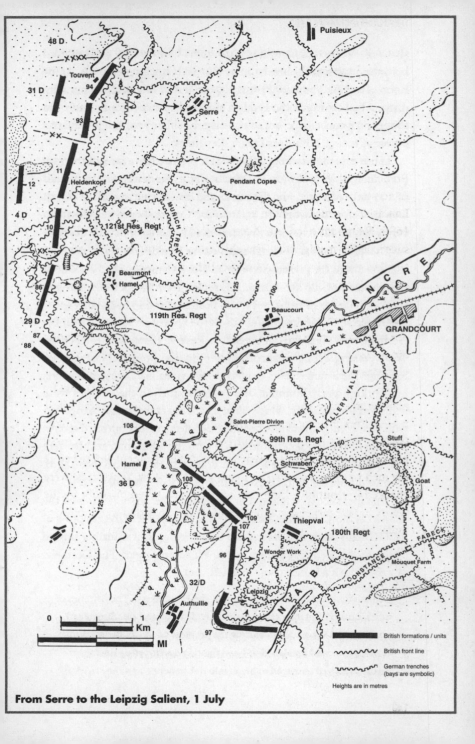

From Serre to the Leipzig Salient, 1 July

Puisieux

48 D.
XXXX
Touvent
94
31 D
93
Serre
11
12
Heidenkopf
Pendant Copse
4 D
10
121st Res. Regt
MUNICH TRENCH
125
100
86
Beaumont Hamel
29 D
87
119th Res. Regt
Beaucourt
88
ANCRE
GRANDCOURT
108
100
125
Saint-Pierre Divion
99th Res. Regt
150
Stuff
Hamel
ARTILLERY VALLEY
Schwaben
36 D
108
Goat
109
107
Thiepval
180th Regt
96
Wonder Work
FABECK
Mouquet Farm
125
100
CONSTANCE
32 D
Leipzig
Authuille
97

0   1
Km

MI

British formations / units
British front line
German trenches
(bays are symbolic)
Heights are in metres

Redan Ridge was the name given to the spur of downland that extended between Serre and the low-lying Beaumont Hamel to the south. At the top was a space about 200 yards square. 'From this patch the ground drops a little towards the English side and stretches away fairly flat towards the enemy side, but one can see far either way, and to have this power of seeing, both sides fought desperately.'[15]

In this case the attacking infantry were preceded by a creeping barrage (something of a novelty for the British), which was descending by bounds of 100 yards at a time, and the smoke and dust helped to pull the British forward before the weak 1st, 2nd and 3rd Companies of the Württembergers of the 121st Reserve Regiment could emerge from their dugouts.

The quadrilateral of trenches called the 'Heidenkopf' (on the crest to the south of the present Serre Road No. 2 Cemetery) had once been the keystone of the defence on this sector, for it swept the broad and shallow valley to its front, but it had been battered so badly during the preliminary bombardment, and it was so exposed on its flanks that the Germans now considered it untenable. Reserve Lieutenant Eitel of the Württemberg Pioneers accordingly prepared powerful charges for blowing. The arrangements went astray when the machine gun covering his working party jammed, and in the confusion the charges were exploded prematurely, which blew up the machine-gunners together with the engineers, and blocked the exits of the neighbouring dugouts. The site of the Heidenkopf together with the adjacent trenches were now seized by men of the 8/Royal Warwicks (a Territorial battalion borrowed from the 48th Division) and the 1/Rifle Brigade.

This first success could not be sustained. The grisly failures of the British divisions on either side of the 31st exposed it to the attention of the Germans on its two flanks, and British progress was further slowed by the resistance being put up by the Württembergers. The Germans saw the British advance come to a halt, and

we later found many bodies in front of the Heidenkopf. The batteries of our 52nd Division intervened magnificently to protect our threatened position, and succeeded in barring the progress of the following British waves. However bitter hand-to-hand fighting developed against the British who had managed to break into our trenches, and they tried to lodge themselves there with the help of all the gear they had brought with them – machine guns, mortars, and signalling equipment in the shape of telephones and flares. After just one hour the positions of the 121st Reserve Regiment were once more free of the enemy, with the exception of the place where they had broken into the Heidenkopf. Reinforcements from our III Battalion were quick to arrive, and in a series of bloody combats the enemy, who were defending themselves obstinately, were pushed back step by step. But again and again they stood their ground anew, by covering themselves with sandbags and bringing machine guns and Lewis guns into position.[16]

It was impossible to get ammunition to the leading British troops, who began to extract themselves in the evening. They left 1,800 dead comrades behind them, and their total losses amounted to about 4,700 men.

29th Division (Regular Army), Major General H. de B. de Lisle
The 86th Brigade, which made up the left wing of the 'Incomparable 29th', was facing defences that might have stood for everything that was formidable about the German positions on the Somme. Redan Ridge reared up to the north, and Hawthorn Ridge to the south, and between the two elevations the narrowing valley was swept by fire from the fortified village of Beaumont Hamel. Miners from the Rhineland and central Germany had been burrowing hereabouts since the winter of 1914/15, and now whole companies were able to shelter in the great tunnel-like dugouts.

The damage caused by the preliminary bombardment to the shelters had been minimal. The defending Württembergers of the 119th Reserve Regiment were, moreover, in a state of the highest alert. In addition to the warning of a general offensive just received from the high command, the 10th Company had beaten off a British trench raid and taken in a British deserter, the Russian-born Jew Joseph Lippmann (see p. 37) who told them that they were going to come under attack.

The British had miners of their own, in the 252nd Tunnelling Company of the Royal Engineers, who placed a gigantic charge below the redoubt on Hawthorn Ridge. As is known to anybody with even a passing acquaintance with the events of 1 July, the British command had settled on blowing the charge at 7.20 in the morning, which was ten minutes before zero hour, in the hope that advance parties would be able to seize the crater before the main assault opened. The whole fire of the artillery of the VIII Corps simultaneously lifted from the German front line to the rear, which left the British on the whole corps sector devoid of close support when they attacked ten minutes later.

'We felt a queer dull thud,' recorded a Lancashire Fusilier in the valley below, 'and our trench fairly rocked, and a great blue flame shot into the sky, carrying with it hundreds of tons of bricks and stones and great chunks of earth mixed with wood and wire and fragments of sandbags. The great mine had gone up.'[17] The 40,000 pounds of ammonal had not so much blown the top off the hill, as heaved the earth and chalk up in a great dome which dispersed down the slopes; even nowadays the ring of trees around the edge of the hole can summon up an eerie vision of the collapsing debris. As seen by the Germans at the time, 'the ground became all white, as if it had been snowing, and a gigantic crater forty or fifty metres wide and twenty deep gaped on the hill'. The greater part of the first platoon of the 9th Company of the German 119th Reserve Regiment had disappeared, and the British infantry moved forward. 'Wave after wave left the enemy trench and came steadily on. Their bayonets were glinting in the sunshine.'[18]

Two platoons of the 2/Royal Fusiliers climbed the slopes, filed around the sides of the crater and established themselves with four machine guns on the further lip. By an accident they had also arrived on top of the dugout of the German 9th Company's commander. Three of the exits had been blocked completely by the explosion, while the fourth was reduced to a small hole, and the British shot the sentry who was trying to clear it from the inside. 'Behind him on the steps were standing Reserve Lieutenant Breitmeier, the company commander First Lieutenant Mühlbayer and a number of their men. As it fell, the sentry's body sent them tumbling down the steps. *Vizefeldwebel* Davidsohn fired a flare directly into the faces of the British, but they then drove him and the rest of the defenders back into the dugout with grenades and smoke bombs.'[19]

The first wave of the main attack was supposed to consist of the

1/Lancashire Fusiliers on the left and the 1/Royal Dublin Fusiliers on the right, but the British creeping barrage had meanwhile marched on, and the Germans were sweeping the hillside and the valley by hidden batteries and by machine-gun fire from the quarry to the north of Beaumont Hamel.

Geoffrey Malins had caught the eruption of Hawthorn Ridge with his ciné camera. Only one human being is in sight, and the vision is entirely impersonal; the same does not apply to his footage of the Lancashiremen waiting opposite the quarry in the Sunken Lane. They had advanced overnight to this dangerously exposed position so as to be nearer their objectives when the attack opened. Many of them were shot down there at 7.25 a.m., and most of the rest fell in the field when they rushed forward five minutes later. The Germans learned from survivors that 'the battalion on the left wing [i.e. the Lancashire Fusiliers] is said to have reached as far as the third German trench, but there it lost contact over to its right and was surrounded. Their losses were heavy, and reinforcements did not arrive.' The 'contact to the right' had been lost because the Dublin Fusiliers were also being wiped out.

By the middle of the morning the disintegration of the 86th Brigade was complete. From the German reconstruction of events 'the 1/Lancashire Fusiliers and the 1/Dublin Fusiliers were committed as assault battalions, with the 16/Middlesex and the 2/Royal Fusiliers assigned to follow up. Prisoners from the latter two battalions maintain that they lost all touch with the leading battalions.'[20]

Up on the hill the Germans emerged from their half-buried dugouts and found themselves among the troops of their intact 11th Company. The lip of the crater was garlanded by a ring of their own dead,

and meanwhile Private Schneider of the *Landsturm* noticed that a number of the British, who had appeared to be dead, were now raising their heads. He spoke perfect English, and called out to them to come into the German trenches. After some hesitation a number of the unwounded soldiers carried in their first lieutenant, who had been badly hit. When the other wounded saw that their comrades were being treated well, they lifted their hands in supplication and asked for help. Men of our 9th Company went out to them, and together with a

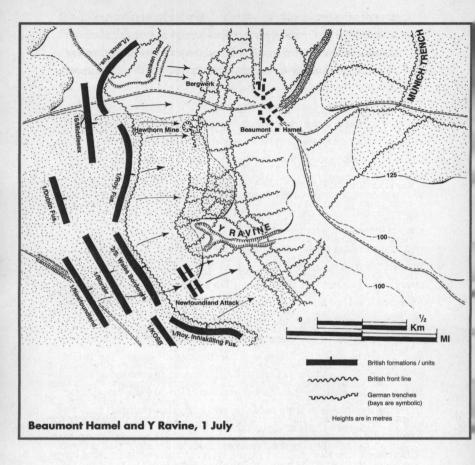

Beaumont Hamel and Y Ravine, 1 July

number of wounded British ... they retrieved thirty-six casualties, five of them officers. Orders of some consequence were found on the regimental adjutant. A number of British batteries continued to fire on the positions of the neighbouring 10th Company, but not a shell fell among the men who were engaged in the rescue.[21]

Two further British brigades, the 87th and the 88th, were stacked up on the right wing of the 29th Division and had the task of taking the positions in the neighbourhood of the notorious Y Ravine, a gully 500 yards long and thirty or forty deep, which cut into the eastern slopes of the Hawthorn Ridge and forked towards the British end. The defenders were once again the tough and dour Württembergers of the 119th Reserve Regiment, and their dugouts here were among the deepest and most elaborate on the Western Front. The German enemy had excavated 'shelters of unusual strength and size. He sank shafts into the banks, tunnelled long living rooms, both above and below the gully-bottom, linked the rooms together with galleries, and cut hatchways and bolting holes to lead to the surface as well as to the gully. All of this work was securely done, with baulks of seasoned wood, iron girders, and concreting.'[22]

Finally the conformation of the ground was such that, by chance, it matched the tactical desiderata as defined by the Germans much later in the campaign. For once the British were attacking downhill, and the first German trench had been traced along the reverse slope where the ground descended towards Y Ravine. The German riflemen were therefore concealed until the assaulting troops came within close range. The ground, as it rose again to the east of the ravine, offered elevated sites from where the German machine-gunners could keep the attackers under fire during the whole time of their advance across the lengthy 500 yards of no man's land, scything them down in association with the German artillery.

By about 8.15 in the morning the Germans had shredded the 87th Brigade. Major General de Lisle was unaware of the extent of the disaster, and he ordered up the 88th Brigade from reserve. By now the British forward trenches were obstructed by the wounded and blocked in places by shell-holes, with tragic consequences for the 1/Royal

Newfoundland Regiment. Its native island maintained a proud legal identity apart from the rest of Canada, and for the present purposes the Newfoundland troops formed part of de Lisle's division. In order to get into the fight the Newfoundlanders climbed into the open, and suffered heavy losses before they so much as reached the line of the first British trench. More men dropped when they crowded together at the gaps in the British wire, and almost all of the survivors fell in no man's land or before the German wire. By one estimate the battalion lost 710 of its officers and men, or nine-tenths of its effectives.

The defeat of the incomparable division was total; 5,240 of its personnel were killed, wounded, prisoners or missing, and by one in the afternoon the German 119th Reserve Regiment had beaten off the attacks along its entire frontage. 'The no man's land presented a frightful sight. The chlorine gas had turned the landscape yellow and eaten at the grass. Khaki-brown dead and wounded lay by the hundred between the two sets of wire.'[23] John Masefield saw them again in 1917. 'The rats burrow in them and their heads lie all over the place and their boots and feet and hands.'[24]

X CORPS, LIEUTENANT GENERAL SIR THOMAS MORLAND
36th (Ulster) Division (New Army), Major General O. S. Nugent; 49th (West Riding) Division (Territorial Force), Major General E. M. Perceval

Elements of the first wave broke through to the fourth German trench, where they found little resistance and are said to have taken many prisoners. In the course of the day, however, their losses were very great. Some of the men were captured when we were in the process of retaking the third and second German trenches. ('Preliminary Findings')

The German positions which faced the British X Corps were among the most visually striking of the Somme battlefront. In the north the Serre–Beaumont Hamel ridge sloped down to the marshy bottomed Ancre valley, 'river, lake, lagoon, marsh, reedbed, osierbed and river coppice all in one'.[25] The chalk highlands rose again to the south of the valley, and for nearly three miles marched roughly south-south-east, receding from the river in the process. The ridge was in German hands, and its dominating feature was the buttress-like Thiepval plateau.

The Thiepval position proper consisted of the fortified village of that name, with its deep cellars, and the pronounced spur of the Leipzig Salient, projecting between the deep Ancre valley to the west and Nab Valley to the east. The château of Thiepval mentioned in so many accounts was not a 'castle' in the English sense, but the ruined brick-built mansion of the comte de Bréda. To the rear the Thiepval position was bolstered by the formidable Schwaben Redoubt, a triangle of trenches, machine-gun emplacements and dugouts up to 600 yards long by 200 deep. Its location on the German *Höhe 151* gave the Schwaben views to the north-west and north across the Ancre valley as it curved to the north-east, and the hamlet of Saint-Pierre Divion, with its machine-gun positions and peculiarly elaborate underground shelters, could be regarded as an outpost of the Schwaben beside the river. Extending to the north-north-east of the Schwaben plateau, Artillery Valley (Vallée Caronesse; *Artilleriemulde*) offered the Germans a sheltered site for their artillery and views down to the upper Ancre by Grandcourt.

A shallow basin extended for about a mile to the east and south of Thiepval to an outer rim of downland, which the Germans exploited to form a line of inner defence. Running from 'one o'clock' to 'five' were the Stuff (*Stauffen*) and Goat (*Zollern*) redoubts, the fortified Mouquet Farm, and the elevations which were crowned by the transverse Constance and Fabeck trenches – all locations that were to be contested until the final stages of the battle.

Now at the beginning of July the defence was co-ordinated by Major General von Soden as commander of the 26th Reserve Division (Württemberg). His 99th Reserve Regiment held the northern sector, embracing the Schwaben Redoubt (so-called after the Swabian race of the Württembergers). The regiment had a generally good reputation, though it had been recently made up to strength by drafts from a number of different regiments, and its positions had taken 'a particularly heavy battering for days on end. There was literally nothing left of the trenches. The belts of barbed wire had been torn apart, and most of the dugouts had caved in under the shelling. The 9th Company to the west of the Schwaben was in an especially bad way, thus creating ideal conditions for the impending enemy attack.'[26]

Thiepval and the nearby defences were the treasured responsibility of the 180th Regiment, which had held the position without a break since September 1914, and kept up a system of internal reliefs company by company from its base at Bapaume. 'The men actually in Thiepval were survivors of the original first-line troops of the German army, high in spirit, intensely proud of their record and their regiment, of splendid physique, and pledged to hold Thiepval to the death.'[27] The 180th had laboured on the defences for twenty months, and the work on the defence of the Thiepval positions as a whole had received a fresh impetus when Major von Fabeck arrived on 15 April 1916. He designed the immense dugout complex down by the river at Saint-Pierre Divion, and gave his name to the much-contested Fabeck Trench just mentioned.

The Germans knew virtually nothing of the character of the opposing British 36th (Ulster) Division. It was overwhelmingly Protestant in its personnel, and drew heavily from the Ulster Volunteer Force, which had been raised in 1914 for the purpose of fighting (with obsolete rifles shipped by the Germans) against Irish nationalists, and if necessary, against the British Army if the London government had sought to impose Home Rule on Ireland.

As a 'political' formation – like the 16th (Irish) Division on the other side of the fence – the 36th had been plagued with an unusually high proportion of indifferent officers, but for the great attack on 1 July the divisional commander Major General Oliver Nugent had prepared very well in the tactical sense. He brought his troops forward silently into no man's land up to thirty minutes before zero hour, to give his men a better chance of winning the crucial 'race to the parapet', and the artillery support was of a high order.

The division's left-hand brigade was the 108th. It had two battalions on the right bank (9/Royal Irish Fusiliers and 12/Royal Irish Rifles), which advanced against the German positions on the slopes of the northern ridge, but came under enfilade fire from Saint-Pierre Divion on the far side of the river. They were pinned down with heavy losses.

The two right-hand battalions of the 108th Brigade (reinforced by a third from the 107th Brigade) were devoted to the attack on the southern heights. The climb was steep but short, for the British had been established well up the slope, and an element of concealment was provided by Thiepval Wood. At 7.30 in the morning the Germans observed the approach of a wall of dense smoke, and shortly afterwards the Schwaben Redoubt came under attack by the 9/ and 10/Royal Inniskilling Fusiliers. By a German account 'the ploughed-up earth was covered with khaki-brown specks. Here and there you could see a man throw his arms in the air – which is a sure sign that he has been struck by a mortal bullet. Wounded men were hurrying back or sheltering in shell-holes, while others took a bad hit and collapsed to the ground. But there was no doubting the courage and determination of the attacking troops. The waves hastened their steps, disappeared for minutes on end in dead ground, then rushed forward again in agile bounds.'[28]

According to a German official history, the 12th Company of the 99th Reserve Regiment succeeded in beating off the first attack, but the two machine guns with the 10th and 11th Companies got off only a few rounds before they were overrun by the furious assault, while a crucial machine gun in the Schwaben had already been put out of action by a direct hit. First Lieutenant Hille, the commander of the 10th Company, was killed in the fighting, and on this sector 'dense khaki masses broke through in the direction of the Hansa Position. They then wheeled to the south to come at the rear of the Schwaben. They occupied this strong-hold, and pressed over the Hansa Position into Artillery Valley and went to ground there about 400 metres in front of the batteries.'[29]

The Germans were describing a remarkable achievement. The Ulstermen had broken the centre and right of the 99th Reserve Regiment, and the advance to Artillery Valley was the work of the reserve brigade, the 107th, which leapfrogged through the leading troops and drove down the western side of the valley to within about 1,200 yards of Grandcourt village – a point which was to be reached again by the British only after stupendous efforts in the middle of November.

It had taken the Germans some time to come to their senses, and only when the troops swarming over the Schwaben were recognised as being British did the German machine-gunners at Thiepval turn their fire in this direction. Finally in the late afternoon von Soden developed a counterattack in the shape of three companies of the 108th Regiment, climbing from Grandcourt, and four of the 8th Bavarian Reserve Regiment which advanced against the south-east corner of the Schwaben. The Ulstermen lost Goat Redoubt, and they needed support and fresh supplies of ammunition if they were to continue to hold the Schwaben.

The difficulties of concerting the action of the divisions within a British corps now became evident. The X Corps' reserve formation was the 49th Division of North Country Territorials. All that the Germans discovered of its movements on this day came from a captured officer of the 5/York and Lancaster, who told them that 'the British had kept its presence a close secret, and had hoped that it would remain completely unknown to the Germans. After the division had been withdrawn from Ypres it had been deployed for just a few weeks south of the Ancre, and it had come as a most unpleasant surprise when a German raid had taken a number of prisoners. After that the division spent the next few weeks in a rest area. According to the prisoner it was good enough at holding the line, but was no kind of assault division.'[30]

The luckless 49th Division had marched up from Martinsart, and in the course of the day it had crossed the Ancre and was committed, as far as it was committed at all, mostly in partial or tardily cancelled attacks in support of the 32nd Division further south. The 5/York and Lancaster was, however, sent over to the left to help the Ulstermen. According to our officer

> he and his men made their way at four in the afternoon from Thiepval Wood towards the *Feste Schwaben* (he uses the German name for this strongpoint). In the process they came under a hot fire from the German artillery, and it seems that they were hard pressed by the German counterattack which arrived from the south [by the 8th Bavarian Reserve Regiment]. He himself was wounded by a rifle bullet. But for this counterattack they would have continued to press to the north-east and cut off the German division in the neighbourhood of Saint-Pierre Divion. They simply did not have the strength to accomplish this mission and at the same time beat off the thrust from the area of Thiepval.[31]

The Ulstermen in the Schwaben were now running out of ammunition, and the combined artillery of the German 26th Reserve Division was now intervening in the fight. It brought down a great concentration of fire to bear in front of Thiepval, and at nine in the evening it began to mete out the same treatment to the enemy in the Schwaben. Major

Peacock was left with no alternative but to order the Schwaben to be abandoned. The reinforcements from the 49th Division were caught in the retreat, and the officer from the York and Lancasters believed that his whole battalion had been cut off and captured.

The 36th Division had lost 5,100 officers and men, or more than one-third of its complement of infantry. The German losses are unknown, though they included the five hundred or so prisoners who were taken in the initial assault, some of whom failed to survive their journey back through the advancing Ulstermen.

32nd Division (New Army), Major General W. H. Rycroft

No clear picture emerges from the statements so far made by the prisoners, but it appears that the losses must have been very great. ('Preliminary Findings')

The 32nd Division was a predominantly New Army formation of Kitchener Men from the north of England and Glasgow, with an admixture of Scottish and Ulster Regulars. The division was not of the best, and Major General Rycroft, who was reputed to get on badly with his staff and brigade commanders, was later dismissed.

The division was assaulting the Thiepval bluffs head on, and the German positions were, and seemed to be, as formidable as anywhere on the battlefront. The 96th Brigade was attacking directly towards Thiepval village. The 15/Lancashire Fusiliers climbed the slopes swiftly in two strung-out columns, gaining useful cover from trees and dips in the ground, and broke through the Germans on a sector where the III Battalion of the 180th Regiment had been pounded severely by the preliminary bombardment. At 9.10 in the morning the Lancashiremen were glimpsed on the far side of the village, and they then vanished forever, probably eliminated by troops of the 99th Reserve Regiment coming from the north.

No support had been forthcoming. Five minutes after the last sighting the companion 16/Lancashire Fusiliers emerged from their trenches and were cut down by machine-gun fire in no man's land. Some troops of the 16/Northumberland Fusiliers to their right were kicking a football as a sign of sporting defiance, but the Germans had their machine guns trained on the gaps in the wire and the battalion was mown down before it could so much as reach the first enemy trench. The Germans describe these bloody episodes in gloating detail:

> As the British barrage moved forward, dense attacking waves of the 16/Lancashire and 16/Northumberland Fusiliers advanced towards the centre of Thiepval under the cover of banks of smoke and artificial fog. The British believed that it would just be a question of harvesting the fruits of their seven-day bombardment and wiping out or taking prisoner such troops as had survived. They were sorely deceived! When their protecting smoke dispersed a murderous fire spewed against them from foxholes, shell-holes and what was left of the trenches. The gaunt and dust-covered shapes of our soldiers, some of them in shirt sleeves, hastened out of their collapsing cellars and ploughed-up shelters. Seized by an indescribable lust for battle they stood, kneeled or lay flat as best enabled them to send a murderous massed fire into the continuous ranks of the British … who, directed by the little flags and sticks of their officers, were advancing in immaculate order against the 99th Regiment. Wave after wave was being cut down by the accurate fire which was being maintained by our officers, NCOs and men, regardless of hands which were bleeding from contact with the red-hot barrels of their rifles. Many victims too were claimed by our machine guns, which were aiming perfectly. Before long the leaderless masses of the British began to come to a halt. Their hesitations were converted into consternation, and finally into a panic-stricken flight when shells tore broad gaps in their ranks. A wall of British dead was growing in front of our positions. Not a single man reached the wire barrier of the 7th Company. The British continued to advance against the 5th Company and the right wing of the 6th, protected by the remains of the trees of the little wood which used to stand in front of their trenches. Men of the two companies threw themselves against the enemy with a thunderous cheer, and there ensued a wild hand-to-hand combat.[32]

The Germans on this sector have little to say about their one significant reverse, when they lost the tip of the Leipzig Redoubt south of Thiepval to the 97th Brigade. This was the work of the 17/Highland Light Infantry (Glasgow Commercials), who filtered out of their trenches in a skulking manner before zero hour, then at 7.30 a.m. covered the remaining thirty or forty yards of no man's land to win the race to the parapet. The Leipzig spur was one of the most visually striking features of the battlefront, but the salient was weaker than it seemed, for the tip was very narrow, and the very steepness of the slopes offered the British dead ground. A machine gun in the Wonder Work behind prevented the Glaswegians from exploiting through the multiple lines to the rear, but they were reinforced in the salient by successive reinforcements being fed by the 14th (reserve) Brigade, which was otherwise pinned down in Authuille Wood in the Ancre valley.

III CORPS, LIEUTENANT GENERAL SIR WILLIAM PULTENEY

The open landscape and gentle slopes in front of III Corps were not as obviously daunting as the heights which overlooked the Ancre valley to the north, but they were none the less deadly on that account, for they offered wide fields of fire and the defences had been developed in considerable depth. The German positions conformed with the lie of the land, which was that of a succession of low but commanding spurs and fire-swept intervening valleys – the Nab, which sloped upwards between Leipzig spur and Ovillers, the gentle Mash Valley in the centre between Ovillers and the far-projecting la Boisselle and the *Schwabenhöhe*; in the south Sausage Valley (so-called after a German observation balloon) was a much more considerable feature than Mash, and the German line on the far side projected in such a way as to enable the defenders to lay down an enfilade fire in front of the *Schwabenhöhe*. High hopes were nevertheless invested in the success of III Corps, for Haig hoped that a breakthrough on this sector would open the way to his cavalry to exploit in great depth.

8th Division (Regular Army), Major General H. Hudson

After suffering heavy losses only a few elements of the assaulting troops reached the wire, where the attack collapsed completely. We have not yet established whether the losses of the attackers were the same along the whole front.

('Preliminary Findings')

The officers and men of the 8th Division were Regulars. These precious troops were over-extended and had been set a near-impossible task. Here the no man's land was up to 750 yards wide, and lay under fire from the

Thiepval heights from the north, from the fortified village of Ovillers to the front, and from the la Boisselle spur to the south. Moreover the frontage of attack was so wide that Major General Hudson had to deploy his three brigades in a single line, instead of keeping one in reserve as was the usual practice.

Units of the leading battalions of all three brigades carried their attack beyond the first German trench, the greatest penetration being made by the 70th Brigade in Nab Valley under the Leipzig Salient. The 25th Brigade in the centre had the shortest stretch of no man's land to cross, but their advance brought them directly against Ovillers. That location was 'a hell on earth. It is on one side of a narrow valley, about 150 yards across and at the most 100 feet deep, quite a narrow place, but all be-Boched and mined and enfiladed, as well as trenched and ranged on, till it was as strong as death.'[33] The 23rd Brigade on the right was caught in the cross-fire from Ovillers and la Boisselle, and made the least progress of all.

The gains in all sectors were too tenuous to be held against counter-attacks, and the supports were cut down in no man's land or stopped on higher orders before they could sally from the British front line. The division had lost 5,121 officers and men, of whom more than 1,900 had been killed, leaving in front of Ovillers 'a field littered with broken skulls and bones.'[34]

34th Division (New Army), Major General Edward Ingouville ('Inky')-Williams

In spite of coming under heavy artillery fire and machine guns firing in enfilade a number of units succeeded in penetrating as far as the third German position. The losses were heavy. We cannot discover any more, since there was only one prisoner (an officer) taken from this division, and he fell into German hands in a communication trench just after the attack began. ('Preliminary Findings')

While the Regulars of the 8th Division could scarcely be considered expendable, their sacrifice figures less in the commemoration of the Somme than do the losses of the 34th Division, which was attacking to their right. It was not just its 6,380 killed, wounded and missing, but the fact that it was one of the most heavily tribal of the New Army formations, taking in the Tyneside Scottish (102nd Brigade) on the left, the Tyneside Irish (103rd Brigade) in reserve, and on the right the 101st

Brigade with its two Edinburgh City battalions (15/ and 16/Royal Scots) alongside two battalions from eastern England (10/Lincolns and 11/Suffolks). Finally the high-lying Lochnagar Crater remains even now one of the most spectacular relics of the battle, and the view from the lip takes in the assembly area of the attacks on the Usna and Tara hills, the spires of Albert, la Boisselle, the ground on either side of the Roman highway as it rises in the direction of Pozières, the ascent towards Contalmaison, and Sausage Valley over to the right.

The German salient at la Boisselle was 1,000 yards wide, and projected 500 yards beyond the general alignment of the German positions. The no man's land there was very narrow, so narrow that both the French and Germans had already resorted to mining on this sector in 1915, which produced a line of huge craters on either side of the Roman Road. Even today the intact zone of mounds and craters just south-west of the village gives an indication as to the intensity of the struggle. For the purposes of the present attack the British had tunnelled beneath the two shoulders of the salient and planted two charges – the Y Sap mine (40,600 pounds) north-west of la Boisselle, and the formidable Lochnagar mine (60,000 pounds) under the *Schwabenhöhe* to the south-east.

The mines were blown at 7.28 a.m. on 1 July. That under the *Schwabenhöhe* produced a crater ninety yards wide by seventy deep, 'as white as cherry blossom',[35] and for a minute the fragments of chalk rained down on the neighbouring German 110th Reserve Regiment. The assaulting troops left the trenches, and through their binoculars the enemy 'had a clear view of the British, laden down by their knapsacks. Their grey-green helmets caught the light and could be seen from a great distance.'[36]

The Tyneside Scottish penetrated on both sides of la Boisselle, the advance of the component 21/Northumberland Fusiliers being facilitated by the Lochnagar explosion. On the frontage of the 101st Brigade to the right the leading elements of the 10/Lincolns and the 11/Suffolks were unable to progress beyond the crater, being checked there by the men of the 110th Reserve Regiment. 'Wave after wave was emerging from the British trenches ... and dense columns followed from the Wood of Bécourt ... the Badeners with their machine guns awaited the approach of the enemy in silence. When the assaulting waves were a matter of metres from the outer line of shell-holes a hurricane of fire broke into the compact hostile ranks.'[37]

The Lincolns and Suffolks veered to their right and were reinforced from the reserve by the Tyneside Irish. As the Germans saw it, 'more and more lines of infantry came on and filled the gaps in the ranks. The men of our 2nd Company stood and shot as if they had been on a firing range. They had their pipes in their mouths and they grinned at their lieutenant. They were happy fellows. This was better than all that endless digging!'[38]

The Tynesiders and the men from Lincolnshire and Suffolk did what they could to support a narrow breakthrough being made by the two Edinburgh City battalions. The Scots were lashed by fire from la Boisselle and Sausage Redoubt, which threw them to the right out of the axis of their advance, but they recovered their direction and a party of the 16/Royal Scots advanced up the slopes as far as Quadrangle Trench in front of Contalmaison before being wiped out. The advance was impossible to sustain, and isolated parties of survivors fell back during the night.

Elsewhere the British had been forced back from everything except the Lochnagar Crater and a patch of ground to its front. 'The battlefield had been crowded by the enemy [the British], but in less than a minute it appeared empty. Then small parties, then whole bodies began to fall back towards Bécourt, and finally it seemed as if everyone was bent on making themselves scarce. The Germans fired after them. Our fire had been crackling ceaselessly for two hours as we defended our positions, but the combat fizzed out once the British reached the hollow of Bécourt.'[39]

XV CORPS, LIEUTENANT GENERAL SIR HENRY HORNE

21st (New Army) Division, Major General Sir David ('Soarer') Campbell

Out of this division only two waves of the assaulting troops managed to advance as far as the third German trench. The few men who broke into it were driven out again by bombing parties. By all accounts the losses of those two waves must have been extraordinarily heavy. Only half of the men engaged succeeded in getting as far as the third German trench, and some of the prisoners were among the men who were cut off there. ('Preliminary Findings')

The village of Fricourt stood immediately behind the first German position, which was where the line of battle began to incline to the east.

The defenders belonged to the 28th Reserve Division, recruited mainly from Baden on the upper Rhine. Its 111th Reserve Regiment held the village proper, while the 110th Reserve Regiment to its right was responsible for holding la Boisselle, as we have seen. Both regiments had been 'pretty badly knocked about by the bombardment',[40] which had smashed many of their dugouts and best observation posts, and left gaps in the wire. Morale was poor in the 110th, which comprised a significant percentage of Alsatians, and the German prisoners stated that they had 'all been expecting an attack but in no case had certain knowledge of when it was to take place. Several thought it was to take place yesterday and the attack this morning at 7.30 was a complete surprise to most of them.'[41] This is strange, because an alarm had been given by a 'Moritz' listening station not far away.

The lie of the German positions invited a converging attack in the style of the operation against Gommecourt, in this case with the 21st Division assigned to break through to the north of Fricourt, and the 7th Division (p. 160) coming up from the south, the two to meet behind Fricourt on the Willow Stream. Between these two flanking attacks a slope covered with tiers of trenches and emplacements rose to the village, where the deep cellars had helped the Germans to convert the place into a fortress.

The onerous task of attacking Fricourt directly fell to the Yorkshiremen of the 50th Brigade. At 7.29 a.m. three medium-sized mines were exploded under the Tambour strongpoint outside the village, which was supposed to make the 50th Brigade's task a little easier, but the subsequent attacks went in piecemeal and were beaten off, the most celebrated example being that of a company of the 7/Green Howards, which mistakenly went over the top at 7.45, well before the rest of the battalion. It was massacred.

The 63rd Brigade to the left fared little better, even though two companies of the 4/Middlesex tried the usually successful trick of infiltrating into no man's land before zero hour. To the left again the tactic was applied to better effect by the 64th Brigade, and a slow and systematic creeping barrage of 18-pounder shrapnel helped to carry the attack as far as Crucifix Trench, which was short of Willow Stream, but still emplaced the Yorkshiremen on the northern flank of Fricourt.

7th Division (Regular Army), Major General Herbert Watts

With the 7th Division, XV Corps' right-hand formation, we take up the story of the forces that were attacking the south-facing German positions from Fricourt as far as the boundary with the French just beyond Montauban. The ground that the British gained here was not only continuous but deep, which stands in remarkable contrast to the story of their attacks elsewhere on the Somme battlefront. There is no single explanation for the difference.

Along this sector the Germans no longer had the advantage of commanding ground. They had given priority to building up their forces on the right wing of the Somme front, and their troops here on the left wing were battered and thinly spread. Their artillery was likewise reduced to ten field batteries and thirteen heavy batteries, which put it beyond their power to lay down the weight of *Sperrfeuer* that interposed a barrier between the leading British troops and their supports in the actions further to the north. Conversely the British assaults, and those of the XIII Corps in particular, were well prepared, the barrages were systematic and effective, and the troops advancing on Montauban were in addition supported by the potent French artillery.

The recent history of the sector must also be allowed a part. In 1915 the fighting hereabouts between the French and the Germans had not been particularly intense, and there had been little obvious activity by the British in the earlier months of the present year. The German 109th Reserve Regiment moved into position around Mametz and Montauban on 16 and 17 June and found that 'the whole state of our new regimental sector indicated that the trench warfare had not been fought with the same bitterness as at la Boisselle and Ovillers. The works were pretty feeble, and we were very conscious that our telephone communications were defective. On the right-hand sector of our battalion, for example, there was just one telephone line, which led to our 1st Company. Essential stocks of provisions and ammunition were not at hand. Stores would have to be brought up in great quantities, if we were to put the position into any kind of state to resist a major attack with a chance of success.'[42]

It is significant that the efforts of the British 7th Division were the least successful on its left wing, but a good deal more productive on the right, where the British adjoined the well-commanded 18th Division of the XIII Corps. In such a way the left-hand 22nd Brigade failed entirely in its task of turning Fricourt from the south, as its part in the pincer movement that had been designed to pinch out the Germans (see p. 159).

The 7th Division's particular mission was, however, to evict the Germans from Mametz, which was one of the obstacles in the way of an eventual British advance against the German second position that extended along the woods and the chalk ridge to the rear. The 20th Brigade, in the division's centre, reached the village, only to be turned out by a counterattack; but the prize fell in the afternoon to the right-hand brigade, the 91st, where the 1/South Staffords and the 22/Manchesters fought their way into the eastern part of the village and forced the remaining two hundred Germans to surrender.

XIII CORPS, LIEUTENANT GENERAL SIR WALTER CONGREVE

18th (Eastern) Division (New Army), Major General Ivor Maxse; 30th Division (mainly New Army with some Regular battalions), Major General J. S. M. Shea
The battered Germans made little distinction between the two British divisions that dealt them such heavy punishment in the neighbourhood of Montauban. They made up the XIII Corps, at the right-hand extremity of the British line of battle. Its commander, Walter Congreve, was described as a slight, sickly individual who was driven by a strong sense of purpose.

The left-hand division, the 18th, had a wide recruiting base of volunteers from the south-east Midlands, East Anglia and the Home Counties, but acquired remarkable cohesion under its abrasive commander Ivor Maxse. 'Quick and energetic, he did not suffer fools gladly, but at the same time he never failed to encourage initiative among his subordinates; he drove them hard, but one and all ... realised the soundness and value of his training, and thanked him for it.'[43] The uncompromising spirit was maintained throughout the division by men like Lieutenant Colonel Frank Maxwell, who commanded the 12/Middlesex in the 54th Brigade. He had won the VC in the Boer War, and afterwards was famous for having thrown an objectionable young officer out of the window of his regimental mess. In the present war he had no time for 'shell shock', and when he once saw a runner wincing at every explosion he called out 'Send that man here!' He ordered the nearby soldiers to stand in a line. 'Give him a kicking and pass him along!'[44]

The scattering of Regular battalions among Shea's companion 30th Division did not dilute its essential character, which derived from the preponderance of Pals from Liverpool (the King's Regiment) and Manchester. Although the 18th Division was the more famous of the two, it was the 30th that made the deepest gains in the great attack.

The British were opposed by two battalions of the German 23rd Reserve Regiment which was defending Montauban and its immediate approaches, while the 109th Reserve Regiment (see p. 160) held the line extending to the west. The headquarters of the 23rd Reserve had been destroyed by a shell on 23 June, and the German positions as a whole were subjected to a systematic bombardment which by 1 July had devastated the heavy artillery back in Caterpillar Valley, cleared the wire, and made the trenches virtually untenable. The defenders took shelter in shallow support trenches, or in deep dugouts, the exits of which were in turn frequently blocked by the continuing bombardment.

Uniquely among the British formations on 1 July, the XIII Corps gained and held all its objectives, which extended to more than 1,000 yards in depth on the sector adjoining the French and twice that at Montauban and to its west.

Montauban itself fell to the forces that were stacked up in great depth on the left wing of the British 30th Division. The initial assault was led by the 21st Brigade, which almost at once broke into the feebly defended positions of the I and II Battalions of the 109th Reserve Regiment and just over a battalion's-worth of the Bavarian 6th Reserve Regiment. As happened so often on this day, however, the British began to take heavy casualties when they came under enfilade fire from flanking positions (in this case a machine gun which enfiladed the 18/King's from Railway Valley), and when the Germans recovered from their shock and climbed from their dugouts.

This was the stage when the advance might have been expected to stall. For once the reserves were deployed in depth, and the British were able to sustain the assault by a leapfrogging motion. In such a way the reserve brigade, the 90th, passed through the first line and opened its attack at 8.30 in the morning, with the 2/Royal Scots Fusiliers in the lead. Conversely the supporting German unit (the III Battalion of the 109th) had been wrecked and its headquarters forced to retreat into a dugout, while at 8.50 the commander of the I Battalion, Captain von Schirach, was disabled by a machine-gun shot in the leg.

A wounded soldier of the 17/Manchesters later told the Germans how the advance had been driven forward. At 9.30 his battalion got on the move in four waves, each wave corresponding with a company. The Manchesters traversed the captured German trenches, now held by the Scots, and continued towards Montauban, where the leading troops arrived at 10.05, and found it empty of Germans, except for the dead bodies piled up in the cellars – victims of a sustained pounding by a battery of French 240 mm mortars.

Our soldier had been lagging behind, because he had been grazed by a bullet and had stopped to have himself patched up. He joined a company of Pioneers (of the 11/South Lancashire Regiment), which was bringing up entrenching equipment. 'The prisoner saw a large number of British wounded, many of them only slightly hurt. The wounds had been inflicted mainly through rifle bullets, and apparently they had suffered little through machine-gun or artillery fire.' The Manchesters dug in at Montauban in expectation of a counterattack, which did not materialise until the following day.

The Germans noted that 'although the man under interrogation had arrived with a batch of replacements only six weeks before, he made a really excellent military impression. He has a very poor opinion of his officers. In spite of the weak German resistance he speaks of a "disorderly, scattered advance", to use his own words. Some extremely precious hours were lost at the church of Montauban because there was nobody to lead, or rather the officers there had no idea of what leadership was and did not know how to exploit the opportunity.'[45]

Mopping up (a speciality of the 30th Division) continued in the positions that had just been overrun, and the beleaguered staff of the III Battalion of the German 109th Reserve Regiment had to surrender in the middle of the afternoon. 'Hour by hour the first day of July drew towards its end. It was a pitifully small remnant which the regimental commander [Lieutenant Colonel von Baumbach] was able to gather about him in the evening.'[46]

The Bavarian 6th Reserve Regiment had suffered under the bombardment and its right wing had been caught up in the fighting at Montauban. According to its commander it had been 'completely wiped out. Of 3,500 men there were only 500 survivors. They, for the most part, were men who had not taken part in the battle. There remained also two regimental officers and a few stragglers, who turned up the following day. All the rest are dead, wounded or missing: only a small fraction fell as prisoners into the enemy's hands. The regimental and battalion staffs were all captured in their dugouts.'[47]

On the right wing of Shea's division his 89th Brigade did not have the same depth of support, but in compensation it was advancing alongside the 39th Division of the excellent XX French Corps. Indeed Lieutenant Colonel B. C. Fairfax, the commander of the Liverpudlians of the 17/King's, the southernmost British unit on the Western Front, was marching arm in arm with Commandant Le Petit, who led the 3rd Battalion of the French 153rd Regiment. There was little opposition from their opponents, the left wing of the 16th Bavarian Reserve Regiment.

The French Sixth Army of General Emile Fayolle had been almost uniformly successful, and its 39th Division had been piqued only because it had failed to take the high ground at Hardecourt. This feature might have been within the British grasp if the British had exploited east from Montauban to take the Bernafay and Trônes Woods. This had not been impossible, but improvisation on the spot was lacking, as we have seen, and Lieutenant General Congreve had achieved what had been asked of him by the high command.

Congreve's gains had in fact pushed the British right wing forward in a way that determined the development of the battle over the following weeks. From the swell of ground west from Montauban to the Pommiers Redoubt the British now had a clear view across the open landscapes to a wide swathe of the German second position as it ran in front of Mametz Wood; now visible also was the clear ground which separated that wood from Bazentin Wood; then High Wood, standing proud, and the cottages of Longueval nestling against Delville Wood.

THE GERMAN EVALUATION

At the time of writing almost a century has passed since the Battle of the Somme. That interval of time is still probably not long enough to enable us to gauge its full impact on British life. The effects certainly fell short of those inflicted on Anglo-Saxon England by Hastings in 1066, or on Highland society by Culloden in 1746, but the fact that such comparisons can be ventured at all must command our attention. The first day of the battle has come to stand for the cost of the whole offensive, because of the disparity between high ambitions and paltry attainment, and losses that amounted to nearly half of the 120,000 British troops committed, namely a total of 57,470, of whom 19,240 had been killed and 2,152 were missing. These figures exceeded the British combat losses in the Crimean, Boer and Korean wars taken together, and make it the worst day in the history of the British Army. Hunter-Weston's VIII Corps and Morland's X Corps had been badly knocked about, and were shortly to be subsumed into Gough's new Reserve Army, while the unique volunteer culture of the Pals battalions had been wiped out along with most of their men, and the progress of all-out conscription was thereby hastened.

The Germans recognised at once that something of moment had taken place, and not all of it was to the disadvantage of the British. The German high command abandoned altogether its intended offensive by its Sixth Army to the north, and on 11 July suspended its attacks at Verdun. Already by 4 July the German press had registered that the attack on the Somme was an integral part of a concerted offensive on the grand strategic scale. The *Kölnische Volkszeitung* acknowledged that 'for the first time since the commencement of the war, unity of action on the fronts of the Quadruple Alliance has become a fact, on which our enemies can congratulate themselves. We have got to face a Russian, an Italian and a Franco-English offensive at the same time ... Although we are supremely confident, the present hour is of very great significance, and perhaps decisive.' Major Moraht, writing in the *Frankfurter Zeitung*, chose to focus on the Somme where, in his opinion, the most significant effort was made by the British. He referred only incidentally to the 'French divisions which are fighting on the right wing of the English.'[48]

German intelligence was already working to make sense of what happened on the tactical level. In general it was clear that 'nine divisions had scored virtually no success whatsoever. Progress was made only on the sector between Fricourt and Maricourt, and that was on account of the long drawn-out destruction of the trenches.'[49] One of the most productive sources was the evidence given by fourteen captured British officers and 160-odd other ranks who were being treated for their wounds in the hospital at Caudry. They had all been engaged on the left wing between Gommecourt and Fricourt.

> In general they attribute the failure to the following five causes:
> 1. The reinforcements for the attacking troops arrived in an irregular way, arrived too late, or often did not arrive at all. The prisoners do not know why, although the plan of attack had been worked out in the greatest detail. The consequence almost everywhere was that the positions won at such a sacrifice had to be abandoned under the pressure of German counterattacks.
> 2. The German wire was in many places in astonishingly good condition, in spite of seven days of bombardment, so that even the first attacking waves could make no progress.
> 3. The Germans put up an unexpectedly strong resistance in their first and second trenches, whereas the troops had been persuaded that the real battle would begin only in the third trench. This accounts for the casual way in which they advanced across the intervals between the German trenches – sometimes in dense masses – so that they suffered heavy losses before they could fire a single shot.
> 4. The fire of the German machine guns was such that a breakthrough proved unthinkable. The German machine-gunners opened up only when the British were thirty or fifty metres from the trench under attack, and the element of surprise therefore threw them into disorder.
> 5. NCOs and men are furious at the inexperience and uselessness of the young officers, which were manifest in an appalling degree. Many of the troops had, with indescribable sacrifices, managed to penetrate through the German lines. But then their officers failed completely. They just stood there perplexed and paralysed! [ratlos und tatenlos] The lack of leadership on the part of the officers had made the men very pessimistic about the future.[50]

The Germans knew in general terms that a British division was a formation of about 19,000 troops, organised into three brigades. The Germans believed that two of the brigades were deployed for the assault as Storm Troops, and they thought it possible that the third brigade was held back in the trenches as reserve.[51] The assessment was not entirely accurate, for the British commanders expected the third brigade to come forward in support of the leading brigades, and the reason why the troops of the reserve sometimes failed to cross their own front line was due to the weight of the German fire. The 8th Division (III Corps) and the 18th Division (XIII Corps) had untypically attacked with all three brigades abreast.

While they waited to attack, the British had received the attentions of the German artillery. The troops talked disparagingly about the 77 mm 'whizz-bangs', which had a purely local effect, but they had more respect for the light field howitzers and the 100 mm long guns, while the 150 mm (5.9-inch) howitzers were 'veritable brutes'.[52]

The British left their trenches by companies in four waves, separated by intervals of eighty-five yards. The formation seemed to be unvarying, even if the relationship between the successive waves was not entirely clear, 'as it often happens that one of the leading waves was running back at the same time as the rearward waves wished to exit the trenches for the assault'.[53] Trench mortars were usually deployed on either flank of the first two waves, and in some divisions the battalion bombers were incorporated in the first wave to the tune of a ten-man section in each platoon.

'What are called "clearing parties" mostly advanced with the last of the four attacking waves, to clear out the captured trenches and bring back the prisoners. They are usually in the strength of two platoons. The fourth wave was also accompanied by the battalion commander, and an artillery observation officer and his men. Close behind came the brigade machine guns and their ammunition bearers, the carrying parties of the headquarters company with spare ammunition and grenades, trench ladders and so on. Last of all follow the Pioneers, who are to put the captured trenches in a defensible state.'[54]

British historians have pointed out that tactics could vary from division to division or even from brigade to brigade, but nothing of the sort was noticed by the Germans. 'Just like us, the French deploy in combat with the smallest possible sub-units. The British attack in masses, and are willing to accept the severe losses among their inexperienced new regiments ... The French soldiers are better trained and more skilful than the British. When their leaders are lost the troops show more independence, for they have a better grasp of the tactical situation.'[55]

Along some sectors the British were met with such a blast of fire as has been depicted in many films, and most familiarly and misleadingly in the footage (taken on training) that has Tommies picking their way forward through low wire, while one of their comrades on the right is supposedly hit and slides backwards down the parapet. The British had expected to encounter devastated and deserted trenches, as we have seen, but instead they met Germans who took them calmly under aimed fire, and sometimes even stood on the parapets to give themselves a better view. They were in little danger, for if the British answered at all, it was by a wild and inaccurate fire. There was something worse. 'Machine-gun fire. That was beyond doubt the main strength of the German defence, against which the attackers stood "no chance", as they called it. The destructive power of the machine gun is the cause of the enormous losses they sustained, and the first impetus of the attack was on many occasions broken just by the fire of the machine guns in the first German line. The machine-gunners were magnificent, and so was the way their weapons were sited. All the prisoners, including the officers, are unanimous on that point.'[56]

There were nevertheless places where the first wave won the race to the parapet and entered the nearest German trenches without opposition. Only afterwards did things go wrong, as was indicated by the quantities of prisoners taken by the Germans between the first and second lines. A number of processes were at work. 'The prisoners believe that in most cases it was impossible to bring reinforcements to the newly captured line. Resupplies of ammunition were again totally absent, as the assaulting troops lost all contact with the rear.'[57] By then the German artillery was bringing down a barrage on no man's land, and the German infantry were climbing out of their dugouts and emerging in the rear of the leading British troops. Even now great gaps might still lie open in the rearward German positions, but the British seemed to be incapable of grasping the prizes that were theirs for the taking, partly as the direct result of the heavy casualties among the officers, and partly due to an over-rigid system of command.

The survivors who fell into German hands made no secret of their shock and depression. Far from being the 'walk-over' they had been expecting, the attack had been a nightmare in which whole battalions had been wiped out,[58] and the Tommies refused to believe that the men who had been lucky enough to get back to their trenches could ever be used in such a way again, 'and yet the British character is such that that we can be pretty sure that they will continue to pursue their aim by new attacks, perhaps backed up by even more artillery and ammunition. Even the better-educated among the prisoners speak in such terms, saying that it is a political necessity which must be obeyed. The British have invested too many hopes in the success of this attack for them to be deflected from their course by an initial failure.'[59]

CHAPTER EIGHT

The Battle Carried Forward, 2–14 July

THE CONTINUING EFFORT

In British cultural history, as remarked already, the Battle of the Somme began in the morning of 1 July and ended just as darkness fell. The truth of this assertion may be tested against the writings on the battle, in most of which the events of 1 July figure more largely than the rest of the happenings on the Somme put together. The battle had nevertheless more than four months to run, as one element in the continuing efforts of the allies – the British, French, Russians and Italians – to win back the initiative.

The events on the Somme battlefront on 2 July mostly concerned leftover business from the day before. Rather than be cut off in Fricourt, the Germans abandoned the place overnight, with all its lavishly appointed dugouts. This was one of the first positions of the kind that the British had ever seen, and they marvelled at 'the living rooms with electric light, the panelled walls, covered with cretonnes of the smartest Berlin patterns, the neat bunks and the signs of female visitors.'[1] On the otherwise fatal 1 July the British had achieved one notable success on their right wing, where they had taken ground on a frontage of three miles, including Mametz and Montauban. The British had expected a counterattack, and it arrived very early on 2 July, when the Germans flung in their 12th Reserve Division, which had yet to recover from the battering it had received at Verdun. The Germans were stumbling forward from the north and east in the darkness, there was no co-ordination between the regiments, and when daylight arrived the scenario resembled that on the first day of the battle in reverse, for the British at Montauban held the higher ground, while the Germans were exposed to British and French shrapnel fire. Small parties entered Montauban, but they were driven out again by bombers, and the Germans fell back on every sector.

Near-panic overtook some quarters of the German high command. False reports for a time persuaded the 28th Reserve Division that its two flanks were under threat: 'Such messages were a sign that the troops were in need of imminent relief, having been for eight days under ferocious British artillery fire and engaged for two days in heavy combat.'[2] South of the Somme the German XVII Corps (General von Pannewitz) abandoned its sector of the second position to the French, a move which left the flank of the German forces north of the Somme hanging in the air.

Haig was still unaware of the extent of the bloodletting under his command. He noted in his diary that British losses amounted to rather more than 40,000, and (in words which have furnished ammunition to the enemies of his reputation ever since) he added 'this cannot be considered severe in view of the numbers engaged, and the length of the front attacked'.[3] As for the state of the enemy, 'the prisoners were a very poor looking lot but their morale on the whole is very good'.[4] By 7 July Haig's chief of staff Lieutenant General Sir Launcelot Kiggell was confident that the Germans were not only in confusion (which had an element of truth) but were dispirited and very weak along a number of crucial sectors.

Haig deduced that he must capitalise on whatever success the British had so far achieved, by advancing his right wing to such a position as would enable him to take the German second position by a full-blooded assault towards the middle of July. He could then exploit north-east towards Bapaume. Such an advance would (as the Germans indeed feared) unseat the strongpoints around Thiepval and make the positions north of the Ancre untenable.

The scheme made pragmatic sense, in the light of the way the battle was already developing, but the French commander-in-chief General Joseph Joffre argued that the British must again attack in great force at Thiepval, which was just where the German defences had been at their strongest on 1 July. Haig could not agree, and from that time onwards the British and French efforts on the Somme scarcely counted as a joint offensive.

Rawlinson had shared Joffre's inclinations, but he was overruled. He was to undertake the offensive on the right wing with his Fourth Army, now somewhat truncated, for on 5 July he lost his VIII and X Corps to a new left-hand neighbour, Lieutenant General Sir Hubert Gough's Reserve Army. Haig had decided that the battlefront could no longer be managed from a single army headquarters. The rather odd name 'Reserve' came from the fact that Haig hoped to use the army later in the battle as a disposable force to exploit the great breakthrough that would be effected further to the south.

On 2 July Major General Fritz von Lossberg had arrived at Saint-Quentin as the new chief of staff of the Second Army. He writes that the Germans expected rightly where the weight of the new offensive would fall.[5] However, his very presence on the Somme was a sign of the turbulence in the German command, for he was there to replace Major General Grünert (sacrificed on account of the retreat of von Pannewitz), whom General Fritz von Below had been very sorry to lose.

The British took la Boisselle on 4 July, and Contalmaison and Mametz Wood on the 10th – the latter after very heavy fighting which cost the heavily 'political' 38th (Welsh) Division more than 4,000 men. The British were being contained at Ovillers and by means of a ferocious struggle for Trônes Wood, but reports of breakthroughs continued to unnerve the German senior officers. Concerning the state of affairs at Ovillers the new commander of the 26th Reserve Division, Major General Burkhardt, reported on the 7th that 'the crisis has been overcome *for the time being* ... My order at the end of the day is this: "hold out to the last man!"'[6] The German high command had not been surprised by the offensive on the Somme, but it was astonished by the weight and continuing ferocity of the attack, and it had to call on its reserve and on Rupprecht's Sixth Army to yield up the forces (fourteen divisions by 9 July) to stave off collapse.

The reinforcements were on the march in an atmosphere of general perturbation. Coming from the north, the 27th Regiment discovered that 'the wildest rumours were abroad, and it was supposed to be worse than at Nôtre Dame de Lorette [near Vimy Ridge] ... The thunder of artillery reverberated ceaselessly from the fighting along the Somme, and now and then swelled to a continuous pounding, which told every one of us that a great and bitter battle was in progress.'[7]

Troops like these were being committed piecemeal, for when it came under genuine pressure the German system of devolved 'mission' command was more fragile than its admirers proclaim, and the front-line battalions were now being left entirely to their own devices, devoid of all guidance.[8] 'Every battle brings with it a considerable mixing-up of forces, but here on the Somme this unwelcome phenomenon assumed dimensions which made an orderly conduct of the battle extremely difficult. The root cause was that the enemy were launching attacks in overwhelming force, and we had to put together all the possible units at hand and throw them into action where the need was the most urgent.'[9]

British historiography represents the period from 2 to 13 July as a prolonged chapter of wasted opportunities, in which forty-six ill-conceived attacks cost the British 25,000 casualties. It is supposed to stand in contrast to the brilliantly conceived assault on Bazentin Ridge on 14 July. In the German perspective, however, the two episodes ran together, for they were aware that they had lost the initiative and were being kept constantly off balance.

The Germans reserved their organisational masterstroke for the night of 13/14 July. Falkenhayn had concluded that the Somme battlefront must come under unified control, which was not a bad idea in itself. However the detail was handled in an awkward way. The river Somme was taken as the internal line of demarcation, dividing the component First Army in the north from the Second Army in the south. This was again rational, but the overall commander of the new Somme Front, General Max von Gallwitz, not only directed the operations of both

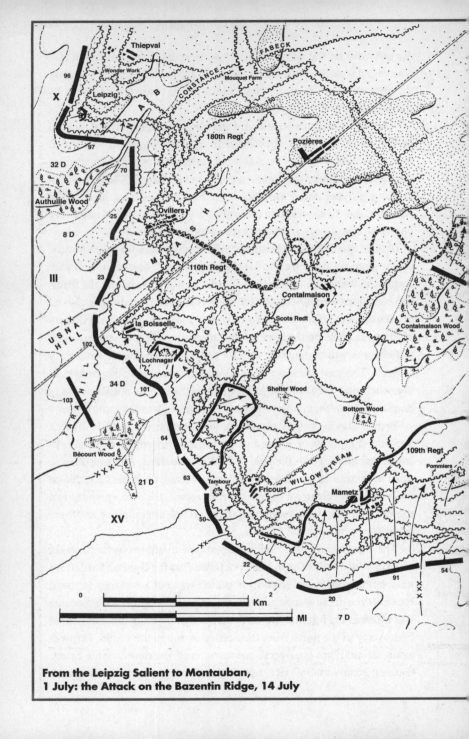

**From the Leipzig Salient to Montauban,
1 July: the Attack on the Bazentin Ridge, 14 July**

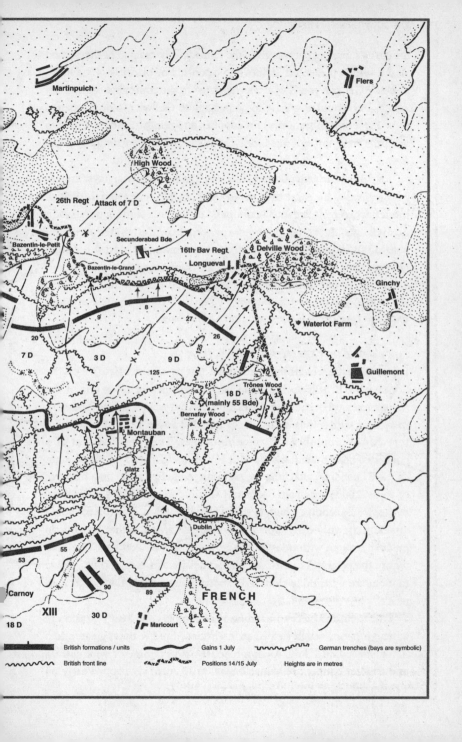

Martinpuich

Flers

High Wood

26th Regt   Attack of 7 D

150

Bazentin-le-Petit

Secunderabad Bde

16th Bav Regt

Delville Wood

Longueval

Ginchy

Bazentin-le-Grand

8

9

27

26

Waterlot Farm

125

20

7 D   3 D   9 D

125

Trônes Wood

18 D

(mainly 55 Bde)

Bernafay Wood

Guillemont

150

Montauban

Glatz

Dublin

53   55

21

90   89

Carnoy

XIII   30 D

18 D

Maricourt

F R E N C H

	British formations / units		Gains 1 July		German trenches (bays are symbolic)
	British front line		Positions 14/15 July		Heights are in metres

armies as supremo, but was given the immediate command of the Second Army, which presented an inevitable conflict of priorities. The hard-done-by General von Below was relegated to the command of the First Army, and would now have to go begging to Gallwitz (who happened to be his junior in seniority) for supplies and reinforcements. The two generals were 'pronounced individualists, and not particularly good friends'.[10]

As part of the general reorganisation, the German corps system was transformed at the same time into something that resembled the British model, whereby it became a command cadre for a shifting population of divisions. The refashioned corps were now designated *Gruppen*, bearing the names of their respective commanders, and three such *Gruppen* were responsible for holding the Somme front, (from north to south) the *Gruppe Stein* (XIV Reserve Corps), the *Gruppe Sixt von Armin* (IV Corps) and the *Gruppe Gossler* (VI Reserve Corps), all these arrangements to take effect in the early hours of 14 July.

THE BATTLE OF BAZENTIN RIDGE, 14 JULY

In the almost unrelentingly gruesome history of the offensive on the Somme, the British operation on 14 July is remembered as one of the more successful of the enterprises, and showed what it was still possible to achieve within the constraints of trench warfare. It was the coming-together of a number of happy influences. The form was that of a concerted blow by four divisions of XV and XIII Corps on the far right of the British line, attacking the German second position on a frontage of some 7,000 yards from Bazentin-le-Petit to Trônes Wood, and taking in the two Bazentins, Longueval and Delville Wood. The troops would attack in the very early morning, which was a notion that Rawlinson pushed through with unusual vigour in the face of doubts by Haig, to whom the proposal to form up whole divisions in the darkness was 'a manoeuvre which one cannot do successfully against flags in time of peace!'[11]

One thousand pieces, including 311 howitzers and heavy guns, were to lend support, which yielded an intensity of fire five times greater than that achieved on 1 July. A comprehensive programme of wire-cutting and counter-battery fire, which began on 13 July, was capped early on the 14th by a five-minute hurricane bombardment by all the artillery. The Germans heard a snarling and hissing in the air, and 'in a matter of seconds the whole landscape to front and rear as well as our own positions were enveloped in smoke, dust and fumes. It was a furious and mighty fire which made the terrors of Nôtre Dame de Lorette seem almost like child's play.'[12] The designated infantry had meanwhile advanced into no man's land, and opened their attack at 3.15 a.m., still under cover of the night and keeping close behind the creeping barrage.

The attack came as a total surprise to the German high command, and hit the left wing of the *Gruppe Sixt von Armin* and the right wing of the *Gruppe Gossler* just when the new commanders were taking over their responsibilities, which was somewhat inconvenient for them. The German forward units were guided only by what they could see or hear of the battle. Visibility was in any case restricted in the area of the two Bazentins, where the close-set country of little woods and valleys was not typical of the general open landscape on this wing of the battlefront. On the sector of the 77th Reserve Regiment the three surviving machine guns of Lieutenant Borelli's 106th Machine Gun Company had been planted in front of Bazentin Wood, in other words squarely in the path of the British 21st Division, the left-hand attacking formation of XV Corps. 'The enemy were storming in something like six waves, not in orderly lines, but by concentrated clumps of soldiers. There were heavy casualties among my gunners, caused by the British who took cover in the shell-holes just to our front, and kept throwing grenades which landed round about us.' When daylight came Borelli was able to drive his tormentors back, and he could register hits when the bullets exploded the grenades that the enemy were carrying in belts.[13]

The attacking troops were probably those of the Leicestershire Regiment, the leading unit of the 110th Brigade. Fifteen minutes later Borelli's attention was drawn to his left by a low-flying aircraft, and he saw that compact British formations had broken through at Bazentin-le-Grand. He could not have beaten off a second attack, for one of his guns had been disabled by a grenade, and the other two had run through 6,000 rounds each. The crackle of rifle fire from the wood and village of Bazentin-le-Petit in his rear told him that it was time to leave, and after removing the locks of his guns he and his party stole away.

What Borelli heard was the sound of the 21st Division's assault on Bazentin-le-Petit wood and village, and the fighting to his left was the combined effort of the adjoining divisions of XV and XIII Corps against Bazentin-le-Grand. The aircraft in question was one of those plaguing the 26th Regiment behind the village. 'We could see the pilots and hear distinctly a staccato tick-tack. "They are sending messages," said one of the veterans, "now we are going to catch it!" But this time he was wrong. It became all too clear that the supposed morse signalling was machine-gun fire. Aircraft were shooting at infantry! We could scarcely believe it, at least not until a couple of our men were hit in the back. We opened a long fusillade at the aircraft, but they carried on with their work regardless, and we were unable to shoot any of them down.'[14] By the end of the day, in spite of counterattacks, the Germans had been driven from all but the northernmost edge of the two Bazentins.

The main body of XIII Corps was attacking the thinly spread 16th Bavarian Regiment on the sector east from Bazentin-le-Grand to Delville Wood. Here the essential purpose was to widen and deepen the salient which the British had already driven north-east into the German positions, and so gain a base for further operations across a wide arc from High Wood to Ginchy and Guillemont. Crucial to the British success was the need to reduce the little village of Longueval, which huddled against the western side of the dense Delville Wood.

The 9th (Scottish) Division was given the task of taking Longueval, and in the darkness of early morning the troops climbed from Caterpillar Valley close behind a creeping barrage of high-explosive shells (a departure from the usual barrage of shrapnel). In the fighting in and around Longueval the Scots established machine guns in deadly enfilade positions, and 'with extraordinary skill the British brought up mortars … on little one-horse carriages and planted them at a range of 150 to 200 metres.'[15] The defending Bavarians were losing men fast, but in the afternoon they were reinforced by a battalion of the 26th Regiment, and the Scots were pushed from the lower-lying northern part of Longueval and were checked in front of Delville Wood.

Along the right-hand flank of the British salient the 18th Division renewed the assault on Trônes Wood, much contested in recent days. The German forward troops had no support from the artillery of their parent 12th Reserve Division, all smashed by the British counter-battery fire, and 'conditions especially favoured the advance of the British infantry and machine guns. They could assemble for the attack in the former German positions, and they brought up supplies through the old German trenches in Bernafay Wood, which they improved. Moreover in the preceding days the British had won ground on both sides of Trônes Wood ... which made it possible for them to open outflanking attacks against the wood from both north and south. In this operation the British made extremely skilful use of their numerous machine guns.'[16] The troops were those of the 6/Northamptons, the 7/Royal West Kents, and the 12/Middlesex under its ferocious commander Colonel Francis Maxwell, VC. Trônes Wood fell to this model operation, though the Germans were still holding out to the rear in Waterlot Farm (actually a sugar factory).

Early in the afternoon the British had to consider whether they should exploit to their further objectives, which extended to Martinpuich and the elevated ground at High Wood. The wood appeared to be empty of Germans, and the British had made good progress in that direction by taking the two Bazentins, all of which indicated that the effort ought to be made by the reasonably intact 7th Division of XV Corps.

The day was well advanced before Lieutenant General Horne released the division in question. After various delays and confusions the troops opened their attack at seven in the evening, and two battalions of the 7th Division proceeded to fight their way into High Wood. However, the Germans had by now arrived in strength, and by determined counterattacks they forced the British infantry to dig in just over halfway into the wood. What might have been achieved by a timely advance was shown by an unlikely success on the part of the division's right-hand screening force, made up of one squadron each of the British 7th Dragoon Guards and the 20th Deccan Horse. They both formed part of the Secunderabad Cavalry Brigade, which helped to make up the total of 90,000 troops of the Indian Army that fought on the Western Front.

The first Germans to see the cavalry were those of the III Battalion of the 26th Regiment. 'We could make out the heads of horses in the sunken road by the ruined mill, and through the binoculars we could discern the riders. Was it new artillery coming up? A messenger was dispatched to the battalion headquarters! All of a sudden several squadrons [sic] of

British cavalry surged from behind the mill in immaculately dressed lines. We had seen nothing of the kind before, and a cavalry attack had never crossed out minds.'[17] The Germans opened fire with two machine guns, and the sight of some riderless horses convinced them that they had defeated this rash enterprise completely. In fact the cavalry was now breaking through the gap between the II and III Battalions, and wheeled around the flank of the 10th Company north of Bazentin-le-Grand. The axis of the advance lay along a hollow, and the reserves of the 3rd *Garde* Division were in no state to bring down effective fire, for they had been shredded by British machine guns while moving up to support the 26th Regiment at Bazentin-le-Petit. German machine guns opened up against the horsemen from Longueval, but they were silenced by the machine guns attached to the Secunderabad Brigade. The German artillery too was ineffective, for the heavy guns were being moved back out of harm's way, while the light artillery was unable to register on this new and mobile target.[18]

Attacking at the trot, the two squadrons killed or captured about one hundred Germans in the open cornfields. They made no attempt to attack High Wood, which was the objective of the infantry, and they dismounted to the south-east to take up the fight with their rifles and supporting machine guns, which was their normal mode of combat. The cavalry had lost eight dead and less than one hundred wounded, and held their ground outside the wood until they were ordered back the next day. It had been a creditable little action, and Haig noted that 'all the cavalry are much heartened by this episode and think that their time is soon coming'.[19]

By this stage it did not take long to twang the highly strung nerves of the German high command. Fritz von Lossberg, as chief of staff on this front, was already aware that a gap existed between the Bazentins and Longueval, and at midnight on 14/15 July he received two reports to the effect that the British were breaking through on that sector. He transmitted the alarm to Falkenhayn, and three German divisions were dispatched, mainly on lorries, to make a counterattack. Not until ten the next morning did it transpire that the British in question were prisoners who were being escorted to the German rear.[20]

CHAPTER NINE

The Wasting Battles, 15 July – 31 August

OVERVIEW

General Haig devoted the high summer essentially to a struggle to evict the Germans from their second position as it faced the British along the central and southern sectors of the battlefront. Pozières (on the direct way to Bapaume, and also the key to the Thiepval position) was a 'new' objective, but the British had already reached or come within striking-distance of the others by 15 July, which was when the impetus of the first attack had expired.

The attack on Pozières became the responsibility of the Reserve Army under the command of the impetuous General Gough, who committed the Australians (inexperienced in the ways of the Western Front) to costly assaults on this undeniably important objective. The management of the battle south of Pozières was in the hands of General Rawlinson, as commander of the Fourth Army, and the character of the fighting there was influenced by his way of taking on limited but difficult objectives with inadequate forces.

At the higher level there was a divergence between the desire of the French commander-in-chief, General Joffre, for the allies to mount concerted, large-scale offensives, and Haig's reluctance to undertake anything on the grand scale before he had gathered all the necessary resources (not least the tanks) and gained the most advantageous jumping-off points. It was, moreover, difficult to establish a common axis of effort, when the French were driving generally east, and the British were pushing north-east in the direction of Bapaume and simultaneously trying to unseat the German salient at Thiepval. Even when the allies settled on some undertaking, the operation was likely to be postponed or disrupted on account of bad weather. Gough complained that 'it was supposed to be summer in "La Belle France", but the amount of rain which fell would have shamed the Green Isle'.[1] Some of the British operations (20 July, the night of 22/23 July, and 16 and 18 August) were timed to coincide with those of the French. To that extent Haig was willing to give way, but after a last and costly affair on 24 August he could state with a reasonably clear conscience that he could not put the British to further risk before he was ready to take part in the coming great offensive, which could not open until 15 September at the earliest.

THE THIEPVAL BASTION

For the Germans the plateau of Thiepval stood as 'the unshakeable corner stone of the old front line'.[2] The British had gained a foothold on the Leipzig Salient on 1 July, which was one of the few successes they had to show north of the Bapaume road. Now the British were represented here by the left wing of Gough's Reserve Army, and they were engaged in a battle of attrition for the plateau, a contest in which the advantages of position were with the defenders, and those of resources very much with the British, as is clear from the German regimental histories.

There was a typical episode on 20 July, when the German 15th Reserve Regiment arrived at what was left of Thiepval village. The unsuspecting German officers were taking in one of the magnificent sunsets that could be enjoyed from this viewpoint, when their regiment was enveloped by four hundred gas shells. Again on the evening of 18 August an attack by the British 48th Division broke through a sector of the 29th Regiment, and the rest of that unit, together with the neighbouring 68th Regiment, were caught up in the subsequent collapse. 'Our infantry up front had come gradually to the belief that they had been abandoned. We cried once more and in vain for some help against the aircraft. Our liaison with the artillery was also bad ... When the British broke into our position they opened an especially intense fire with their trench mortars, and there was scarcely an interval between the noise of the discharge and that of the bursting bombs.'[3] One of the German prisoners testified that 'the behaviour of the enemy was altogether that of gentlemen. All our officers were allowed to keep their side arms, in recognition ... of our conduct.'[4]

The parent German 16th Division was almost completely burnt out by the time the 4th *Garde* Division took over the sector from south of Thiepval to Mouquet Farm on 25 August. Gough wondered why the Germans did not organise an altogether overwhelming counterattack to drive the British from the Leipzig Salient, but it was the German Guards' second tour on the Somme and their senior officers had pleaded in vain that they were still in no fit state to return because of the literally incessant battering by the British artillery.

FROMELLES, POZIÈRES, MOUQUET FARM AND THE AUSTRALIANS
The story of the Australians' commitment to the Western Front is identified with the long drawn-out agony of the fighting for Pozières, but we have take up the story thirty-five miles to the north of the Somme battlefront at Fromelles on 19 July. That was the first and formative action of the Australian Imperial Force in France, and the one that enabled the Germans to form a comprehensive picture of these newcomers.

Major General the Hon. James Whiteside McCay's 5th Australian Division had been formed in Egypt out of reinforcements from Australia and a minority of survivors from Gallipoli, and it had arrived in France at the end of June. It was earmarked for the Somme, and Haig put it under no obligation to attack elsewhere, but McCay and General Sir Charles Munro decided to blood the new division in spite of some very adverse circumstances. The companion British 61st (2/South Midland)

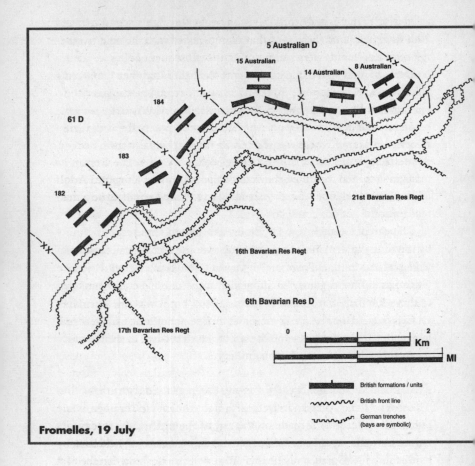

5 Australian D

15 Australian

14 Australian

8 Australian

184

61 D

183

182

21st Bavarian Res Regt

16th Bavarian Res Regt

6th Bavarian Res D

17th Bavarian Res Regt

0		2

Km

MI

British formations / units

British front line

German trenches
(bays are symbolic)

Fromelles, 19 July

Division (Territorial Force) over to the right was in poor condition and down to half its establishment, having supplied numerous drafts to other formations. The weather was bad, the Australian staff officers were inexperienced, and there had been no time to co-ordinate the action of the infantry and artillery. The Australians and British together were outnumbered two to one by the 6th Bavarian Reserve Division, and the defences immediately opposite were manned by the 16th Bavarian Reserve Infantry Regiment (the List Regiment), which was in decline, but still up to the task of holding the position. (One of the survivors of its original core of volunteers was the dispatch runner Corporal Adolf Hitler, who held the Iron Cross and was showing himself to be a man of boundless courage and good will.)

The attacking forces stood under the overall command of the XI Corps of the British First Army, and consisted of three brigades of Australians on the left wing, and three of the British 61st Division on the right. The Germans pieced together many of the details afterwards from what they were told by their prisoners. By their account Australian rank and file had been informed of the operation only on the actual morning of the attack, on 19 July, but they were assured that the artillery had already wrecked the German defences. There had been some upsets from the start, for the first wave of the 14th Brigade in the centre attacked too early, at 5.30 in the morning, and ran into friendly artillery fire. Conversely the 8th Brigade on the left lagged behind the barrage, while the 15th (Victoria) Brigade on the right apparently did not leave its trenches at all, or at least did not get very far (it was being held back by the staff of XI Corps, and released only on the supposition that the 61st Division would be capable of mounting a second attack). The initial casualties among the 14th (New South Wales) and 8th Brigades were believed to have been light, for the German artillery was ineffective, and the wire had been flattened by the Australian and British artillery, as had been promised.

The Australians took the first German trench against light opposition, and established themselves some way beyond, but confusion and dismay set in when the enemy emerged from their dugouts and regained the trench in the rear of the attacking troops. Then 'at first light they came under a fire of machine guns and shrapnel which, to use the words of one of the captured officers, "made Gallipoli seem like a firework display". They reckoned that casualties must have been 30 or 35 per cent at the least.'[5]

As far as the Australians discovered anything about the British 61st Division to their right, it was that the 2/7 Royal Warwicks delayed leaving their trenches until 6.10 in the morning, by which time the covering barrage had reached the German rear and was of no help to the assault. By the German assessment 'while the Australians gained a temporary foothold in our trenches, the attack on the part of the 61st Division seems to have collapsed at the outset in our barrage. We may deduce something of the respective worth of the two divisions from the fact that we made prisoners from seven different Australian battalions but just *one* of the British.'[6]

The costly enterprise was called off at nine in the morning of 20 July. The 61st Division had lost 'only' 1,607 men as opposed to the Australians' 5,333, which strengthened the Australians in the belief that they had been let down by the British. The work of restoring the 5th Division went on for the rest of the year. Its losses had been in the same order as those of the 36th (Ulster) Division on 1 July. The defending Germans had lost 501 killed and 943 wounded.

The Australians conceived a poor impression of British generalship as a whole, for it seemed to them that they had been 'sacrificed on the altar of incompetence'.[7] 'The captured officers were of the opinion that the entire operation had been flawed from the start by the lack of unified leadership. Another fundamental mistake was the order to hold the second trench, instead of having the troops fall back during the night to the first German trench to consolidate there. At the root of everything was the apparently complete failure of the 15th Brigade, which broke the continuity of the attacking front and deprived it of flanking protection. On that account only was it possible for the Germans to regain their first trench and sever all the rearward communication of the enemy units which had penetrated their position.'[8]

A Lieutenant 'Cuminers' (Cummings?), a veteran of Gallipoli, admitted that 'they had had many setbacks there which were just like the present one. The men would advance with all the spirit of the world for a mile or so until they arrived in front of the enemy batteries.

But then the command failed, and they were cut down or forced back.'[9]

It was clear to the Germans that the Australians were not soldiers in the European sense, but the *Berliner Tageblatt* of 30 July could describe them as 'sturdy lads, with gold in all their pockets, unsophisticated sons of graziers and heirs to the land … What their fathers had brought to the wild colony lay in their bearing and eyes, and they were not to be taken lightly. Good shots, cruel fighters, steel-hard fellows.'[10]

The action at Fromelles had an importance that transcended its limited scale (the British official publicity tried to pass it off as a trench raid writ large). For the Australians it defined some of the basic ingredients of what was to become the Anzac Legend. It was a source of pride to Munich, the home of the List Regiment, and helped to maintain Bavaria's fighting credibility among the other states of Germany. After the war it contributed to building Hitler's claim to be the archetypal *Frontsoldat*, and was one of the experiences that helped to convince him that the key to success in the defence was to hold on to every last inch of ground.

The Australians had yet to establish their reputation as assault troops to compare with the Canadians, and many painful lessons were to be learned by their 1st, 2nd and 4th Divisions in the prolonged fighting for Pozières, which was becoming a significant axis of British effort. The open and gentle slopes here led to a little plateau which happened to be the highest point on the battlefield. Once in possession of this feature, the British would have gained a view of the valleys of Martinpuich and Pys to their front, and the German battery positions on the high ground beyond would also be exposed. No less importantly the British could mount an attack against the deep left flank of the Thiepval salient, for they would now have it within range of their field artillery, and be able to develop an advance by way of Mouquet Farm. All of this was well known to the Germans, who had fortified themselves here very strongly. Concreted blockhouses were a rarity on the Somme battlefront (dugouts in the chalk did service instead), but the Germans had two of them at the two entrances to Pozières – Gibraltar at the tip of the village facing the Australians, and the fortified Windmill basement on the summit to the rear in the direction of Bapaume.

On 17 July the last of four British attacks against this position failed in the fog and rain, and on that day the I Anzac Corps was transferred to the command of the Reserve Army. Gough decided to commit the 1st Australian Division ahead of the rest on his sector of the battlefront. He was an impetuous man, but the present move made sense, for the division had come as a formed and cohesive unit from Gallipoli (unlike the 5th), and time had been given to establish tactical principles, and to liaise with the South Midlanders of the 48th Division who were to attack to the left.

The new bombardment of the German positions at Pozières opened on 19 July. On the night of the 22nd the Australians crept forward to within 200 yards of their first objective, then attacked at twenty minutes past midnight on the 23rd. Forty minutes later they were rooting the Germans out of the southern fringes of the village and reaching out to the 48th (South Midland) Division, which was advancing up the shallow Mash Valley to the east.

Over the following hours the two divisions gained further ground in and around Pozières, which was just when Below had planned to counterattack with his newly arrived IX Reserve Corps. Gallwitz as the overall German commander had his doubts about the whole enterprise. Orders were muddled, and the German artillery was totally overwhelmed by the British fire. 'The sky was flecked with the bursts of shrapnel. The gigantic and phantasmagoric shapes of the high explosive could be made out through the yellowish grey dust, which extended over the boiling earth and reduced the sun to a dull yellow disc. Long plumes of smoke stretched over the land from burning stores of ammunition and the blazing houses.'[11]

The Australians could see large bodies of Germans appearing on the crest of the Windmill Hill north-east of the village at 8.30 in the morning, and then wilting under that mighty artillery fire. The effort had cost the Germans 2,000 men, and Falkenhayn demanded to know why so much of Pozières had been lost in the first place, and why the counterattack had collapsed. Gallwitz could only attribute the first to the exhaustion of the defending troops. As for the abortive counterattack, it was due to ignorance of the newest tactics. 'We had invariably employed *Sturmtrupps* at Verdun, but here the forces had been stuck on the defensive for a long time, and lacked the relevant knowledge and training.'[12]

By the time of the next British push, on 29 July, the 2nd Australian Division had relieved the 1st, and was now committed on both sides of the Roman Road to Bapaume. The operation was mounted in some haste, and the initial gains were lost, except for a little ground that was retained by the 6th (Victoria) Brigade on the left. The Australians had been unlucky, in that a German battalion had just arrived to relieve one already in position, and two companies of the 163rd Regiment found themselves at an angle to the Australian advance and were able to lay down an enfilading fire. The Australians also lacked tactical finesse, in that they were fighting with a primitive fury, and large numbers of them were jammed and massacred in a sunken road leading from Pozières. 'When daylight came we could see that countless Australians were lying ... in a carpet, in some places two or three on top of one another. An appalling sight ... A few Australians were brought back as prisoners. They were big, stalwart lads, who made a good impression as soldiers. They were magnificently equipped.'[13]

By 6 August the Germans had been pushed completely out of Pozières. 'Ten thousand men were killed in that plateau and buried and unburied and buried and unburied till no bit of dust is without a man upon it.'[14] The ground now in contention was the Windmill Hill (*Höhe 161*) to the north-east. Late on 6 August the Germans put in a new counterattack. Thirty batteries were in support, and the Upper Silesians of the 63rd Regiment were in a state of some excitement, for they had just been issued with the new steel helmets, and they were under the impression that they were going into action against Canadians – 'Americans from the Wild West'. The Germans lost a number of men to hand grenades, torn apart or blown down. They pressed on, 'and right in front of us we made out fleeing figures. Just then we came under a furious storm of concentrated fire from right and left – the roaring crackle of British machine guns, and collapsing Germans could be seen in the harsh light of the flares.'[15] The Germans fell back with heavy losses.

At first the Germans believed that Pozières had been regained, but 'the British are obstinate people who do not give up'.[16] By the morning of the 7th it was confirmed that the German 9th Reserve Division (IX Corps) had been driven back to its original start line in front of the Windmill Hill. One of the German survivors was appalled to see a battery of four German pieces take up a hopeless duel with the British artillery. In less than half an hour it had been spotted by aircraft and wiped out by the enemy guns. He was equally shocked when two of his comrades saw an opportunity, rushed to the site of the wrecked battery and came back with two tins of pork.[17] Gallwitz took Below to task for having occasioned another useless bloodbath, albeit in accordance with the tactical doctrine of the time, which was to counterattack at all costs.

From prisoners the Germans established that they had been facing the 4th Australian Division, which had just undergone its first experience of combat on the Western Front. 'Veterans from Gallipoli are few in number. It consists almost entirely of inexperienced replacements, and is made up of the 4th, 12th and 13th Brigades.'[18]

After the excitements of 6 August the line stabilised north-east of Pozières across the Windmill Hill, and the attention of the Germans turned to holding the ground to the north and north-west of the village against the pressure of successive Australian divisions (the 4th, 1st and 2nd). The *ne plus ultra* of the German defences was the fortified Mouquet Farm (Moo Cow Farm), with the Fabeck Trench extending to the east, and the Skyline, Constance and Zig-Zag trenches reaching to the west. The Germans were only too aware that a breakthrough there would bring the enemy to the rear of the Thiepval plateau, rendering it totally untenable.

An attack by the 4th Australian Division on 11 August penetrated a gap of 300 yards, which yawned between two newly arrived German divisions, and for a time it precipitated fears of a complete collapse. A counterattack recovered some of the losses, but the Australians were left in possession of a gain 600 yards deep. Another 700 yards were yielded on 12 August, and the Germans noted that even their 'successful' defensive actions were accompanied by a loss of ground.

On 17 August Gallwitz made his way to Hill 124.5 north of Warlencourt to gain an overview. 'We filed along a trench to a periscope. It took in a good wide view which embraced our outer line from Mouquet Farm by way of Courcelette, the Windmill Hill at Pozières, the sugar factory, the position which we lost today, and High Wood and Delville Wood, both of them so disordered that they scarcely deserved the name of wood. In general our line ran along the horizon, but the enemy had made a number of salients which gave them viewpoints from where they could supplement the observation from their aircraft and balloons. The Windmill Hill at Pozières was especially prominent.'[19]

From 21 August onwards the Germans were defending Mouquet Farm itself and the nearby trenches. The operations on this sector as a whole were by no means an exclusively Australian affair (nor, despite a general impression nowadays, was the Gallipoli campaign), and the British 48th (South Midland) Division was attacking parallel and to the left of the Australians. On the night of 27/28 August the Germans captured a sergeant and nine men in the course of an abortive British attack to the west of Mouquet Farm. What they had to say was of unusual interest to the Germans, for it told them something about the new troops who were now diluting the British ranks. The battalion had been detached to the 4th Division for the attack on 1 July, and only two hundred men had come back. It had been brought up to strength with Derby Men, and returned to the front line only on 25 August. On the night of the unfortunate 27th 'their captain had been killed right at the start, when they were still climbing the parapet. They say that their two lieutenants fell into a panic and that their own artillery knew nothing of the attack. The battalion consisted mostly of Derby Men, not a single one of whom had ever been in an attack, and in the absence of leadership nobody had the foggiest idea what to do. They ran off in confusion and tried to shelter in shell-holes, where they were blown to bits by artillery fire, mostly from their own guns ... The attack was a complete failure. When first light came the prisoners tried to escape from the shell-holes, but they lost their way and were captured. They are all thoroughly tired of the war and glad to have been taken prisoner.'[20]

On 31 August Major General Arthur Currie's 1st Canadian Division was marching up to relieve the Australians. 'Guns of all calibres were lined up in Sausage Valley almost wheel to wheel; the air was thick with cordite fumes; half-naked gunners toiled in the murk amid great piles of brass cartridge cases; and the noise of the firing was nerve-racking. At the front the Canadians found the ground littered with the corpses of German and Australian dead, their discoloured, yellow faces and blackened mouths half-hidden by swarms of flies.'[21] The three Australian divisions had lost altogether 23,000 men, and Haig commented that 'some of their divisional generals are so ignorant and (like so many colonials) so conceited, that they cannot be trusted to work out unaided the plans of attack'.[22]

THE CONTEST FOR THE WOODS

HIGH WOOD

The isolated High (Foureaux) Wood crowned a shoulder of downland at roughly equal distances from the two Bazentins to the south-west, Martinpuich to the north-west, and Longueval to the south-east. That village lay close under the western side of Delville Wood, and partly descended the reverse slope towards Flers. The distance between the edges of the two woods, High Wood and Delville, amounted to just 3,500 yards along a north-west to south-east axis, and corresponded to the lie of a battlefront contested between the British and Germans from the middle of July until early September, at enormous cost to both sides.

Haig was determined to conquer the crest as the base from which he intended to mount his ultimate grand offensive against the German third position. General Below, as commander of the opposing First Army, was just as determined to hold the ground or win it back, for the loss would amount to a 'further and most unwelcome addition to the problems of our army's defence'.[23] The disintegrating woodlands and the ruins of Longueval helped to give the subsequent contest its particular character, for command and control were so easily lost in this tangled landscape, and in a way that made neither a conquest totally secure nor a defence altogether hopeless. The Germans wondered at 'the grim obstinacy with which the enemy just kept coming at us, day and night. Sleep was out of the question, for we were in constant danger. We had to stand there with parched tongues and dehydrated bodies, physically and mentally exhausted.'[24]

In the great push on 14 July two battalions of the 7th Division had entered High Wood and the Secunderabad Cavalry Brigade had gained the open country to the south-east. The British were not to have this prize so easily again. Afterwards a German protested that 'the British said in their army reports that High Wood was furnished with all the

British prisoners of war en route to the Reich. (IWM Q 54823)

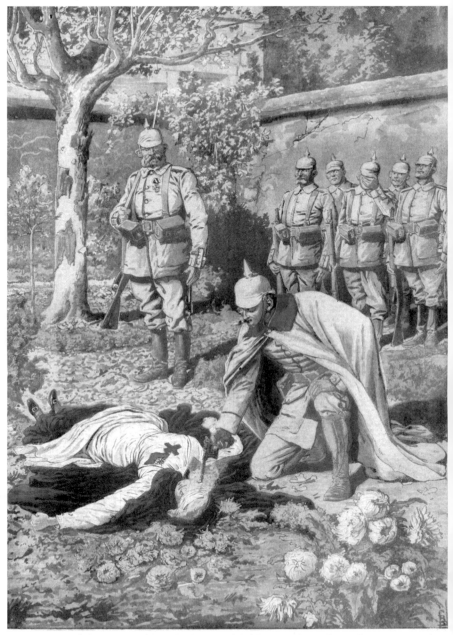

Un crime allemand qui a indigné la conscience humaine

L'ASSASSINAT DE MISS EDITH CAVELL

TOP LEFT The Englishman. Edgar Hamer of Lancaster.
TOP RIGHT The Irishman. O'Brien of Limerick.
ABOVE LEFT The Scot. MacWhinney of Edinburgh.
ABOVE RIGHT The Canadian. William O'Rourke of Sault
Ste Marie, Ontario.
Portrait studies by Otto Stiehl.

OPPOSITE Nurse Cavell. The coup de grâce. (Mary Evans)

ABOVE Tyneside Irish hastening to support the attack on la Boisselle, 1 July 1916 (IWM Q 53)

BELOW A rearward wave of British troops leaving cover to advance to the attack. (Corbis-Bettman/UPI)

British troops in the primitive gas masks on issue in 1916. (Mary Evans)

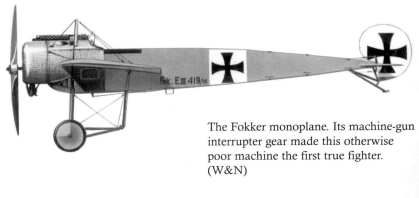

The Fokker monoplane. Its machine-gun interrupter gear made this otherwise poor machine the first true fighter. (W&N)

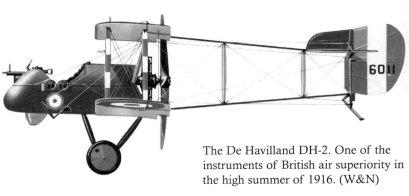

The De Havilland DH-2. One of the instruments of British air superiority in the high summer of 1916. (W&N)

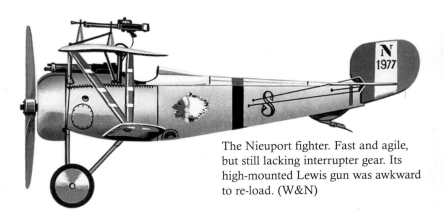

The Nieuport fighter. Fast and agile, but still lacking interrupter gear. Its high-mounted Lewis gun was awkward to re-load. (W&N)

LEFT Oswald Boelke. His gaunt appearance betrays the strain of combat. (IWM Q 58027)

BELOW German motorised anti-aircraft gun. (IWM Q 23779)

RIGHT Unequal
battle. British tank
against unprotected
German infantry.
(Mary Evans)

BELOW British
9.2-inch howitzers
in action.
(IWM Q 7269)

means of field fortification. In fact the position scarcely amounted to a trench, and there was not a metre of wire.'[25] Lieutenant General Horne decided that the gain was untenable, and on 15 July the 7th Division and the supporting cavalry were pulled back. The Germans were free to reoccupy the wood in the evening.

The 7th Division renewed its attack on High Wood under much more adverse conditions on 20 July, and made some deep local penetrations, but was finally driven back to the south-western edge. Early on 23 July the 4/Gordons and the 9/Royal Scots of the 51st (Highland) Division advanced behind a creeping barrage, and the German 165th Regiment could make out 'wave upon wave of khaki-clad forms, followed by dense columns, advancing against our shot-up trenches. Then red flares soared into the sky, and all at once the curtain of a deadly barrage descended in front of our entire position, cutting down the enemy by whole ranks ... But the British are persistent! Again and again they attacked ... in some places as much as four or five times over. Everywhere they failed, and not a single one of the British reached our regimental positions.'[26]

The Highlanders attacked High Wood again on 30 July, and on 24 August it was assailed once more when XV Corps began to sweep it as part of a more general push against the whole sector between there and Delville Wood. The Germans were still in possession of the greater part of High Wood when, at the end of August, they undertook the most ambitious of their counterattacks (see p. 197–8).

DELVILLE WOOD

When they were attacking Delville Wood the British had to contend not only with the inevitable difficulties of combat in heavily contested woodlands, but also with those of advancing from a pronounced and narrow salient that was open to German action from three sides – by infiltration from Longueval from the west, by artillery fire arriving on a wide arc from north-west to south-east, and by machine-gun fire and counterattacking infantry from Ginchy to the east and Guillemont to the south-east.

The British XIII Corps was striving to expand its holdings north through Longueval, and at the same time drive eastwards into the adjacent wood – an episode that precipitated the epic battles of the

9th (Scottish) Division and the newly arrived South African Brigade between 15 and 20 July.

The South Africans had landed in France in April, and on 14 July became the 3rd or reserve Brigade of the 9th Division. With the Scots suffering such heavy losses the South Africans were taken out of reserve and went into action on 15 July in the strength of 121 officers and 3,032 men. The 2nd, 3rd and 4th Battalions entered Delville Wood at six in the morning and in the course of just three hours succeeded in clearing the entire wood and establishing machine-gun nests along the northern edge. By a German account 'the enemy emplaced these machine guns with some skill, and they proved to be decisive for the course of the combat over the following days ... for the enemy now had observation over the sunken road which leads from Longueval to the north, and we could bring up our messages, reinforcements and so on only at the cost of heavy losses.'[27] The South Africans beat off a counterattack, and their 1st Battalion entered the wood in the evening. The Scots simultaneously began to fight their way back into Longueval and reduce Waterlot Farm to the right of the wood.

On 18 July the Scots and South Africans together came under a most determined counterattack on the part of two German divisions. The 26th Regiment drove halfway up the length of Longueval, while three further regiments assailed the South African Brigade in the wood. One of them, the Thuringians of the 153rd, suffered 'many casualties' from 'snipers who sat in the trees'. The regiment was supported by flame-throwers and Storm Troops, but it was counterattacked by the South Africans and by the end of the day had been forced back to the middle of the wood.[28] Coming from the east, the German 107th and 104th Regiments were repulsed without ever reaching the wood.

On 19 July the 3rd (Transvaal and Rhodesia) Regiment of the thinly spread South Africans failed to see two companies of the 153rd Regiment approaching from the north-west, and five officers and 195 of their men were taken prisoner. The fact that they were spared indicates that there was even now an element of give and take among the enemies, though one German account has the enemy murdering wounded as they lay helpless on the ground.[29]

The Germans had still not regained the southern part of Longueval or Delville Wood. At 6 p.m. on 20 July the South Africans were relieved by the British, and the acting commander Lieutenant Colonel E. F. Thackeray came out with two other wounded officers and the surviving other ranks. When the South Africans were paraded the next day they numbered only 755 officers and men.

AS THE BRITISH NOW SAW IT, the front was stabilising along a line that extended from the near edge of High Wood south-east to Longueval, which was still in dispute. From Longueval, a British salient reached through the embattled southern part of Delville Wood. The line retreated opposite Ginchy and Guillemont, which were still in German hands, and apart from a little bulge at Waterlot Farm (now held by the British) it ran almost due south to join the French opposite Maltzhorn Farm.

On 27 July a concerted attack by the British XV and XVIII Corps opened with a sudden barrage of 125,000 shells, which was the highest intensity achieved by the British in the war so far. 'The shells plunged into the bodies of the British who were lying to our [German] front, and together with the acrid fumes of the explosives the stench formed a stinking cloud over the trenches and took your breath away.'[30]

On the 28th the Germans abandoned the ruins of Longueval to the British, though the 76th Reserve Regiment was still holding the ground to the west and the men took the opportunity to rummage through the knapsacks of the enemy casualties, 'it being well known that the British have some pretty good kit. Also it would have been a pity to leave their binoculars, razor blades and other shaving gear to disappear in the mud.'[31] On the same day the Germans were forced back to all but the northern extremity of Delville Wood, which 'probably had more shells in it than any other part of the battlefield'.[32] Most of the remaining ground there was lost by the Germans one month later.

The prolonged fighting for the woods enabled the Germans to take the measure of the British Army at a time when it was undergoing a considerable transition. The old Regulars were fast dying off, or rather being killed off, and Lieutenant Schulze of the 76th Reserve Regiment made the acquaintance of two of the survivors outside Longueval. They had been crawling towards the Germans, and were admitted to the trenches. The second of the men arrived in a very poor state, and according to Schulze 'he was from Kent, married with four children. He could not believe his luck, and from his wallet he drew out a dirty, much-thumbed photograph of his family, and showed it to me. He was grateful and glad to be with us, without having received any ill-treatment. He gave me his shoulder insignia with the brass letters *R. W.K.* (Royal West Kent).'[33]

Among the Territorials the 51st (Highland) Division was acquiring, at a very heavy cost, the experiences which were to make it (in its own estimation at least) one of the elite formations of the army in the last years of the war. On 11 August the German 134th Regiment was holding out in High Wood amid the wreckage of the Highlanders' attacks. 'A filthy stench of corruption lay over our position. There were dead decayed Scots, and a skull with a helmet crowned the parapet. The shells buried the bodies, then ploughed them up again. Thousands of fat black flies.'[34]

There was evidence of increasing turbulence in units like the composite 13/Middlesex of the 24th Division (New Army), which was hit by a counterattack by the 5th Bavarian Regiment near Longueval on 31 August. In addition to its core of west Londoners it had taken in a consignment of young men who had enlisted in the West Kent Yeomanry at the end of March. Among them was a clerk of a coal mine who had joined up, 'in his own words, because in England now a young man who is not in uniform dare not show his face'. To his surprise, he and 169 companions were shipped off to Boulogne to fill out the depleted 13/Middlesex. The battalion had been almost wiped out on 18 August, and 'the veterans were said to have grumbled mightily at having been sent back to action so soon after such heavy losses. They had counted on a number of weeks in a rest area. They say that the battalion does not hang together any more, as about two-thirds of the men arrived ... in various batches of replacements.'[35]

In their innocence these new arrivals began to draw courage from the trenches, which were well built and offered them good cover against artillery fire. 'The attack by the German infantry therefore came as a great surprise, and the officers of the battalion did not have the slightest idea what to do. The battalion suffered very heavy losses in the close-quarter combat which followed. The prisoner can supply no figures, though he believes that few of his company could have survived ... An

attack had been so far from their minds that they had not even got around
to cleaning their rifles, which had become plastered with mud during
the march to the trenches.'[36]

Newcomers had caused more disruption still in the 7th Division,
which could still be counted as Regular when it attacked on 1 July. We
may take the case of the 1/South Staffords, which was all-Regular when
it fought on that day. The battalion went into action again at High Wood
on 14 July, and was mauled so badly that it was only 350-strong when
it was withdrawn to Amiens. The survivors were reinforced by a draft
of four hundred troops, some of them recovered sick and wounded from
Gallipoli, but the rest what the Germans called 'Derby Men' – their
blanket term for both the morally coerced Derby volunteers proper, and
the outright conscripts. The sergeants and the surviving Regulars now
stood out as strangers, and complained that 'the Derby Men, who are
now in the front line for the first time, have no idea what combat means.
All they know is that they are being led into some trench or other – and
there they are buried by shell fire or end up being taken prisoner.'[37]

The state of troops like these had a great deal to do with whatever
local success the Germans enjoyed when they tried to take back Delville
Wood and Longueval on 31 August.

THE GERMAN COUNTERATTACK, 31 AUGUST

For weeks now all the going had been made by the British. Towards
the end of August, however, the II Bavarian Corps and the German
XII Corps positioned themselves to make a great counterattack,
which was designed to win back Longueval and Delville Wood. The
outcome was a disappointment, for the Germans were checked north
of the village, and succeeded only in winning isolated patches along
the northern and eastern edges of the wood. They would probably
have gained even less if it had not been for the fragility of the British
battalions just mentioned.

On the frontage of the 24th Division the composite 13/Middlesex
had collapsed in the face of the 5th Bavarian Regiment and had been
driven back towards Longueval. The boundary with the companion 7th
Division fell awkwardly just inside the eastern edge of the wood, and
as ill-luck would have it this ground was held by the 1/South Staffords,

just mentioned, who came under attack by the German 35th Fusiliers. The South Staffords had taken over this sector only two days before, and had still not established contact with the Manchesters who were deployed somewhere over to their right. They beat off two German probes in the morning, but as the day progressed they were worn down by the bombardment, which included 'Green Cross' di-phosgene shells, and by some very accurate sniping. A final German attack late in the afternoon found the South Staffords exhausted and off their guard. The Germans took ninety prisoners, who seemed to be the only survivors of the A, B and C Companies.

Otherwise the Germans had little to show for the resources they had put into the attack, and so they yielded the initiative once more to the British and French.

CHAPTER TEN

The Second Impetus, September

POSITIONING FOR THE GREAT PUSH, 3–14 SEPTEMBER 1916

In the late summer the German forces on the Somme were under two contending influences – one was a useful sorting-out of command and control at the higher level, and the other was a continuing process of attrition.

On 28 August the German command structure on the Western Front was simplified into two army groups, that of Crown Prince Rupprecht of Bavaria (*Gruppe Kronprinz Rupprecht*), comprising the Sixth, First and Second Armies, from the Channel down to the Somme, and that of Crown Prince Wilhelm (*Gruppe Deutscher Kronprinz*) further south, facing the French exclusively. Inside Rupprecht's group the ambiguous relations between the First and Second Armies were resolved when Gallwitz relinquished overall control of Below's First Army, and reverted to the exclusive command of his Second Army. There was much easing of tension.

On 29 August Field Marshal Paul von Hindenburg replaced Falkenhayn as Chief of the Great General Staff, with General Erich Ludendorff as his assistant. Hindenburg and Ludendorff were on the path to national as well as military leadership, and the commanders in the field knew that they would find support and guidance of an altogether higher order than had been forthcoming from Falkenhayn. Rupprecht's diary for that day has the entry: 'At last!'[1]

Hindenburg and Ludendorff at once tried to get a grip on the Western Front, and on 8 September they assembled the senior commanders at Cambrai to debate matters of fundamental importance. The pair had acquired an almost god-like prestige on the Eastern Front, but they had to recognise that in the West they were confronting little short of a revolution in the waging of war. The issues under discussion embraced the urgent need to replace exhausted divisions, a better direction of the artillery (and especially a more effective co-operation between the batteries and the air forces), the vulnerability of troops when they were packed into forward positions, and in general the requirement to replace the efforts of men with those of machines in the style now being set by the British and French. All of these problems were now addressed in an energetic and realistic way, but in the nature of things there was little that could be done to help the troops in the days just ahead.

At the beginning of September the Germans assessed that on the Somme they were facing altogether thirty-four British and French divisions, twelve of which were in reserve. The twelve German divisions were being burnt out. They confronted odds of nearly two to one in infantry, up to one and a half in artillery, and at least two to one in numbers of aircraft. At roughly 80,000 the German losses on the Somme in August had been less than one-third of those sustained in July, but they were very high in proportion to the small amount of ground that was actually yielded, which suggested that the battle was becoming one of attrition.

General Fritz von Below, now enjoying untrammelled command of the First Army, was correct to identify two axes of British effort against his sector. The one, in the north, was intended to turn the German salient at Thiepval by its left flank and exploit north-east towards Bapaume. The other was directed against High Wood and Ginchy, where the lie of the land was less favourable for defence than that further north, and where Below now had to replace his eight divisions at a rate of a new division every two days.[2]

Haig was aiming to test and wear down the Germans along the whole of their front, but more especially to win ground on his right wing – ground that he considered essential to widen the base for the great combined offensive by infantry, artillery, aircraft and tanks, which he planned for 15 September. As they concerned his left wing, these preliminary attacks were sent against all-too-familiar objectives, and had outcomes that were again depressingly familiar.

RESERVE ARMY

As autumn approached it seemed to the Germans that the striving of the British and French on the Somme was regaining the same intensity as at the opening of the offensive. There appeared to be something ominous about the quiet that reigned on 2 September. 'We felt uncomfortable if shells were not bursting over our company's sector at a rate of a hundred an hour. The whole front had its eyes skinned. From the shell-holes there emerged heads under their dull grey helmets and peered into no man's land, over which there danced just a couple of baby shrapnel bursts.'[3] The offensive broke between 3 and 6 September, when the British and French attacked on a frontage of more than thirty miles on both sides of the Somme.

On 3 September V Corps attacked on the Ancre. The assault by the 39th Division (New Army) north of the stream was the first sizeable operation on this sector since the third week of August, and a captured officer of the 14/Hampshires explained that it was the division's first-ever night attack, 'and that they had to crack the hardest nut along the whole line, one called "Thiepval", and the British failed against it for the second time'.[4] Afterwards the no man's land was covered with British, while the trenches, where there had been hand-to-hand fighting, were literally filled with the dead.[5]

FOURTH ARMY

II Corps

The locations and experiences of II Corps' two attacks on 3 September were horribly reminiscent of events in July. The 49th (West Riding)

Division failed on the much fought-over ground of the Schwaben Redoubt. Its companion on the right, the 25th Division (New Army), was beaten back from the Wonder Work, a strongpoint just behind the front line south of Thiepval. A soldier of the 2/Lancashires fell wounded ten yards short of the first trench. He was retrieved by the Germans and told them that his battalion had been about eight-hundred-strong at the beginning of July, but only two hundred had survived by the middle of the month. They were taken out of the line and reinforced only by two hundred inadequate Derby Men. The battalion survived a period of passive line-holding in Beaumont Hamel, but proved unequal to its new test on 3 September. 'When battalions consist mainly of men like that you should not commit them to attacks. They have no chance of success. They were told that they only had to take two trenches, then they were through, and, as an officer told them, they would meet Australians on the other side near Mouquet Farm. To use the prisoner's own expression, this was just a "bluff" to encourage the younger men to advance. The result was a total failure, as this old soldier had foreseen.'[6] Both Haig and the corps commander Lieutenant General Jacob blamed the failure on the ignorance and lack of offensive spirit of the troops.

Anzac and Mouquet Farm

The attack on the part of the 4th Australian Division was the last contribution to the Australian component of Anzac on the Somme. On the morning of 3 September the Australians were opposed by the 5th Prussian *Garde* Regiment. Just after six one of their lieutenants alerted his men, and 'a magnificent panorama opened before us. As far as the eye could see the whole landscape was bathed in the light of countless flares, while red and green rockets from both sides coursed through the half light in elegant curves. Machine guns hammered away without pause and there was a barking of rifle fire. The earth shuddered with the impact of heavy and super-heavy shells, which were being aimed with great accuracy.' Incendiary rounds were bursting over the trenches, though with little more effect than to singe the troops and their knapsacks.[7]

The Australian objectives were Mouquet Farm and the adjacent Fabeck Trench. 'According to the [Queensland] prisoners the losses in the assault were very few, as the artillery was laying down a barrage which crept slowly forward. The men were coming up behind in a number of waves, although they very soon got intermingled.' The three battalions were able to carry both the trench and the ruins of the farm, but, as had happened before, the Australians were driven out again by counter-attacks, and this time with very heavy losses. The prisoners believed that very few men could have escaped, and that most of the officers had been killed outright. 'They maintain that the attack had been mounted with altogether inadequate forces, and that they had no hope of fighting off the Germans who came storming in from all sides. They had called for support, but the German barrage prevented the reinforcements from getting through.'[8]

The fatal barrage had been something of an accident. The Germans had known nothing of the attack in advance, but they had arranged a test *Sperrfeuer* for what happened to be the time of the assault, and they had a complement of artillery observers up front with full telephone communication with the batteries to correct the fire.[9]

The Australians retained just 300 yards of the Fabeck Trench, and it was inherited by the Canadians, who began to take over their positions on the same day. This gain too was lost, to a counterattack on 8 September.

III and XV Corps in the Woods

The efforts by III Corps were expended in prolonged and inconclusive fighting in High Wood, remarkable only on account of the flame-throwers that the British 1st Division employed on 2 and 8 September.

As its part in the general offensive XV Corps opened an attack on the German toeholds in Delville Wood on 3 September. By the 7th the British managed to clear the Germans from everything they had gained in the last counterattack, and the incoming 14th Bavarian Regiment found that 'the enemy were established on the eastern edge of the wood about 500 yards from the sector we were to occupy. We could hardly make out their positions in the shot-up woodland, which offered them good cover. Conversely the elevated position of High Wood gave them unrestricted view over the whole ground as far as the road from le Transloy to Beaulencourt.'[10] From 7 September the British holdings in that wood were taken over by the 47th Division of London Territorials: 'These look very clean and smart and march well.'[11]

Over in Delville Wood, however, the British were still hemmed in on their eastern flank, and Rawlinson needed to reduce the outlying villages of Ginchy and Guillemont if he was to win a wide enough base for the coming offensive. The 8/ and 9/Devons played the leading role in XV Corps' attacks on the first of these villages. While resting at Ailly the Devons had been reinforced by four hundred men, 'apparently good replacements, most of them Kitchener Men with only a few Derby Men and some returning sick and wounded'.[12] It is interesting to find the Kitchener volunteers now being regarded as effective troops, but even these men were powerless against the machine guns which infested Ginchy and its surroundings. The 9/Devons attacked on 3 September, but were checked 200 yards short of the village and forced to retire.

The attack on Ginchy was renewed on 6 September by both battalions of the Devons, this time supported by the 2/Gordons to their left and the 2/Border Regiment to their right. 'The village of Ginchy was taken towards noon at the price of fairly heavy losses to machine gun and rifle fire. Although the place seemed empty or abandoned, what is described as "invisible" machine-gun fire was coming in from all directions, and made it impossible to hold out there.'[13] Ginchy had to be left once more to the Germans.

XIV Corps and Guillemont

The right flank of the Fourth Army, and therefore by definition of all the British forces on the Western Front, terminated in the neighbourhood of the Maltzhorn Farm, where it met the left flank of the French Sixth Army. The British were very much on their mettle, and every operation of every size had to be concerted with the allies.

The battle hereabouts had at first been the business of the much-vaunted XIII Corps, which discovered that it had resilient opponents in the shape of the 24th (Saxon) and 27th (Württemberg) Divisions. The Germans had beaten off ambitious attacks on 29 and 30 July, and General Gallwitz saw the British prisoners who were assembled at Moislains, 'all in khaki-brown, wearing those saucer-shaped helmets of theirs, with typically British sharp-featured faces beneath ... It was enlightening to learn about the results of the interrogations and conversations with the thirty British who had been taken on the 29th and 30th. They included recruits who had only just arrived at front-line units, and who had been under fire for the first time. In neither appearance or intelligence did they make the same good impression as the men of the first Kitchener Divisions.'[14]

In the middle of August the Württembergers were looking west and saw in the distance 'a dusting of cloud, and above it a perfect blue sky where huge squadrons of enemy aircraft were circling about. Guillemont was invisible, though its location could be made out from the reddish clouds of dust thrown up when shells impacted on its masonry.'[15] The bombardment was in support of Lieutenant General the Earl of Cavan's XIV Corps, which had arrived on 15 August to replace the XIII Corps, and was now given a leading role in the attacks that were designed to put the allies in a favourable position to open their grand push.

At the beginning of September Guillemont was held by the 73rd Fusilier Regiment, one of the historic regiments of Hanover. The Fusiliers were in an isolated position, with gaps to their right and left, and on 3 September the landscape could be seen to be swarming with khaki figures. Over to the left most of the British stood 'upright in the open ground, shooting into the living wall of our troops, who fought on to the last and were shot down man by man'. Over to the Germans' right the British broke into the trenches, and proceeded to roll up the defenders from the flank.[16]

Captain Götz von Olenhausen, the commander of the Fusiliers' I Battalion, was now cut off, and on the report that the enemy were almost on top of him he ordered '"Everybody leave the dugout!" The machine gun was brought up to the exit, but the sentry was killed by a rifle shot, and immediately afterwards something exploded in the dugout. Everyone screamed "Get out! Get out!" and there was a general rush for the exit. Outside ten or so British soldiers and an officer were standing with levelled weapons, and they took the Germans prisoner one by one as they reached the exit, half-unconscious from the gas. I cannot say anything more since I passed out when I reached the exit, and came to again only when a British soldier was ripping my torch and compass from my breast pocket.'[17]

Perhaps the British were held back from doing something worse because they recognised the battle honour *Gibraltar* on the Hanoverians' armbands, recalling the time when British and Germans had defended the rock together against the French and Spanish from 1779 to 1783. The British had advanced on a frontage of 2,500 yards, and stopped only just short of Ginchy.

The 73rd Fusiliers' distant left-hand regiment, the 64th Fusiliers (again from Hanover) were now left totally isolated in the defence of the Braune-Linie and Falfemont Farm, a stoutly built structure of red brick, furnished with deep cellars, which formed an integral part of the German second position. It was sited on a pronounced spur, and to the south it commanded the ravine-like Vallée de Maurepas, along which the French of the Sixth Army must advance if they were to take Maurepas village. The British overran the position in the course of 4 and 5 September, along with most of Leuze Wood to a depth of up to 1,600 yards in the rear. The rest of the wood was cleared on the 6th, and the British thus reached the base of the long and narrow Bouleaux Wood (*Birkenwald*, 'Birch Wood'), which extended to the north-east. These gains were to offer Haig one of his jumping-off points for his offensive on the 15th. 'From here onwards for a depth of about seven miles the land was entirely bare and devastated all round, with plains and low ridges, with no greenery – most desert-like, the ground torn up and covered with shell-holes, the one merging with the other. The earth was greyish, with white chalk showing where the battered remains of trenches existed. There was a great deal of débris on the surface, the remains of barbed wire, smashed vehicles, weapons and broken timber.'[18]

THE IRISH AND GINCHY, 9–10 SEPTEMBER

The Fourth Army had to address itself to one more piece of work if it was to clear its right wing entirely, and this was to reduce the village of Ginchy and thus advance the line into the space between Delville Wood and Leuze Wood. The task was given to Major General W. B. Hickie's 16th (Irish) Division. This body was made up of Irish nationalist and thus predominantly Catholic volunteers, and for the best part of the rest of the twentieth century it was almost eliminated from the historiography of the Great War, while at the same time the achievements of the 36th (Ulster) Division became part of the culture of the Northern Irish Protestants. Some of the references by British officers were disparaging, and Robert Graves, as a former captain in the Royal Welch Fusiliers, wrote that the 16th was careless and casualty-prone, good enough at taking its objectives, but liable to lose them again to counter-attacks. It is worth asking how far comments like this stand up to the record of events at Ginchy on 9 and 10 September 1916.

Neither the attackers nor the defenders of Ginchy were in the best condition. The 19th Bavarian Regiment had only just arrived on this sector, and had not been given the time to familiarise itself with the position. The confusions were confounded by the fact that 'through a mistake and contrary to all the lessons of war, the defence of Ginchy was not assigned to a single formation, but fell on the boundary between two divisions'[19] – the 5th Bavarian Division on the right and the 185th on the left. Some of the 185th were new to infantry work, having been just converted from artillerymen.

On its side the 16th (Irish) Division had been exhausted and depleted by the recent fighting for Combles. For the present task the division was deployed on a frontage of two brigades, the 47th on the right and the 48th on the left. There was no third or reserve brigade to lend support. On 9 September an unusually long interval was left between the opening bombardment (which came down at seven in the morning) and the opening of the infantry attack at five in the afternoon, the purpose being to deny the Germans the time to counterattack in the remaining hours of daylight. Meanwhile the Irish remained under shell fire from both sides, and it was perhaps fortunate that so many of the British shells failed to explode.

The 47th Brigade began to advance up a gentle slope in the open country to the south of the village, but came under a lethal enfilade fire on its right flank from five German machine guns and a body of infantry which had not been detected in time by the British aerial reconnaissance. In contrast the attack by the 48th Brigade on the left carried straight into Ginchy, where the muddle among the Germans had still not been sorted out. According to Crown Prince Rupprecht 'a British battalion infiltrated into this gap piece by piece and without being noticed'. The British proceeded to gain the left flank of the 5th Bavarian Division, which was standing outside the village, and forced it to withdraw.[20] Rupprecht's wording suggests strongly that the Irish had been feeding troops along the stretch of sunken road that led into Ginchy from the south-west.

Some men of the 7/Royal Irish Rifles and the 9/Royal Dublin Fusiliers carried on to the second objective to the rear of the village, but they had to be recalled because the 55th Division of XV Corps was making no progress to their left. The Irish then dug themselves into a semi-circular position, which extended around the northern, eastern and southern sides of the village, and covered the approaches by carefully sited Lewis guns. Few English brigades, and fewer still of the Australians, had ever secured themselves so thoroughly against a counterattack.

The 19th Bavarian Regiment was ordered to retake Ginchy, but, according to its regimental history, 'the British were much too clever to throw large forces into the heap of ruins. They were content to deploy skilfully emplaced machine guns and small units in front of the village, and so make it difficult for us to get anywhere near.'[21] All the German attacks were beaten back short of Ginchy. On 11 September a last coun-terattack failed, and the Germans had to recognise that Ginchy was lost to them for good. Between 7 and 12 September the 19th Bavarian Regiment had lost a crippling 884 men in casualties and missing.

ALTOGETHER BETWEEN 3 AND 14 September the pressure by the British and French precipitated among the Germans a sense of dismay and crisis. On the evening of the 4th the German supreme command described the state on the Somme as 'very serious',[22] and many German post-war regimental histories write of 5 and 6 September as days on which the troops facing the British were at the end of their physical and mental endurance.

Certainly it is possible to maintain that between 15 July and 14 September the Fourth Army had advanced just 1,000 yards on a frontage of five miles and had lost 82,000 men, and was thus 'paying a prohibitive price to secure infinitesimal amounts of territory',[23] but the rising ground just to the north of Ginchy gave the British a clear view to the German third position, and the perspective of the Germans is also worth taking into account. 'It is true that the loss of one piece of ground after another does not amount to much in itself,' wrote Gallwitz on 11 September, 'but the repetition serves to strengthen the enemy and weaken us. Think of all those "missing!" If this game goes on any longer, we will be unable to supply the necessary replacements in men and equipment.'[24] He had been speaking with Major General Lossberg, and had to agree with him that the German batteries were being beaten down by the British low-trajectory pieces, which seemed to offer further proof that the enemy had a greater depth in both material and human resources.

The battered 4th Bavarian Division at Flers warned that 'after the close of the battle for Ginchy we may reckon that the enemy are getting ready to launch a new attack, with all possible resources, against the position which extends along the heights from the south of Flers to the south of Martinpuich. This attack has been in the making over a long period of time. Trench after trench has been prepared for the assaulting troops. A mine attack is in progress in High Wood. A continuous harassing fire of both heavy and light field pieces makes it difficult for us to repair our defences.'[25]

The allied prisoners were themselves showing undiminished confidence, and were happy to tell the Germans how generally feeble the opposition they had encountered had been. The German defensive barrages had opened far too late, while the attacking troops were able to surprise and overrun not only the trench garrisons in their dugouts, but even the forces that had been earmarked for counterattacks.[26]

THE BATTLE OF FLERS-COURCELETTE, 15 SEPTEMBER

Haig determined 15 September as the date for the great push. By that time the 16th (Irish) Division had broadened the salient to the east of Delville Wood, and, although the Germans were still planted in High Wood, the British otherwise had in their possession the forward slope of the main ridge on a frontage of 9,000 yards from near Mouquet Farm to Delville Wood, and the crest of that ridge from Delville Wood to Leuze Wood, which made another 3,000 yards. Recent advances by the French had brought the allies into alignment on the right flank. Haig now proposed to attack the defences between Courcelette and Flers with a view to reducing High Wood and the other remnants of the German second position, breaching the third position and opening the way for an historic arm, the cavalry, to exploit north-east to Bapaume.

The tanks, a new weapon, were to help in cracking open the defences,

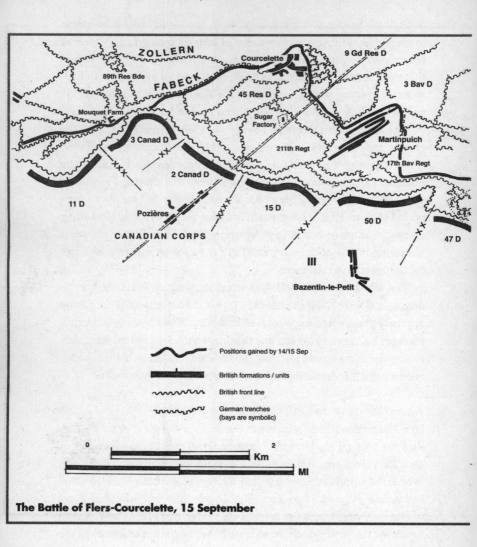

The Battle of Flers-Courcelette, 15 September

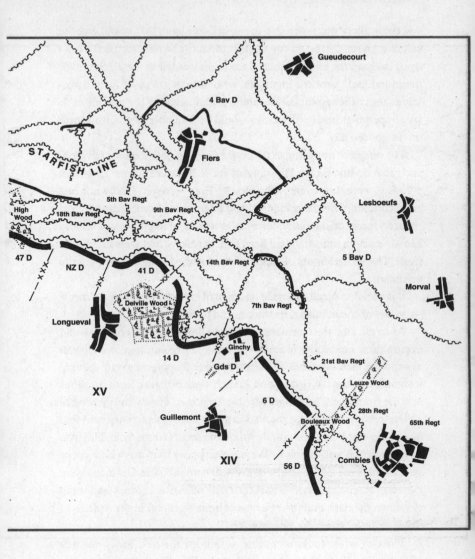

and the artillery was ordered to leave shell-free lanes that would give the vehicles an unobstructed run against the most heavily fortified objectives. In detail the employment of the tanks was left to the discretion of the individual corps commanders, who did not always inform themselves about the unfamiliar capabilities and needs of the machines. It was hoped that nearly fifty tanks would be available to go into action on the chosen day.

The offensive was going to fall on the German 45th Reserve Division, and the 3rd, 4th and 5th Divisions of the II Bavarian Corps. How well prepared were they to meet the attack? They were physically not in a good condition, for the prolonged and intensifying bombardments had reduced many of the outer defences to a zone of shell-holes, and told heavily even on units that had been held in reserve and were nominally fresh. The whereabouts of many of the forward troops were actually unknown.

It is useful to break down the question of surprise into three elements – the fact of the offensive, its timing, and its form.

As to the fact, the Germans were in no doubt that the enemy would exploit their superiority in artillery, stocks of ammunition and aircraft to continue their offensive, and Crown Prince Rupprecht's staff thought it significant that the British and French were bringing fresh divisions into the front line. The *Gruppe Marschall* reported that by the evening of 13 September there was a marked increase in British activity, and that heavy fire was being brought down on the sector south from Thiepval to High Wood and beyond. 'We must consider that the whole corps sector will come under attack in the near future.'[27] The Germans were therefore bracing themselves to meet a new offensive, but they had yet to pin down the date, and their burnt-out units were still in the process of being replaced when the storm broke.

The day when tanks went into action for the first time ever was 15 September 1916, which gives the Battle of Flers-Courcelette an interest that extends beyond the Great War. It would be useful, to put it mildly, to discover how much the Germans knew of what was about to hit them. The most specific evidence of foreknowledge comes from the interrogation of German prisoners who had been facing the British III Corps near Martinpuich.

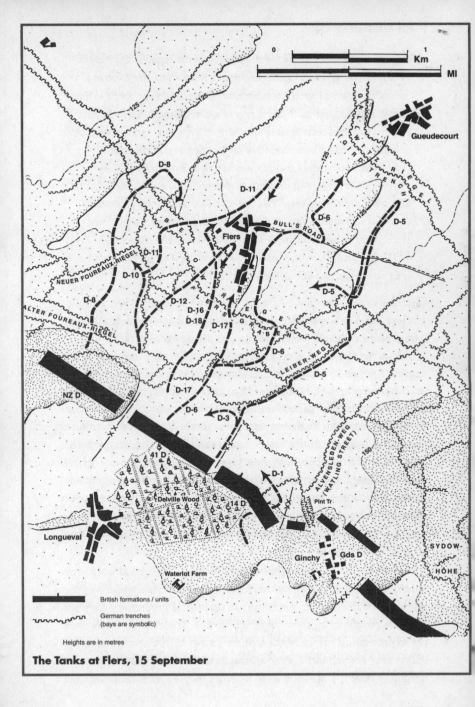

The Tanks at Flers, 15 September

Prisoners state that about six weeks ago [i.e. at the beginning of August] an account of the Land Cruiser had been given over the telegraph in a sort of summary of special correspondence which was circulated to the unit from headquarters. These they read out to the men on parade. In it it stated that land cruisers were armoured to five or six centimetres thick and that they had attacked trenches on a certain part of the front. Infantry were powerless against them as well as field artillery. They were very hard to hit and distinguish and only a 15 cm direct hit was of any use in destroying them. This may be a German agent's account of experiments seen in England. On the 14th they were warned that the British were going to use them on this front and he himself with his F.O.O. [forward observation officer] had seen one through a telescope a long way behind the line and reported this fact.[28]

(The 'he' is not specified.) Another piece of intelligence has armour-piercing S.m.K. ammunition being issued to the defenders of the Quadrilateral near Bouleaux Wood 'for possible use against aircraft'.[29]

All of the foregoing is very puzzling, for tanks were certainly never employed before 15 September. The remaining evidence indicates that the tanks burst upon the Germans on 15 September as a complete surprise. No kind of warning reached the forward troops, and a first lieutenant of the 23rd Bavarian Regiment recalls that three nights before the attack there came from the British side 'a most peculiar gurgling, scraping and grinding, as if from engines of some kind. We had never heard anything quite so sinister, inexplicable or noisy. "They're undermining our whole position," the men surmised, "the British are using engines to drive tunnels all over the place". That was not altogether unlikely, given the situation. As the night of 14/15 September drew to its close there was nothing more to be heard.'[30]

For weeks after 15 September the Germans still could not agree among themselves as to the most basic elements of tank design. On the question of the S.m.K. ammunition, captured gunners of the 5th Bavarian Artillery Regiment told the British '1. The armoured cars were not expected and surprised the units engaged. 2. The armour-piercing bullets were not intended for use against these cars. Their purpose was not definitely stated; a question as to whether they were intended against aircraft also brought no definite answer.'[31] More probably the intended targets were the steel shields that protected British snipers.

Until further sources come to light we cannot rule out entirely the possibility that information of some kind had reached the Germans, and had then been discounted, forgotten, or simply not passed on. When the Heavy Section of the Machine Gun Corps was working up the new machines at Thetford in Norfolk a crewman entered in his diary that 'no outsider is being allowed to attend the experiments and manoeuvres.' On 10 July, however, he mentions that 'we searched the entire camp for a spy who was said to have slipped in. No success.'[32] Brigadier General John Charteris, senior intelligence officer at Haig's headquarters, wrote on 16 September that 'the main argument in favour of their [the tanks] use was that the Germans did definitely know we had some new instrument, but had not yet found out what it was. If we had waited they would have found out and might – we do not know – have found a suitable reply. Also we learn more by one day's active work than from a year's theorizing.'[33]

The Germans had already been under fire for three days when first light dawned on 15 September. 'There was a fresh morning breeze which eased our cramped limbs, but the waiting, the perpetual tension and the uncertainty had left us exhausted. We had just set about getting something to eat when all at once a thousand-voiced throaty scream came at us from the sky, and a long chain of flashing impacts announced that the *Trommelfeuer* had returned.' That must have been at 5.40 on what promised to be a brilliant morning, when every British piece added its weight. 'Smoke and darts of flame, a deafening fizzing and cracking as if the whole world was in a state of disintegration ... A show at once beautiful and terrible was unfolding before the artillery observation officers. Martinpuich and Eaucourt l'Abbaye were shrouded in clouds of black smoke, punctuated with the flames of the bursting shells.' Gas shells were intermingled with the high explosive, and 'white veils shrouded the groaning landscape. The smell was like rotten apples.'[34]

The Germans in the affected sectors had to put on their masks, which made it almost impossible for them to repair their crumbling trenches. Telephone wires were almost everywhere broken, the red flares calling for a defensive barrage were unseen in the smoke, dust and lingering mist.

The British infantry were making ready to attack, and it was no longer a primitive matter of 'going over the top' in the style of 1 July. 'During the night of the 14th to the 15th the enemy brought their assaulting troops forward, and hid them in hollows, sunken roads, shell-holes and dugouts. It was done most skilfully. They made great use of the surviving communication trenches in our former positions, which facilitated greatly the business of advancing their troops under cover.'[35]

A senior officer of the Bavarian Pioneers conceded that 'the co-operation of the British artillery and infantry was admirable. From my viewpoint in the Gallwitz-Riegel [Gird Trench] I could see how the British were bombarding the Below Line in a systematic way, one stretch of trench after another. They then advanced their fire, and under that protection they sent forward a number of well-trained troops to spy out the state of the damaged position and their defenders. They reported back, and on the basis of that intelligence the British either brought the trench once more under a murderous fire, or, if the desired effect had been achieved, they launched their assaulting columns against it.'[36]

The troops advanced from their positions at 6.20 in the morning, and, as before, we shall follow their progress from the left of the British array to its right.

RESERVE ARMY

The Canadian Corps at Courcelette
It was not just the tank that made its debut on the Somme on 15 September, but also, in a major attacking role, the experienced Canadian Corps. Its 2nd and 3rd Divisions formed the right-hand formation of the Reserve Army, and the far-left flank of the forces dedicated to the offensive. The Canadians had infiltrated their way forward overnight, and now, as the Germans saw it, 'the enemy went over to the attack, by advancing waves of troops, divided into section-sized groups and interspersed with machine guns [i.e. Lewis guns] These waves were supported by compact columns. The enemy apparently had recourse to these massive supports as a means of forcing their troops to keep on. They suffered heavily in the process, but their numerical superiority made the cost acceptable.'[37]

The Canadians were attacking Mouquet Farm, the Fabeck Trench between there and Courcelette, and Courcelette itself and its outlying trench system and sugar factory. Mouquet Farm, little more than a pile of bricks and timbers overlying concreted cellars, was taken by a large Canadian raiding party, but lost again to a German counterattack. The Canadians managed to capture and hold long stretches of the Fabeck Trench, and achieved a still more considerable success over to their right at Courcelette. The Canadians were coming at the village from the south in successive waves, ahead of their six supporting tanks, which were destined for a mopping-up role. No shell-free lanes had, therefore, been left for the tanks, and the entire width of the German defences was being pounded by the artillery.

The tanks were grinding up behind, on either side of the Albert–Bapaume highway. One of the machines broke down, three more got stuck, and the remaining two approached the I Battalion of the German 211th Reserve Regiment, where 'a man came running up from the left crying "a crocodile is crawling about in our trenches!" The poor fellow's nerves had cracked.'[38] The tanks could be seen labouring forward, one bearing towards the German left, and the other (probably Captain A. M. Inglis's *Crème de Menthe*) disturbingly close to the right. 'It was a phantasmagoric vision, this giant in the light of dawn, its nose rearing up from a shell-hole, then lurching on, slowly – no doubt – but with a horrid sense of purpose. Now it could be scarcely 100 metres in front of our position.'[39]

Bullets were bouncing off the armour like peas, and the Germans were being shot up at the same time by aircraft and by tanks. The Canadians penetrated the weak boundary between the 211th Reserve Regiment and its neighbour, the 210th Reserve, and the defenders in front of the sugar factory were cut off. 'Some minutes passed before the Tommies broke into our position, not indeed by a proper assault, but by pushing one another forward. They trod on our dead and wounded. They were reeking of alcohol, and offered our men whisky and ciga-rettes, apparently glad to have been spared having to make a bayonet attack. They asked if we had any more men in our trench, because they had come under heavy fire from there. They lifted the tent canvases from the funk-holes and saw – dead and wounded. They told us that they were Canadians, old friends from the fighting in Flanders. That made sense! Medical orderlies came up behind and assembled the wounded, friend and foe together. We were hauled out of the trenches and told to make our way, as best we could, to the British dressing station.'[40]

On the way to the rear the prisoners passed through a third wave of Canadians, 'and behind them there was an officer who was hung about with photographic apparatus and turning the crank of his camera'. Further on still the Germans encountered one battery after another, firing in the open with no attempt at concealment, and heavy guns, which had been planted along the highway, with hydraulic rammers feeding rounds into the hungry breaches. No such concentration of ordnance had ever been seen in the German positions.[41]

Meanwhile the leading Canadian infantry reached the sugar factory, and overcame the fifty defenders with the help of *Crème de Menthe*, which was shooting up the brick and concrete building with its 6-pounder shells. The Canadians resumed their advance, and in the course of the afternoon they gained the greater part of Courcelette and succeeded in holding it against counterattacks.

By yielding ground in this way the German 45th Reserve Division had lost contact with the 4th *Garde* Infantry Division to its right, and for a time Crown Prince Rupprecht feared that the whole German position at Thiepval to the north would be unseated. It seemed to the Germans that the British had achieved their breakthrough, but then failed to recognise or exploit their opportunity.

FOURTH ARMY

III Corps

The 15th (Scottish) Division (New Army) at Martinpuich

With the 15th Division we take up the story of Rawlinson's Fourth Army. The Scots had a secondary place in the general scheme of things, for they were ordered to take the defences of Martinpuich from the southwest, while the neighbouring divisions – the 2nd Canadians to their left and the 50th to their right – were to carry out a pincer movement and meet behind the village.

The opposing troops belonged to the 17th Bavarian Regiment and were at the end of their resources. 'Impact upon impact. The whole of no man's land was a single steaming cauldron ... square metre upon square metre was being ploughed up. Over on the other side from the direction of High Wood we heard a commotion of voices, concentrated pulses of cries. By the time our few survivors came to their shattered senses and came back to reality, it was all over ... wave upon wave ... Not a sound came from our artillery. The communication with our rear was completely broken ... In a state of desperation we loosed off isolated shots at the masses which were storming forward. It was all in vain ... British battalions broke in from every side.'[42]

By three in the afternoon Martinpuich had fallen to the infantry, which had come up close, and at times too close, behind the creeping barrage. No assistance had come from the two supporting tanks. One had broken down, while the other had returned to refuel, and came back only in time to help to clear the trenches after the village had been taken. Martinpuich lay in a narrow valley, out of direct view of many of the German rearward positions, and at ten in the evening Rupprecht received the mistaken report that 'Martinpuich and the position adjoining to the east appear to be once more in our possession'.[43]

The 50th (Northumbrian) Division (Territorial Force), between Martinpuich and High Wood

The 50th Division was under orders to take the eastern edge of Martinpuich, together with the open ground between there and High Wood. The British artillery first put down a barrage on the rearward positions and access routes of the 3rd Bavarian Division, and 'formed an iron wall which made any kind of communication with our [German] rearward units impossible'.[44]

On that morning the 17th Bavarian Regiment heard once more 'that most distinctive roaring of engines, rattling of metal links and so on. There was a gentle swell in the ground about 100 metres in front of our shell-holes, which denied us all view of the hollow beyond. The noise seemed to be coming from over there, and we listened in a state of intense excitement.'[45] Grey metal boxes then heaved themselves into view over the crest.

Two tanks were up with the 150th Brigade on the left, and 'the monsters' motors hummed and droned as they crawled increasingly nearer. They advanced relentlessly, up, down, closer and closer. Holes, hills, rocks, even barbed wire meant nothing. They pursued their goal in a straight line, levelling everything in their passage ... Dense squadrons of enemy aircraft accompanied the attack, in some places descending to 500 metres, and shooting up the trench garrisons and the gun detachments with their machine guns.'[46]

Tank D-24 came to an abrupt halt, and the crew had to get out. The British believed that the machine had been immobilised by artillery fire, though a German account has some of the German infantry inserting grenades in the tracks and stopping it that way.[47] D-25 carried on, and knocked out three machine guns on the eastern edge of Martinpuich. The II and III Battalions of the 17th Bavarian Regiment were effectively destroyed, losing only eighty-seven officers and men as casualties, but a significantly high 547 as prisoners and missing, which testifies to the shock effect of the new weapons.

The right-hand brigade, the 149th, had been assigned a single tank, and this had been diverted over to the right to help the 47th Division, which had been set an almost impossible task (see below). The Germans lining the western edge of High Wood were therefore free to take the right flank of the 149th Brigade in enfilade. The 4/ and 7/Northumberland Fusiliers came under fire as soon as they left cover, and had to be content to establish a flank short of the German first line.

The 47th (London) Division (Territorial Force) at High Wood

Inside the southern edge of High Wood the rival positions were so close that the British artillery was virtually unusable. For that reason there had been no preparatory barrage, while the creeping barrage had to be put down well inside the wood and so was of little use to the attacking troops. As the commander of III Corps, Lieutenant General Sir William Pulteney determined to use tanks as a substitute for the missing artillery firepower. This was contrary to the advice of the tank officers, as passed on by the divisional commander Major General Sir Charles Barter, who were all concerned that the wrecked woodland was the worst possible terrain in which to employ tanks.

The London Territorials opened their attack on a frontage of two brigades, with the inner wings of both brigades advancing from a start line just inside the wood. The 141st Brigade on the left was attacking almost untouched defences, and was pinned down with heavy losses almost at the outset.

The 140th Brigade on the right had the support of tanks, albeit operating under the most adverse conditions. To the troops of the 18th Bavarian Regiment they 'looked in the distance like vehicles laden with wood' (a reference to trench-filling fascines?). One of the tanks (D-13) drove almost due north through the wood and, as experienced by the Bavarians, it then 'broke into the position of our 2nd Company, and proceeded to roll it up. Armed as it was only with infantry weapons, the company was almost defenceless against tanks.' A small remnant managed to escape to the rear under the command of Lieutenant Werry, who was wounded mortally in the process.[48] German infantry were clambering about on the top of the machine, unable to break inside, and D-13 enfiladed a second trench with its machine guns before it came to a halt with engine failure. The motionless vehicle was now knocked out for good by artillery fire, through the crew were able to escape, set fire to the wreck and make their way back on foot.

To the right, D-22 broke out of the wood by its eastern edge, and opened fire on the 6/London Regiment. It was an understandable mistake, and the Bavarians had to report that 'when the British attacked on 15 September the enemy were often taken for our own infantry, for many of our officers had not been issued with binoculars.'[49]

There were no intact tanks left inside the wood, and it took an improvised mass bombardment by Stokes mortars to break the resistance of the Bavarians, which occurred towards eleven in the morning. The leading British troops now gained the far edge of the wood, and in front of them the open ground descended in a gentle slope. It was time to commit the reserve, and the 142nd Brigade was accordingly brought up to attack the Starfish Line, which lay up to 1,000 yards beyond. The Germans retrieved some of the details from two survivors of the 21/London Regiment (1st Surrey Rifles). 'The prisoners are rather elderly men who joined up at the beginning of the war. One of them is a corporal and both make a good military impression.' They had remained in the trenches in the morning, then received the order to move forward in the afternoon. 'During the advance they received a sustained fire from heavy-calibre pieces, which caused a number of casualties. They climbed the hill without encountering German infantry, but when they descended the further slope they came under a violent fire from a German position about 500 metres away, which inflicted heavy losses and halted the attack.' That was probably towards six in the evening, when British accounts mention that the brigade was stopped just short of its objective.

The two men went to ground in shell-holes, but were captured overnight. 'Yesterday [15 September] morning A Company numbered five officers and about one hundred men. They say that all the officers and NCOs fell in the attack on the German position, so that the captured corporal took over the command. They believe that half a dozen or less of the company survived.'[50]

XV Corps

On 15 September the battlefront extended for a total of about 8,000 yards to the west of Flers, and about 3,500 yards to the south-east. However, the concentration of tanks for XV Corps' attack on and about Flers was the heart of the offensive, and the name of the village is now applied to the battle as a whole. It was the scene of the most celebrated episode of the action (the advance of Hastie's D-17 up the high street), and the first appearance of the tank in warfare (Mortimore's D-1, by a few minutes).

The New Zealand Division to the West of Flers

This day was the New Zealanders' baptism of fire on the Western Front, even if they arrived there as respected veterans of Gallipoli. For the present enterprise they formed part of XV Corps, not of Anzac, and were assigned a narrow (900-yard) but important sector on the west wing of the great concentration of force in front of Flers, with the task of pushing to the left of the village and establishing a defensive flank on the high ground to the north-west. Four tanks (Ds-8, -10, -11 and -12) gave support, and the New Zealanders stood in need of all the help they could get to carry them through the multiple lines of trenches.

On this sector the creeping barrage was something of a failure, for it left much of the wire uncut, yet moved too slowly for the New

Zealanders' liking. These people were moreover exposed to flanking fire on their left, for the 47th Division was making heavy weather in High Wood. In compensation all the assigned tanks were in the thick of the combat. D-10 was disabled by shell fire short of the Flers Lines, but all the others got across. D-12 on the New Zealanders' right survived initial damage from artillery, penetrated the north-west corner of the village, and only on its return journey was it hit a second time and set on fire. The crew, like that of D-10, managed to escape. The other two machines (Ds-8 and -11) sustained the momentum of the division's attack beyond the Flers Lines as far as Grove Alley, and D-11 continued some distance towards Gueudecourt before turning back.

The division gained nearly all its final objectives, and consolidated beyond the Flers Lines. The troops had been stacked up deeply on their constricted frontage, and the Germans learned of the experiences of the supporting elements from the diary of a private of the 2/Canterbury Battalion of the 2nd New Zealand Brigade. His unit had come into position with High Wood to the left, Delville Wood to the right, and a little treeless hill just in front:

> 14. September. Our guns were making a worse racket than ever. The endless crashing really gets on your nerves.
>
> 15. September. This was the day of our big push. We had our usual packs, with a dozen sandbags extra, two grenades and a shovel or pick The fire swelled up at 6.30. First of all arrived four of those 'Caterpillar' machine gun vehicles. Then the barrage came down by bounds of fifty yards at a time. At 7.20 we went over the top. Our artillery opened a rapid fire, and the Germans did everything they could to stop us. Shells were bursting all over the place. Twenty-two balloons were in the air behind us, and I counted twenty of our aircraft circling in the sky – it was blue, and it was a splendid day. But there were shocking sights as we advanced – dead everywhere, most of them Germans who had been killed a few days earlier. Some of the wounded were being brought back by our stretcher bearers. Other wounded collapsed to the ground, or limped or crawled to the dressing station. We dug in about 300 yards in front of our front line. It was hard work, but we just had to keep digging, and shells were bursting around. Two of our mates were

buried, but we were able to dig them out. Two others were badly hit. At two in the afternoon we went forward to the crest and began to dig a position. On the way we saw the same sights as before. Our lads were bringing a whole lot of German prisoners back, and some of them had to carry our wounded. Our troops were advancing by wave after wave. We had only just begun work on our position when the Germans began to bombard it with heavy shells. These kinds of explosions are frightful. We dug as fast as we could. We were tired, hungry and thirsty, but the work just had to be done. At five we ate a slice of bread and cheese and a couple of hard biscuits. We were getting along well with our work, but we had to give it up for a time when the fire redoubled.[51]

The man was killed not far away five days later, and his diary was found by the Germans.

The 41st and 14th Divisions, Flers Village

Together, the British 41st and 14th Divisions were supported by fourteen of the eighteen tanks that had been allocated to XV Corps, and this concentration of force, together with the emphasis placed by the British high command on breaking through the whole depth of the German defences by way of Flers to Gueudecourt, made this sector the main point of effort of the British attack on 15 September.

The first tank to see action here, and in the annals of warfare, was Captain Harold Mortimore's D-1, out on the far right of the 14th Division. Conscious of his historic role, Mortimore set out from just south-east of Delville Wood at 5.15 in the morning. His career was nevertheless very brief, for D-1 seems to have fallen behind the two associated companies of the King's Own Yorkshire Light Infantry, and was halted by artillery damage to its steering gear not far behind Hop Trench.

The rate of ditching and breakdowns among the other tanks was high, and only about seven machines survived to carry the attack deep into the German defences. On the left flank D-12 (assigned to the New Zealanders), D-16 and D-18 all succeeded in crossing the double German line just to the west of Flers, and the enemy were in addition assailed by D-11, which had drifted over from the New Zealand sector. D-12 was the first casualty among this group, and was abandoned by its crew (see

p. 223). The others were still active towards the middle of the afternoon in support of the New Zealanders and the 41st Division. D-16 and D-18 returned to the British lines before the day was out, but the adventurous D-11 probed towards Gird Trench (*Gallwitz Riegel*) before turning back, and was one of the few tanks still in operation the next day.

The British public fastened on the action of Lieutenant Stuart Hastie's D-17 and the 122nd Brigade of the 41st Division. Hastie contrived to shoot down an enemy observation balloon (or at least persuaded the Germans to haul it down) on his approach, and an observer of the Royal Flying Corps then saw him advancing through Flers, accompanied by three hundred assorted troops. The resulting report was then transmitted through the British press as 'a tank is walking up the High Street of Flers with the British infantry cheering behind'. There was no officer at hand to exploit the success, and persistent engine trouble made Hastie turn about in the square at the far end of the village. On his way out he found British infantry digging in at the southern end, and minutes later his tank was hit by shell fire and had to be abandoned. Some histories assume that the impetus of the infantry was spent, but several German accounts describe the British as then advancing in force from Flers towards Gueudecourt.

The country to the east of Flers was wide and open, which helped to make it the first setting of one of the classic confrontations of twentieth-century warfare, namely between tanks and artillery. D-6 (Lieutenant R. C. Legge) advanced smartly up the road to Flers, veered to the right and skirted the eastern edge of the village, and by engaging the machine guns on that side he was able to help the 124th Brigade of the 41st Division forward. Legge then devastated a battery in the Bull's Road track on a little rise to the north-east of Flers, and made direct for Gird Trench in front of Gueudecourt, where he brought two more batteries under fire. The unequal duel came to an end just short of the line, when D-6 was hit and caught fire. One of the gunners (Garner) was killed outright. The others escaped from the tank, but Legge was killed by rifle fire, and just three survivors were able to reach the British lines.

To the east again, D-5 (Second Lieutenant Blowers) covered a greater distance than any other tank that day. Taking advantage of a long and shallow valley Blowers followed the eastern lip of a sunken track and compelled the detachments of two 77 mm guns of the Saxon artillery to abandon their pieces. Beyond Bull's Road the tank entered the cutting, and progressed along it as far as Gird Trench, which was the outlying defence of Gueudecourt village. By now Blowers had outdistanced the infantry of the 14th Division, and after his remarkable achievement he turned back. On his return journey he was diverted in the direction of Flers by a plea to help 5/King's Shropshire Light Infantry to overcome a German strongpoint. D-5 was finally stopped south-east of the village by direct hits from artillery. Two of the crew were killed, Blowers and one more were wounded, but a further crew member was able to remove a machine gun from the tank and return fire before he too was wounded.

Among the tanks that now fell out of action nearby, D-10 was disabled about 850 yards to the west of Flers, while D-17 was immobilised just outside to the east.

The destructive work of the German artillery cannot be pinned down to individual batteries with total confidence, but the fates of D-5 and D-6 appear to be linked most closely with the batteries of the 12th Bavarian Artillery Regiment, which were scattered to the east of Flers. The hasty flight of the German infantry gave the guns a clear shot at the village, and then at the British troops who began to push from there towards Gueudecourt.

Lieutenant Klitta was watching the scene from a viewpoint to the north of Ginchy, and 'we took turns at the binocular periscope – powerless spectators of the British who were advancing north-west of us from Flers towards Gueudecourt. We could also observe tanks, something we had never seen before. We were altogether delighted when one of the monsters was laid on its side by a shot from a heavy battery.'[52]

On a wider perspective the German affairs in the Flers sector were in a state of crisis, for the British had penetrated between the 9th and 14th Bavarian Regiments to the east of Flers, and then wheeled against the left flank and rear of the 9th and captured its I and II Battalions almost intact. By the middle of the morning the signs of a breakthrough were unmistakable, for the British were now advancing from Flers along both sides of the road to Gueudecourt, 'and at the same time we caught sight of a large armoured vehicle [probably D-11] driving northwards over Hill 150 to the west of Flers.'[53] It was clear to the German divisional commander Lieutenant General Endres that the British had now broken through the second line of both his 9th and 14th Bavarian Regiments, and that he had no reserves with which to seal the gap.

XIV Corps

The Guards Division to the East of Flers

At seven in the morning a thick fog still lay over the positions of the 7th Bavarian Regiment behind Ginchy. When the vapours dispersed the Germans could see a dense swarm of infantry pushing to the north-west towards Flers and Gueudecourt, followed by multiple platoon columns and two tanks, and accompanied by up to thirty low-flying aircraft. Before long it was the 7th Regiment's turn to receive attention, for the Guards Division was advancing against the Bavarians over the broad and open country from Ginchy on a frontage of 1,200 yards. Out of its sixteen tanks, the XIV Corps had allocated ten to the Guards Division, although only three of them seem to have got into effective action.

Every now and then Lieutenant Klitta of the Bavarian artillery returned to his periscope to observe the events at distant Flers and Gueudecourt with a professional interest. He was back there at noon, and his first look through the eyepieces showed him a British platoon only forty yards away and magnified monstrously. He crashed into his dugout and yelled 'The British are here!' He and his men ran for their lives. 'My initial wound was a shot in the shoulder which bowled me over ... The British were behind us and firing wildly. I got another shot in my left lower arm, and just afterwards I experienced a frightful blow in the head which threw me to the ground. A bullet had hit my steel helmet and made a sizeable hole. We kept on running like hunted beasts and tripped repeatedly over the telephone wires which cross-crossed the ground.'[54] He was being pursued by the Guards, who had just broken through the first and second trenches of the 7th Bavarian Regiment.

The attack by the Guards Division nevertheless proved to be one of the most costly episodes of the whole British operation. Three of the tanks designated for the left wing had wandered into the sector of the 14th Division, and, in spite of the inspired leadership of Lieutenant Colonel J. V. Campbell, the 2/ and 3/Coldstreams (1st Brigade) were able to advance only halfway to the objective at Lesboeufs. The 2nd Brigade on the right wilted under the fire from the Sydow-Höhe, which was defying the efforts of the British 6th Division to the east. The 2nd Brigade's single effective tank, Second Lieutenant Clerk's 'B', did well to knock out six German machine guns and waddle as far as Low Road, before running low on petrol and having to turn back.

6th Division (Regular)

This formation made only minimal progress towards its final objective at Morval, being checked by the unsubdued fire from the *Sydow-Höhe*, which lay in one of the untouched 'artillery lanes'. This feature was not so much a hill in the conventional sense, but a huge and open swell of ground that was located in an enfilading position and commanded an excellent field of grazing fire. The British histories have a powerful redoubt, the 'Quadrilateral', sitting on this elevation, but the German sketch maps show nothing beyond an ordinary trench with a couple of pieces of fragmentary trench behind. On 15 September, at least, the strength of the position derived from the lie of the ground and the front.

The sector was held by the 21st Bavarian Regiment, which describes three large vehicles as advancing against it from Ginchy and Leuze Wood. The machines were at first taken to be ambulances of some kind, on account of the red and white crosses painted on them, but they then opened up with machine guns and rapid-fire artillery pieces, and 'one of the vehicles halted for some time in front of the trench of the 6th Company and showered it and the sunken road with a destructive rain of bullets'. Rifle fire and grenades proved unavailing against the tank. 'Only artillery could be of any help, and in fact, without being asked, it brought down its fire against the fat monsters, finished one of them off, and forced the other two to fall back.'

British aircraft then appeared over the smoke and dust, directing the fire of the artillery, and shooting up the German positions with machine guns. At 8.30 the fire ceased all of a sudden, and five or six lines of densely packed infantry came sweeping forward. 'They were cool and determined lads ... but (thanks be to God) at last an enemy we could hit. Before long we could make out their steel helmets, their rifles with fixed bayonets, and down the left side of their chests the sacks which carried the grenades for close-quarter combat. We responded in a fury – our machine guns with prolonged bursts of fire and our troops by rapid rifle fire … The ground was covered with hundreds of dead or badly wounded British.'[55] The defenders beat off the attack along the whole regimental front, though they had to seal off their right flank, for the enemy on that side had broken through the 7th Bavarian Regiment (see p. 231). A particularly aggressive NCO of the Durham Light Infantry was captured in the fighting between the rival bombing parties.

The account is pretty circumstantial, though it is at some variance with the British sources, which mention that two of the supporting tanks (C-20 and C-22) were driven off not by artillery, but by small arms fire (probably with S.m.K. armour-piercing rounds) which starred the periscopes and caused bullet splashes inside the tanks. The machines withdrew from the action.

The 56th (London) Division (Territorial Force) and Bouleaux Wood

At the far eastern end of the battle line the 56th Division attacked from Leuze Wood with the task of winning ground towards Morval and so establishing a secure right flank for the British advance as a whole. The infantry made little progress, chiefly because the long and narrow Bouleaux Wood enabled the Germans to feed up reinforcements under cover and put the London Territorials under enfilade fire. The two assigned tanks, 'huge grey boxes',[56] were engaged very closely indeed, and their fate is important to our story, for it gave the Germans their first chance to recover documentation and explore one of the new machines.

On 14 September tank C-16 was in position 'to the right of a wood. Nearly all the trees have been shot down, and the place is covered with crosses and crucifixes to mark the graves of German soldiers. It's noon precisely, and the enemy are bringing fire down on the wood. I imagine they are trying to search us out. After it's dark today we will set off to where we are going to go into action. It will be hot work tomorrow'[57]

On the day of the battle C-16 did good work by knocking out machine guns as it advanced to the junction of Loop and Combles trenches, where a British 'short' artillery round broke a track. The crew managed to fight off the swarming German infantry until the 169th Brigade came to the rescue, whereupon they set fire to the tank and joined their deliverers. They had escaped intact, though one of the crew dropped a diary which was retrieved by the enemy, who copied out the entries just mentioned.

As the Germans saw it, 'an armoured vehicle actually preceded the attack, advancing against our left wing from the south-east corner of Leuze Wood. It was able to drive up close to our foremost trench and take it under heavy machine-gun fire. This vehicle later caught light ... perhaps set on fire by the British themselves after their infantry fell back. They removed the machine guns from the vehicle and emplaced them further to the rear.'[58]

The other tank, Lieutenant Arnold's C-14, worked along the north-west-facing side of Bouleaux Wood, and progressed as far as Beef Trench, where it stuck in a shell-hole and was assailed by German bombers, who contrived to set its petrol tank on fire. As a 'female' tank, C-14 was bristling with machine guns. The crew were able to take away two of them, but had to be content with removing the locks of the others and leaving them in the machine. By the German account the tank 'supported the enemy attack by an overhead fire of its machine guns, then drove across the open ground to within thirty metres or so of the right wing of our position. We threw hand grenades at it, and one of them apparently exploded near the petrol tank, upon which flames and a great deal of smoke rose from the vehicle, and its machine guns at once stopped firing. A hatch opened and a pigeon flew out. *Note*: A few days later we broke open the hatch and took from the vehicle six machine guns, heavily reinforced with steel, along with 10,000 cartridges in belts.' The Germans also recovered a set of tactical instructions from a dead crew member. It confirmed what they were being told by prisoners, that 'the tanks were to drive through the German lines and shoot them up from the rear. They were also to make for strongpoints and run over them.' Both the tactical instructions and the other crewman's diary were translated into German and circulated among the army groups on 23 September.[59]

THE AFTERNOON AND EVENING

In the middle of the afternoon Crown Prince Rupprecht climbed to the upper storey of a house and took in the view over the field. 'The battle was in full swing. The *Trommelfeuer* was resounding like the noise of some great waterfall, every now and then abating, then swelling violently up again. It was a gentle rolling landscape which fell to the north-east in long tongue-like spurs from the knoll [le Becquet, 154 metres] south-east of Martinpuich towards High Wood (which rose sharply from the horizon) and the plateau between there and Delville Wood. To judge by the clouds of smoke, a counterattack was in progress with the aim of recovering Martinpuich [Rupprecht later believed that it had succeeded] The village itself could not be seen, for it lay in a hollow, and the same applied to Flers, which was apparently also in possession of the enemy.'[60]

The British had in fact made gains on most of the frontage of their attack, and penetrated to a depth of about 2,000 yards on the sector between Courcelette and Flers. A great void existed to the left of the German 211th Reserve Regiment, and when, at 6.30 in the evening, the order came to counterattack at Courcelette, the I Battalion found itself isolated and altogether outnumbered and was forced to go to ground among the shell-holes.

It was much the same story at Flers, where a great counterattack on the part of the 4th Bavarian Division, which was ordered early in the afternoon, was reduced to an unsupported advance by the 7th Bavarian Regiment. One of the battery commanders was trying to open fire on his own infantry. He knew nothing about the counterattack, and had to be told 'with Bavarian bluntness' to desist.[61]

The confusions, however, were not confined to the Germans. The tanks had nearly all run their course, the British communications generally were much degraded, the 122nd and 125th Brigades had suffered grievous casualties at Flers, and the rallying, gap-sealing and counterattacks by the defenders seemed much more impressive to the British than they did to the Germans themselves. At three in the afternoon, at about the same time as Rupprecht was surveying the battle, Rawlinson ordered an end to operations for the day. From the experi-ence of the 7th Bavarian Regiment it appeared that the British would have had it in their power to take the thinly garrisoned Gird Trench (*Gallwitz-Riegel*) of the German third position. 'We had the impression that the British junior command failed, after the first objectives had been attained and unexpected opportunities then opened up. Only when the enemy had specially trained troops immediately available could they score a number of small local successes. Those groups had been prepared for quite specific tasks, and acted as supports for the main body of the infantry. But when they were not at hand the performance of the mass was much diminished.'[62]

By the standards of their earlier attacks the British had made some impressive gains of ground. They had finally taken the whole extent of the second German position along the Bazentin Ridge, with its facility for artillery observation, and won ground on a total frontage of about nine miles. High Wood was at last theirs, even if the terrain that sloped away to the north was littered with the casualties of the last attack by the London Territorials of the 47th Division, 'specks of black and grey ... When you approached the black patches rose into a thick buzzing swarm of bluebottles, revealing underneath a bundle of torn and dirty grey or khaki rags, from which protruded a naked shin bone, the skeleton of a human hand, or a human face, dark grey in colour, with black eye holes and an open mouth, showing a line of snarling white teeth, the only touch of white left. When you have passed on again a few yards, the bluebottles settle again, and quickly the bundle looks as if covered by some black fur.'[63]

The Germans had also been pushed back to the north of Courcelette, Martinpuich and Flers. To the east their positions bulged forward again to take up the former line at Combles, but that low-lying place was now threatened by the loss of Flers, which Crown Prince Rupprecht considered to be a serious affair in every regard. The 4th Bavarian Division had evacuated Flers in the face of the artillery bombardment, and then failed to realise how speedily the British infantry were able to establish themselves there. He was also concerned by an accusation that Courcelette had been allowed to fall because the enemy had found a gap between the 45th Reserve Division and the 3rd Bavarian Division, and taken the village in the flank and rear.[64]

Haig had nevertheless failed to achieve the breakthrough for which he had been husbanding his resources for weeks. In terms of his high ambitions the tanks had certainly fallen short. Altogether only eighteen of the machines had progressed beyond the start line on 15 September, and probably only a couple of these could be counted as reasonably good 'runners' by the end of the day. The detail is somewhat more impressive. Just five or six of the tanks had been lost to direct enemy action, and 'only' nine crew members had been killed. There were locations, notably at High Wood, where the tanks had been committed under patently adverse conditions, but the happenings at Courcelette and Flers indicated that the opposition collapsed rapidly whenever they were able to get a good shot at their objective. After the war the German official historians concluded that the tanks had made a major contribution to the British gains.[65]

Under the immediate impact of events Lieutenant Stephen of the 17th Bavarian Regiment wrote that 'the success of the British attack was due to two important factors:

1. The complete failure of the defensive barrage

2. The extremely close co-operation between the enemy infantry and artillery, which was made possible by the remarkable achievements of their aviators.'[66]

The choice of the word 'success' is interesting, and Stephen's comments are typical of the German judgements at the time, which assessed the battle by conventional criteria, with at best only incidental reference to the tanks. The Germans were aware not just of the way their artillery had let them down, but how worn down and over-stretched their infantry had been, and how their communications had collapsed. Crown Prince Rupprecht, as we have seen, was concerned about failures at the divisional level of command.

The Germans remarked how the opening British bombardment had been both intense and precise, and that its effects had been monitored diligently. When the British infantry went forward a number of them were seen to be carrying signs such as large white flags with green or black stripes to advertise their whereabouts to the friendly artillery and aircraft. 'The British aviators followed the progress of the infantry attack with close attention', while at the same time 'there was not a single one of our aircraft to be seen.'[67] Artillery observation officers were well up with the attacks, and were capable of getting new forward observation posts, complete with telephone communication, in operation within a few hours.[68]

AFTER THE BATTLE, 16–24 SEPTEMBER

At Courcelette the events of 16 September confirmed the verdict of the big battle on the day before. The German 45th Division failed in a counterattack, and the British were able to capture the staff of the 211th Reserve Regiment in their isolated dugout.

In the centre the main British effort was devoted to a vain attempt to exploit the break-in at Flers. On the left the New Zealand Division, supported by a single tank (D-11), made some progress to the east of the village. To the right the newly arrived British 21st Division was making from Flers directly against the formidable stretch of the German position (Gird Trench, *Gallwitz-Riegel*), which extended in front of Gueudecourt. The start of the attack was delayed by rain, and the advance of the infantry was finally nailed down by the German artillery short of the objective.

The two supporting tanks carried on alone. The fate of Second Lieutenant Court's D-14 was described by a senior officer of the Bavarian Pioneers.

> A vehicle of peculiar shape was moving to the north-east exit of Flers along the track which ran towards our positions in front of Gueudecourt. It was driving slowly but it kept on coming. At first our men observed the monster with interest, which turned into considerable astonishment at its advance. Rifle and machine-gun fire poured down on the machine, which continued on its way regardless, and now all curiosity was changed into a sense of dumb horror. The armoured vehicle continued along the road unchecked, halted behind our positions, and shot up Gird Trench from the rear with its machine guns. But a battery of field artillery had meanwhile observed what was happening, and now took aim and finished the vehicle off by a direct hit at the third round. This lifted the frightful spell, and when the seven crewmen jumped from the exploding machine they fell rapidly victim to the fury of our men.[69]

D-9, another 'female' tank, advanced initially behind D-14 along the same path to the north-east of Flers, then veered to the left, passed through the flagging 9/King's Own Yorkshire Light Infantry, and, after sustaining successive damage from artillery, was finally disabled by a shell not far short of Gird Trench. Two gunners were killed, but the other six crew members escaped. Both tanks had probably been destroyed by a few rounds aimed by Lieutenant Schneider of the 12th Bavarian Field Artillery Regiment.[70] The defence of this sector had been the responsibility of the 7th Bavarian Regiment, which was relieved in the evening after having lost 1,208 men.

The final act of the Flers offensive was some business left over from the 15th, namely the reduction of the defences on the high ground (the *Sydow Höhe*) between Ginchy and Combles. Here the British 6th Division returned to the attack early on 18 September, when a heavy fire descended on the III Battalion of the 21st Bavarian Regiment, and 'a dense row of figures emerged running from the curtain of mist. They were making for the 11th Company and the centre of our position. They were thrown back by the fire of our rifles and machine guns. But soon afterwards altogether overwhelming masses came pressing against the right flank, namely from Leuze Wood and Bouleaux Wood, against the companies of our III Battalion. A wild and desperate close-quarter combat ensued.'[71]

From the German rear British troops could be seen spilling over the *Sydow Höhe*, and it became clear that the 21st Regiment had lost the position. Afterwards the surviving Bavarians were annoyed to find the episode represented in Haig's report and in *The Times* as a triumphal storm of a fortress-like stronghold, the fabled 'Quadrilateral'. 'It was no fortress at all, this position of the 21st. In what did it consist? In rifle trenches which were repeatedly ploughed up into heaps of rubble ... and in shell-holes, where thirsty men with hollow cheeks, blackened with dust, crouched with burning eyes ... determined to defend the position entrusted to them with the last breath.'[72]

The 5th Bavarian Division was relieved the next day, having been depleted by about 5,400 men in the recent fighting. The remaining defenders of the Somme battlefront drew breath, and no more than a scattering of British fire was falling on their positions. A captain of the German anti-aircraft artillery seized the opportunity to take a stroll from Achiet-le-Petit, and halted at the civilian cemetery at the northern end. The blast from British aerial bombs had blown over some of the crosses, and the paper flowers of the wreaths had a pathetic look about them.

'The sky was a clear blue above the cemetery hill, but it became progressively dimmer as it sank into the perpetual greyish-black cloud which lay over the front line. You could distinguish clearly the impact of the various calibres by ear, while the explosion of heavy enemy shells resounded in the background like a distant rolling of drums.'[73]

THE CULMINATING ATTACK, 25–30 SEPTEMBER

The events on the Somme in the last week of September were not a cataclysmic drama to match those of 1 July, nor did they have the high technical interest of the battle of Flers-Courcelette which had just been fought. They do not present themselves as a unified whole, for they feature in history as two battles, those of 'Morval' and 'Thiepval Ridge'. With all of that, they present together probably the supreme effort of the British on the Somme, and the one that brought the Germans closest to collapse.

Haig was unaware of the opportunities of the moment, for he was thinking ahead to the next winter and spring, and how the British could best position themselves to beat off counterattacks, gain a springboard for a great offensive in 1917, and meanwhile build up depots, communications and reserves undisturbed by the enemy. Up on the left wing by the Ancre the British had still failed to evict the Germans from their first position in and around the bluff at Thiepval, but even a small gain in this sector would push the enemy from the highest ground and deny them the view down the Ancre valley towards Albert. There was a further task to be addressed on the right wing, this time dating from the middle of September, when the British attacks on the third German position had run out of momentum only just short of Gueudecourt, Lesboeufs, Morval and Combles.

The operations on the two wings were planned as an entity, with the Fourth Army's attack on 25 September helping to distract attention from the Reserve Army's push north of the Bapaume road on the next day. The preparatory bombardments were to be of unprecedented intensity, and a heavy and systematic barrage was to march just ahead of the infantry on the entire frontage of the assaults.

In the course of 22 September the German high command became convinced that a new and major allied offensive was impending. In the south the fire of the British and French swelled across the Combles sector, and the Germans discovered a document on a British body which 'gave valuable information as to the British intentions.'[74] Gallwitz, as commander of the Second Army, warned that 'the British gained their considerable success [an interesting phrase] on 15 September by attacking early in the morning … after a heavy *Trommelfeuer*. It is probable that they will use the same tactic and choose the same time for the powerful attack which is coming. I demand the most acute vigilance, especially for the troops in the most advanced positions and for the artillery in the half-light of morning.'[75]

THE BATTLE OF MORVAL, 25–29 SEPTEMBER

The German command had expected the attack to fall on 23 September, but it did not arrive until the 25th, and then later than the hour anticipated by Gallwitz. The British fire descended in the early afternoon, and 'our trenches became our graves. In Gueudecourt the walls crashed down and buried the defenders under their rubble.' Later in the afternoon 'the fire sprang back and simultaneously dense lines of enemy infantry came surging up from the direction of Flers … flares soared up, and our defensive barrage set in. The British sank to the ground in hundreds, but wave upon wave continued to rise from the enemy trenches. Our own machine guns opened up with a rattle and threw 16,000 rounds into the charging British masses. They fell like flies, and yet it did us no good at all, because fresh waves were coming up from behind.'[76] The British found a gap in the 13th Bavarian Regiment, charged through and took the II Battalion of the 6th Bavarian from the rear.

This was the work of the British 21st Division. A number of the platoons forced their way across the double Gird Trench (*Gallwitz-Riegel*) and made for Gueudecourt. They might have taken the place there and then if some of the German machine guns, according to a new tactical doctrine, had not already been moved out of harm's way, and opened up from rearward positions, forcing the British back.

Over to the right, the scattered units and feeble positions of the German XXVI Corps were crumbling in the face of an attack by the Guards Division and the 6th and 56th (London) Divisions. Lesboeufs fell without so much as a fight, while the British took advantage of the deep hollow south of Morval to break through the 239th Reserve Regiment, work around to its rear and fall on its III Battalion. In a now familiar scene the British arrived at the dugout of the battalion head-quarters, threw gas and incendiary grenades through the entrance, and waited outside with levelled rifles. 'The first to crawl out was the battalion doctor ... who indicated his red cross armband and asked them not to fire on the ones who would be following him. He also asked them to rescue the wounded from the burning dugout, as he was not allowed to do so, and in fact they were now retrieved by the British.'[77]

For publicity purposes the names of individual objectives now counted for a great deal, and the Germans found that the British news-papers were elevating Morval to a fortress to compare with Verdun. In fact it was scarcely defensible, and 'even so this achievement – whole divisions against a single and well under-strength battalion – could be attained only with the help of alcohol', or so at least the Germans concluded, after they had captured a British soldier who was so drunk that he was incapable of giving coherent answers.[78]

The British were now advancing in force to the west of the hollow of Combles and the French to the east. The little town itself was held by the troops of the 235th Reserve Regiment, who concluded that they had survived so far only because Combles lay on the boundary between the British and the French. In fact the advance had been planned as a pincer movement from the beginning, and Captain von Hochwächer made a wise chose when he decided that the whole position must be abandoned overnight. 'I had seen the loss of Combles coming,' wrote Crown Prince Rupprecht. 'The place was completely surrounded and thoroughly gassed. Just two hundred men of the garrison ... were able to break out through the enemy.'[79]

The British had failed only at Gueudecourt, and the omission was put right on 26 September, when the 21st Division cleared the double Gird Trench, and wiped out the I Battalion of the 6th Bavarian Regi-ment with the help of a tank. On the same day the French captured Bouchavesnes, on the important lateral road (N 17) that ran behind the German battlefront. The 'battle of Morval' was almost complete, and was prolonged only by minor actions over the next two days.

THE BATTLE OF THIEPVAL RIDGE, 26–30 SEPTEMBER

Even after eleven weeks of fighting the German positions on the commanding bluff at Thiepval represented part of the original front line as it had existed on 1 July. Thiepval had beaten off every British attack on that day and every occasion since. The slopes leading up to it became 'a litter beyond comparison of half- and quarter-buried men, with broken gear and dud shells and old bombs ... helmets torn into spirals, gas masks, rotten sandbags, bones, backbones, old legs, boots, old wheels, miles of bedevilled wire, packsacks ... rifles, bayonets, bits of spines, tins, canteens, socks, gloves, and a litter of burst shells and a pox of shell-holes.'[80]

The repeated repulses had served to impress the name on the British public. By the same token the 180th Regiment from Württemberg drew fresh inspiration from a location they had built and defended over the course of two years. A little ground had been lost towards Schwaben Redoubt just to the north, but the main erosion had been out to the left flank, where the line had been driven in to such an extent that it now ran east-north-east by way of Mouquet Farm to just north of Courcelette.

Mouquet Farm was second in notoriety only to Thiepval, for the stubborn defence of the trenches and cellars there had put a term to the advance of both the Australians and Canadians against the far left rear of the Thiepval plateau. By now, however, the symbolic importance of Mouquet Farm exceeded its practical use for the Germans, for it lay about 350 yards in front of the nearest supporting trenches. 'It would certainly have been capable of putting up a stout defence, if it had been incorporated in our lines. But now it lay well ahead of our front, and was connected to it only by a single, half-filled trench. It continued to suck in units of our troops, who were weak enough in any case ... and in such a way sapped the strength of our own position instead of adding to it.'[81]

This conformation, probably as much as the skills of Ivor Maxse's 18th Division, explain the outcome of the complicated little battle of Thiepval Ridge. On the critical 26 September Maxse's right-hand attacking brigade, the 53rd, climbing from Nab Valley, made creditably speedy progress in order to outwit the German defensive barrage. However, the supporting tanks broke down, and the assault failed under

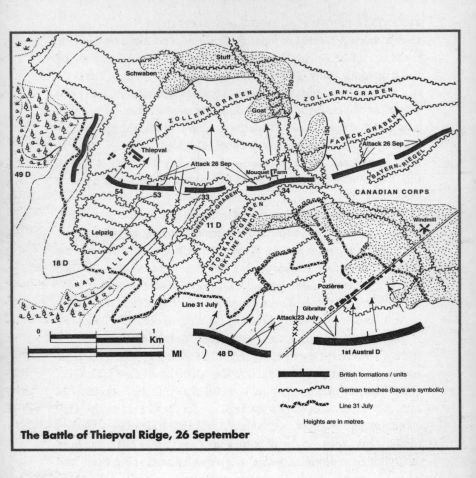

The Battle of Thiepval Ridge, 26 September

Heights are in metres

British formations / units

German trenches (bays are symbolic)

Line 31 July

fire from the German trenches. The 54th Brigade to the left did well to make a lodgement in the south-western part of Thiepval village, where a tank helped the troops to overcome a troublesome machine gun in the ruins of the château.

The British might have been thrown out again if the Germans had not also been attending to a crisis over to their left in the area of Mouquet Farm, where the British 11th Division was breaking through the German positions to the west of the ruins, at the same time as the 1st Canadian Division penetrated to the east. The defending troops of the 6th Company of the German 165th Regiment were now cut off in the farm and could be eliminated at leisure. Corporal Heinemann and his men were sealed off in a dugout without access to air or water, and finally realised that their only hope of survival lay with the enemy. The Germans beat on the topmost steps of the dugout, and began to hear picks and spades at work. 'The voices from outside became more and more distinct, and finally a plate-sized hole appeared at the exit and air and light streamed in. Soon the opening was large enough to allow us to leave, creeping out one after another. Outside stood two of the British [*sic*] with aimed rifles. Some tufts of grass survived at the exit, and we tore them up so as to cool our parched tongues with the dew. The enemy must have felt sorry for us as they gave us each a mug full of water. Never in my life will I forget that wonderful drink ... The trench was in the possession of Canadians, who had already arrived as reliefs.' Heinemann thanked his lucky stars that he had not encountered the original British assaulting troops, from whom he would have received different treatment.[82] The good Canadians were probably men from Ontario or Toronto.

The 11th Division's breakthrough to the west of Mouquet Farm opened up the defences of Thiepval from the left flank and rear, and the 180th Regiment together with three companies of the 77th Reserve Regiment were now taken in a trap. Major Weeber, commander of the I Battalion of the 180th was last seen in the late evening engaged in grenade fighting at the well by Thiepval church. He must have been killed shortly afterwards, and only a lieutenant and one hundred men were able to break out. In such a way this cornerstone of the German West Front fell after a final twenty hours of combat.

There were some ugly details. In the British 18th Division the for-midable Lieutenant Colonel Frank Maxwell had ordered his troops to take no prisoners. He now admired the German resistance, 'and probably no more than three hundred to five hundred put their hands up. They took it badly out of us, but we did ditto, and I have no shame in saying so, as every German should be exterminated. I don't know that we took one. I have not yet seen a man or officer who did, anyway.'[83]

In the morning of 27 September the Germans lost their last toehold in Thiepval village, and the British could now claim to hold the western extremity of the chalk ridge which had been in contention since 1 July. Perhaps it was because the names of Thiepval and Mouquet were so familiar that British officialdom could claim that the battle of Thiepval Ridge had closed on 30 September. In reality there was a lot to do, for the Germans still held most of Schwaben Redoubt (which was in heavy contention) along with the slopes down to Saint-Pierre Divion by the Ancre. Over to the west, the 1st Canadian Division and the British 11th Division were fighting to clear the successive trench lines behind and to the west of Courcelette. By 1 October they had advanced to an average depth of 1,000 yards, but left the Germans in possession of Regina and Stuff trenches.

In terms of ground, therefore, the gains by the British alone were not genuinely great. However, the advances on 25 and 26 September by the British and French together were the largest since 1 July, for between Thiepval and Bouchavesnes the German positions had been driven in across a breadth of more than fifteen miles and to an average depth of one mile.[84] More significantly, the cumulative impact of the British efforts in September had brought the Germans very close to breaking point – closer, possibly, than for two years to come.

For the Germans, the month that had just ended bore a distinct and universally horrific character. Quite apart from the advent of the tanks, which proved to be of terrifying but localised impact, the British had made more effective use of their artillery than ever before, whether through their brief but intensive preparatory bombardments, or through bringing down walls of fire in front of their advancing infantry. The new German Storm Troops and the new generation of aircraft and fighter aces had scarcely registered any effect on the ground, nor did the heavily promoted tactics of defence in depth. Rupprecht observed that 'the success of the enemy attacks had much to do with the way most of our machine guns in the wretched forward trenches were being totally buried by the exploding shells. General Below fears more than anything else a continuation of the enemy attack in the direction of Bapaume, for it is just there that our trenches are the most inadequate.'[85]

The German artillery was failing badly, while it contrived to use up greater resources than ever. The expenditure of ammunition by the field artillery on the Somme had risen from about 1.5 million shells in August to 4.1 million in September, and that of the heavy howitzer batteries from 643,000 to 907,000,[86] and in the big engagements about one-quarter of the pieces were falling out of action from mechanical failures alone. The artillery of Below's First Army was giving out a vast volume of unaimed and unsystematic fire, much of it onto its own troops,[87] while at the same time a misplaced economy limited the duration of defensive barrages to three minutes at a time – a practice duly noted and exploited by the British infantry.

The First and Second Armies had lost nearly 135,000 men in the course of September, which made it the Germans' most costly month in the Battle of the Somme.[88] More disturbing still was the way so many were being lost, as prisoners. The German supreme command began to doubt the powers of resistance of its men for probably the first time, and demanded an explanation of the reasons, without trying to allocate any blame. 'Hitherto our infantry had been inferior to that of the enemy in numerical terms, but in quality it had been superior. Now the heavy losses, and especially those among the officers and NCOs, has reduced this qualitative advantage to a considerable degree.'[89]

CHAPTER ELEVEN

October – the Ancre Heights, Warlencourt and le Transloy

The year was advancing to its end. Haig was unaware of the desperation among the Germans, but he was still striving to win advantages before the weather closed down operations. In essence, the Fifth Army (the new designation for the Reserve Army) was to expand the British holdings through the extraordinarily tough defences that still overlooked the Ancre from the rearward part of the plateau of Thiepval. On the centre and right, Rawlinson's Fourth Army was supposed to advance on a frontage of about nine miles, from near the Butte de Warlencourt by way of le Transloy to the boundary of the French, who would attack Sailly-Saillisel. It was hoped that Rawlinson would be able to overrun the mostly sketchy defences facing him, and win useful ground in the direction of Bapaume and Cambrai.

Ambitious enough in outline, the British plan translated in local terms to narrow-front attacks, which, to the despair of Joffre, became miniature battles of attrition.

THE BATTLE OF THE ANCRE HEIGHTS

The great bluff at Thiepval had defied all the British efforts in one of the most hideous episodes of 1 July. The Reserve Army had breathed fresh life (if that is the apposite term) into the deadly battle on this sector by taking the remains of Thiepval village and gaining lodgements in the Schwaben Redoubt late in September. Now, towards the middle of October, the work was completed by the British II Corps.

The 10/Cheshire Regiment stormed Stuff Redoubt behind the Schwaben on 9 October, and on the 14th the British 39th Division evicted the Germans from their last toehold in the Schwaben itself. A wretched soldier of the 110th Reserve Regiment (a cigar-maker in peacetime), had been sheltering with a lieutenant and eighteen men in a dugout when the attack on the Schwaben arrived in the afternoon. 'Upon the sound of heavy firing the officer ordered them to get their accoutrements on and to man the trench. Before any of them had time to get out, hand grenades were thrown into the dugouts and fifteen killed, the officers and four others survived and remained hidden until 10 a.m. on the 15th, when they crept out and surrendered. He says he and several of his comrades had always intended to surrender at the first opportunity as they knew they would be well treated when captured. This is a general gossip in his regiment, and [he] heard it from home through prisoners.'[1] Crown Prince Rupprecht registered his astonishment at 'the persistence with which the attacks are continued. This simply cannot last.'[2]

In September the veteran Württemberg troops had been appalled to learn that Thiepval village had fallen, but now some German officers believed that the loss of the Stuff and Schwaben redoubts was more serious still. The position of the 109th Reserve Regiment and the 28th Reserve Division as a whole was now compromised, for the whole of the Ancre valley and the ruined village of Grandcourt lay under direct fire, and Grandcourt itself had become an exposed salient. 'The British just had to manage to advance to left or right and they would cut off the retreat from Grandcourt; it was a real death-trap. Nothing like a proper position existed any longer ... The trenches had been levelled, and the only way to get about was from shell-hole to shell-hole, by difficult and indistinct tracks where it was all too easy to lose your way. And losing your way meant in many cases falling into the hands of the British.'[3]

Rupprecht and Ludendorff favoured abandoning altogether the forward position at Saint-Pierre Divion and the salient north of the Ancre at Beaumont Hamel, but the supreme command decided otherwise, under pressure from Below as commander of the First Army. All the German effort was put into counterattacks, the first of which was a scrambled affair mounted by survivors of the 109th Regiment against the Schwaben Redoubt on the night of 14/15 October, just hours after it had been lost. The enterprise collapsed in chaos, and the regimental history admits to 'lack of time to orientate the attack, insufficient knowledge of the terrain, exhaustion of the attacking troops due to the long approach march and the weight of the assault packs, absence of any kind of inter-communication on account of the nature of the ground – all churned-up as it was with shell-holes, no proper support from the artillery before the attack'.[4] Prisoners told the British that the men of the 6th Company 'refused to go out of the trenches saying that they feared that their own artillery, owing to lack of observation, would only fire on them as it had often done before. The actual attack was carried out by "Storm Troops", which had very heavy casualties. Prisoners are not clear as to what division or regiment this troop belonged. After the attack had failed the 12th Company was ordered to assault, but the men refused to move out of the trenches.'[5]

In view of the advantage of the ground gained, and the damaging effect on the Germans, the 39th Division's exertions in October yielded one of the major British 'successes' of the whole of the Battle of the Somme. It is difficult to identify anything comparable along the rest of the Fifth (Reserve) Army's front. By the evening of 21 October the British 25th and 18th Divisions and the 4th Division of the experienced Canadian Corps had advanced to a depth of some 500 yards on a broad front, but had still not succeeded in clearing the whole of Regina Trench.

THE BAPAUME ROAD AND THE BUTTE DE WARLENCOURT

The Bapaume road, an ancient Roman highway, slanted from south-west to north-east through the positions of the rival British III Corps and the 6th Bavarian Reserve Division, and crossed the double system of Gird Trench (*Gallwitz-Riegel*) just behind the Butte de Warlencourt. When the attack opened here on 1 October the Bavarians were pushed from Flers Trench (*Below-Riegel*) and for a time also from the thick-walled farm complex of Eaucourt l'Abbaye, which the Londoners of the 47th Division took with the aid of two tanks.

The 17th Bavarian Reserve Regiment saw the vehicles approaching to the west of the Flers–Rancourt road, and soon enough the tanks opened a lively fire of machine guns and 6-pounders, accompanied by low-flying aircraft which joined in with their own machine guns. The tanks crossed the remains of Flers Trench, and drove along the far side, which forced the Bavarians to abandon that stretch of the defences. The tanks then came to a halt, for reasons that were unknown to the Germans (they had bogged down). 'Upon this some of the crewmen abandoned the tanks and tried to get into our rearward trenches. They were shot down in short order. The rest ran towards the Eaucourt-Flers road, apparently after they had set the tanks on fire. At any rate the vehicles burst into flames immediately.'[6]

The 47th (London) Division returned to the attack on 2 and 3 October, and this time it was able to take firm possession of Eaucourt l'Abbaye. 'The loss of this place was no surprise to me,' wrote Crown Prince Rupprecht. 'When I last talked with General Below I empha-sised that the trenches to the south of the village formed a narrow salient and were untenable. But General Below refused to order them to be abandoned, for they enabled us to bring a good cross-fire to bear on the ground to the front.'[7] Just over to the west, le Sars fell to the British 23rd Division on 7 October, after repeated assaults.

The ground descended gently all the way from Martinpuich to Eaucourt l'Abbaye. Beyond that again a rise corresponded with the lie of the German third position, based on which the Germans were able to halt any further advance along the axis of the Bapaume road for the rest of the year. Among their outlying defences the most notorious was the prehistoric Butte de Warlencourt. The mound proper was a chalk hillock, surmounting a bare plateau about half a mile wide, and had been dismissed in an earlier British topographical report as a low-lying feature of no interest (see p. 120).

The Germans thought otherwise, and dug themselves in there comprehensively and deeply. The work proved its value in October, by when the British had grasped the importance of the position and made it one of the principal axes of their efforts. The defenders in their turn were under orders to defend the mound to the utmost. 'The commanding ridge of the Butte de Warlencourt afforded us unobstructed views as far as the Windmill Hill at Pozières, the hotly contested Hill 154, and the short stumps that were all that were left of High Wood and Delville Wood. From the Butte also we could see into the intervening no man's land, and our artillery was able to take in enfilade the deep hollow of Martinpuich which constituted the best approach for enemy forces to the battlefront. The distance to the elevations which formed the horizon was five or six kilometres, which meant that the British had to bring all but the longest-ranged of their offensive batteries forward into this ground.'[8] Now at last the German gunners could take up the duel with the British artillery on more equal terms.

The power exerted by the Butte was more than a question of physical topography, for it had a nightmarish quality all of its own. 'That ghastly hill, never free from the smoke of bursting shells, became fabulous. It shone white in the night and seemed to leer at you like an ogre in a fairy tale. It loomed up unexpectedly, peering into trenches where you thought yourself safe: it haunted your dreams. Twenty-four hours in the trenches before the Butte finished a man off.'[9] To the Scots of the 9th Division the Butte became the most grisly place, 'guarded by slime and weather', on which they ever fought in the war, and that experience had included hideous Delville Wood.[10] The Scots found a long line of the dead of the London Regiment lying face-down in front of the Butte, and they added to the number in the course of a costly and unsuccessful assault against the 16th Bavarian Regiment on 12 October.

The 104th Regiment took over the guard of the hillock on 13 October. The Germans were doing well enough until two of their companies were ordered into a counterattack on the 17th. It turned out badly, and then we were overtaken by an unforeseen misfortune. All of a sudden a gigantic iron 'dragon' came rattling and wheezing forward, reeling like a drunkard, but crossing the shell-holes and all the uneven ground with ease. Like some mythical antediluvian monster the British battlewaggon seemed to breathe fire from mouth, nose and eyes, and whenever it detected a German position it would proceed to spray it with bullets and small-calibre shells from its machine guns and rapid-fire cannon. Even the bravest among us were stricken with horror. We were seeing and meeting this new enemy for the first time, and we were literally paralysed ... machine-gun fire and rifle fire were useless, and grenades just bounced off ... In such a way the tank, which unfortunately had not been spotted by our artillery, drove along the whole length of the 9th Company's sector and virtually wiped it out. Encouraged by its success, the monster paid Gird Trench a visit and then returned the way it had come, quite unmolested.[11]

Towards five in the morning of 18 October a deluge of artillery fire was followed by a determined attack of infantry, in which the Cape Province Battalion of the South African Brigade took a leading part. The Germans beat back the first wave by machine-gun fire, but then new columns 'came flooding forward in a wild surge'.[12] At that moment the German machine guns jammed, and a sequence of attack and counter-attack ended with the South Africans in possession of the Butte.

In the course of the following night the Germans returned in very considerable force (the 104th and 181st Regiments and a Prussian storm battalion) and began to force the South Africans from the mound, and by 22 October 'the masses of British dead in front of our position were giving forth such a stench of corruption that our brave defenders could not touch their food. The weather was wet, and our rifles and machine guns were rusting and covered with mud.'[13]

The British advance up the Bapaume road had reached its full extent.

THE BATTLE OF THE TRANSLOY RIDGES

XV CORPS ON THE LEFT

As it extended to the east, the German third position clung to the low spurs in front of Riencourt, Beaulencourt and le Transloy and thus still allowed the Germans the continued use of a long stretch of the N 17 behind their front. On the sector of the British XV Corps the 41st and 12th Divisions opened the battle on 7 October. They were beaten back. The 12th Division returned to the attack two days later, and the Germans later identified their assailants as the 7/Norfolks, 7/Suffolks and the 8/ and 9/Royal Fusiliers. They, too, were shot down as they came forward with rifles slung. The Prussians of the 64th Regiment were tempted by such easy targets to stand in the open ground, but they paid the price when they came under a devastating fire of howitzers.

The 30th Division was fed into the attack on 18 October. Such success as the British enjoyed was due to the 2/Wiltshires, who gained a temporary lodgement in Bayonet Trench. Afterwards the Germans collated the evidence from these people, together with that from prisoners of the 18/King's and 2/Green Howards. 'They lost heavily to the German machine-gun fire, and such men as reached the German trench were overwhelmed by hand grenades. It was really impossible for these battalions to take the German trenches, as they lacked all communication to right and left and to their rear. They also suffered from dropshorts from their own artillery. The prisoners themselves say that the British attack was a total failure.'[14]

XIV CORPS ON THE RIGHT; THE BRITISH INFILTRATIONS
On the far British right the XIV Corps closed up the British line of battle on the Western Front. On this sector the Transloy battle opened at nine in the morning of 7 October with a battering by the adjacent British and French artillery. West of le Transloy the British shells were bursting among and just above the 84th Reserve Regiment, and 'the whole position lay under a dense, sulphur-yellow shroud, all mixed with dust and mud ... steel and iron splinters of every size were cutting through the air with a hissing sound'. Early in the afternoon the fire suddenly lifted from the forward trench. '"Listen. They're comiiiiing!" Now it was a battle of man against man, and our machine guns hammered into the enemy ranks, which were being thinned at the same time by our hand grenades.' It seemed that the British were falling back, but 'our brave defenders are aware that the British are obstinate people',[15] and sure enough news arrived that the enemy (the 20th [Light] Division)

had destroyed the 9th Company and broken into the positions of the nearby regiments.

A definite pattern was building up and was now repeated many times over. The 78th Reserve Regiment was holding positions in front of le Transloy when the British attacked early in the afternoon of 11 October, 'supported by an aircraft which shot up our forward line. The British left their trenches in dense columns, with their rifles slung, and carrying grenades and knives in their hands ... never had we seen such casual behaviour.'[16] The Prussians knew that the enemy were inflicting heavy casualties, but then found that their regiment was being rolled up from its right flank.

For the 78th Reserve Regiment the British effort on the 12th qualified as a mighty *Grosskampftag*. Once more the infantry attack arrived early in the afternoon, and was signalled when the bombardment lifted to the German rear. 'My batman was the first to see the Tommies climb from their trenches,' recalls Lieutenant Wittneben, '"Lieutenant, sir, here they come!" ... Wherever you looked you saw a swarming and a seething as if of a horde of ants ... our rifles were exacting a heavy toll among the advancing British, but they were as unconcerned as if they had been on an exercise, and it did not seem to matter to them if here and there one or another crashed to the ground.' The British overran the 2nd Company on the right wing, and the Germans were unable to reply, for the British had brought their Lewis guns forward to give covering fire and were taking back large numbers of German prisoners. 'The Tommies were in a fine good mood. They waved to us and blew us kisses.'[17]

On 18 October the British infiltrations had some bizarre consequences on the sector of the 15th Bavarian Regiment. Very early in the morning the Germans had brought down hundreds of British in front of their position, and it was reasonable to suppose that everything was over. A little later forty of the enemy were discovered to have found their way to the rear of the regiment, and were busy digging in. A lieutenant and an English-speaking NCO were sent to negotiate, and were able to persuade the intruders to surrender. It was still only about six in the morning when a party of up to sixty 'Germans' were reported to be coming up as reinforcements. These, too, were found to be British, whereupon the Germans brought two machine guns into action and shot most of them down.[18]

By 20 October, the date given in the British official history as the close of the 'battle of the Transloy Ridges', the British XV and XIV Corps had effected a shallow, saucer-shaped salient into the German defences, measuring 2,000 yards across, and 800 yards deep at its furthest penetration. However, the British and French were still attacking shoulder to shoulder towards Sailly-Saillisel on the extreme right. On 28 October two companies of the 12th Bavarian Regiment fell victim to a typically British process of infiltration and envelopment, and on the next day the allied efforts were rewarded with a foothold in the defences of Sailly-Saillisel. Crown Prince Rupprecht noted that 'the recapture of Sailly is a matter of urgency, since from there the enemy will have a good view over our battery positions and trenches in the direction of Lesboeufs'.[19]

OCTOBER IN PERSPECTIVE

In terms of ground the exertions and sacrifices of the allies in October had not brought commensurate rewards. The capture of the Schwaben Redoubt and the neighbouring defences was of tactical significance for the command of the nearby Ancre valley, but the advance towards Bapaume had been checked on a level with the Butte de Warlencourt. To the east, Ligny-Thilloy remained in German hands, and from there the German third position snaked to the disputed high ground at Sailly-Saillisel. Geographically, the British gains in the Battle of the Somme were almost at an end.

Possibly the British could have achieved more if they had been aware how badly shaken the Germans were in the second week of the month. Company after company was being lost to the British, who were now expert at penetrating gaps in defences. German soldiers were choosing to surrender in significant numbers, and there were distinct signs of frayed nerves among the officers. On 15 October Rupprecht visited the excellent 17th Reserve Regiment from Hamburg, and could not help noticing that its distinguished commander had trembling hands.[20]

German confidence had recovered somewhat by the time the allies opened their atttack on Sailly-Saillisel on the 23rd. Otherwise there followed a wholly unusual pause, which lasted until 3 November. By the end of October the German losses since the beginning of the Battle of the Somme had reached a total of 420,000, but the 85,000 lost in October represented a considerable fall on the 135,000 recorded in September, which had been the truly critical month for the defenders.

As for the future, the intelligence branch of the German Great General Staff concluded on 12 October that the British had only four fresh divisions in reserve in France, and that these would probably be employed in small-scale attacks south of Arras.[21] Two days later the Bavarian representative at supreme headquarters nevertheless reported that 'in spite of hints as to further offensive operations by the British left wing, it is believed that the scene of the former attack on the Somme will continue to be the main offensive. The big blow is supposed to descend at the end of October or the beginning of November, and it will be accompanied by demonstrations of strength on other sectors.'[22] By 26 October three separate reports by German spies indicated something big for the beginning of November. 'The combat will then, as far as the weather allows, be sustained all through the winter, and renewed with fresh forces in the spring.'[23]

THE FOURTH ARMY'S LAST OFFENSIVE, 5–8 NOVEMBER

The weather did not in fact 'allow', for the cold and wet persisted through the first week of November and a little beyond, and it seemed that only an obsession was driving the attacks on the part of the left wing of Rawlinson's Fourth Army along the axis of the Bapaume road.

On 5 November the Durham Light Infantry of the 50th (Northumbrian) Division attacked the Butte de Warlencourt and gained a little ground. Thereafter the attack fragmented and the British were driven back. Early the next day the Germans believed they had identified an isolated pocket of eight or ten men who had been left behind. Sergeant Kuhre of the 179th Regiment was sent with a section to investigate. When he called out a few British emerged and gave themselves up. They were followed, to his astonishment, by unsuspected forms who climbed from shell-holes and scrapes in the ground and brought the number of prisoners to three officers and seventy-two men.[24]

Over to the 50th Division's right the preparatory bombardment had reached a crescendo after eight in the morning of 5 November, and fifteen minutes later the 5th Prussian *Garde* Regiment came under attack by the 1st Australian Division north of Gueudecourt. The Australians were moving over deep, churned-up ground, and in columnar formations that suffered heavily under the German defensive barrage. The Germans threw the Australians out of everything they had gained, except on a sector where a company counterattack 'failed on account of the superior throwing range of the British egg grenades'. A second German company came up in support, but this too was beaten back, 'the main reason being the efficacy of a well-placed machine gun.'[25] The Australians evidently owed a great deal to the Mills bomb and the Lewis gun.

CHAPTER TWELVE

The Final Actions: Gough's Fifth Army and the Last Battles of the Ancre, 13–14 and 18–19 November

The last major effort by Rawlinson's Fourth Army had spent itself, and the initiative in the final episodes of the Battle of the Somme lay with Sir Hubert Gough's Fifth Army to the north. It faced locations like Serre and Beaumont Hamel, whose names recalled the events of 1 July, and indeed the positions of the rival forces had hardly changed since then, with inevitable effects on the landscape. A Thuringian field artillery regiment arrived to find that 'the land around our position was pock-marked with shell-holes every bit as densely as Hill 304 in front of Verdun. Wherever you looked there was nothing to see but ploughed-up torn-apart earth, brown mud, and the sites of former battery positions which had been so thoroughly shot-up as to be nothing but a dismal mash of iron, timber and earth.' The much-vaunted exploits of the late

Boelcke's *Jasta* 2 seemed to count for nothing, for the sky was still swarming with British aircraft. The new regiment's batteries were under surveillance from at least thirty captive balloons, and were now being destroyed one by one. 'The pieces were being shattered by heavy-calibre shells, the exits of the dugouts received hit after hit and collapsed. Ammunition stores blew into the air and our own shells burst in a wide circumference around us. For the first time we came under systematic fire by gas shells, and we had to put on our masks.'[1]

The right wing of Gough's army spanned the marshy Ancre valley as it curved from the north-east to the south, and in the deteriorating weather the war in this part of the world took on a character of its own. The slopes down to the river became muddy slides, and the channels had disappeared, being replaced by a murky lake several hundred yards wide. Supreme efforts were needed to bring troops, rations and materials forward, and to evacuate the wounded, and only an unofficial but regular and strictly observed morning truce made conditions remotely tolerable for the combatants.

The frontage of Gough's planned attack extended for more than 6,000 yards from the north of Serre to beyond Saint-Pierre Divion south of the Ancre. It would, if successful, push the Germans from Serre, and from Beaumont Hamel and the broad and high ridge between there and Beaucourt. The British would then be better placed to carry the battle forward in 1917, and, more immediately, have something to show for their efforts when the French and British commanders met at Chantilly in the middle of November. The historians Prior and Wilson (2005) aptly termed this a 'political battle'.

Gough was able to benefit, at second hand, from the months-long experience of Rawlinson's Fourth Army, and he was eager to put into effect some promising new notions. At the same time he had to exploit to the full anything that might tend to surprise, for the fact of the coming attack could scarcely be hidden from the Germans, as was underlined by an article in *The Times*, which conveniently gave notice that the attacks on the Somme would continue.[2] The British artillery hammered away ceaselessly from 7 November, and among the Germans south of the Ancre 'there was no way of preventing the gradual psychological decline among the soldiers. They became discontented, sickly and embittered, and went about their duties with a deepening lack of hope.'[3]

In the north the British XIII Corps had the task of pushing towards Puisieux and Serre, and thereby covering the flank of the Fifth Army's push. The 31st Division launched its operation at 5.45 in the morning of 13 November to the north-west of Serre, and only a few hundred yards from where it had attacked on 1 July. The outcome was tragically similar, and not just on account of the failure, but because its 92nd Brigade was a great rarity, namely an intact formation of Pals Battalions, which had been held back in reserve on 1 July and therefore been spared the fate of the others. Now the leading troops, the 12/East Yorkshires (Hull Sportsmen) and the 13/East Yorkshires (t'Others) were cut down with losses of more than eight hundred men.

On the right, the 3rd Division came to a stop amid the mud and uncut wire. Both divisions were unfortunate to be facing one of the best German formations, the 52nd Division from Baden, and, in spite of the dense fog, the Germans had detected the British digging in no man's land overnight, and a patrol had seen and reported the first approach. The Germans were therefore on high alert, and their regiments and battalions put in powerful counterattacks without waiting for further orders.

The attack to the south by V Corps was an altogether bigger affair, which engaged the 2nd, 51st (Highland) and 63rd (Royal Naval) Divisions on a frontage of more than 4,000 yards, against the German defences from Redan Ridge by way of Beaumont Hamel to the Ancre in front of Beaumont.

Attacking to the north of Beaumont Hamel, the 5th Brigade of the 2nd Division moved close behind the creeping barrage, and made some creditable progress towards Redan Ridge. This day was nevertheless remembered as the making of the 2nd Division's right-hand neighbour, the 51st (Highland). Like the others, it was attacking positions that had remained essentially unchanged since 1 July. Beaumont Hamel and Y Ravine were places of the most evil memory, and the exploding of a new mine (30,000 pounds of ammonal) under Hawthorn Ridge was a forceful reminder of the earlier operation. There the resemblances ceased, for the Highlanders opened their initial attack from the closer and more realistic distance of 250 yards from their initial objectives, they were screened by fog, and they enjoyed the support of tanks, a good creeping barrage, and one of the novel machine-gun barrages, which in this case caught many of the Germans when they were out of their trenches. Hawthorn Ridge, Beaumont Hamel and Y Ravine were all in possession of the 51st Division by the end of the day, and the Highlanders took more than 2,000 prisoners, including the whole of the I Battalion of the 23rd Regiment, which heard a great explosion through the fog (the Hawthorn mine), and was then overwhelmed by a mass of British infantry that emerged from the direction of Beamont Hamel.

The German First Army ordered an investigation, and found that:

- The loss of these positions, which had been brought to the best state of defence over two years, is to be sought in the following causes:
- For weeks the positions had been under heavy fire, some of it from the flank and rear. The wire was destroyed and the trenches were shot up badly, though the dugouts of the original position had six to eight metres of overhead cover and mostly survived. Every morning over the previous days the enemy had put down an intensive and sudden bombardment, with the intention of sapping the vigilance of our troops.
- The attack took place between six and seven in the morning of 13 November, though reports differ as to the exact time. It was preceded by a quarter of an hour of *Trommelfeuer*.
- The defensive barrage failed on account of the fog, which is an important point.
- It was left to our unsupported infantry to throw back the first enemy to penetrate our positions.

In detail the findings were extremely critical of the performance of the 12th Division, recruited from the heavily Polish Upper Silesia. Along its sector 'the enemy achieved surprise in the fog. Despite all the orders which had been given the security measures did not work well. The troops were too slow to reach the fire-steps from the dugouts. Our men were taken by surprise, and were plunged at once into a hand-to-hand combat in which the heavy numerical superiority of the enemy told to full effect. It was a tough fight, which could have been sustained only by a force which was solid and well-disciplined. The 12th Division was not a

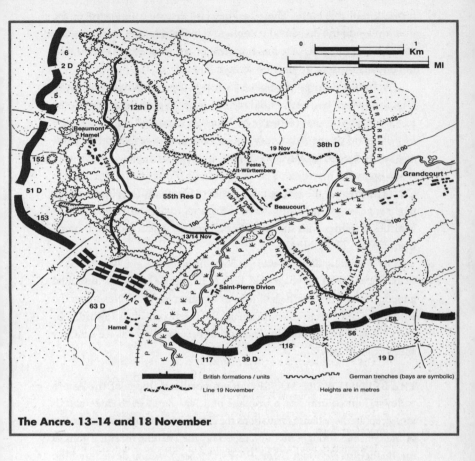

The Ancre. 13–14 and 18 November

formation of this kind.' There had been no display of initiative at the unit level, and the divisional command remained totally inert until the early afternoon, when the headquarters of the First Army had to take the management of affairs into its own hands.[4]

The British V Corps' right-hand formation was the 63rd (Royal Naval) Division, which had been raised in 1914 from shipless personnel of the Royal Naval Volunteer Reserve by Winston Churchill, in his capacity as First Lord of the Admiralty. It had seen action at Ostend in 1914, and been engaged heavily at Gallipoli, and now its depleted ranks were made up by the insertion of an army brigade of four battalions and the City gentlemen of the Honourable Artillery Company (HAC). However its strange ways and ethos derived from its two battalions of Royal Marines, together with six battalions of sailors, which took their name from famous old admirals.

The defending division was the 38th, from Thuringia, which was in better repute than the disgraced 12th to its right. One of the attached gunners records that 'in the half light of the morning of 13 November the British fire burst forth most furiously. We threw ourselves towards our pieces. Red flares soared up and at that precise moment we sent our shells on their way.'[5]

THE BRITISH WERE MASSED down northern slopes of the Ancre valley in four columns on a frontage of 1,200 yards, each three battalions deep. In these dense formations the British were vulnerable to the fire of the German strongpoints, and especially the bristling machine guns of the Beaucourt Redoubt (*Feste Alt-Württemberg*), which devastated the Hawke and Nelson Battalions in the right centre. None of the British reached the ultimate objective of Red Line beyond Beaucourt, and the operation would have been accounted a failure but for the remarkable advance of Lieutenant Colonel Bernard Freyberg's Hood Battalion on the far right, which destroyed the German dugouts that extended in a great complex in the railway cutting close to the Ancre. Supported by the Drake Battalion and the 1st Company of the HAC, the Hoods overran the 55th Reserve Regiment in front of Beaucourt and established themselves in the village. By the German report 'not a great deal can be found out concerning the events in the first position, because few men of the two battalions deployed there ever came back ... The direction of the 55th Reserve Regiment failed because the headquarters seems to have been already put out of action in the morning of the 13th – it is always risky when regimental commanders are too near the front line.'[6]

In the course of the day Freyberg withdrew his troops from the edge of Beaucourt. They had come under the fire of heavy artillery, and (according to the British version) it had been considered prudent to put the force beyond reach of the powerful counterattack that was sure to arrive. The German report has the survivors of the 55th actually driving the British back.

South of the Ancre the British 39th and 19th Division were fortunate enough to catch the Germans when their 38th Division was being relieved by the 223rd – a scratch force that had been put together only four weeks before. On this side of the river, too, the preparatory bombardment had been carefully targeted, as well as being very heavy, to the extent that a 4.5-inch howitzer was aimed at the entrance of every known dugout and tunnel. The British took a total of 1,380 prisoners, and the major prize in terms of ground was the hamlet of Saint-Pierre Divion, down by the Ancre, together with its great system of tunnels. In this muddy terrain a single tank managed to get ahead of the British infantry, and broke down usefully just in front of a dugout.

The British renewed their attacks in full force on 14 November. On the German side a regiment of Lorrainers, the 144th, came up by way of Miraumont as part of the incoming 223rd Division and was thrown in piecemeal on both sides of the Ancre early in the morning. The III Battalion reached Beaucourt at four, when 'the position presented an appalling sight. The dead were lying in heaps, having been caught by the barrage ... other objects had just been left littered about – postal sacks stuffed with letters and parcels, bits of equipment and boxes of ammunition and rations. It was difficult to see anything which resembled a trench, and precious few dugouts had survived the artillery fire.'[7]

The new arrivals could establish no contact with the disintegrating 55th Reserve Regiment, which they were supposed to be relieving, and now an intense fire of the British artillery descended on the scene. The first probing British troops were shot down, but at eight in the morning 'the British, under cover of fog, got around our right flank, reached our rear and attacked us from the east! ... after that the British materialised immediately in front of our trench and called out, with their fingers on their triggers, "Hands up".[8] Two tanks bogged down but continued to give supporting fire with their 6-pounder guns, and by 10.30 in the morning the British had established themselves in the western end of Beaucourt and they consolidated themselves there overnight.

The German high command believed that the fighting at Serre, Beaumont Hamel and along the Ancre must have been the last episode in the months of British striving on the Somme, and that a period of sullen attrition had settled in. Gallwitz applied for a three-day break in Brussels (though he did not have a chance to take it), while Rupprecht departed for a spell of leave in Bavaria. They had no reason to suspect that Gough, buoyed up by what he had achieved on the 13th and 14th, would have persuaded Haig to commit the Fifth Army to yet another attack.

Early on 18 November the Germans had scarcely registered that the landscape was covered with some of the first snow of winter when 'a wild *Trommelfeuer* descended like a blow. The earth was shaking, and the battlefront was veiled in clouds of smoke and dust ... Miraumont had been a prettily situated place up to now, but this day's fighting gave it a totally different aspect. The last roofs of the houses disappeared under the hail of shells, and in the Ancre valley the trees, which had withstood gales over the course of centuries, were now smashed and overset as if by a giant fist.'[9]

North of the Ancre the attack was the business of the newly arrived 32nd and 37th Divisions. The 32nd was advancing from the area of Beaumont Hamel against Munich Trench and the defences south of Serre. The attack turned out to be a costly failure, but it was very much to the credit of the 2/Manchesters and the 2/King's Own Yorkshire Light Infantry that they got into Serre, came at the Germans from the rear and captured the headquarters of the III Battalion of the 77th Reserve Regiment. There was no support, and Second Lieutenant Davidson of the Manchesters was captured during the inevitable retreat. He was probably the officer who told Lieutenant Stratmann that 'the troops who made the attack had come straight from London. At the end of nine hours of marching they were thrown into the storm in the morning fog, and had huge losses. The British who appeared in our [German] rear belonged to the forces which had broken through over to our left and made our battalion staff temporarily captive.'[10]

All unknown to the Germans a group of about 165 cut-off British had gone to ground in dugouts 300 yards behind the front line. They remained there peaceably, content to take prisoner any Germans who wandered by, until somebody finally noticed on 23 November. The *Engländernest* beat off two attacks the next day, but the British were finally captured by Storm Troops on the 25th.[11]

Further towards the Ancre the British 37th Division, which had relieved the Highlanders and the Royal Naval Division, pushed along the northern bank as far as 600 yards beyond Beaucourt by the close of 19 November. It was a good effort, but not good enough to give the necessary flanking support to the British forces on the far side of the river.

As its contribution to the general offensive on 18 November, the 19th Division had the task of smashing the German defences in front of Grandcourt south of the river. Major General Tom Bridges protested in vain at what was being asked of his troops, for in this quagmire they would have to begin the assault in an already exhausted state, and the artillery was being required to hit invisible targets on a reverse slope. Again, the acting commander of the 8/North Staffords believed that an attack on Grandcourt made no sense unless the British kept pace on the north bank of the Ancre.[12]

The outcome was like that of the last round of a contest between two utterly spent boxers. In spite of everything, the British effected an important breakthrough on the sector of the 106th Regiment towards the centre of the German array, 'and for the first time in this campaign our regiment, with heavy hearts, had to leave a trench in the hands of the enemy'.[13] The British were now able to take the German right wing from the rear and destroy the I Battalion of the 120th Reserve Regiment. 'It was sad, very, very sad. We had many men lost as missing, which was something new.'[14] To the Germans at this time 'missing' signified troops who had chosen to surrender.

The 144th Regiment and the 29th Regiment, both of them already shaken by the events of 14 November, were left to defend Grandcourt itself. The 29th was broken, and its remains thrown into the right flank of the 144th. The British penetrated Grandcourt, but they had over-extended themselves badly, and in the course of the day they had to retreat up the near side of Artillery Valley to a position a good 700 yards from the western edge of the village. The British perception of the operation against Grandcourt was therefore one of failure, but the German losses had been extremely heavy, and they became heavier still when the 172nd Regiment opened fire on masses of troops who were seen streaming away from Grandcourt, not realising that they were German prisoners.

The one British defeat on 18 November was sustained by the 8/North Staffordshire Regiment, attacking south of Grandcourt. At 6.30 in the morning the curtain of the British creeping barrage had approached the defending 173rd Regiment, 'and at the exits ... of the dugouts we waited expectantly for the moment when the fire would descend to the rear. Upon that the sentries darted out and cried "*Alles raus, der Tommy kommt!*"'[15] By then the Staffords had actually passed over the remains of the German trenches without noticing them, and the Germans emerged in the rear and cut them off so completely that they became a 'lost battalion', whose fate remained unknown to the British even after the war.

The original battalion commander, Lieutenant Colonel Parish, had departed with 'shell shock' a few days earlier, and the command had been assumed by Lieutenant Colonel Anderson of the South African Light Horse. He told the Germans that he had been coming up behind the last wave when his left arm was shattered by a shrapnel ball. 'He lost consciousness for some time, and when he recovered his senses he saw that he was surrounded by German soldiers. The British had attacked with two companies in the first line and another two in the second, each in two waves. Visibility was lost in the driving snow, and he thinks that for that reason the attack on Grandcourt Trench must have failed as well.'[16]

By the afternoon of 18 November the snow had been succeeded by rain which turned the ground into brown mud. The wet weather persisted over the following days, and the Germans tried to cheer themselves up with the thought that 'things must be just as bad for the Tommies. Patrols which crept up to their wire heard a constant slapping of spades, the working of pumps, and the splashing of drained water over their parapets.'[17] It was at best a dismal consolation, and the continuing rain and the endless exhausting labour brought the morale and combat-worthiness of the Germans to the lowest ebb of the year.[18]

Unknown to the Germans the British high command had 'closed down' the last offensive on 19 November. By the end of the month Rupprecht allowed himself to think that the British and French had desisted in their efforts, and by 10 December he was still more confident that a term had been put on the battle, which he believed to have been 'the greatest, the longest and the most costly of the war'.[19]

It was very far from being the end of that war, and not even the end to the killing on the Somme. 'On the 29th [of December] at two in the afternoon, an enemy patrol approached the right wing of our sector and threw a number of grenades. Our sentries opened fire and brought one of the British down. When our sentries came up to retrieve him he pointed his pistol and refused to give himself up. We took him prisoner anyway and brought him back to our position, where he later died of his wounds. On the same occasion we found another of the British hanging in our wire. He too declined to surrender, and he fell under our rifle fire. Both were of the Grenadier Guards.'[20]

PART FOUR

WEAPONS AND TACTICS

CHAPTER THIRTEEN

The British Style of Combat

The British wire was neither as thick-set nor as deep as that of the enemy, but to the Germans it seemed to be planted with considerable cunning. In April they noted that the British 'deploy their wire according to accurate and meticulous prescriptions. As well as barbed and smooth wire they employ so-called "French wire", which falls into coils when it is unrolled and is much favoured for setting up obstacles at speed.'[1] In September German Captain Gum reported on an exemplary layout where, amongst other refinements, triangular projections of the belt were designed to funnel the attacking troops towards gaps, where they could be massacred by machine guns.[2]

What the Germans knew of official British defensive doctrine as a whole came from a captured army order of 22 June 1915, which laid down that the first line was to be defended at all costs. By February 1916, however, the most recent practice indicated that 'the British now follow the French model, and the order in question seems to be out of date … A number of prisoners say that three or four machine guns per company are dug into the outermost trench, but that most of these weapons are emplaced further to the rear in support trenches, from where they can lay down overhead or enfilade fire.' A paper by one Captain Batty advocated withdrawing the infantry to a support trench 100 yards in the rear, leaving the defence to the foremost trench solely to well dug-in machine guns.[3]

Otherwise almost everything the Germans knew about the British style of war came from the British being on the attack. Just before the opening of the Battle of the Somme the Germans at Thiepval launched a spectacularly successful trench raid against the Dorset Regiment. This was an exception, for the British were under constant pressure from Haig to maintain the offensive spirit and carry the war to the enemy, and they undertook 106 trench raids in the six months before 1 July, and another 310 between then and November.[4] By a German account 'the British detected immediately whenever forces on our side were in the process of being relieved, and a favourite tactic of theirs was to launch an attack. It would succeed more often than not, for our new troops would not have had the time to orientate themselves in this difficult ground.'[5]

On 7 May 1916 Crown Prince Rupprecht registered his dismay at what the censor of letters was discovering about the poor spirit among the reserve divisions which were drawn from Germany's industrial areas. A man of better stock, a miner who was attached to one of these dismal formations, wrote home that

> the British are treating our men like children. One evening not long ago they betook themselves with their lethal clubs as far as the third trench, and proceeded to knock a number of men down and drag them off. The rest of our men ran for their lives! They were back here again yesterday. They caught the sentry crouching in a dugout and beat him on the behind. They clubbed down several of our troops and took them prisoner, and they captured our consignment of post, which held amongst other things a parcel for a corporal – let's call him 'Striefe'. Some time afterwards they called out, 'Corporal Striefe, here is your post!' and they duly handed it over. In fact a constant trade is going on, and the British often send things across. When a rat scuttles in the wire during the night it is quite enough to make all our men cower![6]

Probably the most remarkable of such British achievements in 1916 was the 'lifting' of the entire 112-strong 8th Company of the 17th Bavarian Regiment in broad daylight west of Martinpuich on 29 August. It was accomplished in total silence, and the neighbouring German units knew nothing of the event until they found that the enemy had taken up residence in the company's position.[7] This must have been the work of either the Australians or the 15th (Scottish) Division.

The Germans were naturally on the alert for signs of something bigger. Their 'Moritz' (Arendt) listening stations were capable of picking up messages or fragments of messages from earthed Morse buzzers up to a distance of about 1,500 yards, and, usefully for the Germans, the British rarely used code words. Most of the interceptions were of little value, like the frequent complaints that telephone wires were being broken by grenade training.[8] However, the Arendt stations were good at giving warnings of impending British artillery strafes,[9] and a fragment of an inspirational message from Rawlinson at 4.15 in the morning of 1 July gave a last-minute warning that something big was about to happen.

Other indicators were particularly useful. Before the first attack on the Butte de Warlencourt on 5 November 'there was lively traffic for day after day behind the trenches, and carts and light railways were bringing up material from a considerable distance … it was then taken forward from le Sars and Courcelette by carrying parties'.[10] The British frequently obliged by moving troops to their assaulting positions across open ground, apparently indifferent to the artillery fire that was being brought down on them,[11] 'and as a sure sign of a coming attack we take the way they fill their line with patrol-sized parties and small groups, a process which goes on for hours on end'.[12]

For all their professed confidence, the Germans still had no guarantee that they could identify the weighting, the method, the hour, the day or even the basic fact of a British offensive. Towards the end of June 1916 the German calculations were complicated by the two-day postponement of the opening of the grand offensive, and on the actual day, 1 July, the sustained impetus of the XIII Corps attack at Montauban never allowed the Germans to recover their balance. Again, at the opening of the battle of Flers-Courcelette on 15 September, quite apart from the employment of the tanks, the British in some locations took the Germans unawares by having infiltrated troops to close assaulting distance overnight. The battle of Bazentin Ridge on 14 July and the last attack on the Ancre on 18 November present themselves as examples of total surprise.

Early in October the Germans had tried, not very successfully, to identify some kind of pattern in the timings.

Signs of Enemy Attacks. The larger attacks usually follow intervals of five or six days. The assaults open at various times. In the smaller attacks on 3 and 8 September they arrived in the afternoons and evenings, but in the more considerable attack on 15 September at 6.15 in the morning. The attacks on the 3rd and the 8th were preceded by an artillery preparation which lasted for several hours, and which on the 8th intensified all of a sudden after midday and continued at a rate which indicated that an attack would follow. The preparations for the attack on 15 September began on the 13th, with the registration of the heavy pieces, and firing for effect in the course of the 14th, while the following night and the time immediately before the infantry attack were relatively quiet. There was nothing out of the ordinary to be noted before the enemy infantry surged forward en masse at 6.15 in the morning.[13]

British infantry tactics at their crudest were represented by the sight of the leading troops flooding forward in successive waves, followed by supports that marched up in compact little columns. It was clear that in the first attacks on the Somme 'the British were relying too heavily on the effect of their artillery fire. After they had brought their *Trommelfeuer* to bear it seemed impossible to them that any kind of resistance could stir in the German lines. Astonished and uncomprehending, the troops as they stormed forward saw that men were crouching in the torn-up ground and that machine guns were being brought into position.'[14]

The state of the wire might also come as an unwelcome surprise. The British high command had dismissed or ignored the potential of the bangalore torpedo for blowing gaps in the wire,[15] and the artillery provided no guarantee of destruction. 'Whatever you did, however long the time you gave to cutting the wire, it never disappeared entirely; vile, treacherous strands stuck out of the earth like brambles, stakes remained upright with waving lengths of wire to grab you by the sleeve or the trousers.'[16] When the leading troops did find gaps, they were likely to discover themselves cut off from support when a barrage descended in their rear, and unsuspected Germans emerged from shell-holes or dugouts.

The reinforcing columns had troubles of their own, for they made rewarding targets for artillery, and the Germans found that rifle fire proved effective against them up to a range of 850 yards. A British attack near Sailly-Saillisel may stand for many others. The German fire sliced among the unsupported troops 'like a giant sickle, and scattered the men who were yet unwounded. Only isolated parties still tried to come on. On reaching the hollow in front of our position they were beaten down by our rifle fire and by our *Minenwerfer* which were making excellent practice.'[17]

The men who were prepared to face such losses were extraordinarily brave and determined. 'Something which compels our astonishment and highest admiration was to see the enemy attack again and again over the same ground – ground that was littered with the victims of their earlier attempts, and whose bodies were fast corrupting in the heat of high summer and filled the air with their sweet stench.'[18] The British were repeatedly observed to be kicking footballs in front of them, which the Germans had at first taken to be a monstrous form of grenade.

There had always been exceptions to the episodes of blundering sacrifice, and in the course of the Battle of the Somme they reached such dimensions that they began to command the serious attention of the Germans. By the middle of September British infantry had clearly benefited by better training,[19] and on the *Grosskampftag* on the 15th individuals and small parties went forward to assess the effect of the artillery, and the fire was adjusted accordingly. The spotting and the fire support by the Royal Flying Corps was now being integrated into the attacks in a way that could truly be considered an advance in the art of war.

The mass attacks could still be as clumsy as ever, 'but on the other hand individual machine-gun crews, patrols, bombing parties and the troops who were assigned to seal off trenches were behaving very well. The explanation is that they were trained in independent action ... If it was a question of seizing smaller sectors of trenches, the British pushed forward small groups or simple bombing parties which advanced cautiously, in that they made skilful use of ground, but also in an aggressive spirit. Once they had broken in they lost no time in exploiting to the flanks and planting their light machine guns.'[20] As early as the beginning of August the British were seen to be making use of 'assaulting troops up to battalion strength ... It was noticeable how the enemy sought out weak points or locations of especial tactical importance. That was where they would bite into our lines and seek the next opportunity to develop their success.'[21]

On 18 November an officer of the German 29th Grenadier Regiment was facing le Sars and Courcelette when the fog lifted, 'and I was able to watch the progress of a British patrol which an officer was leading ... across our trenches. There they found a number of Germans and duly sent them back as prisoners. The patrol was advancing with great skill, with the officer at the head, and the men echeloned back in arrow-head formation. They covered the ground swiftly, making use of the cover afforded by every shell-hole, and yet without losing cohesion. I got the impression that the British officers were bold men who knew what they were doing.'[22]

It was still striking to the Germans that the British were so rarely capable of 'raising their game' to take full advantage of the opportunities they were creating for themselves. Such a chance had clearly existed, for example, in the gap in the German positions to the west of Windmill Hill at Pozières on 5 August.

> The reason is to be sought in the training of the British commanders and soldiers. On our side the leaders never cease to impress on the men that whatever orders and instructions might have been given, they will prove inadequate in the event of anything serious, for the situation will change from one moment to the next. Success might open an opportunity which must be exploited without loss of time, while somewhere else a situation might develop which demands a change of plan. Thus our officers and men develop as independent strategists. They work within the broad concept of the orders and guidelines, but the decisive action is often the work of officers – and men as well – who are acting on their own authority. The passing chance would have been a matter of history if they had tried to seek the approval of the higher circles.[23]

The British were found to be working on different premises, 'something rigid and calculated on the mass'.[24] Some of the British officers and NCOs themselves were critical of the complicated and formulaic style of command,[25] and a German memorandum drew attention to the fact that 'every order goes into the tiniest detail, in striving to tie down the officers and men in advance'.[26] In the margin a German officer entered the word *Ungewandtheit* (lack of skill), which touches on the fact that there were still not enough British officers of the calibre to supply what was needed. A man of the 17/Sherwood Foresters, taken north of Beaumont Hamel on 3 September, said that his captain had been the only officer in his company who had any front-line experience; the other four officers had not even been in the trenches before.[27]

The outcome was to be seen again and again in the actions on the Somme in the late autumn and early winter, when local British break-throughs and outflanking movements could capture whole German units at a time, but often ended with the British going to ground inside or even behind the German positions in the typical *Engländernester* (improvised strongpoints). Once they had established themselves the British could prove very hard to dislodge, for they might have their Lewis guns and trench mortars with them, and they were astonishingly speedy diggers. A German, told off to investigate a group of the intruders, raised himself cautiously over the edge of a shell-hole. 'Good heavens! I could scarcely believe my eyes! Moles seemed to be at work scarcely forty metres to my front. The very earth was in motion among flying clods. There then appeared a brown face and one of the flat saucer-shaped helmets. A harsh foreign voice carried to my ears. Spades were clinking. There were more saucer helmets. The Tommies were digging themselves in here.'[28]

The German army and corps commanders had to issue weighty warnings to the effect that the British were managing to identify and penetrate chinks in the German positions, and 'repeated experience confirms that in the course of the Battle of the Somme these so-called *Engländernester* invariably become the starting-point for major new attacks, if they are not at once eliminated or sealed off. These lodgements are small and can easily escape detection, yet the British are extraordinarily skilful at enlarging them little by little and using them as the foundation of fresh assaults'.[29]

The British were finding their way towards the tactical revolution that spread through their armies on the Western Front in 1917, when the platoon was made the basis for fire and manoeuvre, in a way that combined something of the tactical skills of the pre-war Regulars with the mobile firepower of the Lewis gun. In the long run it was to prove a more promising development than that of the celebrated Storm Troops, who remained a minority within the German Army, and who in 1918 sucked the unimproved masses of the German infantry forward to be massacred by aircraft and machine guns.

CHAPTER FOURTEEN

Weapons of Close Support

THE MACHINE GUN CORPS, THE VICKERS AND THE LEWIS GUN

The machine gun of the Great War was a predominantly defensive weapon, and the combat on the Somme is associated so strongly with the carnage wrought by the German machine-gunners that it is possible to overlook the fact that the British had machine guns as well, and were using them in novel and effective ways.

The Machine Gun Corps owed its short existence principally to the limitations and remarkable capacities of the Vickers gun, a belt-fed, water-cooled weapon firing the same .303 cartridge as the infantry rifle. Although lighter than the original version, the .45 Maxim, it still weighed 58 pounds and was much heavier than the Lewis gun, which was introduced in 1915 to fight alongside the infantry. Rather than see the Vickers dethroned altogether, Captain George ('Boss') Lindsay tried to persuade the authorities that the Vickers' ability to lay down accurate, predictable and sustained fire to a range of 2,800 yards could best be exploited by trained personnel who were acting under expert direction.

Lindsay succeeded only in part. The Machine Gun Corps was established by royal warrant on 22 October 1915, albeit in diluted form, and acted almost entirely under the orders of the infantry brigades or cavalry squadrons. Its most exotic manifestations, and the ones that came closest to the original inspiration, were the Motor Machine Gun batteries, which, as the Germans concluded, 'serve apparently as a mobile reserve, and will be brought together in larger formations for particular purposes. They are transported as follows: the crews on motorcycles, with the guns on carriages attached to the sides – the so-called "sidecars".'[1]

The Brigade Machine Gun Squadrons were attached to the cavalry squadrons, and were equipped with the strip-fed French Hotchkiss. However, by far the greater part of the corps served in the infantry-support companies, which (after the introduction of the Lewis gun) came under the orders of the infantry brigades. In such a way 'the Machine Gun Corps does not appear as a recognisable entity, but is rather more of an administrative organisation. Each brigade has at its disposal a number of machine guns. The quantity varies greatly, and the numbers of machine guns assigned to the individual companies and battalions differ still more. Most of the companies have between two and four machine guns, of which two are Vickers and the others Lewis guns.'[2]

The Germans learned that for purposes of the attack the Vickers were 'deployed as far as possible on the flanks. They work best when they are sited in such a way that they can keep up their fire for the greatest length of time, i.e. exploiting for as long as possible their capacity for sustained fire. In the attacks reaching to a greater depth the machine guns are to be brought forward by stages. Covered positions will have been prepared for them in advance by designated detachments of the attacking infantry.'[3]

Such was the ideal, but the Vickers guns 'offer a comparatively big target and require a stable foundation for their fire',[4] and it was evident from the stories of the prisoners that it was difficult for the British to bring the guns up. Once in open ground these bulky weapons had no shelter from fire, and men of the machine-gun company of the 93rd Brigade (31st Division), captured in front of Serre on 27 July, said that it had been impossible to position the guns before their infantry had been beaten back.

'In the defence [so the Germans deduced] it seems that the machine guns of the Machine Gun Corps are employed in the foremost trenches only by individual weapons. Most of them are strongly emplaced in the second or third trenches and at considerable intervals. The intention is probably to lessen their exposure to the enemy *Trommelfeuer*, for they are otherwise easily buried, become unserviceable and all too readily fall into the hands of the assaulting enemy infantry. Their firepower is primarily intended for use against counterattacks, and as far as possible from flanking positions.'[5]

In such positions the Vickers could also act as a weapon of interdiction to compare with artillery or poison gas, and its design suited it eminently to keep up 'a mass fire of long duration'.[6] '"Overhead" means firing at high trajectory, as opposed to low trajectory. The Vickers has a better "overhead fire" than the Lewis gun.'[7] In a celebrated episode the ten guns of the 100th Machine Gun Company fired nearly one million rounds at High Wood in the course of 14 August. Exploiting his weapon's considerable range, a good Vickers gunner could harass Germans in their rearward positions, and Lieutenant Ernst Jünger of the 73rd Fusilier Regiment was 'especially irritated by one machine-gunner who sprayed his bullets at such an angle that they came down vertically, with acceleration produced by sheer gravity. There was absolutely no point in trying to duck behind walls.'[8]

The Lewis gun was a gas-operated weapon, which was served by a gunner and up to five hard-put-upon assistants who carried the replenishment magazines in canvas buckets. The magazines were cumbersome and notoriously difficult and slow to reload, but at 30 pounds the gun with its magazine in place weighed only just over half as much as the Vickers, which opened all sorts of tactical possibilities. The Germans described the guns as 'air-cooled automatic weapons, which look like a rifle with a very thick barrel. They have a rotary magazine which holds fifty [sic] rounds, and can fire three hundred rounds a minute. The gun gets hot quickly, which rules out a sustained fire. A special tripod (with no aiming apparatus) enables it to fire up to 300 metres.'[9] The potential of the Lewis was tested and proved on the Somme, and as the first genuinely effective portable machine gun the weapon became an essential foundation of the new tactics adopted by the British platoons in 1917.

The Germans followed the progress of the Lewis on the Somme with meticulous attention. By 24 February 1916 the gun was being identified on battalion sectors, and ambitious programmes for training the operators indicated that the British believed that the weapon had a future. The men had at first resented the Lewis as an inadequate replacement for the Vickers, which was no longer at the immediate disposal of unit commanders, but in the course of May many prisoners told the Germans that they now preferred the Lewis 'on account of its greater mobility'.[10]

Further evidence emerged on 29 July, when the Germans captured thirteen NCOs and men of the 2/Rifle Brigade, who had served recently on the Somme. Six of them had operated the Lewis gun, and they said that their battalion was equipped with ten of the weapons, to be increased shortly to sixteen. 'Special emphasis is being put on training every machine-gunner with the Vickers and the German machine guns as well. After the men have completed their training in England, and before they come to the front, they undergo theoretical and practical instruction in schools which have been set up for that purpose in Saint-Omer.'[11]

By October experience showed the Germans that the Lewis out-classed both the German *Muskete* and the French *fusil mitrailleur* as a provider of light automatic firepower, and eclipsed totally the M 08 (the German equivalent of the Vickers) in the offensive role. 'The light British Lewis machine guns are superior to our heavy versions in mobility. Our machine gun is unfortunately too heavy to accompany our shock troops at their own pace. The British Lewis machine gun can be carried by one man, and is better suited for that purpose.'[12] In detail,

> the Lewis guns are to work forward individually under cover of the ground, then plant themselves in forward positions and support the advance of the infantry. After the sector under attack has been gained, they free some of the infantry from the task of consolidating the captured position, and they simultaneously bar the enemy communication trenches and thereby protect the flanks. Their mobility and the speed with which they can bring a concentration of fire to bear makes them especially suitable for exploiting opportunities as they present themselves. The actions on the Somme have proved that, after a

position has been captured, the facility to bring forward a *large* number of Lewis guns at speed endows the newly won British positions with great strength.[13]

On the defensive, 'the Lewis guns are assigned to the companies according to need, and are always deployed in the forward line or in advance posts. They are not solidly dug in, but change their positions as circumstances dictate.'[14] On 31 August, at Delville Wood, this facility enabled the British to advance their Lewis guns 200 yards into no man's land, and so evade a destructive bombardment which was falling on the trench to their rear.[15]

HAND GRENADES ('BOMBS')

Hand grenades were the private artillery of the infantryman, and in both the British and German armies the soldiers prized the weapon for its capacity to inflict damage without exposing the thrower to view. For the same reason both British and German officialdom believed that it could sap the momentum of the attack, and in the second half of 1916 they began to discourage its use in all but exceptional circumstances. The stick grenade, along with the coal-scuttle helmet, nevertheless remained a symbol of the German soldier in two world wars, while a derivative of the Mills was in use among the British until the 1960s.

Earlier in 1916 the Germans had found that the British grenades and their throwers demanded the most serious examination.

The usual method in an operation is to bring together small detachments, led by an NCO, and made up of two riflemen, two trained bombers, two grenade carriers and two replacements. The bombers have a broad belt wrapped around them, with the grenades inserted in little pockets. Down their sides they have a knobkerry with an iron-bound head, but otherwise they carry no weapon, so as to have both hands free to throw the grenades. The two riflemen are assigned for their protection, and have their bayonets fixed permanently in constant readiness for close-quarter combat. The men who carry the spare grenades are also fully trained in throwing them. In the trenches the grenades are usually stored ten or twelve at a time in little niches, disposed along the whole line.[16]

By the end of 1915 the Mills bomb No. 5 was fast supplanting the great and alarming variety of explosive devices that had been current in earlier times. The Mills grenade was a heavy weapon, weighing up to one pound nine ounces, and a number of soldiers at the time and most of the histories since have maintained that the German stick grenades and their little egg grenades were more effective in themselves, and were capable of being thrown to greater distances.[17]

In 1916 the weight of the opinion in the two armies held otherwise. Where the stick grenade went off with a loud *ping*, and relied for its effect solely on blast, the Mills exploded with a thunderous *bang*: 'it was a killing weapon which broke into black slugs the size and shape of sugar-lumps'.[18] The German allowance of grenades for most units was believed to be too small, while the awkward length of the stick grenade, when it happened to be available, prevented it from being carried in the same quantity as the Mills bomb. Oval grenades of any kind were more convenient to carry, and early in September the Bavarians reported that the enemy used them 'successfully and on a large scale when they attacked from Delville Wood'.[19]

Training and habituation also had to be taken into account. The commander of a German regiment complained in October that his troops consisted 'almost two-thirds of replacements, who had no acquaintance with hand grenades, and therefore did not stand a chance against the British, who are very well trained in this respect. Our few good grenade-throwers had been reassigned almost immediately, and we received nobody to take their place.'[20]

Here the notorious British *Sportsidiotismus* proved to be a distinct asset, for the Germans had no ball-throwing equivalent of the British cricket. There was a classic incident at Thiepval on 27 September, when Second Lieutenant Tom Adlam of the 7/Bedfords earned the VC by launching a one-man bombing attack on the Germans, utilising the same skills as had enabled him to throw a cricket ball 100 yards in peacetime. Three days later Second Lieutenant J. Wightman of the East Surreys repeated the feat at Schwaben Redoubt, where 'the enemy knew the ground. Also they were armed with "egg bombs" with which they ought to have been able to out-throw our bombers. But Lieutenant Wightman was an extremely powerful thrower and actually out-bombed the Germans with the Mills bomb.'[21]

The Germans discovered another devotee in a wounded officer of the 5/York and Lancaster Regiment, captured north of Thiepval on 2 July. 'He claims – and it has been confirmed by other soldier and officer prisoners – that the Germans, evidently on account of insufficient training, not only are bad at throwing grenades, but do not throw them far enough, and that the German hand grenades are pretty ineffective. They maintain that the British "Mills No. 5" is much more impressive, and claim that captured German officers have told them the same thing.'[22] Again, an order of the 21st Bavarian Reserve Regiment lamented at the end of the month that 'a few Englishmen throwing grenades from their trench can thoroughly frighten a crowd of Bavarians. That must not be allowed to go on.'[23]

The range of the grenades was extended considerably when designed to be fired from a rifle, which made them, in the opinion of a German captured in September, 'one of the most effective weapons of the British'.[24]

The prowess of the British bombers was celebrated in verse by James Norman Hall:

> The first to climb the parapet
> With the 'cricket balls' in either hand;
> The first to vanish in the smoke
> Of God-forsaken No Man's Land...
>
> Full sixty yards I've seen them throw
> With all the nicety of aim
> They learned on British cricket-fields,
> Ah, bombing is a Briton's game!...

(James Norman Hall, *The Cricketers of Flanders*, 1916)

In the last years of the war the Americans claimed the same advantage on behalf of their baseball pitchers.

TRENCH MORTARS

The work of the British artillery proper was supplemented by thin-tubed, smooth-bore pieces known generally as 'trench mortars', which employed a small charge to launch a relatively heavy bomb in high trajectory. The most common German equivalent was the ugly *Priesterwerfer*, a short-ranged spigot mortar that shot a serrated cylinder with projecting fins. The *Minenwerfer* were scaled-down siege howitzers, which were accurate and much feared by the British, but even the lightest version was too heavy to be risked in a forward trench, let alone accompany troops into the attack. In this branch of killing there was never any doubt that in 1916 the British had gained the upper hand.[25]

The British ascendancy owed much to the advent of the 3-inch Stokes mortar, which was accepted into service in 1916, and operated by detachments of trained infantrymen. The bomb carried up to 430 yards and was 'a devilish thing, for when it bursts it makes a terrific bang and sends out flakes of jagged steel which account for anyone standing within fifty yards'.[26] The original mortar was supplemented by 4- and 6-inch models and by a massive 9.45-inch mortar, which discharged a 150-pound 'Flying Pig' to a range of 1,000 yards. Termed by the Germans as 'aerial torpedoes' or 'clothes baskets', the huge bombs were clearly visible when they coursed through the air and 'soon occasioned the most extraordinary fear. No dugout was capable of withstanding the fearful power of their explosions.'[27]

More oafish still was the 60-pound toffee-apple, which was fired from a 2-inch spigot and reached to 600 yards. It was probable that the British did not know just what an effective weapon it was, for they were content to install the mortars individually in complicated little shelters. By German accounts the explosion of the monstrous globe had 'an appalling effect on nerves and eardrums'.[28] Its splinters could smash through the stoutest timbers, and the blast and fragments were very effective at levelling trenches and tearing barbed wire to rags. As with most shells, however, the blast exited through one of the sides, and the Germans found that when the remaining husk was hung up by its stalk it made a rather good gong for gas alarms.

The heavier mortars came under the command of the Royal Garrison Artillery, and were brought most frequently to bear against identified strongpoints. All too often the result was a ponderous routine. Early in July the German 62nd Regiment learned that it would come under fire predictably at 7.30 each morning. The British would pause after two hours, then continue their attentions for a further two. 'We could hear the dull crash of the explosions, and every time the lights in the bunker were extinguished by the blast. It was impossible to sleep, and we just groped around in the dark and listened to the showers of stones as they bounced down the steps and the sand as it sifted through the timber framework.'[29]

The 3-inch mortars were more effective in their way, for they could prove deadly at night against unsuspecting German working parties, and they could be brought forward like Lewis guns to support assaulting troops. The Germans observed how in the battle of Flers-Courcelette, 'light and mobile mortars were at hand with astonishing speed when the forward attacking troops encountered obstinate resistance.'[30]

CHAPTER FIFTEEN

Artillery

Where the enemy gained any successes in the Battle of the Somme, they owed them chiefly to the excellent deployment of technical resources, and above all to the unprecedented and huge quantity of their artillery and ammunition, and the co-operation between their infantry, artillery and aircraft – a co-operation in the dimensions of both time and space. (KA 3 ID, Bd 77, Below, *Erfahrungen der 1. Armee in der Sommeschlacht 1916* [24.6.–26.11.1916])

For the British troops on the Somme a constant source of pride was in the power of their artillery, and at one remove in the achievements of their munitions industry.[1] For the German survivors of the battle, the most enduring memory was probably how their trenches had been stamped into the ground by the British guns. In the considered assessment of the commander of the Pioneers of the 4th Bavarian Division 'in the course of the Battle of the Somme the enemy facing us (in our sector the British) have assembled a quantity of artillery which is overwhelming in numbers and calibre, and deployed it with consummate artistry with regards to both tactical positioning and tactical employment. They have brought it against a trench system which we had hitherto regarded as impregnable, and which had been made stronger still on the basis of the most recent technical advances. With all of this the British were able, in a comparatively short time, to batter it so comprehensively that even our brave and death-defying infantry found it impossible to hold their wrecked positions against the mass storms which followed.'[2]

In 1916 the Germans learned little about the interior workings of the Royal Artillery, for the artillery observers were whisked away out of their reach if they were in danger of being captured, and 'the troops are forbidden to linger in the neighbourhood of the batteries. Information concerning the artillery is consequently as scanty as before.'[3] Most of the German information, therefore, came from the simple fact that the Germans were the targets of this mass of ordnance.

In the middle of August the Germans were told that 'the artillery of the 11th Division has consisted hitherto only of light and medium calibres: 4.5-inch (114 mm) pieces have been the heaviest pieces up to now. But heavy artillery is now on the way; 7.9-inch (200 mm) pieces are now expected, amongst others.'[4]

In the course of the battle the Germans became better acquainted with the whole variety of pieces at the disposal of the British infantry division – its thirty-six 18-pounder field guns, its brigade of eighteen of the excellent 4.5-inch howitzers just mentioned, and its quartet of long-ranged 60-pounder guns. The 18-pounder gun of 1916 could reach to 6,525 yards, and the 4.5-inch (114 mm) howitzer to 7,300, which out-ranged its nearest German equivalent, the 105 mm howitzer, by 1,000 yards, and gave it a useful capacity for counter-battery work. The unmodified 60-pounder gun (the heaviest piece that could be towed by horses) carried to 10,300 yards.

The 60-pounder was just the younger brother of the heavy low-trajectory guns, which were held at the corps level of command, in which the British held a near-total superiority over the Germans. 'In spite of the many duds, the shells of the heavy low-trajectory pieces have a considerable physical impact, by burying many of our troops, and they have a shattering effect on morale when they burst.'[5] If the variety of heavy howitzers are added, the British had the means of taking both the first and second systems of the German defences under fire without having to resite their heavy batteries.[6]

Shrapnel made up about two-thirds of the British preparatory fire for the first day of the Battle of the Somme, and in one way or another it remained the chief German-killer for the rest of the campaign. These air-burst shells had the most immediate effect against men in open ground or shallow trenches, and thus against relieving or departing troops, or forces assembling for counterattacks. Actuated by a time-fuze, the shrapnel shells burst with a 'sharp, concentrated vicious snap'[7] and 'shook loose their little balls in a dense cloud, and the empty cases rasped after they were gone'.[8] The bursting charge was black powder, which gave British shrapnel its characteristic ball of white smoke. Shrapnel, along with the globular toffee-apple, was still the only weapon of any utility at the disposal of the British for clearing wire, and then only if the fuzes were so adjusted as to burst the shell immediately over the entanglements.

Shrapnel, less obviously, was the chief agent of neutralisation, for, by forcing the German infantry to seek shelter, it helped the British infantry to get forward, while posing the Germans with difficult questions of timing. They had only to cover the short distance from their cover to their firing positions, 'but those few steps needed to be taken in the instant of a great crescendo of fire before an attack'.[9]

Cover itself was no guarantee of protection against high-explosive shells. 'Narrow and steep-sided trenches once again proved to be deadly, and led to far heavier casualties (through being buried) than broad and shallow trenches. This experience is based on the fact that the fragmentation action of most of the British shells is inferior to their shock effect.'[10]

The German infantrymen felt vulnerable in open trenches of any kind, and like their British counterparts they excavated little funk-holes (*Kaninchenlöcher*, or rabbit holes) in the forward sides. The sense of security was an illusion, for the shelters undermined the parapets and made them liable to collapse on their occupants. Captain Georg Lang of the 6th Bavarian Regiment believed he was safe when he was sheltering in a niche in Gird Trench north of Flers on 22 September.

> There was a hiss – and the earth cover collapsed on top of me and I
> found myself buried. I automatically threw up my hand in a defensive
> gesture. I drew myself up on my legs and pushed up with my shoulders,

but could not move an inch. I was hemmed in. Deep night had closed in on my eyes … Air became scarcer and scarcer, and my breath shorter and more laboured … Hot sweat broke out all over my body. My breathing was now a rattle … there was a roaring and buzzing in my ears and my thoughts became confused. I then felt a blow, and a pain in my right hand – air came streaming in. My men, led by Corporal Dehling, were hauling me out … I know what it is to die.[11]

The ordeal was much longer for men who were trapped in deep dugouts, where twenty or more men at a time could be entombed.[12]

The British artillery fire over the Somme never actually ceased, and by the second half of September the British were hitting the German First Army with four times as many shells as they received in return. Crown Prince Rupprecht reported to the supreme command on the 27th that 'the British make up for their deficiencies by the gigantic artillery preparations for their attacks. It is this enormous expenditure of artillery ammunition which is wearing down our infantry. There is a great deal of shirking even in the good units.'[13]

The German positions on the Somme would probably have become totally untenable if so many of the fuzes of the British shells had not failed. The proportion of duds reached 50 per cent or more in the heavy calibres, and a Saxon NCO informed the British that on 7 August in Courcelette 'he saw two 38 cm [15-inch] duds. [The] prisoner, who had never seen German shells of this calibre, said that he could just reach from base to nose by extending his arms.'[14] There were innumerable reports of the same kind. However, the quantity of effective shells was still shocking enough to the Germans, and one of their gunners told the British that 'the accuracy with which the range is lengthened or the fire lifted, or the barrage develops is commented upon by the German artillery officers. Our shrapnel is considered excellent, good burst and no "blinds". Our medium heavy calibres give "blinds", but not many. [The] prisoner said that a blind which was a direct hit on a dugout often knocked it out more thoroughly than if it burst on top.'[15]

Under the leadership of Brigadier General Hugh Trenchard, the Royal Flying Corps gave a high priority to artillery spotting, while the observers of the Royal Artillery took advantage of every possible post

– up in observation balloons, in positions in the second or third trenches of the first line, or perches in houses or trees. New observation posts were established as the fighting moved forward, and the Germans noted that 'in the position which the enemy occupied in the evening [of 15 September], and which they had in their possession for only a few hours, we found that they had already planted an observation post for an NCO of the artillery, complete with periscope and telephone.'[16]

The German front-line troops were scarcely aware of the British advances in artillery survey, but they repeatedly recorded their astonishment at the precision with which the British could bring their fire to bear. An officer 'observed ... with silent admiration how they were shooting up our communication trenches with 75 mm [18-pounder] shells. The pieces were being pointed with amazing exactitude. Each shell cracked ten metres in front of the last, and every one just over the trenches.'[17] The entrances to dugouts were identified and blown in as a matter of routine. 'The British would casually throw in gas shells in this orgy of destruction', and the 95th Regiment recorded on 12 November how 'two heavy shells shattered the entrance of a dugout not far from the regimental quarters. Of the occupants, just one half-conscious individual was able to work his way out through the greenish-yellow cloud, and there was no saving the nine others.'[18]

The British artillery kept the German rear areas under constant harassing bombardment. In the German experience the French fire at Verdun as a whole was heavier, 'but there was a difference in the way with which the rearward communications and accommodation on the Somme were subject to interdiction fire to a considerably greater depth and with a gigantic expenditure of ammunition. Here the British also made particular use of long-barrelled naval guns.'[19] These heavy pieces made some of the villages untenable, and forced the Germans to establish headquarters and batteries in open ground that was devoid of distinguishing landmarks. Such targets invited the use of tear gas shells, as well as those filled with chlorine or phosgene, the intention being to make the locations impossible to use over a length of time. German gunners were issued with only two masks each, which was not long enough to see them through a prolonged gassing.

The one besetting sin of the British interdiction fire was its habit of falling into predictable patterns. 'The British routine seemed to be the same from day to day, and they apparently did not wish to be disturbed. In the mornings and evenings our trenches came under *Trommelfeuer.* Always at the same time. The rearward communications were targeted evening after evening. It was a wonderful sight to see the length of the horizon flare up with the flashes of the countless pieces as they fired. Then we would hear a whistling and sighing in the air above us, followed by the muffled explosions of the shells far to our rear. Two pieces drew our attention by their red muzzle flashes. They were sited immediately behind Auchonvillers.'[20]

As for the detailed targeting, the trenches would be shelled methodically from one end to the other, which permitted the Germans to evacuate the next section that was going to come under fire. In the same way it was possible for German reinforcements to traverse the shrapnel-strewn zone of the communication trenches with minimal cost.[21] In contrast with the rigidity of the British interdictions, the French batteries were 'deployed more artistically'. They varied their targets more frequently, and were clever at bringing sudden and unexpected concentrations of fire to bear.[22] Perhaps comments like these were not altogether fair to the British gunners, for predictable routines of fire could be 'a form of ritualised aggression fully compatible with [the convention] of live and let live'.[23]

Counter-battery fire was usually the work of the 4.5-inch howitzers, the 60-pounders and the heavier calibres, and the Germans could see for themselves that this branch of gunnery was in a state of constant evolution. The 4.5-inch howitzers were out-ranged by the German 120 mm howitzers, if not by the 105 mm version, and by the middle of October the losses among the forward batteries were persuading the British to place a greater reliance on the longer-reaching pieces.[24] One month later the German batteries along the Ancre were being taken under a particularly destructive fire, and it seemed to the Germans that the British had learned the lessons of month after month of combat and were applying them to beat down the German gun positions one after another.

Fire of every kind intensified during the days of bombardment which led up to a *Grosskampftag.* All calibres of guns and howitzers were called in for this work, with the 18-pounder field gun being assigned the vital task of cutting wire by its low-bursting shrapnel. This kind of work was cumulative, but the effect of artillery on the enemy troops and weapons was related not so much to the weight of shell over the duration of the bombardment as to the intensity of fire within a given span of time. When the German 55th Field Artillery Regiment returned to the Somme in the autumn 'we very soon ... noticed something new. In August, when a major attack was impending, we had frequently lain under a preparatory fire for several days and nights on end. But now it was clear that the enemy were trying to concentrate their destructive fire more tightly in terms of time, and to bring it to a still higher intensity in the chosen period.'[25]

The impact of the preparatory bombardment was monitored closely by the Royal Flying Corps and the observers of the Royal Artillery, and from 15 September onwards the British 'utilised pauses in this fire to keep pushing forward larger or smaller parties of infantry to sound out the defensibility of our forward positions. As soon as a weakening could be identified they would send their infantry into the attack.' Another new technique was to combine *Trommelfeuer* along a wide frontage with heavy local concentrations designed to smash holes in chosen sectors, so enabling the infantry to exploit the gaps and take the defenders of nearby sectors from the rear.[26]

Once the British infantry went over the top they received more and more help from the 'creeping barrage', a curtain of shells that descended ahead of them by bounds of 150 yards or less, and gave the Somme battle-scape its characteristic appearance. Charles Carrington remembered having seen the Durham Light Infantry attack the Butte de Warlencourt on 13 November, and commented that 'battles in the First War were rarely spectacular, since the shrapnel obscured visibility. A great noise and a smoke-filled cloud filled the valley in which now and then one saw distant figures moving, aimlessly it seemed, like ants on a disturbed anthill [the same image occurred to the Germans]. I am sure I saw them swarming over the lower slopes of the Butte de Warlencourt which I'm sorry to say they did not capture.'[27]

The practice varied from one division's artillery to the next, but in general high explosive began to replace shrapnel, the bounds became shorter, and the fire dwelt longer on each bound. Unmistakable descriptions of the barrage appear in the German histories and memoirs, and the

Germans recognised that when the line of shells moved to the rear of the outlying positions the British infantry was almost upon them, and that it was time to win the 'race to the parapet' or at least to the lip of the shell-hole. Gallwitz observed as a curiosity that between 20 and 22 August the British 'screened their advances at High Wood by firing little bombs eighty to a hundred metres to their front, which then took fire and spread dense clouds of smoke'.[28] It is doubtful whether the Germans grasped the essential principles of the technique. Not all the Germans understood that the timing and the spatial intervals of the bounds of the creeping barrage were determined in advance, and at the battle of Flers-Courcelette they attributed the progression to the aircraft following the progress of the attacking infantry.[29]

The further the assault progressed, the more difficult it inevitably became to co-ordinate the action of the British artillery and foot soldiers. British troops repeatedly came under fire from their own guns, but something of the kind has occurred ever since artillery has been invented, and on the Somme in 1916 the inter-working of the British arms was far better than anything achieved by the enemy. German officers saw how the advances were signalled to observers by flags or lamps, and commented ruefully that there was a lack of any kind of communication to their own batteries.[30] Thus a body of German infantry could find itself under fire from the same German battery for days on end and have no means of transmitting its displeasure.

In this, as in so much else, the Germans registered an advance in British effectiveness. 'We must note the technical skill with which the British have on several occasions widened their break-ins – evidently after having satisfied themselves completely as to the depth and extent. They then bring down an accurate fire of heavy pieces on the adjacent German lines, destroying them and forcing the defenders to one side, after which the British establish themselves in the sectors of trench which have been shot-up or abandoned.'[31] When German units tried to recover the lost ground they were likely to be spotted from aircraft or observation balloons, and 'magnificently directed artillery fire would inflict appalling and almost instantaneous losses upon them ... they would continue to advance with whatever troops were left, or they would not advance at all'.[32]

CHAPTER SIXTEEN

Gas

Gas accounted for a tiny proportion of fatalities on the Western Front, the British losing a 'mere' 1.2 per cent of their 487,004 deaths from this cause, but the sufferings of the victims were horribly evident to eye and ear, and more than any form of killing it seemed to be a matter of subjecting human beings to an industrial process. Gas was objectively useful, oddly enough, on account of the very measures taken to counter its effects, for the gas masks or 'helmets' were stifling, sweaty bags with goggles that were liable to mist over, and while they might preserve life they degraded every kind of military activity.

The Germans unwisely took the initiative in the business when they released chlorine gas from banks of cylinders to blow over the French and Algerians at Ypres on 22 April 1915. 'Unwisely', because on the northern part of the Western Front the wind favoured the Germans on average for 32 per cent of the days of a year, but the allies for 44 per cent, and nobody in particular for the rest of the time. The first British response was a cylinder-launched chlorine attack at Loos on

25 September 1915. It brought mixed results on this occasion, on account of the light and fitful wind, but the British went on to become enthusiastic gassers and began to surpass the Germans in the quantities of their attacks. To the enemy, the British gas looked like an accumulation of white vapour or an advancing white wall, which then caused the birds to fall dead from the sky, withered fruits and leaves, left the ground and the bottom of the trenches strewn with dead moles, mice and snails, turned rifles a rusty red, and coated shell splinters and bare steel with a green patina.

The Germans regained the technical lead in December 1915, when they began to deploy di-phosgene, which was by itself about six times more toxic than chlorine, and more likely to be inhaled by the intended victims, for it caused little or no irritation and struck only several hours later. A little of the highly volatile chlorine was added to the heavy phosgene to help it to disperse, and both gases worked by filling the lungs with plasma from the blood.

By now the British were taking anti-gas precautions seriously. In the middle of November they began to issue the pig-snouted P Mask, followed by the improved though 'hideous' and 'vile-smelling'[1] PH model in January 1916. The Germans were impressed by the rigour of the countermeasures among the British, 'where great emphasis is put on ... meticulous obedience to the precautions in force'.[2] Every item of anti-gas equipment was inspected daily, and the practice alerts were taken every bit as seriously as the genuine alarms. Prisoners from a New South Wales battalion explained that 'before the battalion went into the line they were trained by being placed in a trench, and gas blown towards them in a whitish-green cloud. A number of the men had not put their masks on properly and were affected by the gas, though they recovered very quickly.' A German officer commented that this was 'an excellent idea'.[3]

Some casualties were inevitable, in spite of every precaution. Corporal P. J. Jones of the 8/Royal Dublin Fusiliers told the Germans that the 16th Division had had a useful warning of a gas attack early on 28 April 1916, for deserters had betrayed what the Germans had in mind, and at five the troops could hear the gas as it was being released from the cylinders a good three minutes before it reached the trenches. Jones testified that 'the gas masks are very good ... The front-line troops and the reserves were at once ready for action, and the whole sector was prepared to meet an enemy attack. After every gas attack the trenches are sprayed with a chemical solution, and once the men have survived an attack of this kind they have more faith in the precautionary measures and are not so nervous on the next occasion. But it is a terrible thing to die from gas. I had a very bad time, because my mask had been damaged, and I would have died if I had not been taken prisoner as soon as I was ... After attacks like that the dead are collected and buried very deep.'[4]

A dedicated branch of the Royal Engineers, the blandly named Special Brigade, came into being in May 1916 to manage this new branch of warfare, and on 26 and 27 June a cylinder attack on a mass scale was integrated into the process of softening up the German defences before the opening of the Battle of the Somme. Afterwards the British and German investigations reached the same general conclusion, that the gas had had little effect against troops who had put on their masks in time. However, the German report added the significant rider that the British had released their gas under particularly unfavourable conditions of weather, 'and the result was that our troops began to underestimate the effects of the enemy gas. Later on the enemy launched smaller attacks in suitable weather, and the same units now suffered, which can be attributed in part to carelessness.'[5]

Cylinder gas attacks were already falling out of favour among the Germans, 'because ... we had insufficient quantities available, and because the release became impossible in the prevailing wind'.[6] The Germans staged their last attack of the kind (in Flanders) on 8 August. A strike with shells filled with liquid gas could be delivered with far greater precision, was affected much less by the weather conditions, and it had, moreover, a better chance of taking the enemy by surprise, for the shells could so easily be mistaken for duds. The Germans employed 'Green Cross' (*Grünkreuz*) shells filled with di-phosgene against the French in June, and similar attacks against the British followed in July, August and September, and caused at least 2,800 casualties.

The British were inevitably spurred on to reply. Their formulation of phosgene was marginally more lethal than the German di-phosgene, and by German accounts it smelt not unattractively of mature hay or ripe fruit, which gave rise to the rumour that it was deliberately designed to encourage the enemy to savour the aroma. Batteries became a favourite target, along with crossroads and villages. In such a way a strafe by gas shells caught the 15th Reserve Regiment by surprise in Martinpuich just after midnight on 22 August. 'Upon impact the shells made a dull thud and threw up a cloud of dust from the dry ground. "Duds, unless I'm mistaken," commented Captain von Forstner at the exit of the dugout. But Corporal Kasprzak called out to him: "Gas! Put on your mask straight away, Captain!" "But you don't have one yourself!" "Yes, but I'm a miner and used to gas. I'll just smoke a cigar" … we were being treated to a gas attack with deadly phosgene, a new enemy. All the companies except the 3rd were fortunate enough to pass through the village later on or by-passed it altogether. Most of our men experienced no discomfort from the ripe, mephitic smell of the gas, and they just wanted to get out of the zone as quickly as they could. But that was the devilish thing about it, because they now took the gas into their labouring lungs.' Sixty-five men of the 3rd Company were killed or disabled.[7]

For closer-range work the British began to employ mortar bombs or Captain F. H. Livens' projector, which was an array of tubes that were embedded in the ground in rows, and fired large phosgene-filled bombs up to 1,375 or 1,700 yards, depending on the version. The tubes took a lot of setting up, but they had the capacity to dump large quantities of gas on unsuspecting Germans before they had time to put on their masks. The first use of the Livens projector was at Beaumont Hamel on 28/29 October, and it was to be employed on a mass scale at Arras on 9 April 1917.

CHAPTER SEVENTEEN

The Tank

To Germans of a philosophical turn of mind the arrival of the tank on 15 September 1916 appeared to be a further episode in the 'ever-lasting and gigantic contest between Germanic manpower and Anglo-French technology'.[1] Where the tanks succeeded in getting into action on that day they came as a total surprise. By a British intelligence assessment 'prisoners ... appeared to be terror-stricken by it. They said they had never seen anything like it, it was not war but bloody butchery. A machine-gunner says he fired frantically at one, but could see nothing but blue and red sparks. One tank got astride their trench enfilading it both ways, and prisoners said there was no getting away from it.'[2]

It was natural to suppose that the initial shock would wear off, and on 28 September Captain Weber of the German military intelligence would commit himself no further than venturing the opinion that 'only time will tell whether this new weapon will have the success which the enemy expect from it'.[3] More than a month after the epoch-making 15 September the machine still retained its power to shock troops who had never experienced its impact at first hand,[4] but towards the end of the year German military intelligence registered that 'the original enthusiasm of the [British] soldiers … has abated, after they have seen that the tanks can be employed successfully only under unusually favourable conditions. All the same they still hope that the experiences up to date will bring about improvements, and especially – as they believe – the Germans will be unable in the near future to build anything of the kind or to devise effective countermeasures.'[5] Only through the mass tank attack at Cambrai on 20 November 1917 were the Germans convinced of the true capabilities of the weapon.[6]

It had not taken the Germans long to grasp the essentials of the British armoured doctrine. As early as 5 October 1916 the headquarters of the Sixth Army was able to circulate the following:

The British seem to intend to hold a great number of these vehicles in readiness in concealed positions behind the sector of attack, and employ them to support and accompany the assault directly. So far they have been unable to bring forward more than two or three machines at the same time. Some of them drive immediately behind the first wave of infantry, and support it by the overhead fire of their machine guns; others actually go out ahead of the infantry, who come up smartly behind in dense columns. The machines then halt near our first line, and spray it with rapid fire.

If a gap opens in our line somewhere or other, the vehicles will exploit it most skilfully in order to break through. A number of the machines drive along behind the intact sectors of our line and shoot the defenders down from the rear. Others exploit in the greatest depth possible, and are fond of making for our command posts, observation posts and batteries. They have put several of our battalion headquarters out of action, which made it very difficult for us to direct the combat.

When a larger number of tanks, acting simultaneously, have effected a wider breach, it is also clear that the British have intended to throw cavalry into the gap.

The vehicles have in fact brought the British a number of successes. But this is to be attributed mainly to surprise. Every new technical device brings with it an element of the unfamiliar, and it is the same here. At first our troops were inclined to discount or laugh at the giants as they crept forward. But when they came nearer with apparent impunity the result in some places has been a panic.[7]

ON 21 OCTOBER THE headquarters of Crown Prince Rupprecht's army group added that 'a number of the tanks are brought forward as far as possible under the cover of darkness or fog. From these positions, as soon as the light allows, they plunge into the battle directly, or at least after having only a short distance to cover before coming into action … In spite of their size their dirty grey paint renders them almost invisible in dull weather and at long distances.'[8]

Again, the Germans were very soon informed as to how the 'Heavy Section of the Machine Gun Corps' was formed, trained and brought into action. A prisoner told them that at Thetford in Norfolk 'the machine was tested and approved, but oddly enough never across ground like the terrain which it had to cross just recently south of Flers. He reckoned that the speed was one English mile per hour. The noise, fumes and heat were very considerable. To use his own expression, passing over uneven ground made it a "dreadful" journey ("Common sense ought to tell anybody that it is rot!").'[9] Much detail was also forthcoming about the shipping to French ports, the loading-up of the tanks on rail cars, and the protracted and sometimes difficult journey across northern France and the unloading at the far end.

When the Germans knew so much, it almost defies belief that for many weeks after 15 September they were uncertain as to what tanks actually looked like. It was natural for the British to assume that the enemy were much better informed on this point than they really were. Towards the end of November the chief censor Sir Frank Swettenham told Haig that he was worried that the press reports of the tank might be of use to the Germans, but Haig reassured him that there could be little that they did not know already. By the account of his chief of intelligence, John Charteris, 'one of these was for several hours in German hands, and we knew that it was examined and parts of its fittings taken away. Several more are lying out of action in full view of the Germans. Full information has also already been given in French newspapers, far more than any we have published.'[10]

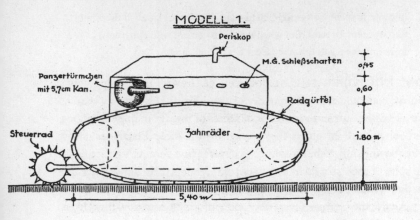

MODELL 1.

Periskop

M.G. Schließscharten

Panzertürmchen
mit 5,7 cm Kan.

Radgürtel

Steuerrad

Zahnräder

0,45

0,60

1,80 m

5,40 m

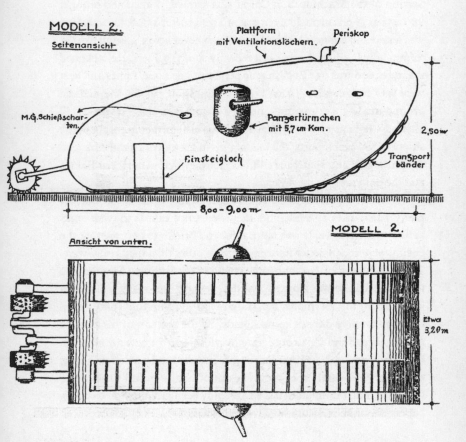

MODELL 2.

Seitenansicht

Plattform
mit Ventilationslöchern.

Periskop

M.G.Schießschar-
ten.

Panzertürmchen
mit 5,7 cm Kan.

Einsteigloch

Transport
bänder

2,50 m

8,00 - 9,00 m

MODELL 2.

Ansicht von unten.

Etwa
3,20 m

MODELL 3.

Seitenansicht.

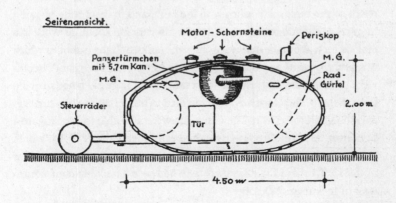

Motor - Schornsteine

Periskop

Panzertürmchen
mit 5,7 cm Kan.

M.G.

M.G.

Rad -
Gürtel

Steuerräder

Tür

2,00 m

4.50 m

Vorderansicht   ### Hinteransicht.

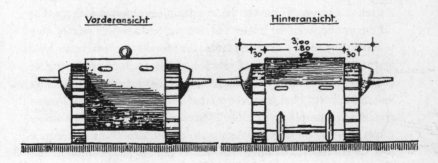

3,00
7.80

30   30

MODELL 4.

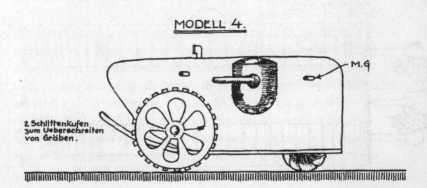

M.G

2 Schlittenkufen
zum Ueberschreiten
von Gräben.

Some of the earliest descriptions had been the best. One such was furnished by one of the first captured crewmen. 'He had escaped unhurt from a tank which had exploded; for days he trembled and shook as a result of the nightmare journey in the tank, and in this frame of mind he gave, going into the minutest details, information about his work in a tank factory, about the construction of the tanks, and the extent to which this new engine of war was being manufactured ... The sergeant's details were so complete that a model of a tank could have been constructed from them.'[11] The Germans were inclined to think that the information was too good to be true. The Germans were also able to interrogate a soldier of the 14th Division, who had examined Court's D-14, which had blown up north of Flers on 16 September,[12] and a talkative sergeant of the 13/Durham Light Infantry who had seen a tank in action south-west of le Sars on 7 October.[13]

With all these advantages, the Germans were unable to distinguish the reliable accounts from the wilder imaginings reported to them. The differences between the 'male' and 'female' tanks, which related only to armament, seem to have implanted the idea that there were multiple and radically different types of vehicles, and the seeds of a most terrible confusion were sown by a German officer who had seen one of the tanks wrecked north of Flers, and believed that it was driven by a great 2-metre wide single caterpillar track. On 28 September the intelligence officer Captain Weber included the details along with a much more accurate description and had to admit that 'we are still not in a position to give an authoritative and clear picture of the construction of these vehicles, which come in several models. There is particular variance between the descriptions of the size.'[14]

Another red herring or startled hare must be laid to the account of NCO Tauscher of the 104th Regiment, who had witnessed the execution wrought by a tank on 18 October. He described the machine as having a skid and two large cogged wheels towards the front, and a single wheel set with shovels at the back. His monster looked like a beast from the margin of a medieval manuscript, but this too was forwarded by Captain Weber and was duly circulated on 21 October. Towards the end of the month the headquarters of the Sixth Army confessed that it was as baffled as ever. 'There are just too many discrepancies between the reports and sketches furnished by the eyewitnesses. There is even word of a vehicle with trailers ... It has not been possible to establish the length of the runners which go around the front wheels and come into action when the machine crosses shell-holes.'[15] On 15 November the Germans believed that they had identified four different models, one of them still derived from Tauscher's monster. Most probably the various fantasies derived from genuine sightings of destroyed tanks whose anatomies had been rearranged in drastic ways by German artillery or British 'dropshorts'.

Hard experience began to tell the Germans what weapons might be of some avail against the tanks. German infantry swarmed out like bees when a tank got stuck near Thiepval on 28 September, and 'although the covered batteries of the vehicle showered them with bullets, they tried with the strength of desperation to storm the armoured fort and kill its crew. Defying the continuous machine-gun fire they hauled one another up and climbed onto the roof. They were evidently hoping to find some gaps or cracks in the monster's armour, but they might as well have been attacking a battleship with spades.'[16]

Rifle fire was found to be useless, and so was machine-gun fire, except possibly when concentrated on a single spot with armour-piercing S.m.K. rounds, which was probably the ammunition that compelled C-20 and C-22 to withdraw from the fight on 15 September. On 5 October Crown Prince Rupprecht was inspecting two regiments of the IV Corps when a lieutenant told him how 'a British armoured vehicle was coming on at the speed of a running man and a panic broke out among his troops. He calmed them down by shouting out: "There are only six men inside!" [There were actually eight.] At this call the troops rallied and threw hand grenades, one of which exploded under the vehicle, which then drove slowly back and halted at a distance of 300 metres. Not long afterwards they saw a large cloud of smoke ... The petrol tank had evidently exploded.'[17] The reference is possibly to Arnold's C-14 on 15 September.

The weight of opinion nevertheless held that individual hand grenades were ineffective, and an instruction of 29 October maintained that the best way to put a sufficiently powerful charge together was to set six grenade heads in a star around a central grenade with an intact stick;

the heads of all the grenades were seated on a circular board, and were bound to the board and to each other by wire. This heroic device was supposed to be heaved against the tracks, but the document continued with the despairing counsel that 'ultimately the infantry must be trained in the belief that, even if they are defenceless against the vehicles for a few moments, they can protect themselves by lying still, whereas flight signifies certain destruction'. By a process of elimination 'artillery is therefore the weapon to be used against the vehicles, for they advance slowly and make good targets.'[18] Even then the Germans distrusted the effect of a piece of anything less than 60 mm calibre firing in low trajectory, and the gun still had to be hauled out of its pit and expose itself in the open ground.

The Germans as yet gave little consideration to anti-tank defence of the passive kind. Roads might be secured against what would now be called a 'thunder run' by felling wayside trees and establishing barricades, though anti-tank ditches as such do not seem to have been specified. Mines were rejected, because they would interfere with the movement of one's own troops, and were certain to be touched off prematurely by artillery fire. If the British had invented tanks, the Germans were now in the process of inventing anti-tank warfare.

CHAPTER EIGHTEEN

The Royal Flying Corps

THE SWING OF THE PENDULUM

It is both tempting and misleading to describe the place of airpower in the Battle of the Somme in terms of the 'knights of the air'. Except in a figurative sense nobody can 'command' the air any more completely than they can command the sea, and in any case the sole benefit of dominance is the use to which such an advantage can be put. Individual daring and skill could still determine the issue of aerial combat in 1916, but this year is the first in which it is proper to speak of 'air forces' in the collective sense, and that had more to do with machines, organisation and doctrine.

In large part gaining of air superiority, relative though it might be, depended on the technology available. From July 1915 until the spring of 1916 the Germans dominated the skies through their Fokker E I ('E' standing for *eindecker*, monoplane), an aircraft which was unique in its time in being equipped with Anton Fokker's interrupter gear, which linked the revolutions of the engine with the firing mechanism of its fixed machine gun, and gave the weapon a clear shot through the revolving propeller. On 8 April 1916 a German Fokker pilot misidentified the junction of a road with the la Bassée Canal, and flew the wrong way along the canal until he ran out of fuel and made a forced landing at Renescure. The machine itself proved to be unremarkable, for it was a straightforward copy of the French Morane-Saulnier Type L Parasol, and a captured British pilot later told the Germans that the Fokker was 'a very poor machine, difficult to fly. A British pilot had flown it and found it an unsatisfactory experience.'[1]

The Fokker's chief British opponent, or rather victim, was the general-purpose two-seater BE2 C biplane. Shot-down pilots and observers told the Germans early in 1916 that 'five months ago the machines were state of the art, but they have now fallen behind the times'.[2] The BE2 C was actually too stable to lend itself to sudden manoeuvres, which was a great disadvantage in a combat plane, and was embarrassed by an awkward arrangement of its machine guns. There were three pivots, 'one each to left and right front of the observer, and one behind him, though never more than two guns were carried, one to his front and one to his rear. If the plane is flying by itself, it carries the forward machine gun on the left-hand side, but if it forms part of a squadron the gun is placed on [whatever is] the outer side, and therefore depends on the aircraft's assigned place in the squadron. It is said to be virtually impossible to change the place during the flight. The rearward machine gun has the better field of fire, for it is not obstructed by the propeller. The forward machine gun, according to all the planes which the prisoner has seen, has to fire clear of the propeller, which is painted white so as to make its whole circumference visible. The prisoner has never heard of firing through the propeller.'[3]

Lawrence Wingfield was shot down in such a machine as late as 1 July 1916 and retrieved by the Germans. 'I asked what they proposed to do with my aeroplane and was informed that the 2 C was considered so ancient and at the same time a survival of such historical interest that it would be handed over to the proper authorities for exhibition in a museum in Berlin.'[4]

A companion of the BE2 C in misfortune at this time was the Vickers FE DD. Second Lieutenant Sydney Littlewood and his observer Captain

D. Lyall Grant had scarcely the time to become acquainted with the aircraft before they were shot down on 1 June. They believed that their plane was capable of reaching eighty miles per hour and (over-optimistically) that it could climb to more than 9,000 feet in twenty-five minutes, 'and there are several machines of the same type in the park at Farnborough. They will be flown across here shortly.'[5] However, there were persistent criticisms of the Rolls-Royce engine as being under-powered, and the FE DD was believed to be 'unsuitable for combat on account of its poor rate of climb and inadequate armament'.[6]

The British began to claw back the advantage when the grand battle approached. They admitted that 'they would not get around very quickly to the secret of shooting through the propeller, as in England they are "damned slow" about such things'.[7] As the British indeed still had no means of firing through a forward-mounted propeller, except by armouring it with deflector plates, they resorted to the crude expedient of mounting the engine and propeller to the rear of the pilot in a 'pusher' conformation. The result was represented by two machines, the FE2 B and the DH 2, which looked as if they hailed from a much earlier stage in the history of aviation. The fuselage was reduced to a pod, and the detached tail was supported by two sets of struts that splayed out widely to the two wings to give plenty of space for the propeller. Neither machine was designed specifically to counter the Fokker monoplane, but they became available at a time that was particularly convenient for the Royal Flying Corps.

The general-purpose FE2 B carried a pilot and an observer, the latter operating a pivot-mounted Lewis gun from his place in the forward nacelle. The large Beardmore engine restricted the view to the rear, but 'an excellent field of fire from the front made them quite potent fighters. Indeed ... the FEs were famous for their follow-my-leader tactics ... each plane circling in formation and able to contribute accurate fire from his quarters while depending on its fellows to protect its rear.'[8] Shortly before his death Boelcke noted concerning this machine and the FE2 D 'Good field of fire forwards, sideways and upwards, blanketed only by the pusher propeller. Attack from behind on same level or slightly below ... Both ... can take a lot of punishment because the crew are shielded by the engine.'[9]

The De Havilland DH 2, similar in general appearance to the

FE2 B, was a dedicated single-seater 'scout' (fighter), a fragile-looking but sturdy machine. Its forward-mounted Lewis gun was capable of a limited traverse.

The British ascendancy was consolidated by some capable aircraft of conventional 'tractor' conformation. The two-seater Sopwith 1½ Strutter was powered by a 110 hp Clerget rotary engine, which gave the machine a claimed speed of up to 105 mph, though a downed pilot told the Germans that 'there are said to have been repeated accidents in steep dives. The pilot says that he knows of four such cases.'[10] More importantly, the Strutter was the first British aircraft to be equipped with interrupter gear to fire through the propeller.

Most of the French-built 'saucy little'[11] Nieuport scouts were hogged by the Royal Naval Air Service, but captured pilots of the Royal Flying Corps were enthusiastic in the machine's praise. 'The 120 hp Nieuports are now by general consent far superior to the Fokkers. They have a speed of 100 English miles per hour, and can climb to 10,000 English feet in nine and a quarter minutes. They have in addition the same advantage of the fixed forward-mounted machine gun.'[12] The opinion of the RFC was confirmed by a German pilot, who testified that it was 'easily the best' of the machines available to the British.[13] According to Boelcke the Nieuport was 'very manoeuvrable and fast. Armament and firepower as in German single-seaters. Tends to lose height in combat, especially up high. Get on its tail, preferably at short range.'[14]

The big 120 hp Beardmore engine reappeared in the British-built Martinsyde Elephant. Opinion among the pilots was divided. Some ranked it with the Nieuport. Another encountered 'a frightful struggle' to force the machine up to 8,000 feet,[15] while the lieutenants G. E. Maxwell and A. Cairnduff informed the Germans that 'their squadron has had a great many accidents with them, and sometimes so many that their squadron had only one machine capable of flying'.[16]

The impact of the new British machines was cumulative, and the downfall of the Fokker monoplane was symbolised on 18 June 1916 when Lieutenant MacCubbin in his FE2 B shot down the ace Lieutenant Max Immelmann. Less than a month later another British pilot found himself a guest of the Germans. His first interrogator 'seemed a very nice fellow, and was full of praise for the audacity of the RFC and was most interested to learn that Long (my observer) had dropped the wreath for Immelmann. This wreath had been dropped on a German aerodrome a few days before, as a token of respect which the RFC felt for a great pilot.'[17]

The cult of the ace was proving dangerous for the Germans in more ways than one. The hero was almost inevitably doomed, unless taken out of active service, and it was no coincidence that Immelmann's associate Oswald Boelcke was almost immediately whisked away to make a tour of the Balkans. More significantly, the adulation of the skyborne warriors distracted attention from what the exercise of airpower was all about. At the epoch-making conference at Cambrai on 8 September Ludendorff argued that 'artillery and flyers must be brought closer together. A combat high in the skies brings them the prospect of high decorations and mentions in dispatches, and has become more attractive and splendid in their eyes than the business of observing for the artillery, which we have not got at all right. An understanding of the high importance of artillery spotting is something which can be awakened only over the course of time.'[18]

The British superiority in the air in the middle of 1916 would therefore have counted for far less if Brigadier General Hugh Trenchard, commander of the RFC since August 1915, had not been dedicated to the support of the ground forces to the best of his powers. He was an enemy of the cult of the individual, and General Sir Hubert Gough wrote in the same vein that 'the adoption of a system of "star turns", of "aces" in the air, or of "Storm Troops" on the ground, may lead to some brilliant exploits, but it is a wrong system ... and it does not maintain a high average sense of duty and efficiency'.[19]

Utilising the greater numbers of aircraft at his disposal in 1916, Trenchard combined squadrons under the command of wings, and wings in their turn into ground-assigned 'brigades'. As early as May the RFC was implementing 'a policy of relentless and incessant offensive'[20] by compact formations, which before long were dominating the space above the German lines and rear. The German forces did not attempt to contest British airspace, and wasted their resources in an attempt to set up an 'air barrier' (*Luftsperre*).

The contrast became all too evident to the Germans on the ground.

Scarcely had the sun conquered the mist than the British aircraft made their appearance – six, eight, a whole dozen at a time. Like buzzards who had fixed on their prey, they cruised ceaselessly and almost at ground level above our trenches and shell-holes. They experienced no disturbance from our anti-aircraft guns or our air forces. There was something sinister about the buzzing of their engines, and more sinister still were the peculiar signals by which they communicated with their artillery. They swooped down to within 200 metres, seeking out every strongpoint, every machine gun, and fastening on the least movement … The men holding the trenches were like mice, pressing themselves into funk-holes, or crouching at the bottom of the trenches.[21]

Medical officers reported that men were being shot through literally from head to toe, and some of the planes were descending so low that the Germans could smell the exhaust fumes, and were persuaded that the British were reading the regimental numbers on their shoulder straps. Any attempt to answer by rifle or machine gun was certain to draw down a hellish fire.

In such a way the British exercised a near-total mastery of the air for the opening ten weeks of the Battle of the Somme. On 15 September, the day of the Battle of Flers-Courcelette, a Bavarian regiment reported 'they were performing downright brilliantly, as all our men had to admit. They were flying at 50 or 100 metres above our trenches, and directing artillery fire onto individuals. Nothing was being done on our side to interrupt them, and they could observe our every movement at their leisure.'[22]

The British domination was over in a matter of days. On 19 September the attention of German anti-aircraft gunners at Achiet-le-Petit was drawn to the east by the sound of engines. 'Over there, where the blue of the sky was becoming lighter, there appeared silhouettes of aircraft … silver-grey, short, stubby … they were coming up at speed, bigger and bigger, in compact battle array. Seven machines in a formation, led by the commander's plane which was distinguished by a long streamer, while the other six were echeloned back on either side.' The leading aircraft drove a British machine almost down to ground level before finishing it off with a short burst of fire. More and more planes were being fed into the combat by both sides, and soon more than sixty were wheeling in the sky, which was 'filled with the humming of the British rotary engines, the growling of their German counterparts, the tick-tack and roar of the machine guns. Phosphorous rounds ... were describing vicious grey streaks across the blue of the sky. Here and there burning machines were falling among fumes and smoke. Others, out of control, were just clumsy lumps plunging earthward.'[23] The battle ended with the British making back towards their lines.

The suddenness of the thing was deceptive, for the Germans had been busy reorganising their relevant forces since 4 July. The air wing and the anti-aircraft artillery now had a common telephone network, and each army division was supported by an air squadron (*Flieger-Abteilung*) specifically for artillery observation, with a protecting *Kampfstaffel*. 'The maintaining of a defensive air barrier, which had led only to the dispersal of our own forces, was now forbidden. In contrast, all pilots were duty-bound to carry the attack across the enemy lines to gain the upper hand in aerial observation and reconnaissance.'[24] Specialised roaming *Jagdstaffeln* had the main role in the battle for airspace, and of these the most famous was *Jasta* 2, set up at Bertincourt by Boelcke after he returned from his Balkan tour on 27 August.

A trio of new aircraft was now at the Germans' disposal, namely the Fokker DII, the Halberstadt DII, and the streamlined Albatros D of which *Jasta* 2 took delivery on 16 September (the 'D' standing for *Doppeldecker*, biplane). Machines of all kinds were now available in greater numbers for the Somme, now that the Germans had closed down offensive operations at Verdun. On 21 September the Badeners of the 239th Reserve Regiment saw that the process of beating down the British and French air forces was now in full train. 'On that morning half a dozen of the British and French were eliminated in very short order. One hour after Boelcke's planes appeared in the sky not a single enemy aircraft was to be seen over our lines on the sector from Combles by way of Morval to Lesboeufs.'[25]

The business extended into October. A downed British pilot told the Germans 'how he and his comrades were taken by surprise by Boelcke's intervention ... which was not a particularly happy experience. All the same this young sportsman in his pilot's uniform was very glad to have matched himself against an enemy who excelled the British in the very skills in which they took such pride, and who showed an aggression which they could only envy. This slight, wiry little lieutenant became quite excited when he talked about it.'[26] As for the all-important impact on the ground, the German infantry noticed that 'German airmen were once more in evidence, which was a great boost to our morale'.[27]

Boelcke himself did not outlive the month. On 28 October his squadron was engaged against two De Havillands, and he crashed into the positions of the 181st Regiment.[28] His last flight was seen from the position of the 104th Regiment, here described in language typical of a peculiarly German cult of airborne death:

> When his *Jagdstaffel* was embroiled in a major dogfight his aircraft happened to be brushed by one of his comrades. He broke away from his squadron and entered into a steep but steady dive. When his plane approached the Bapaume–le Sars road we all hoped that this intrepid leader would be able to effect a smooth landing on open ground. But then the wings broke off [a besetting sin of the Albatros] and the fuselage crashed into the ground, burying its pilot beneath it. At that very moment the evening sun broke victoriously through the veils of haze and smoke … and its rays bore the soul of this beloved of God up to Valhalla.[29]

Boelcke's death underlined how fragile the command of the air could be. There is a tendency to assume that the new period of German domination extended without a break until its apogee in Britain's 'Bloody April' in 1917, but we are presented with a clear contradiction with the perspective of the German ground forces, who speak with near unanimity about a British resurgence in the late autumn and early winter of 1916. The crucial evidence comes from regiments returning to the Somme after spells on other fronts. Thus the German 107th Reserve Regiment had the unwelcome experience of being engaged at Pys and Courcelette in the period from 24 October to 19 November, when 'the pronounced superiority of the enemy in the matter of aircraft and captive balloons was more unpleasant than it had been when we were on the Barleux sector of the Somme'.[30] There were many other testimonies of the same kind.

The reasons are not easy to identify. They certainly had nothing to do with any decisive improvement in the allied aircraft, which was not evident until May the next year. The explanation may lie in a more deeply ingrained offensive doctrine among the allied forces, a greater willingness to fly in adverse conditions, the fact that the *Jagdstaffeln* came and went as 'guest artists' (rather like the Storm Troops on the ground), or a continuing unwillingness of the German air forces to engage in ground support. At no stage in the Battle of the Somme did the British troops have to endure punishment of the same kind that the RFC was inflicting on the Germans.

THE RFC IN GERMAN PERSPECTIVE

The Germans learned that the British parcelled out sectors of their front to assigned 'wings', which comprised a greater or lesser number of 'squadrons' according to the importance of the sector, though two or three seemed to be the norm. 'As a general rule each squadron has a specialised role and accordingly consists of aircraft of the same type. In such a way No. 8 Squadron has machines for artillery observation; on occasion, however, it executes general-purpose reconnaissance flights in the enemy deep rear and provides both the reconnaissance planes and the escorts. Other squadrons are primarily for combat and are made up entirely of "fighting machines", mostly Vickers.'[31] Becoming bolder in May, the British began to employ full-scale offensive operations by formations of scouts, the equivalent of the later German *Jagdstaffeln*. The squadron in turn held between twelve and fourteen aircraft, increasingly of a uniform type, as just indicated.

The Germans learned that 'almost all reconnaissance missions are couched in very general terms – establishing rail and road traffic (which are the most important indicators for a coming offensive), identification of new positions, and so on. The British ground commanders set great store by long-range reconnaissance, but the aviators themselves are much less convinced, for they have to fly too high to be able to make out any detail. In any case the German rail traffic is heaviest during the night, as is also the case with the British.'[32]

The sometimes delicate relations between the pilot and observer were familiar to the Germans in general from the experience of their own air forces. Lieutenant W. Black, an observer in No. 11 Squadron, was shot down on 20 October 1916. He was careful to explain to the Germans that it should not have happened, for his real pilot was a Lieutenant Harvey. But he made his last flight with another pilot, and the others prophesied that neither of them would come back, for the new man was too reckless.'[33]

Other tensions were of particular interest to the Germans. 'Very often the sorties are made when the weather is bad and even when the visibility is virtually nil, just to counter the objections of the General Staff that the flying arm is not doing enough. The commanders of the ground forces leave the weather conditions entirely out of account when they give their orders. The flyers believe that night sorties are generally useless, and they should be ruled out for the British in France.'[34]

The British squadron commander was described to the Germans as being in an unenviable position. He was forbidden to fly over enemy lines, 'and there is a general complaint that the really good flyers are employed as squadron commanders, and therefore divorced from the actual business of flying. In such a way all the best men end up "on the ground".'[35] The desk-bound squadron commander could protest to his wing commander if he considered a particular mission to be unfeasible, but he had no power to cancel it on his own authority, and he then had to pass on the order to such a pilot as Lieutenant C. B. Wilson, who was shot down on a reconnaissance flight on 19 January 1916. To Wilson it was an object lesson in a rigid and dictatorial style of command, 'and the result is that British flyers are often forced to undertake pointless sorties, which accounts for the high rate of recent losses'.[36]

When it came to the detailed purposes of the RFC, the Germans had to concede that the British flyers gave excellent support to the ground forces. 'Every aircraft in a squadron has its assigned place. Just one machine carries out photographic reconnaissance, while the others serve as escorts. High-flying scouts accompany the squadron, and they dive down on any aircraft which might attack it.'[37] Both single- and two-seaters were employed for the photography. German batteries were objects of particular interest, along with machine-gun nests and dugout entrances, and complete photographic coverage was made a duty.

In an aircraft shot down on 23 April 1916 it was found that the plates had to be loaded individually into the camera, and the observer and his pilot spoke very disparagingly about their equipment.[38] Matters seem to have improved by 31 May, for 'the British now have exclusively magazines with eighteen interchangeable plates, and they are very pleased with them'.[39] As soon as the plane had landed, the exposed plates were rushed to the wing commander and thence to the intelligence officers at army headquarters. During the flight the pilot or observer would have been making entries on small map tables, which could be dropped to friendly artillery in a cassette.

Immediate liaison could be effected between air and ground by Morse messages transmitted by the 20-pound Sterling wireless. 'Both pilot and observer are trained in wireless communication. The codes are positioned by each seat. So far they can transmit messages, but not receive them.' Beside the last words a German officer noted: 'It's just the same with us! The noise of the engine makes reception impossible.'[40]

Targets of opportunity could also be designated by flying in circles above the object, bringing it under machine-gun fire, or sounding horns or sirens. The wails put Ernst Jünger 'in mind of the cries of a fabulous creature, hanging pitilessly over the desert'.[41] The artillery's response could arrive with astonishing speed. The German 5th Regiment relates an unsuccessful attack on the part of its I Battalion on 31 August. The troops had crouched in readiness in the shallow trenches, covering themselves with tent canvas in the hope of escaping detection. 'The assaulting companies made their way forward at a crawl, then in a crouch, and finally at the run. Upon this they were detected by an airman who gave the alarm by his machine gun, and scarcely a minute later the first heavy shells landed on the trench exits which had been prepared for the assault.'[42] All of this was in addition to the facility of bringing targets under direct attack by machine-gun fire or bombing.

Specific bombing raids were a specialised form of long-range attack, mounted at the order of the high command. German airfields were a favourite target, along with nodal points of communication like the railway station at Saint-Quentin. In the middle of the afternoon of 1 July two German battalions were about to entrain when British aircraft appeared overhead. 'Only one bomb fell on a shed which was filled with ammunition and caused a big explosion. There were two hundred waggons of ammunition in the station at the time, sixty of them caught fire and exploded; the remainder were saved with difficulty. Those allotted to the transport of the troops and all the equipment which they had placed on the platform were destroyed by fire. The men were panic stricken and fled in every direction. One hundred men of the 71st Reserve Regiment and eighty of II Reserve Jäger Battalion were either killed or wounded.' None of the British aircraft returned to base, but the disruption they had caused to the Germans had been invaluable.[43]

For most of the campaign the British were able to deploy their observation balloons in complete safety, and the Germans had to accustom themselves to the sight of a western horizon that was festooned with these objects, 'from which we believed that the British could recognise and observe individual soldiers or machine guns, and direct artillery fire down on them ... It is true that at the beginning ... we had some balloons in the air as well, but they were all destroyed one by one. The enemy aircraft flew down on them, and released incendiary material which descended like a rain of fire. The balloons took light immediately, and we could see the observers jump out with parachutes.'[44] As early as 25 June the aerial observation of the German XIV Reserve Corps was wiped out when the British downed all its balloons. Even at the end of the year Major General von Lindequist, the commander of the 3rd *Garde* Reserve Division, complained that for every German balloon in the air the British had fifteen.[45]

In descending order, British pilots and observers fell into German hands through three main causes – the action of German aircraft, engine failure and anti-aircraft fire. The British could not agree among themselves how effective that fire was. A second lieutenant remarked that 'it was downright astounding how accurately and speedily our anti-aircraft fire was able to register the altitude of the targeted aircraft. Fourteen days ago his machine was riddled and nearly brought down by our anti-aircraft guns, and he was able to land behind his own lines only with difficulty.'[46] Others were inclined to be dismissive, but all the airmen conceded that a few German batteries shot particularly well, and they singled out a battery behind the Bois de Biez, an anti-aircraft train at Vimy, a battery at Lens, and the 'Professor's Battery' at Fampoux, all of which happened to be located to the north of the Somme battlefront.

In general, Germans shooting at British aircraft seem to have put themselves at more risk than their targets. In September a standing order laid down that 'when enemy aircraft are near the fundamental rule is to lie motionless in the trench or find concealment in the funk-holes. For defence against enemy machines it is expedient to site machine guns in dispersed positions behind the first and second trenches, and have them open fire against exceptionally low-flying aircraft. When parties of infantry in the front line open fire against the planes, they just draw even more artillery fire on themselves.'[47]

On 18 September Captain Hans Jancke arrived at Puisieux-au-Mont with his motorised anti-aircraft artillery from Flanders. Unacquainted with conditions on the Somme, he made the mistake of opening fire against a circling British aircraft. Writing of himself in the third person, he describes how 'the shrapnel ... looked like balls of cotton wool in the early morning. But it did no good. The enemy was not to be driven away ... The British aircraft described a curve, and now through his binoculars the captain could see plainly the wireless antenna as it hung from the aircraft. Artillery registration by aerial observations and correction of the fire by wireless – you can't have anything more modern than that! But this was a period when the new technology did not always work, and the captain hoped that this would now be the case. He was wrong. The impact of the shells came closer and closer, and more and more dangerous.'[48] Jancke gave up the duel and sped away to a site between two field batteries, where the officers made it clear to him that he was not at all welcome, for he would be drawing fire on them as well.

If aircrew came to ground relatively intact, they would at once try to set their machines on fire with matches, and they might well succeed if the petrol tank had been holed already. Lawrence Wingfield did not have the chance, for he discovered that he had landed his BE2 C on a German drill square. 'My machine and I were immediately surrounded by German infantry, and I found myself among men who knew London and Brighton well, and who were all questioning me as to the condition of those places. Did I know them? Had they suffered much through the war? And so on. I was able to reassure them on those points.'[49] The reception by the German troops was indeed generally good, in spite of all they had to suffer from the RFC.

The prisoner might well then find himself in the company of cheerful and hospitable German aviators at the nearest airfield before he was driven away to be interrogated. The experience was thoroughly disorientating, and it was difficult to keep a guard on the tongue, when, as sometimes happened, the man was invited to sit in the cockpit of a German aircraft. With the single exception of a pilot officer, originally of the 1/Canadian Mounted Rifles,[50] the Germans learned something useful from every pilot and observer who was shot down on the Somme in 1916.

One branch of aviation remained a mystery to the Germans, for 'the maritime squadron, the "Royal Naval Air Service", never works with the squadrons of the army. Relations between them are bad, which gives rise to frequent complaints.'[51] 'We can establish no details concerning the maritime aircraft. The one thing which stands out is the evidence of bad feeling between the naval officers and the naval aviators. The former deliberately turn their backs on the whole idea of aerial reconnaissance, and are still more dismissive of the personnel of the naval aviation, as being for the greater part assembled from the lower orders of society ("no gentlemen"). Most of them are mechanics, locksmiths and the like, and carry little weight with the naval officers, few of whom volunteer as observers.'[52]

The Germans had looked very closely at the RFC in 1916, and their official historians concluded after the war that the German aviation in the early summer of that year had been defective in every respect.

In contrast the attacking forces – and especially the British – deployed large numbers of compact formations of fighter aircraft which, moreover, were technically superior at that particular time. As early as May they won a palpable superiority in the airspace, and were able to develop a novel way of conducting aerial warfare, aimed at implementing three tasks:

• An aggressive battle to win superiority in airspace which extended well behind the enemy front

• The systematic beating-down of the German batteries in concert with their own artillery

- Combat reconnaissance for the infantry, combined with lending support in the attack, and, together with designated balloons, assuring communication between the fighting troops and the command.

In such a way the RFC exercised a decisive influence on the character of the fighting in July and August, and established the principle that the mastery of airspace over the battlefield was a precondition for success on the ground.[53] These striking statements run counter to the conclusion of a distinguished historian that 'ultimately, the opening of the Somme campaign served to show that the most the RFC could contribute must remain a small part of the whole. Command of the air in this war would never make the difference between success and failure on the ground.'[54]

The Reckoning

The ground won by the British during the four and a half months of attacks on the Somme extended across a frontage of about thirteen miles, and reached a maximum depth, namely to the foot of the Butte de Warlencourt, and just beyond Gueudecourt, of not quite six miles. The Germans were never evicted from Serre at the northern end of the fighting front. The last British attacks had won Beaumont Hamel of terrible memory and the Ancre valley to just short of Grandcourt. From there the gains began to extend significantly to the east almost as far as the Butte de Warlencourt, before inclining southwards to take in Flers, Lesboeufs and Morval and reach the boundary with the French near Sailly-Saillisel. The Germans held Serre, as already noted, along with their third position, and they kept Bapaume and Péronne altogether out of the allies' reach.

In the course of the battle the terrain had been of literally vital tactical importance from one moment to the next, but the subjective link between human sacrifice and the ground gained was soon to be devalued almost to the point of irrelevance. On 24 January 1917 British patrols began to find the German positions empty, and a party of Australians pushed on to Bapaume without encountering any opposition. 'The officer ... came back to his colonel and said, "They've hopped the bloody twig. They're out of it." Colonel: "Who? The Boche? Out of Bapaume?" Officer: "Yes, the bloody place is empty." Colonel: "You're a bloody liar." Officer: "Bloody liar be damned. You give me the bloody battalion and I'll take the bloody place, right now."'[1]

The Germans had disengaged cleanly, and were in the process of withdrawing to the Hindenburg Line. It was one of those rare genuine 'strategic retreats', for the new line offered them a shorter and more systematically prepared defence than the positions on the Somme.

We must clearly look beyond the winning and loss of ground to identify the significance of what happened on the Somme. The management and the impact of the campaign are much more profitable subjects of enquiry, and here the comparison of the British and German sources offers some useful perspectives.

As regards the conduct of operations at that time, all the combatants had to confront some basic technical problems, one of which had been identified by Crown Prince Rupprecht early in 1916, namely that 'a breakthrough can succeed only when at least two enemy-defended lines can be taken in the first onrush.'[2] On the Somme, at least, the Germans were on the operational defensive and therefore had the simpler task. Their artillery, for example, was spared one of the major responsibilities of the British gunners, which was to destroy trench systems and belts of wire and open the way for infantry assaults. The Germans could concentrate their energies on developing defences in depth, all the way from their improvised *Trichterstellungen* back through their three trench systems and ultimately to the grand Hindenburg Line which was being built well to the rear.

When so many of the British attacks failed, it is worth pointing out that the Germans, too, failed in their offensive at Verdun, and that they never found an effective means of reclaiming lost ground on the Somme. Their hasty counterattacks mostly broke down through lack of co-ordination, while the better prepared ones gave the British time to dig in and plant their Lewis guns and Stokes mortars. The Germans had no equivalent to this mobile firepower, and their flame-throwers were bulky and liable to explode. The Storm Troops remained alien implants from Verdun.

The German knowledge of their British opponents was patchy. In 1916 they discovered virtually nothing about the high command, logistics or the personnel of the artillery. After 15 September a mass of information was available to the Germans concerning the tank, but it was processed and assessed very badly by the military intelligence. The Germans nevertheless learned a great deal from prisoners about conditions on the British home front, the tensions in Ireland and in the Empire, together with the experience and mentality of all the British and Imperial regimental ranks, the weapons and tactics of the infantry, and every aspect of the Royal Flying Corps.

Much could be deduced by the Germans from the simple fact that they were the object of the British attentions, as manifest most obviously in the brute force of the British preparatory bombardments. Due note was also taken of the creeping barrages, which were linked so closely with the progress of the British infantry. All the same it was evident that the British high command consistently demanded more of its troops than they were capable of giving, that there was a consequent gap between aims and attainment, that the British military intelligence was poor at identifying the times when the Germans had been reduced to a state of genuine exhaustion, and that the degree of British training and the prescriptive British system of command were unequal to converting a local success into a breakthrough.

The tanks had a devastating local impact, and never more than when they went on single-tank rampages; but the machines were few in number, and the Germans reserved judgement as to their utility in general. The Germans were nevertheless aware of the advances in British minor tactics in the later actions on the Somme, and again and again we encounter references to paralysing artillery strikes, and penetrations and envelopments that gobbled up whole battalions and companies at a time. Once the British established themselves, they proved very difficult to root out on account of their man-portable firepower, their skill at digging-in, and the speed with which they established communications back to their artillery. All of this lends some credibility to Rawlinson's penchant for a progression 'step by step.'

The Germans were impressed above all by the skill that the British brought in 1916 to co-ordinating the action of artillery, aircraft and infantry. The verdict of the Germans at the time was confirmed by the German official historians after the war, and it is fair to regard this phenomenon as the birth of twentieth-century mechanised warfare, and to date it consequently to 1916, and not, as some historians would have it, to the last years of the war. The misconceptions probably arise from the mistaken ambition on the part of writers to fit the advances into a 'learning curve'. A curve is by definition something smooth, whereas the progression in the Great War was more of a series of steps, some of which led downwards. It was, if anything, a learning or re-learning *process*. More generally, to relate the experience to a 'learning curve' is to imprison the historian in an artificial framework of reference to compare with the notion of a 'Military Revolution' which distorted the study of early modern military history for decades from the 1950s. The distinctive character of individual actions and campagins can thereby be overlooked.

In such a way the expertise which the pre-war British Regulars brought to the tactics of fire and manoeuvre was lost when the ranks of the professionals were thinned in the early battles, and the army was bulked out by the Kitchener Men. 'Those British Regulars who survived the first months of fighting would see the level of training and skills that they took for granted within their battalion become diluted and deteriorate to the same levels they witnessed in the German ranks in 1914.'[3] The preparatory fire at Neuve Chapelle in 1915 had been a genuine lightning bombardment, albeit dictated by forces of circumstances (shortage of shells), but nothing of the kind was seen again until 14 July 1916. In the later months of that year the Kitchener Men were at last attaining true proficiency when the ranks were filled out once again by a fresh influx of inadequately trained recruits, in this case the 'Derby Men'. Until the end of the campaign the Royal Flying Corps was able to harass the German ground forces as ruthlessly as ever, in spite of the work of the famed *Jastas*, but that advantage was lost over the coming months, an ordeal which culminated in the 'Bloody April' of 1917.

Few people even in 1916 would have disagreed with Rupprecht when he stated that 'the measurement of the success or failure of the two sides is to be found less in winning or losing land than in the relative loss of men and material'.[4] On the Somme the casualties, prisoners and missing of the combatants stood at about:

- French: 204,000

- British: 420,000, of whom about 150,000 had been killed. The average strength of the infantry component of a division on active service was roughly 11,000, and the odds against your surviving happened to be the grimmest in two New Army Divisions, the 30th (losses of 17,374), and Ivor Maxse's 18th (13,323) which was evidently paying highly for its reputation.

- Germans: Estimates vary wildly, from about 230,000 at the lowest to a still less credible 680,000, but the best sources put it at about 500,000.[5]

- (A loss of an entirely unquantifiable kind was the end which the war had put to a fast-developing Anglo-German society, in which German connections had so signally enriched British industry, commerce and the arts.)

On the face of it the balance in favour of the Germans was about 20 per cent. But that was not the whole story. In 1929, in a heavily selling book, which was dedicated to Hindenburg, the right-wing official historian and novelist Werner Beumelburg could state that a break-through on the Somme lay beyond the power of the British and French, in the same way as success at Verdun had eluded the Germans, 'and yet the roots of the outcome of the war lay in just these battles. The work of uncovering them is more a matter of feeling than calculation.'[6] If the allies lost more men, they could afford to lose more. The allies could replace their material losses, and so could the Germans, but not over the long term. The German soldier lost hope in the improvement of his situation, 'and here we have something which was invisible but decisive, the moral element'. The best, the longest-enduring type of German soldier emerged from the grinder 'to all appearances unbroken and healthy. What we could not see that inside he had become another man. He knew nothing of it himself. The second experience of *Trommelfeuer* brought him that more quickly to the point of exhaustion, and the third more rapidly still. His psychological constitution had become more sensitive to the effects of the battle of matériel. His resilience had diminished.'[7]

The words *Zermürbungskrieg* and *Erschöpfungskrieg*, both signifying 'war of attrition', had long been current in the German high command. The wearing-down process extended well beyond the erosion of manpower and material resources, as Beumelberg suggested, and it is worth asking what the agents of attrition were, and why in the end they affected the Germans more than the British and the French.

The evidence is oddly inconclusive, when we try to relate the damage to the nature of the fighting on the Somme. The average daily loss of the British on the Somme stood at 2,943, which was higher than at Third Ypres ('Passchendaele', August–November 1917), but lower than at Arras (April–May 1917) and the victorious Hundred Days (August–November 1918).[8] On some days in Normandy in 1944 there were heavier British losses than on some days on the Somme. When put in those terms the relative cost of the Somme might not seem excessive, but this was a very long drawn-out offensive, when there was a marked disparity between the times and along the sectors when not much was happening, and the wholesale massacres on what the Germans called 'big battle days' (*Grosskampftage*) when the experience was unforgettable or terminal.

When the Germans drew comparisons with other theatres, they agreed that enemy artillery fire was heavier and more shattering at Verdun in April, and in Champagne and at Third Ypres in the next year, but that the Battle of the Somme proved to be an unparalleled ordeal on account of 'the unbelievable state of the ground. Our positions were well built, but the ways up to them, and the positions themselves were filthy and muddy due to the autumn weather and the continuous rain. The shell-holes became ponds, the trenches kept falling in and were transformed into swampy channels. The deep dugouts were often filled with water.'[9] It will appear strange to the British to find the mud on the Somme being described as worse than at Ypres, but at Ypres the Germans on the whole occupied the better-drained ground.

The service of the German 173rd Regiment on the Somme proved to be every bit as bloody as the tour at Verdun, but the more open terrain enabled the sub-units to keep better together, without the isolation that was imposed by the steep woods and deep valleys at Verdun.[10] Conversely the broken terrain at Verdun offered some protection against aerial observation, whereas any movement on the Somme in daytime was likely to attract the attention of aircraft and draw down bombing or machine-gun attacks or artillery fire.

What was truly destructive to the Germans on the Somme was probably less the experiences in the front line than the lack of restorative time out of it. The long arm of the British artillery and aircraft reached well into the German rear. Moreover recreation and useful training were often sacrificed to trench-digging and other labours, and the infantrymen were returned to the front line too soon and in an exhausted state. For the gunners 'there was really no rest of any kind, whether for the gun detachments, the drivers, the observers, the signallers or the runners! And yet the time by which the infantry were designated as being "burnt out" was much shorter than that for the artillery or the other arms.'[11] Elements of a division's artillery might well be retained in the front line when the division marched off to somewhere quieter, which could prolong the gunners' ordeal for weeks on end.

Such was the indirect but telling result of the greater depth of resources open to the British. It extended beyond numbers to technology, which the British in particular were exploiting to the limits of the time. Ludendorff put it succinctly when he summoned up one of the discussions at the conference at Cambrai on 8 September 1916: 'We found that among the enemy infantry the power of the men had already been enhanced to a comprehensive degree by that of the machine. Our efforts, on the contrary, depend too much on the men.'[12]

Much of that effort had been called forth by the need to counter the British, who were present on the Western Front in altogether unexpected strength. By September 1916 the British and Imperial forces in France amounted to about 1.4 million troops, made up of forty-seven divisions of British infantry, four of Canadians, another four of Australians, and one of New Zealanders, along with a brigade of South Africans, three divisions of British cavalry and a brigade of Canadian cavalry.

The fact that the British were therefore able to mount a weighty and, above all, sustained offensive on the Somme forced the Germans to scale down and ultimately abandon their offensive at Verdun, and, what is less generally appreciated, call off an intended further offensive against the British forces between Arras and the Somme front. Neither of these important consequences can be related to any strokes of strategic genius on the part of Haig. The allied offensive on the Somme had been conceived before the Germans struck at Verdun, and it was continued long after the Germans desisted in their efforts at that place. The German plans to strike at Arras and to its south remained unknown to him. The allies had nevertheless deranged completely the German plans for the Western Front in 1916, which lends substance to the claim that the offensive on the Somme was, if not a victory, at least a costly strategic success that was important to the outcome of the war.

After the Armistice Grand Admiral Alfred von Tirpitz took the officers of the German General Staff to task for having acquiesced in the representation of the British troops before the war as 'Aldershot Tommies, with little side caps and walking sticks'. On the outbreak of the war he had addressed his concerns to the Chief of the General Staff Helmuth von Moltke, who replied 'we will just have to arrest them', and on another occasion that 'the more British the better'.[13] Tirpitz was irked at having seen his 'plan' for a great naval confrontation with the British set aside from 1906, and Moltke's response seemed to exemplify a delusion of the General Staff, which believed that Germany's problems could be solved by a short war on the Continent in which a British intervention could be swept aside.

The distinguished General Hermann von Kuhl (chief of staff of the First Army, and then of Army Group *Kronprinz Rupprecht*) did what he could to answer the charges. He claimed that Moltke had been very well informed on the British potential, and that his words to Tirpitz in 1914 were intended as a show of optimism. By von Kuhl's account the General Staff had for years reckoned that Britain would be numbered among Germany's enemies, and had monitored carefully Britain's military reforms and the developing military understandings with the Empire and France. The Territorial Force had been called into being to supplement the Regular Army, and the General Staff believed that Britain would not hesitate to resort to conscription should the need arise.

Kuhl passed over in silence the totally unforeseen phenomenon of

Kitchener's New Armies, and conceded that 'we were mistaken on only one point. The British dominance over India and Egypt showed itself to be so firm that no native uprisings of note ever took place. The British were able to draw more troops from India than we had supposed, and even from time to time employ native troops in the European theatre of war. But they scarcely weighed in the balance.'

Kuhl maintained that everything considered, the German General Staff had made as valid an assessment of British capabilities as had been possible before the war. That war, however, had lasted for more than four years, and 'what Britain actually achieved ... went a good deal further. It was impossible to have reckoned on that in advance.' In the event the British were able to deploy forces to Macedonia, the Middle East and the German colonies as well as in France, and 'the mighty reinforcement and reorganisation of the British Army in the course of the war amounted to an administrative achievement of the first order'.[14]

Conscious of their limited and dwindling reserves of men and materials, the Germans in 1916 had consoled themselves with the thought that they retained superiority in mental and spiritual resources. But the Germans' strength was being challenged even there, and by the men who by all reasonable calculation ought to have been the least able to dispute it, namely the British survivors of the prolonged offensive on the Somme. At the end of the year the German intelligence officers concluded that 'the gigantic dimensions of the Battle of the Somme have put the events of the war before 1 July 1916 so much in the shade that in Britain they reckon that the real war began only from that time. The main reason is that it was the time when Britain first came to grips with its real enemy, Germany ... Most of the front-line soldiers too are extremely proud of what they have achieved so far. Again and again we hear from prisoners the self-satisfied question: "Don't you think we have done very well?".'[15]

Notes

ABBREVIATIONS:

KA   Bavarian Kriegsarchiv, Munich

ID   *Infanterie-Division*

RID   *Reserve Infanterie-Division*

Bd   *Bund* (lit. 'bundle'), file

NA   National Archives, Kew
       (formerly Public Record Office)

Introduction

1. Schatz, 1927, 83

2. Stosch, 1930, 257

3. Gruson, 1930, 235

4. Ritter, Albrecht, 1926, 147

5. Ibid., 147–8

6. Reymann, 1923, 41

7. Carrington, 1965, 12

8. Holmes, 2004, xxiii

9. Foley, 2005, 127

10. Edmonds, 1932, I, Appendix 8

11. Gough, 1931, 129

12. Bridges, 1938, 159

13. Eden, 1976, 121

14. Quoted in Pedersen, 1985, 144

15. Bloem, 1940, 7

16. Pafferath, 1930, 245

17. NA WO 157/281, Intelligence II Corps, 'Notes on the examination of a stretcher bearer belonging to the 4th Company, 29th Infantry Regiment', undated, August 1916

18. NA WO 157/281, Intelligence II Corps, 'Extracts from Prisoners' Statements … received up to 6 p.m., 26th August 1916'

19. Tucker, 1978, 80, 53

CHAPTER ONE
Knowing the Enemy

1. NA WO 157/173, Fourth Army Intelligence Summaries, 'Extracts from the German Press, 30th July to 2nd August 1916'

2. Werner Sombart, quoted in Stibbe, 2001, 76

3. Wolff, 1924, 71. See also Brandis, 1930, 279

4. Wilson, 1986, 21

5. Holmes, 24, 545

6. Graves, 1981, 69

7. Gibbs, 1920, 332

8. Nobbs, 1918, 207

9. Charteris, 1931, 179

10. Sassoon, 1928, 309

11. Graves, 1981, 163

12. Morton in Weingartner (ed.), 1995, 176

13. Williams, 1933, 89

14. Testimony of Private James Hazel, 4/Gordons, as transmitted to his grandson Major David Hazel

15. Lawrence, 1993, 39

16. NA WO 157/469, XV Corps Intelligence Summaries, 'Extracts from other summaries', letter of 18 August 1916

17. Vormann, no date of publication, III, 536

18. Gruson, 1930, 245

19. Gallwitz, 1932, 111

20. Goldammer, 1931, 142–3

21. KA 3 ID, Bd 77, III Battalion of the 17th Bavarian Regiment, *Erfahrungen*, 13 September 1916

22. Eyre, 1938, 47

23. *Vizefeldwebel* Paulsen, in Speck, 1937, 93

24. KA 10 ID, Bd 46, *Vernehmung eines Überläufers* (*II. R. Fus., 29. Div., 86. Brig.*), Corps HQ, 26 June 1916

25. KA 6 RID, Bd 35, *Vernehmung eines Sergeanten vom XIII. Dur. L.I., 23. Div., 68. Brig., gefangen genommen am 7. Okt. südwestlich le Sars*, 7 October 1916

26. KA 14 ID, Bd 13, *Vernehmung eines Gefreiten des VII/ Cam'n Highrs. (44. Brig., 15. Div.) gef. gen. 24.12. Mittags nordwestlich le Sars*, Army HQ, 28 December 1916

27. KA 3 ID, Bd 49, *Vernehmung von Gefangenen der 5. Division*, Army HQ, 2 September 1916

28. Nicolai, 1924, 182. See also KA 3 ID, Bd 79, *Nachrichtenwesen*, Army HQ, 2 April 1916

29. NA WO 157/437, X Corps Intelligence Summary, 12 July 1916

30. KA 14 ID, Bd 13, *Stimmungsbild nach Aussagen von Gefangenen aus den Oktober–November Kämpfen an der Somme*, Army HQ, 16 December 1916

31. KA 3 ID, Bd 70, *Über Stimmungen der bisherigen Gefangenen aus der Somme-Schlacht*, Army HQ, 15 October 1916

32. KA 5 ID, Bd 10, report to General Kirchbach, Corps HQ, 7 September 1916

33. Jünger, 2004, 83

34. KA 6 RID, Bd 23, *Aussagen eines Leutnants vom II/V Gloue. R., 184, Brig., 61. Div., Gefangen genommen am 16.8. um 7 Uhr abends südöstlich Fauquissart*, Army HQ, 17 August 1916

35. Harvey, 1920, 9

36. KA 3 ID, Bd 79, *Nachrichtenwesen*, Army HQ, 2 April 1916. See also NA WO 157/174, Fourth Army Intelligence Summary, No. 77, 'Concerning Intelligence Service and Treatment of Prisoners', Gruppe Kirchbach, 28 August 1916

37. Nicolai, 1924, 183

38. KA 3 ID, Bd 79, *Nachrichtenwesen*, Army HQ, 2 April 1916

39. KA 6 RID, Bd 23, *Ergebnis der Unterhaltung mit den gefangenen australischen Offizieren*, Divisional HQ, late July 1916

40. Harvey, 1920, 7

41. Nicolai, 1924, 184

42. KA 6 RID, Bd 23, Crown Prince Rupprecht, *Aussagen eigener Gefangener*, 25 May 1916. See also Stosch, 1927, XXI, 26–7; Graves, 1981, 163

43. NA WO 157/321, III Corps Intelligence Summary, 2–3 October 1916

44. Nicolai, 1924, 185, 188

45. KA 3 ID, Bd 49, *Vernehmung eines 1.9. abends nordöstlich Delville-Wald gefangenen Engländers VI/Conn. Rang., 47. Brig., 16. Div.*, Army HQ, 3 September 1916

46. KA 3 ID, Bd 70, *Über Stimmungen der bisherigen*

Gefangenen aus der Somme-Schlacht, Army HQ, 15 October 1916; KA 2 ID, Bd 81, *Nachrichten von der englischen Front*, Army HQ, 2 April 1916

47. Nicolai, 1924, 186

48. Ibid., 183

49. KA 3 ID, Bd 70, *Aussagen eines verwundeten Offiziers (Oberleut) vom IX. W. York. R., 34. Brig., 11. Div., gefangen genommen in der Nacht vom 10/11.8.16.*, Army HQ, 16 August 1916

50. KA 3 ID, Bd 79, *Nachrichtenwesen*, 2 April 1916

51. Nicolai, 1924, 185

52. Harvey, 1920, 12

53. Jackson, 1989. See also Moynihan, 1978, 61

54. KA 6 RID, Bd 23, *Aussagen eines Leutnants vom II/V Gloue. R. ...* Army HQ, 17 August 1916

55. KA 10 ID, Bd 46, untitled, Army HQ, 8 May 1916

56. KA 10 ID, Bd 46, *Vernehmung des am 5. IV. abends südlich Beaumont gefangen genommen. engl. Leutnants G. W. Phillimore*, Army HQ, 6 April 1916

CHAPTER TWO

The Imperial Troops

1. Pugsley, 2004, 13

2. KA 3 ID, Bd 70, *Nachtrag zu den Aussagen des Gefangenen der 93. Brig. M.G. Komp., 93. Brig., 31 Div.*, Army HQ, 5 August 1916

3. Anon., *Südafrikas Deutsche in englischer Gewalt*, 1916, 19

4. Nicolai, 1924, 189

5. KA 3 ID, Bd 70, *Nachtrag zu den Aussagen ...* Army HQ, 5 August 1916

6. KA 3 ID, Bd 70, *Aussagen eines Mannes der 93. Brig. M.G. Komp., 93. Brig., 31. Div., gefangen genommen ... am 27 Juli 1916*, Army HQ, 29 July 1916

7. KA 3 ID, Bd 70, *Nachtrag zu den Aussagen ...* Army HQ, 5 August 1916

8. KA 14 ID, Bd 13, *Stimmungsbild nach Aussagen von Gefangenen aus den Oktober – und November – Kämpfen an der Somme*, Army HQ, 16 December 1916

9. KA 3 ID, Bd 70, *Aussagen eines schwerverwundeten vom II/South Afr. Brig., 9. Div.*, Army HQ, 19 September 1916

10. Quoted in Cave, 1999, 106–7

11. Vormann, III, 543

12. Stiehl, 1916, 18

13. KA 3 ID, Bd 49, *Vernehmung von Gefangenen der 1. Kanad. Div. ... gefangen genommen 8.9. morgens östlich Mouquet Ferme*, Army HQ, 10 September 1916

14. KA 14 ID, Bd 13, *Stimmungsbild nach Aussagen ...* Army HQ, 16 December 1916

15. KA 3 ID, Bd 49, *Vernehmung von Gefangenen der 1. Kanad. Div. ...* Army HQ, 10 September 1916

16. KA 3 ID, Bd 49, *Vernehmung von 16 Mann (grössenteils verwundet) vom 14. Kanad. Batl., 1. Kan. Div., 3. Kanad. Brig., gefangen genommen am 8.IX morgens im Fabeck-Graben östlich der Mouquet-Ferme,* Great HQ, 8 September 1916

17. KA 3 ID, Bd 49, *Vernehmung von Gefangenen der 1. Kanad. Div. ...* Army HQ, 10 September 1916. See also Fromm, 1920, 74

18. KA 14 ID, Bd 13, *Stimmungsbild nach Aussagen ...* Army HQ, 16 December 1916

19. KA 6 RID, Bd 23, *Ergebnis der Unterhaltung mit den gefangenen australischen Offizieren,* late July 1916

20. KA 3 ID, Bd 70, *Der Angriff auf die 6. Bay. Res. Div in Gegend nordwestlich Fromelles am 19. Juli 1916 nach Schilderung von Gefangenen (meistens Offiziers-Aussagen),* Army HQ, 30 July 1916

21. KA 14 ID, Bd 13, *Stimmungsbild nach Aussagen ...* Army HQ, 16 December 1916

22. Rupprecht, 1929, I, 458–9

23. KA 3 ID, Bd 70, *Der Angriff ...* Army HQ, 30 July 1916

24. Williams, 1933, 77

25. KA 14 ID, Bd 13, *Vernehmung eines Gef. vom 19. Austr. Batl., 5. Austr. Brigade, 2. Austr. Div., gef. gen. 24.12 östlich Gueudecourt,* Army HQ, 29 December 1916

26. KA 14 ID, Bd 13, *Stimmungsbild nach Aussagen ...* Army HQ, 16 December 1916

27. KA 3 ID, Bd 70, *Der Angriff ...* Army HQ, 30 July 1916

28. KA 4 ID, Bd 35, *Ergänzung der Aussagen der am 30.5.16. nördlich Fromelles gefangen genommenen Australier, 3. Austral. Brig., 1. Austral. Div.,* date illegible, 1916

29. KA 6 RID, Bd 23, *Nachrichten über den Gegner,* Army HQ, 17 August 1916

30. KA 14 ID, Bd 13, *Stimmungsbild nach Aussagen ...* Army HQ, 16 December 1916

31. KA 3 ID, Bd 49, *Auszug aus dem Tagebuch eines Mannes vom 53. Austral. Batl.,* Army HQ, 10 September 1916

32. KA 4 ID, Bd 35, *Aussagen der am 31.5.16. bei Inchy gefangen genommenen englischen Flieger,* Army HQ, 3 June 1916

33. KA 3 ID, Bd 70, *Unterhaltungen mit gefangenen Engländern,* Army HQ, 11 September 1916

34. KA 14 ID, Bd 13, *Stimmungsbild nach Aussagen ...* Army HQ, 16 December 1916

35. Dziobek, 1922, 127

36. KA 4 ID, Bd 35, *Aussagen von 3 Gefangenen vom LVIII Batl. 15. Austr. Brig. 5. Austr. Div. gefangen genommen am 15.7.16. abends 11 Uhr nordwestlich Fromelles,* Army HQ, 17 July 1916; KA 4 ID, Bd 35, *Vorläufige Vernehmung von 6 Offizieren und 213 Mann der 5. Austr. Division gefangen genommen am Morgen des 10.7.16. gegen 4 Uhr, nordwestlich Fromelles in der Hufeisenstellung (von den Australiern "horse shoe" genannt),* Army HQ, 21 July 1916

37. KA 3 ID, Bd 70, *Der Angriff ...* Army HQ, 30 July 1916

38. KA 6 RID, Bd 35, *Vernehmung eines Mannes vom II. Wellington Batl. Neuseel. Div. 2. neus. Brig., gefangen genommen in der Nacht vom 1–2 an der Nationalstrasse, wohin er sich verlaufen hatte,* Army HQ, 3 October 1916

39. KA 4 ID, Bd 35, *Ergänzung der Aussagen ...* date illegible, 1916

40. Stiehl, 1916, 21

41. Ibid., 20

42. Ibid., 21–2

43. Ibid., 23

44. Corrigan, 1999, 198

45. KA 3 ID, Bd 70, *Über Stimmungen der bisherigen Gefangenen aus der Somme-Schlacht,* Army HQ, 15 October 1916

46. KA 2 ID, Bd 81, *Nachrichten von der englischen Front im Abschnitt St. Eloi-Loos,* Army HQ, 15 February 1916

47. KA 10 ID, Bd 46, *Anhang zu Nr. 775,* 8 May 1916

CHAPTER THREE
The British Army

1. KA 2 ID, Bd 81, *Nachrichten von der englischen Front im Abschnitt St. Eloi-Loos,* Army HQ, 15 February 1916

2. KA 3 ID, Bd 49, *Vernehmung von 2 am 31.8. abends nordwestlich Longueval gefangenen Engländern des XIII/Middx. (73. Brig., 24. Div., XV Corps),* Army HQ, 3 September 1916

3. KA 3 ID, Bd 49, *Nachrichten über den Feind Nr. 5.,* Army HQ, 5 September 1916

4. KA 3 ID, Bd 70, *Über Stimmungen der bisherigen Gefangenen aus der Somme-Schlacht,* Army HQ, 15 October 1916

5. KA 14 ID, Bd 13, *Stimmungsbild nach Aussagen von Gefangenen aus den Oktober – und November – Kämpfen an der Somme,* Army HQ, 16 December 1916

6. G. M. McGowan in Wolff (ed.), 1992, 184. For a similar effect in the 7th Division at Ginchy on 6–7 September see Atkinson, 1927, 318

7. Rupprecht, 1929, III, 90–91

8. KA 6 RID, Bd 23, *Aussagen eines Leutnants vom II/V Gloue. R. ...* Army HQ, 17 August 1916

9. KA 3 ID, Bd 49, *Vernehmung eines Offiziers und eines Mannes des VI/Shrops. L.I. (6. Brig., 20. Div.), gefangen genommen in der Nacht 4/5/9 zwischen Guillemont und Ginchy*, Army HQ, 7 September 1916

10. KA 3 ID, Bd 70, *Aussagen eines am 20.10.16. bei Monchy-le-Preux, westl. Arras, abgeschossenen engl. Fliegers*, Army HQ, 26 October 1916

11. NA WO 157/319, III Corps Intelligence, 'Further Examination of Lieutenant Schade, 6/181 Regiment, captured ... on 18/8/16'

12. KA 10 ID, Bd 46, *Aus Unterhaltungen mit den im Lazarett in Caudry befindlichen, gefangenen Engländern*, Army HQ, 9 July 1916

13. KA 14 ID, Bd 13, *Vernehmung eines Gefangenen v. II/Gordon Highrs/ 20 Brig., 7. Div., eingebracht 25/11 nordöstlich Beaumont*, Army HQ, 27 November 1916. See also KA 3 ID, Bd 49, *Vernehmung von 2 am 31.8. abends nordwestlich Longueval gefangenen Engländern des XIII/Mddx. ...* Army HQ, 3 September 1916

14. KA 3 ID, Bd 70, *Aus Unterhaltungen mit gefangenen Engländern*, Army HQ, 22 September 1916

15. KA 10 ID, Bd 46, *Vernehmung des am 12.VI/16. südlich Mametz gefangen genommenen Engländers der 'B' Komp., II/Bord. R. (20. Brig., 7. Div.)*, Army HQ, 13 June 1916. See also KA 10 ID, Bd 46, *Vernehmung eines verwundeten engl. Soldaten vom XVII/Manch. R. 30. Div., eingebracht am 2.7. in Gegend Montauban*, Army HQ, 6 July 1916; KA 10 ID, Bd 46, *Vernehmung*, Army HQ, 11 July 1916; KA 3 ID, Bd 70, *Über Stimmungen der bisherigen Gefangenen ...* Army HQ, 15 October 1916; KA 5 ID, Bd 22, Major General Lindequist, late December 1916

16. KA 3 ID, Bd 49, *Vernehmung von 85 Gef. des I/S. Staffs. R., 91., Brig., eingebracht 31.8. abends am nordostrande des Delville-Waldes*, Army HQ, 2 September 1916

17. KA 3 ID, Bd 81, *Aussagen eines Offiziers (und 2 Mann) vom VIII.Rifle Brig., 14. Div.*, Army HQ, 26 March 1916

18. NA WO 157/321, III Corps Intelligence Summary, 2–3 October 1916

19. Rupprecht, 1929, I, 460–61

20. KA 14 ID, Bd 13, *Stimmungsbild nach Aussagen ...* Army HQ, 16 December 1916

21. KA 3 ID, Bd 49, *Vernehmung eines Mannes vom III. Worc., 7. Brig., 24. Div., gefangen genommen am 2.9.16. südwestlich Thiepval*, Army HQ, 7 September 1916

22. KA 2 ID, Bd 81, *Nachrichten von der Englischen Front*, Army HQ, 7 September 1916

23. Kuhl, 1920, 84

24. Dudley Ward, 1921, 2–3

25. KA 10 ID, Bd 46, *Vernehmung von 2 der am 18.III. abends westlich Serre gefangen genommenen Engländer der 'O' Komp, des VI/Glouc. R. (144. Brig., 48 Div.)*, Army HQ, 20 March 1916

26. KA 10 ID, Bd 46, *Vernehmung der bei Hébuterne in der Nacht 16. Gefangen genommenen Engländer der 'B' Komp., IV/R. Berks. R. (145. Brig., 48. Div.)*, Army HQ, 18 May 1916

27. KA 10 ID, Bd 46, *Mitteilungen über die Englischen Armee*, Army HQ, 12 February 1916

28. KA 2 ID, Bd 81, *Unterredung mit dem am 27.2. südlich Hulluch gef. gen. Engl. Hauptmann Hughes S. Walker vom VI/Cameron Highl., 45. Brig., 15 Div.*, Army HQ, 1 March 1916

29. KA 2 ID, Bd 81, *Aussagen eines Offiziers (und 2 Mann) vom VIII/Rifle Brig.*, Army HQ, 26 March 1916

30. KA 10 ID, Bd 46, *Vernehmung der am 20/21 V.16. südwestlich Serre gefangen genommenen Engländer der 'A' Komp., XV/W. York. R.*, Army HQ, 22 May 1916

31. KA 3 ID, Bd 70, *Aussagen eines verwundeten Offiziers (Oberleutnant) vom IX/W. York. R., 34. Brig., 22. Div., gefangen genommen in der Nacht vom 10/11.8.16*, Army HQ, 16 August 1916

32. KA 2 ID, Bd 81, *Aussagen von 3 Gefangenen vom IX/W. Riding R., 52. Brig., 17. Div.*, Army HQ, 28 April 1916

33. Binding, 1929, 92

34. Gibbs, 1920, 33. See also Gough, 1931, 141

35. KA 14 ID, Bd 13, *Vernehmung eines Gefreiten des VII/Cam'n Highrs. (44. Brig., 15. Div.), gef. gen. 25.12. mittags nordwestlich le Sars*, Army HQ, 28 December 1916

36. Binding, 1929, 48. But see also Stormont Gibbs, for whom 'of the public school boys the quiet scholarly types were the best. The smart young men and the athletes would throw their weight around behind the lines but they were not chosen for a nasty job and after a few months' real war they were likely to crack up.' (Stormont Gibbs, 1986, 68)

37. KA 6 RID, Bd 23, *Zur Frage des Englischen Ersatzes*, Great HQ, 15 January 1916

38. Feilding, 1929, 75

39. KA 6 RID, Bd 23, *Zur Frage des Englischen Ersatzes*, Great HQ, 15 January 1916

40. KA 2 ID, Bd 81, *Unterredung mit dem ... Hauptmann Hughes S. Walker ...* Army HQ, 1 March 1916

41. KA 3 ID, Bd 70, *Nachrichten über den Gegner*, General HQ of the Field Army, 31 July 1916

42. KA 3 ID, Bd 49, *Vernehmung von 1. Serg. Und 10 [?] Mann vom VIII. R. War. R., 49. Div., 148. Brig., gefangen genommen in der Nacht 27/28 westlich Ferme de Mouquet*, Corps HQ, 29 August 1916

43. KA 2 ID, Bd 30, *Vernehmung von Gefangenen der 29. Div., 1 Verwundeter vom 1/Essex R., 88. Brig., gefangen genommen 12/10 nachts nördlich Gueudecourt*, Army HQ, 20 October 1916

44. KA 3 ID, Bd 70, *Aus Unterhaltungen mit gefangenen Engländern*, Army HQ, 11 September 1916

45. KA 14 ID, Bd 13, *Stimmungsbild nach Aussagen ...* Army HQ, 15 December 1916

46. KA 3 ID, Bd 49, *Aus Unterhaltung mit einem Gefangenen (XIII/Mddx., 72. Brig., 24. Div.) dessen Zivilberuf in England Theologe (Privatdozent) war*, Army HQ, 8 September 1916

47. NA WO 339/47976, file Mortimer-Phelan

48. KA 2 ID, Bd 88, *Vorläfiges Ergebnis der Vernehmung der am 23.4.. Durch Oberleut. Immelmann und Leutnant Mulrer bei der Mühle von Pelves abgeschossenen englischen Fliegeroffiziere, 11. Abteilung, 13. Wing*, Army HQ, 25 April 1916

49. KA 2 ID, Bd 81, *Fliegerabgaben. Nach Aussagen von etwa 10 Englischen Flugzeugführern und Beobachtern aus der Zeit von Oktober 1915 bis Januar 1916*

50. KA 3 ID, Bd 70, *Aussagen eines am 20.10.16, bei Monchy-le-Preux östl. Arras abgeschossenen englischen Fliegers*, Army HQ, 26 October 1916

51. KA 2 ID, Bd 81, *Aussagen eines am 13.3. gegen 6 Uhr nachm bei Bourlon heruntergeschossenen Flugzeug-Beobachters (P. J. Shaw ohne Rang)*, 16 April 1916

52. KA 2 ID, Bd 81, *Nachrichten von der englischen Front ...* Army HQ, 15 February 1916

53. Allen, 1924, 85–6

54. Tucker, 1978, 80

55. Coppard, 1969, 89

56. Pflugbeil, 1923, 61

57. KA 2 ID, Bd 81, *Nachrichten von der englischen Front ...* Army HQ, 15 February 1916

58. KA 3 ID, Bd 70, *Aussagen eines schwerverwundeten vom II. S. Afr. Inf. Brig., 9. Div., Gefangennahme am 14.9.16. in Gegend östlich Souchez*, Army HQ, 19 September 1916

59. KA 2 ID, Bd 81, *Nachrichten von der englischen Front ...* Army HQ, 15 February 1916; KA 2 ID, Bd 81, *Aussagen von 3 Gefangenen vom IX. West Riding R., 52. Brig., 17. Div.*, 28 April 1916; KA 2 ID, Bd 49, *Vernehmung des am 12.V.15. südlich Mametz gefangen genommenen Engländers der 'B' Komp.,'II. Border R. (20. Brig., 7. Div.)*, Army HQ, 13 June 1916

60. KA 3 ID, Bd 49, *Vernehmung von 5 Krankenträgern des 48. Austrl. Batls., 4. austr. Div. 12. Brig. und 15 Mann der 4. austr. Div. Field Ambulance. Austral. Brig. der 13. austr. Brig. zugeteilt*, Great HQ, 1 September 1916

61. KA 14 ID, Bd 13, *Vernehmung eines Gefreiten des VII. Cam'n Highrs. (44. Brig., 15. Div.) gefangen genommen*

25.12. *mittags nordwestlich le Sars*, Army HQ, 28 December 1916

62. KA 14 ID, Bd 13, *Stimmungsbild nach Aussagen ...* Army HQ, 16 December 1916

63. KA 14 ID, Bd 13, *Vernehmung eines Offiziers vom. 23. Batl., 6. Austr. Div. gefangen genommen 21.11. frühe dicht östlich der Strasse Flers-Ligny-Thilloy*, Army HQ, 23 November 1916

64. Niebelschütz, 1926, 104

65. KA 2 ID, Bd 81, *Nachrichten von der englischen Front*, 2 April 1916

66. Ibid.

67. KA 4 ID, Bd 26, *Allgemeine Schilderung der Verhältnisse an der Somme ... Erfahrungen*, late 1916

68. KA 2 ID, Bd 70, *Aussagen von 2 verwundeten Gefangenen vom VIII. E. Surr. R. (B-Comp.), 55. Brig., 18. Div., gefangen genommen in der Nacht vom 6. Zum 7.8.16. südöstlich Bois Grenier*, Army HQ, 7 August 1916; Nicolai, 1924, 192–3

69. Anon., *Unter englischem Feuer. Die Zerstörungen in Flandern und Nordfrankreich*, 1918, 4

70. KA 14 ID, Bd 13, *Stimmungsbild nach Aussagen ...* Army HQ, 16 December 1916

71. KA 2 ID, Bd 70, *Aussagen von 2 verwundeten Gefangenen vom VIII. E. Surr. R. ...* Army HQ, 7 August 1916

72. KA 2 ID, Bd 81, *Aussagen von 4 Mann vom IX. R. Muns. Fus. (48. Brig., 16. Div.)*, Army HQ, 29 March 1916

73. KA 10 ID, Bd 46, *Vernehmung von 21 bei Hébuterne in der Nacht vom 15. Zum 16.V.16. gefangen genommenen Engländer der 'B' Komp., R. Berks. R. (145 Brig., 48. Div.)*, Army HQ, 18 May 1916

74. Tucker, 1978, 62

75. Nicolai, 1924, 188

76. KA 2 ID, Bd 81, *Nachrichten von der englischen Front*, 2 April 1916

77. KA 10 ID, Bd 46, *Vernehmung der am 20/21/V südwestlich Serre gefangen genommenen Engländer der 'A' Komp., XV W. York. R.*, Army HQ, 22 May 1916

78. KA 10 ID, Bd 46, *Vernehmung von 21 der bei Hébuterne ... gefangen genommenen Engländer ...* Army HQ, 18 May 1916

79. KA 10 ID, Bd 46, *Vernehmung des ... südlich Mametz gefangen genommenen Engländers ...* Army HQ, 13 June 1916

80. KA 3 ID, Bd 70, *Über Stimmungen der bisherigen Gefangenen ...* Army HQ, 15 October 1916

81. KA 10 ID, Bd 46, *Vernehmung der am 19.II. abends westlich Serre gefangen genommenen Engländer von den C und D Compagnien des II/Lanc. Fus., 12. Brig., 4. Div.*, Army HQ, 11 September 1916

82. KA 10 ID, Bd 46, *Aus Unterhaltungen mit den im Lazarett*... Army HQ, 9 July 1916

83. Reimann, 2000, 46–8

84. NA WO 157/319, III Corps Intelligence Summary, 'Extracts from a conversation with a Vizefeldwebel of the 133rd Regiment (Saxon), captured on the 11th inst. by the 4th Australian Infantry Brigade (Anzac Corps)', 15 August 1916. On the apathy of the British troops see also Ferguson, 1999, 347

85. KA 3 ID, Bd 70, *Aus Unterhaltungen mit gefangenen Engländern*, Army HQ, 11 September 1916

86. KA 10 ID, Bd 46, *Vernehmung von 2 am 18.III.... gefangen genommenen Engländern*... Army HQ, 20 March 1916

87. Stiehl, 1916, 16

88. Ibid., 18

89. Binding, 1929, 150

90. KA 10 ID, Bd 46, *Aus Unterhaltungen mit den im Lazarett*... Army HQ, 9 July 1916

91. KA 3 ID, Bd 70, *Aus Unterhaltungen mit gefangenen Engländern*, Army HQ, 11 September 1916

92. KA 10 ID, Bd 46, *Aussagen von 9 englischen gefangenen Offiziere*, 19 July 1916

93. KA 2 ID, Bd 30, *Vernehmung eines Mannes vom II/E.Lanc.R., 24. Brig., 8. Div., gefangen genommen 23/10 nachmittag nordöstlich Gueudecourt*, Army HQ, 25 October 1916

94. KA 3 ID, Bd 70, *Über Stimmungen der bisherigen Gefangenen*... Army HQ, 15 October 1916; KA 14 ID, Bd 13, *Stimmungsbild nach Aussagen*... Army HQ, 16 December 1916

95. KA 3 ID, Bd 70, *Über Stimmungen der bisherigen Gefangenen*... Army HQ, 15 October 1916

96. KA 3 ID, Bd 70, *Aussagen eines verwundeten Offiziers (Unterleut.) vom IX/W. York. R., 34. Brig., 11. Div., gefangen genommen in der Nacht vom 10/11.8.16.*, Army HQ, 16 August 1916. See also KA 2 ID, Bd 81, *Aussagen eines bei Tourcoing am 19.1. heruntergeschossenen engl. Flieg eroffiziers vom 15. Squadron, 2. Wing., R.F.C.*, 21 January 1916; KA 4 ID, Bd 35, *Nachtrag zu den Aussagen des am 21. Mai östlich Cabaret-Rouge gefangen genommenen englischen Offiziere*, Army HQ, 25 May 1916

CHAPTER FOUR

The Home Fires

1. KA 10 ID, Bd 46, *Vernehmung der am 20/21.V.16. südwestlich Serre gefangen genommenen Engländer der 'A' Komp., XV/W. York. R.*, Army HQ, 22 May 1916

2. Ritter, Holger, 1926, 129

3. Reichsarchiv, 1925–44, XI, 32–3

4. Ritter, Holger, 1926, 130

5. KA 14 ID, Bd 13, *Aus Unterhaltungen mit im Dezember 1916 eingebrachten englischen Gefangenen*, Army HQ, 1 January 1917. See also KA 14 ID, Bd 13, *Vernehmung eines Unteroffiziers vom IV/Gren. Gds., 3. Garde Brig., Garde-Div., gef. gen. 17/18 früh nördlich Sailly*, Army HQ, 18 December 1916

6. KA 14 ID, Bd 3, *Aus Unterhaltungen mit im Dezember*... Army HQ, 1 January 1917

7. KA 10 ID, Bd 46, *Vernehmung des am 5.IV. abends südlich Beaumont gefangen genommen. Englischen Leutnants G. W. Phillimore*, Army HQ, 6 April 1916

8. KA 2 ID, Bd 81, *Nachtrichten von der englischen Front*, Army HQ, 2 April 1916

9. KA 14 ID, Bd 13, *Stimmungsbild nach Aussagen von Gefangenen aus den Oktober – und November – Kämpfen an der Somme*, Army HQ, 16 December 1916

10. KA 3 ID, Bd 70, *Aus Unterhaltungen mit gefangenen Engländern*, Army HQ, 11 September 1916

11. Feilding, 1929, 107

12. NA WO 157/284, 'Annexe to IInd Corps Intelligence Summary no. 108 ... Summary of the German Press, 10.10.16. to 1.11. 16.'

13. KA 2 ID, Bd 30, *Aus englischen Briefen*, Army HQ, 18 October 1916

14. KA 3 ID, Bd 70, *Aus Unterhaltungen mit gefangenen Engländern*, Army HQ, 11 September 1916

15. KA 14 ID, Bd 13, *Stimmungsbild nach Aussagen*... Army HQ, 16 December 1916

16. KA 3 ID, Bd 70, *Über Stimmungen der bisherigen Gefangenen aus den Somme-Schlacht*, Army HQ, 15 October 1916

17. Ferguson, 1999, 275

18. Quoted in Welch, 2000, 227

19. KA 10 ID, Bd 46, *Aus Unterhaltungen mit den im Lazarett in Caudry befindlichen, gefangenen Engländern*... Army HQ, 9 July 1916

20. Rupprecht, 1929, III, 17

21. KA 3 ID, Bd 70, *Über Stimmungen der bisherigen Gefangenen*... Army HQ, 15 October 1916

22. KA 14 ID, Bd 13, *Aus Unterhaltungen mit im Dezember*... Army HQ, 1 January 1917

23. KA 2 ID, Bd 80, *Aus englischen Briefen*, Army HQ, 18 October 1916

24. KA 4 ID, Bd 35, *Weitere Aussagen der am 31.5.16. bei Inchy abgschossenen englischen Fliegeroffiziers*, date illegible, 1916

25. KA 14 ID, Bd 13, *Aus Unterhaltungen mit im Dezember*... Army HQ, 1 January 1917

26. Stiehl, 1916, 17

27. Dungan, 1997, 197

28. KA 10 ID, Bd 46, *Aus Unterhaltungen mit den im Lazarett* ... 9 July 1916

29. Nicolai, 1924, 188–9

30. KA 4 ID, Bd 35, *Aussagen eines Mannes vom VI/Irish Regt/'b' Komp., 47. Brig., 16. Div.*, Army HQ, 10 May 1916

31. Feilding, 1929, 121

32. Gough, 1931, 186

33. KA 2 ID, Bd 81, *Aussagen von 4 Mann vom IX/R. Muns. Fus. (48. Brig., 16. Div.)*, Army HQ, 29 March 1916

34. KA 3 ID, Bd 49, *Vernehmung eines 1.9. abends nordöstlich Delville-Wald gefangenen Engländers VI/Conn. Rang., 47. Brig., 16. Div.*, Army HQ, 3 September 1916

35. Anon., 2000, 'Prince Joachim', *The Irish Sword*, XII, No. 87, 112

36. Rupprecht, 1929, I, 456

37. Rintelen, 1933, 131–2

38. KA 10 ID, Bd 46, *Anhang zu Nr. 775*, Army HQ, 8 May 1916

39. KA 3 ID, Bd 70, *Aussagen eines Gefangenen vom 1. Munster Fusiliers, 48. Brig., 16. Div.. Gefangen in der Nacht 4/5/8 südlich Hulluch*, Corps HQ, 15 August 1916

40. KA 3 ID, Bd 70, *Aus Unterhaltungen mit gefangenen Engländern*, Army HQ, 11 September 1916

41. KA 4 ID, Bd 35, *Aussagen eines Mannes vom VIII/R. Munster Fus., 'D' Komp., 47. Brig., 16. Div.*. He had been captured 8/9 May south of Loos

42. KA 2 ID, Bd 81, *Aussagen von 4 Mann vom IX/R. Muns. Fus. (48. Brig., 16. Div.)*, Army HQ, 29 March 1916. It is possible that there is some confusion here with the 9/Royal Dublin Fusiliers

CHAPTER FIVE
The British in France, 1914–15

1. Kuhl, 1920, 94. Also, less forthrightly, in Stein, 1919, 43

2. Kuhl, 1920, 92, 84

3. Ibid., 87

4. Ibid., 93

5. Ibid., 84

6. Ibid., 92

7. Ibid., 84

8. Stein, 1919, 44

9. KA 3 ID, Bd 70, *Aussagen eines verwundeten Offiziers (Oberleutnant) vom IX/W. York. R., 34. Brig., 11. Div. Gefangen genommen in der Nacht vom 10/8/16*, Army HQ, 16 August 1916

10. KA 10 ID, Bd 46, *Aus Unterhaltungen mit den im Lazarett in Caudry befindlichen, gefangenen Engländern*, Army HQ, 9 July 1916

11. KA 10 ID, Bd 46, *Vernehmung des am 5.IV. abends südlich Beaumont gefangen genommen. englischen Leutnants G. W. Phillimore*, Army HQ, 6 April 1916

12. Rintelen, 1933, 246. See also KA 4 ID, Bd 35, *Vorläufige Vernehmung von 6 Offizieren und 213 Mann der 5. Austral. Division*, Army HQ, 21 July 1916

13. Opinion of 1912, in Kuhl, 1920, 87

14. KA 10 ID, Bd 46, *Vernehmung des ... Leutnants G. W. Phillimore*, Army HQ, 6 April 1916

15. Kuhl, 1920, 90

16. KA 10 ID, Bd 46, *Vernehmung des ... Leutnants G. W. Phillimore*, Army HQ, 6 April 1916

17. KA 2 ID, Bd 81, *Unterredung mit dem am 27.2. südlich Hulluch gef. gen. engl. Hauptmanns Hughes S. Walker vom, VI/Cameron Highl., 45. Brig., 15. Div.*, Army HQ, 1 March 1916

CHAPTER SIX
Designs and Preparations

1. Gerster (*Die Schwaben*), 1920, 80

2. Ludendorff, 1921, 216

3. Rupprecht, 1929, I, 470

4. KA 10 ID Bd 46, *Aus Unterhaltungen mit den im Lazarett in Caudry, befindlichen, gefangenen Engländern*, Army HQ, 9 July 1916

5. KA 10 ID, Bd 46, *Vernehmung des am 12.VI.16. südlich Mametz gefangen genommenen Engländers der 'B' Komp., II/Bord. R. (20. Brig., 7. Div.)*, Army HQ, 13 June 1916

6. Binding, 1929, 108

7. Rupprecht, 1929, I, 477

8. Gallwitz, 1932, 87

9. Rintelen, 1933, 242

10. Feilding, 1929, 89

11. Ibid., 82

12. Major General Heynitz, in Gropp, 1932, 143

13. NA WO 157/318, Intelligence III Corps, 'Report on Country between Bazentin and Bapaume', 20 July 1916

14. Ibid.

15. Rupprecht, 1929, I, 415

16. Gerster (*Reserve-Infanterie-Regiment 119*), 1920, 48

17. Kümmel, 1926, 209

18. KA 1 ID, Bd 77, *Erfahrungen der 1. Armee in der Sommeschlacht* (*14.6–16.11.1916*)

19. Möller, 1939, 49

20. Kümmel, 1926, 109; Rupprecht, 1929, I, 484

21. War Office Publication S.S. 480, *Lessons drawn from the Battle of the Somme by Stein's Group*, 8 September 1916

22. Gerster (*Reserve-Infanterie-Regiment 119*), 1920, 50

23. Ibid., 49

24. Frisch, 1931, 132

25. NA WO 157/468, XV Corps Intelligence Summaries, 'Notes on the Examination of numerous prisoners belonging to the 110 and 111 R.I.R.', 1 July 1916

26. *Vizefeldwebel* Wickel, in Frisch, 1931, 134

27. NA WO 157/111, GHQ Summary of Information, 'Effect of Gas attacks on the enemy, 26th–27th June 1916', 21 July 1916

28. Vischer, 1921, 331

29. Vormann, no date of publication, III, 491

30. Gerster (*Reserve-Infanterie-Regiment 119*), 1920, 51

CHAPTER SEVEN
The Catastrophe of 1 July

1. Ewing, 1921, 95

2. KA 10 ID, Bd 46, *Aus Unterhaltungen mit englischen Gefangenen vor der Front des XIV.R. K.*, Army HQ, 6 July 1916

3. Masefield (1917), 1972, 92

4. S.S. 536, *Report on the Defence of Gommecourt on the 1st July 1916* (translation), General Staff (Intelligence), GHQ, January 1917, 8

5. Ibid.

6. Kümmel, 1926, 211

7. Dudley Ward, 1921, 44

8. Forstner, 1929–30, I, 207

9. KA 10 ID, Bd 46, *Vorläufiges Ergebnis der Vernehmung von 9 Offizieren und 301 Unteroffizieren und Mannschaften (Engländern) die in den Kämpfen am 1.VII.16. eingebracht wurden*, Army HQ, 5 July 1916

10. Carrington, 1965, 116

11. KA 10 ID, Bd 46, *Vernehmung* of Corporal Stead and Private Jones of the 6/Gloucesters, captured west of Serre, 18 March 1916

12. Carrington, 1965, 119

13. Lademann, 1922, 33

14. Stosch, 1927, I, 28

15. Masefield (1917), 1972, 97–8

16. Stosch, 1927, I, 28

17. Ashurst, 1987, 90

18. Gerster (*Reserve-Infanterie-Regiment 119*), 1920, 54

19. Stosch, 1927, I, 33

20. KA 10 ID, Bd 46, *Vorläufiges Ergebnis ...* Army HQ, 5 July 1916

21. Gerster (*Reserve-Infanterie-Regiment 119*), 1920, 54

22. Masefield (1917), 1972, 107–8

23. Gerster (*Reserve-Infanterie-Regiment 119*), 1920, 54

24. Masefield, 1984, 230

25. Ibid., 204

26. Stosch, 1927, I, 36–7

27. Nichols, 1922, 80–81

28. Gerster (*Die Schwaben*), 1920, 110

29. Stosch, 1927, I, 37

30. KA 10 ID, Bd 46, *Unterhaltung mit einem verwundeten englischen Offizier des V / York. & Lanc. R., 148. Brig., 49. Div., eingebracht am 2.7. in Gegend nördlich Thiepval*, Army HQ, 6 July 1916

31. Ibid.

32. Stosch, 1927, I, 46–7

33. Masefield, 1984, 243

34. Ibid., 226

35. Masefield (1917), 1972, 134

36. Fiedel, 1929, 123

37. Stosch, 1927, I, 5

38. Fiedel, 1929, 123

39. Stosch, 1927, I, 55

40. NA WO 157/468, XV Corps Intelligence Summaries, 'Notes on Examination of numerous prisoners belonging to the 110th and 111th Reserve Infantry Regiments', 1 July 1916

41. NA WO 157/468, XV Corps Intelligence Summaries, 'Notes on the Examination of numerous German prisoners, both officers and men, belonging to the 109th Reserve, 111th Reserve and 23rd Regiments', 1 July 1916

42. Frisch (ed.), 1931, 121

43. Gough, 1931, 147–8

44. Nichols, 1922, 100

45. KA 10 ID, Bd 46, *Vernehmung eines verwundeten engl. Soldaten vom XVII/Manch. R., 30. Div., eingebracht am 2.7. in Gegend Montauban*, Army HQ, 6 July 1916

46. Frisch (ed.), 1931, 128

47. NA WO 157/11, GHQ Summary of Information, 'Extract from diary of the Officer Commanding, 16th Bavarian Regiment, 10th Bavarian Division', entry for 2 July 1916

48. NA WO 157/11, Annexe to GHQ Summary of Information, 'Summary of the German Press, 27th June, 1916, to 4th July, 1916'

49. KA 10 ID, Bd 46, *Angriff der Engländer*, Army HQ, 14 July 1916

50. KA 10 ID, Bd 46, *Aus Unterhaltungen mit den im Lazarett in Caudry befindlichen, gefangenen Engländern*, 9 July 1916

51. KA 10 ID, Bd 46, *Vorläufiges Ergebnis ...* Army HQ, 5 July 1916

52. Ibid.

53. KA 10 ID, Bd 46, *Aus Unterhaltungen mit den im Lazarett ...* 9 July 1916

54. KA 10 ID, Bd 46, *Aus Unterhaltungen mit englischen Gefangenen vor der Front des XIV.R. K.*, Army HQ, 4 July 1916

55. Stosch, 1927, I, 20

56. KA 10 ID, Bd 46, *Aus Unterhaltungen mit dem in Lazarett ...* 9 July 1916

57. KA 10 ID, Bd 46, *Vorläufiges Ergebnis ...* 5 July 1916

58. Ibid.

59. KA 10 ID, Bd 46, *Aus Unterhaltungen mit englischen Gefangenen vor der Front des XIV.R. K.*, Army HQ, 4 July 1916

CHAPTER EIGHT
The Battle Carried Forward, 2–14 July

1. Masefield (1917), 1972, 137

2. Stosch, 1927, I, 100

3. Haig, 2005, 197

4. NA WO 157/468, XV Corps Intelligence Summaries

5. Lossberg, 1929, 225

6. KA 10 ID, Bd 18, *Gefechtsbericht der Division Burkhardt 7.7.16.–13.7.16.*, Divisional HQ, 23 July 1916

7. Werner, 1933, 140

8. Hase, 1922, 29

9. Fliess and Dittmar, 1927, 94

10. Lossberg, 1929, 231

11. Haig, 2005, 202

12. First Lieutenant Uhle-Wettler, in Werner, 1933, 147

13. Borelli, in Wohlenberg, 1931, 204–5

14. Lieutenant Rählert, in Vornann, no date, III, 526

15. Stosch, 1927, II, 27

16. Ibid., II, 22

17. Rählert, in Vornann, no date, III, 526

18. Palmer, 1917, 159

19. Haig, 2005, 206

20. Lossberg, 1929, 229

CHAPTER NINE
The Wasting Battles, 15 July–31 August

1. Gough, 1931, 144

2. Gabriel, 1921, 61

3. Pafferath, 1930, 269

4. Lieutenant Heibitzky, in Ibid., 271

5. KA 3 ID, Bd 70, *Der Angriff auf die 6. Bay. Div. in nordwestlich Fromelles nach Schilderung von Gefangenen (meistens Offiziers Aussagen)*, Army HQ, 30 July 1916

6. Ibid.

7. Williams, 1933, 68

8. KA 3 ID, Bd 70, *Der Angriff ...* Army HQ, 30 July 1916

9. KA 6 RID, Bd 23, *Ergebnis der Unterhaltung mit den gefangenen australischen Offizieren*, Divisional HQ, undated, July 1916

10. Williams, 2005, 145

11. Klähn, 1925, 133

12. Gallwitz, 1932, 68–9

13. Dziobek, 1922, 126–7

14. Masefield, 1984, 126–7

15. Kaiser, 1940, 138

16. Gallwitz, 1932, 78

17. Speck, 1937, 106

18. KA 3 ID, Bd 70, *Nachrichten über den Gegner*, Great HQ, 7 August 1916

19. Gallwitz, 1932, 88

20. KA 3 ID, Bd 49, *Vernehmung von 1 Serg. Und 9 Mann von VIII. Roy. Wark. R., 48. Div., 143. Brig., gefangen genommen in der Nacht 27/28.9. westlich Ferme de Mouquet*, Corps HQ, 29 August 1916

21. Goodspeed, 1969, 70

22. Haig, 2005, 211

23. Reichsarchiv, 1925–44, III, 95

24. Bloem, 1940, 162

25. Gruson, 1930, 238

26. Fliess and Dittmar, 1927, 102

27. Vormann, III, 512

28. NA WO 157/14, GHQ Summaries, 'Extracts from the diary of a man of the 3rd Company, 1/153rd Regiment, 8th Regiment', Delville Wood, 18 July 1916

29. Cave, 1999, 106–7; Reymann, 1923, 117

30. Schulze, in Gropp, 1932, 157

31. Schulze, in Ibid., 166–7

32. Masefield, 1984, 209

33. Schulze, in Gropp, 1932, 157

34. Walter Schubert's diary, in Schatz, 1927, 77

35. KA 3 ID, Bd 49, *Vernehmung von 2 am 31.8. abends nordwestlilch Longueval gefangenen Engländern des XIII. Midd'x (73. Brig., 24. Div., XV Corps)*, Army HQ, 3 September 1916

36. KA 3 ID, Bd 49, *Aussagen eines Gefangenen vom XIII. Middlesex, 73. Brig., 24. I.D., gefangen durch 5. Bay. I.R. nordwestlich Longueval am 31.18.16*

37. KA 3 ID, Bd 49, *Vernehmung von 85. Gef. des I/S. Staff. R., 91. Brig., 7. Div., eingebracht 31.8. abends am Nordostrande des Delville-Waldes*, Army HQ, 2 September 1916

CHAPTER TEN
The Second Impetus, September

1. Reichsarchiv, 1925–44, II, 3

2. Ibid., III, 94

3. Kohl, 1932, 134

4. KA 3 ID, Bd 70, *Vernehmung von 2 englischen Offizieren der C- und D-Komp. XIV/Hamps. R. (116. Brig., 39. Div.) gefangen genommen 4.0. nördlich Hamel*, Army HQ, 6 September 1916

5. Gerster (*Reserve-Infanterie-Regiment 119*), 1920, 58

6. KA 3 ID, Bd 49, *Vernehmung von 1 Verwundeten vom II. Batl. S. Lanc., 75. Brig.*, Great HQ, 4 September 1916

7. Hüber, in Stosch, 1930, 284

8. KA 3 ID, Bd 49, *Vernehmung von 35 Mann vom 49. Austr. Batl., 4. Div., 13. Brig., wovon 2 Mann verwundet. Gefangen genommen: bei der Mouquet Ferme am 3. September morgens zwischen 10 und 11 Uhr*, Great HQ, 4 September 1916

9. Von der Knesebeck, in Stosch, 1930, 286

10. Anon., *Das K. B. Infanterie-Regiment Hartmann*, 1931, 170

11. Glubb, 1978, 61

12. KA 3 ID, Bd 49, *Vernehmung von zum Teil verw. Des IX/Devon. R. (20. Brig., 7. Div.) eingebracht in Ginchy nach Angriff der Engländer am 6.9.*, Army HQ, 10 September 1916

13. Ibid.

14. Gallwitz, 1932, 72, 77

15. Simon, 1922, 42

16. Mohnkern, in Voigt, 1938, 420

17. Olenhausen, in Ibid., 413–4

18. Tucker, 1978, 63

19. Rupprecht, 1929, III, 105

20. Ibid., III, 105

21. Reber, 1929, 206–7

22. Reichsarchiv, 1925–44, XI, 61. See also Gallwitz, 1932, 110

23. Prior and Wilson, 1992, 205

24. Gallwitz, 1932, 109–10

25. KA 4 ID, Bd 26, 4th Bavarian Infantry Division, *Denkschrift für den Abschnitt der 4. Bayer. Inf. Div. bei Übergabe am 25. Inf. Div.*, Divisional HQ, 12 September 1916

26. KA 3 ID, Bd 77, Army Group *Kronprinz von Bayern* to the First, Second and Seventh Armies, Army Group HQ, 16 September 1916

27. KA 23 ID, Bd 27, *Gruppe Marschall, Abendmeldung*, 13 September 1916

28. NA WO 157/320, III Corps Intelligence Summary, 15–16 September 1916

29. Pidgeon, 1995, 186

30. Reil, in Drexel and Gathmann, 1917, 149

31. NA WO 157/13, 'Extracts from GHQ Summary dated 24th September'

32. KA 4 ID, Bd 26, Captain Weber, *Über die neuen englischen Panzerwagen (Caterpillar)*, Army HQ, 28 September 1916

33. Charteris, 1933, 165

34. Ritter, Albrecht, 1926, 154; Anon., *Geschichte des ehemaligen Königlichen bayerischen 12. Feldartillerie-Regiments*, 1935, 53; Beyer and Scheitzka, 1933, 101

35. Gieraths, 1928, 167–8

36. KA 4 ID, Bd 26, Franck, Commander of the Pioneers of the 4th Bavarian Division, *Beobachtungen und Erfahrungen aus der Somme-Schlacht*, Divisional HQ, 1 October 1916

37. Gieraths, 1928, 168

38. Weinert, in Fuhrmann, Pfoertner and Fries, 1933, 172

39. Weinert, in Ibid., 172

40. Weinert, in Ibid., 173

41. Weinert, in Ibid., 174

42. Kohl, 1932, 128–9

43. Rupprecht, 1929, II, 22

44. Riegel, 1927, 47

45. Reil, in Drexel and Gathmann, 1917, 150–51

46. Ebelshauser, 1984, 85; Riegel, 1927, 47

47. Ebelshauser, 1984, 87

48. Ritter, Albrecht, 1926, 154–5

49. KA 3 ID, Bd 77, 23rd Bavarian Regiment, *Erfahrungen aus der Schlacht an der Somme*, 30 September 1916

50. KA 3 ID, Bd 49, *Aussagen von 2 Gefangenen XXI London Regiments, 142. Brig., 47. I.D. (Gef. in Nacht 15/16 nordöstl. Foureaux Wald)*, 16 September 1916

51. KA 4 ID, Bd 35, *Auszüge aus dem Tagebuch eines am 20.9.16. in der Gegend Flers gefallenen Neuseelandeers vom 2. Batl. Canterbury Inf.-Regiments*, 1 October 1916

52. Klitta, in Beyer and Scheitzka, 1933, 103

53. KA 5 ID, Bd 22, *Gefechtsbericht des bayer. 14. Inf. Regts. Über die Schlacht an der Somme*, undated

54. Klitta, in Beyer and Scheitzka, 1933, 103

55. Reber, 1929, 144–5

56. KA 4 ID, Bd 35, Captain Weber, *Über die neuen englischen Panzerwagen (Caterpillar)*, Army HQ, 28 September 1916

57. KA 4 ID, Bd 35, *Auszüge aus dem Tagebuch eines gefallenen Bedienungsmannes des am 20.9. nordwestlilch Combles zerstörten englischen Panzerfahrzeuges*, Army HQ, 23 September 1916. In fact the man was not killed, and the incident took place near Bouleaux Wood on the 15th

58. KA 4 ID, Bd 35, Captain Weber, *Über die neuen englischen Panzerwagen (Caterpillar)*, Army HQ, 28 September 1916

59. KA 4 ID, Bd 35, *Auszüge aus dem Tagebuch ...* Army HQ, 23 September 1916; KA 4 ID, Bd 35, *Übersetzung eines vorgefundenen Befehls der 56. Engl. Div. zur Verwendung der Panzerfahrzeuge am 15.9.16*, 23 September 1916

60. Rupprecht, 1929, II, 21–2

61. KA 14 ID, Bd 26, Franck, *Erfahrungen aus der Somme-Schlacht ...* Divisional HQ, 1 October 1916

62. KA 5 ID, Bd 22, 7th Bavarian Regiment, *Anhang zur Gefechtsbericht über den Einsatz des Regiments an der Somme. Erfahrungen*, 19 October 1916

63. Glubb, 1978, 68

64. Rupprecht, 1929, III, 102

65. Reichsarchiv, 1925–44, XI, 70

66. Stephen, in Kohl, 1932, 132

67. Stephen, in Ibid., 133

68. KA 5 ID, Bd 22, 7th Bavarian Infantry Regiment, *Anhang zur Gefechtsbericht ... Erfahrungen*, 19 October 1916

69. KA 4 ID, Bd 26, Franck, *Erfahrungen aus der Somme-Schlacht*, Divisional HQ, 1 October 1916

70. KA 3 ID, Bd 70, 3rd Bavarian Infantry Division to the II Bavarian Corps, *Englische Panzerwagen*, Divisional HQ, 13 October 1916

71. Reber, 1929, 158

72. Ibid., 158

73. Jancke, 1939, 105

74. Henning, 1931, 96

75. Vogt, 1932, 145

76. Lang, 1920, 106

77. Schatz, 1927, 88–9

78. Ibid., 89

79. Rupprecht, 1929, II, 33

80. Masefield, 1984, 210

81. Fliess and Dittmar, 1927, 117–18

82. Heinemann, in Ibid., 126

83. Nichols, 1922, 99

84. Reichsarchiv, 1925–44, XI, 76

85. Rupprecht, 1929, II, 36

86. Reichsarchiv, 1925–44, XI, 79

87. Gallwitz, 1932, 120

88. Reichsarchiv, 1925–344, XI, 78

89. Rupprecht, 1929, II, 34

CHAPTER ELEVEN

October – The Ancre Heights, Warlencourt and le Transloy

1. NA WO 157/283, Intelligence II Corps, 'Summary of Information. Received up to 6 p.m. 16th October 1916'

2. Rupprecht, 1929, II, 46

3. Frisch (ed.), 1931, 154

4. Ibid., 159

5. NA WO 157/283, Intelligence II Corps, 'Summary of Information. Received up to 6 p.m. 16th October 1916'

6. Grossmann and Merkt, 1923–6, II, 61

7. Rupprecht, 1929, II, 37–8

8. Wolff, 1925, I, 285. See also Gabriel, 1921, 74

9. Carrington (Edmonds), 1929, 117

10. Ewing, 1921, 168

11. Wolff, 1925, I, 294

12. Ibid., I, 293

13. Pflugbeil, 1923, 63

14. KA 2 ID, Bd 30, *Vernehmung*, IX Reserve Corps, 21 October 1916

15. Speck, 1937, 135

16. Möller, 1937, 181

17. Wittneben, in Ibid., 183–4

18. KA 2 ID, Bd 29, 15th Bavarian Regiment, *Gefechtsbericht über den Angriff der Engländer am 18.10. Vorm.*, 21 October 1916

19. Rupprecht, 1929, II, 54

20. Ibid., III, 46. See also Solleder, 1932, 249; Speck, 1937, 146

21. KA 3 ID, Bd 70, *Nachrichten über den Gegner*, HQ of the General Staff of the Field Army, Intelligence Department, 12 October 1916

22. Rupprecht, 1929, II, 47

23. Ibid., II, 53

24. Goldammer, 1931, 140

25. Stosch, 1930, 198

CHAPTER TWELVE
The Final Actions: 13–14 and 18–19 November

1. Wolff, 1924, 70–71

2. Rupprecht, 1929, II, 63

3. Buttmann, 1935, 171

4. KA 14 ID, Bd 11, Army Group A, *Untersuchungen der Ursachen für Verlust der Stellungen bei Beaumont und St. Pierre Divion*, 27 November 1916

5. Wolff, 1924, 71

6. KA 14 ID, Bd 11, Army Group A, *Untersuchungen ...* 27 November 1916

7. Wilhelm Müller, in Bröcker and Kayser, 1928, 193

8. Müller in ibid., 194

9. Kalbe, 1938, 278; Böttger et al., 1927, 140

10. Stratmann in Wohlenberg, 1931, 243

11. Mücke, 1922, 42–3

12. KA 14 ID, Bd 13, *Vernehmung eines verwundet gefangenen englischen Oberstleutnants, Kommandeur des VIII. N. Staff. R., 57. Brig., 19. Div., eingebracht am 18.11.16. im Grandcourt-Riegel südl. Grandcourt*, Army HQ, 23 November 1916

13. Böttger et al., 1927, 138

14. Fromm, 1920, 75

15. Kalbe, 1938, 279

16. KA 14 ID, Bd 13, *Vernehmung eines verwundet gefangenen englischen Oberstleutnants ...* 23 November 1916

17. Bröcker and Kayser, 1928, 84

18. Wolters, 1921, 62–3; Schmidt, 1922, 111–12; Freund, 1930, 168

19. Rupprecht, 1929, II, 68

20. Wolters, 1921, 63

CHAPTER THIRTEEN
The British Style of Combat

1. KA 2 ID, Bd 81, *Nachrichten von der englischen Front*, Army HQ, 2 April 1916

2. KA 3 ID, Bd 77, 12th Bavarian IR to the 6th Bavarian Brigade, *Erfahrungen aus der Schlacht an der Somme*, 30 September 1916

3. KA 1 ID, Bd 81, *Engländer*, 6 February 1916

4. Ashworth, 1980, 185–91

5. Frisch (ed.), 1931, 154

6. Rupprecht, 1929, I, 469

7. Kohl, 1932, 113

8. KA 2 ID, Bd 81, *Nachrichten von der englischen Front*, Army HQ, 2 April 1916

9. Gerster (*Reserve-Infanterie-Regiment 119*), 1920, 48

10. Böttger et al., 1927, 149

11. KA 6 ID, Bd 59, 6th Bavarian IR to the 6th Bavarian Infantry Division, 12 October 1916; KA 14 ID, Bd 11, 56th Infantry Division, *Erfahrungen während des Einsatzes der Division in der Sommeschlacht vom 24.8. bis 19.9.*, Divisional HQ, 15 September 1916

12. KA 6 ID, Bd 59, 6th Bavarian IR to the 6th Bavarian Division, 12 October 1916

13. KA 3 ID, Bd 77, *Erfahrungen aus der Schlacht an der Somme*, 1 October 1916

14. Klähn, 1925, 156–7

15. Eberle, 1973, 81–2, 90

16. Dudley Ward, 1921, 50

17. Klähn, 1925, 177

18. Wolff, 1925, I, 140–41. See also KA 3 ID, Bd 77, Army to all brigades and regiments, 22 August 1916; Klähn, 1925, 157

19. KA 6 ID, Bd 18, Notification of the III Bavarian Army Corps, 15 September 1916

20. Stosch, 1927, I, 20

21. Wolff, 1925, I, 241

22. Hansch and Weidling, 1929, 315

23. Klähn, 1925, 156

24. Ibid., 156

25. Gallwitz, 1932, 77

26. KA 2 ID, Bd 81, *Nachrichten von der englischen Front*, Army HQ, 2 April 1916

27. KA 3 ID, Bd 60, *Vernehmung* of troops of the 39th Division, captured 3 September 1916

28. Weiland, 1929, 91. See also KA 3 ID, Bd 77, Army to all brigades and regiments, 22 August 1916; Mücke, 1922, 43; Wohlenberg, 1931, 342

29. KA 6 ID, Bd 18, III Bavarian Corps to the 6th Bavarian Infantry Division, 21 September 1916. See also KA 6 ID, Bd 18, General von Below, *Armeebefhel betreffend Engländer- und Französennester*, 22 September 1916; KA 6 ID, Bd 59, 11th Bavarian IR to the 12th Bavarian Infantry Brigade, *Erfahrungsbericht über den Verteidigungskampf und den Stellungsbau in der Somme-Schlacht*, 9 October 1916

CHAPTER FOURTEEN

Weapons of Close Support

1. KA 3 ID, Bd 70, *Die Bewaffnung der britischen Truppen mit Maschinengewehren*, Great HQ, 13 October 1916

2. KA 4 ID, Bd 35, *Nachtrag zu den Aussagen der am 21. Mai östlich Cabaret-Rouge gefangen genommenen englischen Offiziere*, 25 May 1916. The captured officers were Captain G. N. Portman and Lieutenants Gurney and Brooks, all of the London Regiment

3. KA 3 ID, Bd 70, *Die Bewaffnung* ... Great HQ, 13 October 1916

4. Ibid.

5. Ibid.

6. Ibid.

7. KA 4 ID, Bd 35, *Nachtrag* ... 25 May 1916

8. Jünger, 2004, 78

9. KA 3 ID, Bd 70, *Die Bewaffnung* ... Great HQ, 13 October 1916

10. KA 4 ID, Bd 35, *Nachtrag* ... 25 May 1916

11. KA 3 ID, Bd 70, *Aussagen* of personnel of the 2/Rifle Brigade, captured 29 July, Army HQ, 31 July 1916

12. KA 5 ID, Bd 22, *Gefechtsbericht des 7. I-Rs. Über den Einsatz an der Somme*, 18 October 1916. See also KA 14 ID, Bd 11, 13th Infantry Division's *Erfahrungen aus der Somme-Schlacht*, Divisional HQ, 11 October 1916

13. KA 3 ID, Bd 70, *Die Bewaffnung* ... Great HQ, 13 October 1916

14. Ibid.

15. KA 14 ID, Bd 11, 13th Infantry Division's *Erfahrungen* ... Divisional HQ, 11 October 1916

16. KA 2 ID, Bd 81, *Nachrichten von der englischen Front im Abschnitt St. Eloi –Loos*, Army HQ, 15 February 1916

17. E.g. KA 10 ID, Bd 18, *Bericht über die Gefechtstätigkeit des II. Bats. Reserve Infantrie-Regiment Nr. 15 von 7. Bis 20. Juli 1916*. See also Parker, 1964, 49

18. Carrington, 1965, 174. See also Eden, 1976, 70

19. KA 5 ID, Bd 22, First Lieutenant Döge, *Bericht zur Brigade Verfügung vom 20.9.1916*

20. KA 6 ID, Bd 59, 11th Bavarian IR to the 12th Bavarian Brigade, *Erfahrungsbericht über den Verteidigungskampf und den Stellungsbau in der Somme-Schlacht*, 9 October 1916

21. Nichols, 1922, 123

22. KA 10 ID, Bd 46, *Unterhaltung mit einem verwundeten englischen Offizier des V / York & Lanc. R. ... eingebracht am 2.7. im Gegend nördlich Thiepval*, Army HQ, 6 July 1916. The identification of the 5th Battalion is doubtful. On the British faith in the Mills see also Gallwitz, 1932, 77

23. NA WO 157/320, III Corps Intelligence Summary, 29–29 September 1916

24. NA WO 157/282, 'Extract to Reserve Army Summary, No. 171, 20/9/16'

25. Stühmke, 1923, 132

26. Masefield, 1984, 288

27. Gerster (*Reserve-Infanterie-Regiment 119*), 1920, 50

28. Lademann, 1922, 33

29. Reymann, 1930, 129

30. KA 5 ID, Bd 22, *Anhang zum Gefechtsbericht über den Einsatz des Regiments an der Somme*, 10 October 1916

CHAPTER FIFTEEN
Artillery

1. KA 3 ID, Bd 70, *Über Stimmungen der bisherigen Gefangenen aus der Somme-Schlacht ...* Army HQ, 15 October 1916

2. KA 4 ID, Bd 26, Franck, Commander of the Pioneers of the 4th Bavarian Division, *Beobachtungen und Erfahrungen aus der Somme-Schlacht*, Divisional HQ, 1 October 1916

3. KA 2 ID, Bd 81, *Nachrichten von der englischen Front. II. Fortsetzung*, Army HQ, 2 April 1916

4. KA 3 ID, Bd 70, *Aussagen eines verwundeten Offiziers (Oberleutnant) vom IX/W. York. R.*, 16 August 1916

5. KA 14 ID, Bd 11, 56th Infantry Division, *Erfahrungen des Einsatzes der Division in der Somme-Schlacht vom 24.8. bis 19.9.*, Divisional HQ, 15 September 1916. See also Wohlenberg, 1931, 307

6. KA 5 ID, Bd 22, Major General von Lindequist, commander of the 3rd *Garde* Division, to the Chief of the Great General Staff, 29 (?) December 1916

7. Palmer, 1917, 51

8. Jünger, 2004, 80

9. Ibid., 85

10. KA 6 ID, Bd 18, *Erfahrungen des IV. Armeekorps aus der Somme-Schlacht*, 15 September 1916

11. Lang, 1920, 104

12. Kümmel, 1926, 230

13. Rupprecht, 1929, III, 103

14. NA WO 157/319, Intelligence III Corps, August 1916, 'Extracts from a conversation with a Vizefeldwebel of the 133rd Regiment (Saxon), captured near Mouquet Farm on the 11th inst ...'

15. NA WO 157/320, III Corps Intelligence Summary, 21–22 September 1916

16. KA 3 ID, Bd 22, *Gefechtsbericht des 7. Infanterie Regiments über den Einsatz an der Somme*, 18 October 1916

17. Reymann, 1930, 130

18. Buttmann, 1935, 171

19. Bröcker and Kayser, 1928, 187

20. Reymann, 1930, 130

21. KA 13 ID, Bd 77, 1st Infantry Brigade, *Erfahrungen aus der Schlacht an der Somme*

22. Vormann, III, 409

23. Ashworth, 1980, 125

24. Wolff, 1925, I, 286

25. Ibid., I, 286. See also Below's order of 22 October 1916, in Vogt, 1932, 45

26. KA 4 ID, Bd 26, Franck, *Erfahrungen aus der Somme-Schlacht*, Divisional HQ, 1 October 1916; KA 5 ID, Bd 22, XXVI Reserve Corps, *Erfahrungen in der Sommeschlacht. Richtlinien für kükünftige derartige Kämpfe*, 24 October 1916

27. Carrington, 1965, 129

28. Gallwitz, 1932, 90

29. Kohl, 1932, 132

30. KA 5 ID, Bd 22, 10th Bavarian Infantry Brigade to the 5th Bavarian Division, *Erfahrungen an der Somme*, 22 September 1916; KA 5 ID, Bd 22, Baron von Gelbsattel, *Erfahrungen aus der Somme-Schlacht*, 20 October 1916

31. KA 5 ID, Bd 22, III Bavarian Corps, *Erfahrungen aus der Somme-Schlacht*, 30 October 1916

32. KA 5 ID, Bd 22, XXVI Reserve Corps, *Erfahrungen in der Sommeschlacht*, 24 October 1916

CHAPTER SIXTEEN
Gas

1. Williams, 1933, 57

2. KA 2 ID, Bd 81, *Nachrichten von der englischen Front im Abschnitt St. Eloi-Loos*, 2 February 1916

3. KA 4 ID, Bd 35, *Aussagen* of one officer and twenty-one men of the 20/New South Wales Battalion, captured 5 May 1916

4. KA 4 ID, Bd 35, Account of Corporal P. J. Jones, 8/Royal Dublin Fusiliers, captured 28 April 1916

5. KA 3 ID, Bd 77, *Erfahrung der 1. Armee in der Sommeschlacht 1916 (24.6.–16.11.1916)*

6. Wohlenberg, 1931, 207

7. Forstner, 1929–30, I, 350–51

CHAPTER SEVENTEEN
The Tank

1. Gabriel, 1921, 61

2. NA WO 157/282, II Corps Intelligence Summaries, received up to 6 p.m. 16 September 1916, 'Notes on conversations with captured officers of the 209th Reserve Regiment'

3. KA 4 ID, Bd 35, Captain Weber, *Über die neuen englischen Panzerwagen (Caterpillar)*, Army HQ, 28 September 1916

4. Wolff, 1925, I, 294

5. KA 14 ID, Bd 13, *Stimmungsbild nach Aussagen von Gefangenen aus den Oktober – und November – Kämpfen der Somme*, Army HQ, 16 December 1916

6. Kuhl, 1920, 91

7. KA 3 ID, Bd 70, HQ of the Sixth Army to all general commands and the chief of the Great General Staff, *Englische Panzerwagen*, 29 October 1916

8. KA 2 ID, Bd 81, Army Group Crown Prince of Bavaria, *Englische Kampfkraftwagen*, 21 October 1916

9. KA 4 ID, Bd 35, Captain Weber, *Über die neuen englischen Panzerwagen (Caterpillar)*, Army HQ, 28 September 1916

10. Charteris, 1931, 177

11. Nicolai, 1924, 186

12. KA 2 ID, Bd 30, 18th Reserve Division, *Vernehmung von Gefangenen der 56. Div., 47. Div., 14. Div., über die englischen Panzerwagen (Caterpillar Tanks)*, Divisional HQ, 12 October 1916

13. KA 2 ID, Bd 30, *Vernehmung eines Sergeanten vom XIII/Dur. L.I., 68. Brig., 23. Div., gefangen den 7/10/16. Frühe südwestlich le Sars, über Panzerfahrzeuges (Caterpillars)*, Army HQ, 15 October 1916

14. KA 4 ID, Bd 35, Captain Weber, *Über die neuen englischen Panzerwagen (Caterpillar)*, Army HQ, 28 September 1916

15. KA 3 ID, Bd 70, HQ of the Sixth Army ... *Englische Panzerwagen*, 29 October 1916

16. Wohlenberg, 1931, 231

17. Rupprecht, 1929, II, 41

18. KA 3 ID, Bd 70, HQ of the Sixth Army ... *Englische Panzerwagen*, 29 October 1916

CHAPTER EIGHTEEN
The Royal Flying Corps

1. KA 2 ID, Bd 81, *Vorläufiges Ergebnis der Vernehmung der am 23.4. durch Oberlt. Immelmann und Leutnant Mulrer bei der Mühle von Pelvles abgeschossenen englischen Fliegeroffiziere, 11. Abt., 13. Wing*, Army HQ, 25 April 1916. See also Baring, 1930, 139

2. KA 2 ID, Bd 81, *Fliegerabgaben. Nach Aussagen von etwa 10 englischen Flugzeugführern und Beobachtern aus der Zeit von Oktober 1915 bis January 1916*, Army HQ

3. KA 2 ID, Bd 81, *Aussagen eines am 13.3. gegen 6. Uhr nachm., bei Bourlon heruntergeschossenen Flugzeug-Beobachters*, 16 May 1916

4. Wingfield, in Ackerley (ed.), 1932, 292

5. KA 4 ID, Bd 35, *Aussagen der am 1.6.16. bei St. Quentin westl. Lille notgelandeten englischen Flieger*, Army HQ, 3 June 1916

6. KA 4 ID, Bd 35, *Aussagen der am 31.5.16. bei Inchy gefangen genommenen englischen Flieger*, Army HQ, 3 June 1916

7. KA 2 ID, Bd 81, *Vorläufiges Ergebnis ...* Army HQ, 25 April 1916

8. Winchester, 1971, 10

9. Tubbs, in *Purnell's History of the Great War*, 1971, V, No. 3, 1,863

10. KA 5 ID, Bd 63, *Aussagen von 3 engl. Flieger-Offiziere, abgeschossen am 27.9.16. vorm., bei Dury, südwest. Vitry*, undated, September 1916

11. Palmer, 1917, 140

12. KA 6 RID, Bd 23, *Aussagen des am 3.VII.16. vormittags von einem Fokker bei Douai zur Landung gezwungenen engl. Flieger-Leutnants W. Baxter-Ellis vom R. Fl. C., 5. Squadron, 2. Wing*, Army HQ, 3 July 1916

13. NA WO 157/322, III Corps Intelligence Summary, 'Extracts from the Examination of an Observer (Officer) and a Pilot (*Offizier-Stellvertreter*) belonging to the 34th Feld Flieger Abteilung, captured near Flers on the 16/11/16'

14. Tubbs, in *Purnell's History of the Great War*, 1971, V, No. 3, 1,863

15. Strange, undated, 111

16. KA 4 ID, Bd 35, *Aussagen der am, 31.5.16. bei Inchy ...* Army HQ, 3 June 1916

17. Evans, 1921, 8

18. Ludendorff, 1921, 211–12

19. Gough, 1931, 149. See also Reimann, 2000, 71

20. Baring, 1930, 179–80

21. Goldammer, 1931, 100

22. KA 3 ID, Bd 77, 12th Bavarian IR to the 6th Bavarian Infantry Brigade, *Erfahrungen aus der Schlacht an der Somme*, 30 September 1916. See also KA 5 ID, Bd 22, *Gefechtsbericht des 7.* [Bavarian] *Inf. Rs. (Prinz Leopold) über den Einsatz an der Somme*, to the 10th Bavarian Infantry Brigade, 18 October 1916

23. Jancke, 1939, 109, 115

24. KA 3 ID, Bd 77, *Erfahrungen der II. Armee in der Sommeschlacht (2.6.–26.11.1916)*, Army HQ, 30 January 1917

25. Schatz, 1927, 83

26. Jancke, 1939, 132–3

27. Pafferath, 1930, 31

28. Wolff, 1925, I, 301

29. NA WO 157/284, 'IInd Corps Summary of Information. Received up to 6 p.m. 13th November 1916'; Pflugbeil, 1923, 63

30. Reinhardt, et. al., 1928, 274. See also KA 5 ID, Bd 22, Major General von Lindequist to the Chief of the General Staff, 29 (?) December 1916; Hartmann, 1921, 199; Wolff, 1924, II, 70; Kümmel, 1926, 248; Hüttmann and Krüger, 1929, 108; Freund, 1930, 16; Buttmann, 1935, 171

31. KA 2 ID, Bd 81, *Nachrichten von der englischen Front. II. Fortsetzung*, Army HQ, 2 February 1916

32. KA 2 ID, Bd 81, *Vorläufiges Ergebnis ...* Army HQ, 25 April 1916

33. KA 3 ID, Bd 70, *Aussagen eines am 20.10.16. bei Monchy-les-Preux östl. Arras abgeschossenen engl. Fliegers*, Army HQ, 26 October 1916

34. KA 2 ID, Bd 81, *Fliegerabgaben ...* Army HQ, undated

35. Ibid.

36. KA 2 ID, Bd 81, *Aussagen eines bei Tourcoing am 19.1. heruntergeschossenen engl. Fliegeroffiziers vom 15. Squadron, 2. Wing, R.F.C.*, Army HQ, 21 January 1916

37. KA 4 ID, Bd 35, *Aussagen der am 31.5.16. bei Inchy ...* Army HQ, 3 June 1916

38. KA 2 ID, Bd 81, *Vorläufiges Ergebnis ...* Army HQ, 25 April 1916

39. KA 4 ID, Bd 3, *Weitere Aussagen der am 31.5.16. bei Inchy abgeschossenen englischen Fliegeroffiziers*, early June 1916

40. KA 2 ID, Bd 81, *Aussagen eines am 13.3. gegen 6 Uhr nachm ...* 16 May 1916

41. Jünger, 2004, 98

42. KA 3 ID, Bd 27, *Verlauf des Angriffs des I/5 IR am 31.8.1916 und des feindl. Gegenangriffs am 1.9.16. nach Schilderung der Komp. Führer des I/5 IR*, 2 September 1916

43. NA WO 157/281, 'Annexe to the IInd Corps Summary, No. 19, 12/8/16'

44. Ritter, Holger, 1926, 153

45. KA 5 ID, Bd 22, Major General von Lindequist to the Chief of the Great General Staff, 28 (?) December 1916

46. KA 3 ID, Bd 49, *Vernehmung eines englischen Fliegeroffiziers vom 19. Squadron, 9. Wg., abgeschossen bei Grévillers am 26.8.16*, Army HQ, 28 August 1916

47. KA 5 ID, Bd 22, *Bericht zur Brigade Verfügung vom 29.9.26*. See also Goldammer, 1931, 100

48. Jancke, 1929, 81

49. Wingfield, in Ackerley (ed.), 1932, 91

50. KA 14 ID, Bd 13, *Vernehmung eines schwerverwundeten Fliegeroffiziersm 7. Squad., 16. Wing, abgeschossen am 21.12. vorm. zwischen Miraumont und Serre*, 27 December 1916

51. KA 2 ID, Bd 81, *Nachrichten von der englischen Front. II. Fortsetzung*, Army HQ, 2 February 1916

52. KA 2 ID, Bd 81, *Fliegerabgaben ...* Army HQ, undated

53. Reichsarchiv, 1925–44, XI, 110

54. Wilson, 1986, 371

The Reckoning

1. Masefield, 1984, 221

2. Rupprecht, 1929, I, 423

3. Pugsley, 2004, 174

4. Rupprecht, 1929, II, 65

5. Lossberg, 1929, 270; Reichsarchiv, 1925–44, XI, 94–5

6. Beumelburg, 1929, 220

7. Ibid., 221

8. Sheffield, 2003, 151–2

9. Etzel, 1928, 25. See also Brandenstein, 1921, 84; Reinhardt et al., 1928, 274

10. Kalbe, 1938, 287

11. Stenger, 1935, 218

12. Ludendorff, 1922, 253. See also Stühmke, 1923, 132; Wolff, 1925, I, 240; Rupprecht, 1929, II, 64; Gallwitz, 1932, 77

13. Kuhl, 1920, 93

14. Ibid., 89

15. KA 14 ID, Bd 13, *Aus Unterhaltungen mit im Dezember 1916 eingebrachten englischen Gefangenen*, 1 January 1917

Order of Battle

British Order of Battle

British Expeditionary Force – General Sir Douglas Haig

FOURTH ARMY General Sir Henry Rawlinson

RESERVE/FIFTH ARMY General Sir Hubert Gough

THIRD ARMY Lieutenant General Sir Edmund H. H. Allenby

II CORPS Lieutenant General C. W. Jacob

III CORPS Lieutenant General Sir W. P. Pulteney

V CORPS Lieutenant General E. A. Fanshawe

VII CORPS Lieutenant General Sir T. d'O Snow

VIII CORPS Lieutenant General Sir A.G. Hunter-Weston

X CORPS Lieutenant General Sir T. L. N. Morland

XIII CORPS Lieutenant General Sir W. N. Congreve

XIV CORPS Lieutenant General The Earl of Cavan

XV CORPS Lieutenant General H. S. Horne (promoted to command First Army)
   the Lieutenant General J. P. du Cane

I ANZAC Lieutenant General Sir W. R. Birdwood

CANADIAN CORPS Lieutenant General the Honourable Sir J. Byng

GUARDS DIVISION Major General G. P. T. Fielding
1st Guards Brigade
2/Grenadier Guards, 2/Coldstream Guards, 3/Coldstream Guards, 1/Irish Guards
2nd Guards Brigade
3/Grenadier Guards, 1/Coldstream Guards, 1/Scots Guards, 2/Irish Guards
3rd Guards Brigade
1/Grenadier Guards, 4/Grenadier Guards, 2/Scots Guards, 1/Welch Guards
Pioneers
4/Coldstream Guards

1ST DIVISION   Major General E. P. Strickland

1st Brigade
10/Glosters, 1/Black Watch, 8/Royal Berkshires, 1/Camerons
2nd Brigade
2/Royal Sussex, 1/Loyal North Lancashire, 1/Northamptons, 2/King's Royal Rifle Corps
3rd Brigade
1/South Wales Borderers, 1/Glosters, 2/Welch, 2/Royal Munster Fusiliers
Pioneers
1/6th Welch

2ND DIVISION   Major General W.G. Walker

5th Brigade
17/Royal Fusiliers, 24/Royal Fusiliers, 2/Oxfordshire and Buckinghamshire Light Infantry, 2/Highland Light Infantry
6th Brigade
1/King's Regiment, 2/South Staffordshires, 13/Essex, 17/Middlesex
99th Brigade
22/Royal Fusiliers, 23/Royal Fusiliers, 1/Royal Berkshires, 1/King's Royal Rifle Corps
Pioneers
10/Duke of Cornwall's Light Infantry

3RD DIVISION   Major General J. A. Haldane (promoted to command VI Corps) then C. J. Deverell

8th Brigade
2/Royal Scots, 8/East Yorkshires, 1/Royal Scots Fusiliers, 7/King's Shropshire Light Infantry
9th Brigade
1/Northumberland Fusiliers, 4/Royal Fusiliers, 13/King's Regiment, 12/West Yorkshires
76th Brigade
8/King's Own, 2/Suffolks, 10/Royal Welch, 1/Gordon Highlanders
Pioneers
20/King's Royal Rifle Corps

4TH DIVISION   Major General the Honourable W. Lambton

10th Brigade
1/Royal Warwicks, 2/Seaforths, 1/Royal Irish Fusiliers, 2/Royal Dublin Fusiliers
11th Brigade
1/Somerset Light Infantry, 1/East Lancashires, 1/Hampshires, 1/Rifle Brigade
12th Brigade
1/King's Own, 2/Lancashire Fusiliers, 2/Essex, 2/Duke of Wellington's Regiment
Pioneers
21/West Yorkshire

5TH DIVISION   Major General R. B. Stephens

13th Brigade
14/Royal Warwicks, 15/Royal Warwicks, 2/King's Own Scottish Borderers, 1/Royal West Kents

15th Brigade
16/Royal Warwicks, 1/Norfolks, 1/Bedfords, 1/Cheshires

95th Brigade
1/Devons, 12/Glosters, 1/East Surreys, 1/Duke of Cornwall's Light Infantry

Pioneers
1/6th Argyll and Sutherland Highlanders

6TH DIVISION   Major General C. Ross

16th Brigade
1/Buffs (Royal East Kent), 8/Bedfords, 1/King's Shropshire Light Infantry, 2/York and Lancaster

18th Brigade
1/West Yorkshires, 11/Essex, 2/Durham Light Infantry, 14/Durham Light Infantry

71st Brigade
9/Norfolks, 9/Suffolks, 1/Leicesters, 2/Sherwood Foresters

Pioneers
11/Leicesters

7TH DIVISION   Major General H. E. Watts

20th brigade
8/Devons, 9/Devons, 2/Borders, 2/Gordon Highlanders

22nd Brigade
2/Royal Warwicks, 2/Royal Irish, 1/Royal Welch Fusiliers, 20/Manchesters

91st Brigade
2/Queen's, 1/South Staffordshires, 21/Manchesters, 22/Manchesters

Pioneers
24/Manchesters

8TH DIVISION   Major General H. Hudson

23rd Brigade
2/Devons, 2/West Yorkshires, 2/Middlesex, 2/Scots Rifle

24th Brigade '
1/Worcestershires, 1/Sherwood Foresters, 2/Northamptons, 2/East Lancashires

25th Brigade
2/Lincolns, 2/Royal Berkshires, 1/Royal Irish Rifles, 2/Rifle Brigade

Pioneers
22/Durham Light Infantry

9TH (SCOTTISH) DIVISION   Major General W.T. Furse

26th Brigade
8/Black Watch, 7/Seaforths, 5/Camerons, 10/Argyll and Sutherland Highlanders

27th Brigade
11/Royal Scots, 12/Royal Scots, 6/King's Own Scottish Borderers, 9/Scottish Rifles

South African Brigade
1/ Cape Province, 2/Natal & O.F.S., 3/Transvaal and Rhodesia, 4/Scottish
Pioneers
9/Seaforth

11TH DIVISION   Lieutenant General Sir C. Woollcombe

32nd Brigade
9/West Yorkshires, 6/Green Howards, 8/Duke of Wellington's Regiment, 6/York and Lancaster
33rd Brigade
6/Lincolns, 6/Border Regiment, 7/South Staffordshires, 9/Sherwood Foresters
34th Brigade
8/Northumberland Fusiliers, 9/Lancashire Fusiliers, 5/Dorsets, 11/Manchesters
Pioneers
6/East Yorkshires

12TH DIVISION   Major General A. B. Scott

35th Brigade
7/Norfolks, 7/Suffolks, 9/Essex, 5/Royal Berkshires
36th Brigade
8/Royal Fusiliers, 9/Royal Fusiliers, 7/Royal Sussex, 11/Middlesex
37th Brigade
6/Queen's, 6/Buffs (Royal East Kent), 7/East Surreys, 6/Royal West Kents
Pioneers
5/Northamptons

14TH (LIGHT) DIVISION   Major General V. A. Couper

41st Brigade
7/King's Royal Rifle Corps, 8/King's Royal Rifle Corps, 7/Rifle Brigade, 8/Rifle Brigade
42nd Brigade
5/Oxfordshire and Buckinghamshire Light Infantry, 5/King's Shropshire Light Infantry,
9/King's Royal Rifle Corps, 9/Rifle Brigade
43rd Brigade
6/Somerset Light Infantry, 6/Duke of Cornwall's Light Infantry, 6/King's Own Yorkshire Light
Infantry, 10/Durham Light Infantry
Pioneers
11/King's

15TH (SCOTTISH) DIVISION   Major General F. W. N. McCracken

44th Brigade
9/Black Watch, 8/Seaforth, 8th/10th Gordons, 7/Camerons
45th Brigade
13/Royal Scottish, 6th/7th Royal Scots Fusiliers, 6/Camerons, 11/Argyll and Sutherland
Highlanders

46th Brigade
10/Scottish Rifle, 7th/8th King's Own Scottish Borderers, 10th/11th Highland Light Infantry, 12/Highland Light Infantry

Pioneers
9/Gordons

16TH (IRISH) DIVISION   Major General W. B. Hickie

47th Brigade
6/Royal Irish, 6/Connaught Rangers, 7/Leinster, 8/Royal Munster Fusiliers

48th Brigade
7/Royal Irish Rifles, 1/Royal Munster Fusiliers, 8/Royal Dublin Fusiliers, 9/Royal Dublin Fusiliers

49th Brigade
7/Royal Inniskilling Fusiliers, 8/Royal Inniskilling Fusiliers, 7/Royal Irish Fusiliers, 8/Royal Irish Fusiliers

Pioneers
11/Hampshires

17TH DIVISION   Major General T. D. Pilcher (relieved) then Major General P. R. Robertson

50th Brigade
10/West Yorkshires, 7/East Yorkshires, 7/Green Howards, 6/Dorsets

51st Brigade
7/Lincolns, 7/Border Regiment, 8/South Staffordshires, 10/Sherwood Foresters

52nd Brigade
9/Northumberland Fusiliers, 10/Lancashire Fusiliers, 9/Duke of Wellington's Regiment, 12/Manchesters

Pioneers
7/York and Lancaster

18TH (EASTERN) DIVISION   Major General F. I. Maxse

53rd Brigade
8/Norfolks, 8/Suffolks, 10/Essex, 6/Royal Berkshires

54th Brigade
11/Royal Fusiliers, 7/Bedfords, 6/Northamptons, 12/Middlesex

55th Brigade
7/Queen's, 7/Buffs (Royal East Kent), 8/East Surrey, 7/Royal West Kent

Pioneers
8/Royal Sussex

19TH (WESTERN) DIVISION   Major General G. T. M. Bridges

56th Brigade
7/King's Own, 7/East Lancashires, 7/South Lancashires, 7/L. N. Lancashires

57th Brigade
10/Royal Warwick, 8/Glosters, 10/Worcestors, 8/North Staffordshire

58th Brigade
9/Cheshires, 9/Royal Welch Fusiliers, 9/Welch, 6/Wiltshires

Pioneers
5/South Wales Borderers

20TH (LIGHT) DIVISION Major General W. D. Smith

59th Brigade
10/King's Royal Rifle Corps, 11/King's Royal Rifle Corps, 10/Rifle Brigade, 11/Rifle Brigade

60th Brigade
6/Oxford and Buckinghamshire Light Infantry, 6/King's Shropshire Light Infantry, 12/King's Royal Rifle Corps, 12/Rifle Brigade

61st Brigade
7/Somerset Light Infantry, 7/Duke of Cornwall's Light Infantry, 7/King's Own Yorkshire Light Infantry, 12/King's

Pioneers
11/Durham Light Infantry

21ST DIVISION Major General D. G. M. Campbell

62nd Brigade
12/Northumberland Fusiliers, 13/Northumberland Fusiliers, 1/Lincolns, 10/Green Howards

63rd Brigade [2]
8/Lincolns, 8/Somerset Light Infantry, 4/Middlesex, 10/York and Lancaster

64th Brigade
1/East Yorkshires, 9/King's Own Yorkshire Light Infantry, 10/King's Own Yorkshire Light Infantry, 15/Durham Light Infantry

Pioneers
14/Northumberland Fusiliers

23RD DIVISION Major General J. M. Babington

68th Brigade
10/Northumberland Fusiliers, 11/Northumberland Fusiliers, 12/Durham Light Infantry, 13/Durham Light Infantry

69th Brigade
11/West Yorkshires, 8/Green Howards, 9/Green Howards, 10/Duke of Wellington's Regiments

70th Brigade [3]
11/Sherwood Foresters, 8/King's Own Yorkshire Light Infantry, 8/York and Lancaster, 9/York and Lancaster

Pioneers
9/South Staffordshires

24TH DIVISION Major General J. E. Capper

17th Brigade
8/Buffs (Royal East Kent), 1/Royal Fusiliers, 12/Royal Fusiliers, 3/Rifle Brigade

72nd Brigade
8/Queen's, 9/East Surreys, 8/Royal West Kents, 1/North Staffordshires

73rd Brigade
9/Royal Sussex, 7/Northamptons, 13/Middlesex, 2/Leinsters

Pioneers
12/Sherwood Foresters

25TH DIVISION   Major General E. G. T. Bainbridge

7th Brigade
10/Cheshires, 3/Worcesters, 8/Loyal North Lancashires, 1/Wiltshires

74th Brigade
11/Lancashire Fusiliers, 13/Cheshires, 9/Loyal North Lancashires, 2/Royal Irish Rifles

75th Brigade
11/Cheshires, 8/Border Regiment, 2/South Lancashires, 8/South Lancashires

Pioneers:
6/South Wales Borderers

29TH DIVISION   Major General H. de b. de Lisle

86th Brigade
2/Royal Fusiliers, 1/Lancashire Fusiliers, 16/Middlesex, 1/Royal Dublin Fusiliers

87th Brigade
2/South Wales Borderers, 1/King's Own Scottish Borderers, 1/Royal Inniskilling Fusiliers, 1/Border Regiment

88th Brigade
4/Worcestershire, 1/Essex, 2/Hampshires, Royal Newfoundland Regiment

Pioneers
2/Monmouth

30TH DIVISION   Major General J. S. M. Shea

21st Brigade
18/King's, 2/Green Howards, 2/Wiltshires, 19/Manchesters

89th Brigade
17/King's, 19/King's, 20/King's, 2/Bedfords

90th Brigade
2/Royal Scots Fusiliers, 16/Manchesters, 17/Manchesters, 18/Manchesters

Pioneers
11/South Lancashires

31ST DIVISION   Major General R. Wanless O'Gowan

92nd Brigade
10/East Yorkshires, 11/East Yorkshires, 12/East Yorkshires, 13/East Yorkshires

93rd Brigade
15/West Yorkshires, 16/West Yorkshires, 18/West Yorkshires, 18/Durham Light Infantry

94th Brigade
11/East Lancashires, 12/York and Lancaster, 13/York and Lancaster, 14/York and Lancaster

Pioneers
12/King's Own Yorkshire Light Infantry

32ND DIVISION Major General W. H. Rycroft

14th Brigade
19/Lancashire Fusiliers,[4] 1/Dorsetshires, 2/Manchesters, 15/Highland Light Infantry

96th Brigade
16/Northumberland Fusiliers, 15/Lancashire Fusiliers, 16/Lancashire Fusiliers, 2/Royal Inniskilling Fusiliers

97th Brigade
11/Border Regiment, 2/King's Own Yorkshire Light Infantry, 16/Highland Light Infantry, 17/Highland Light Infantry

Pioneers
17/Northumberland Fusiliers[5]

33RD DIVISION Major General H. J. S. Landon then Major General R. J. Pinney

19th Brigade
20th Royal Fusiliers, 2/Royal Welch Fusiliers, 1/Cameronians, 5/Scottish Rifles

98th Brigade
4/King's Regiment, 1/4th Suffolk, 1/Middlesex, 2/Argyll and Sutherland Highlanders

100th Brigade
1/Queen's Regiment, 2/Worcestershires , 16/King's Royal Rifle Corps, 1/9th Highland Light Infantry

Pioneers
18/Middlesex Regiment

34TH DIVISION Major General E. C. Ingouville-Williams (killed) then Major General C. L. Nicholson

101st Brigade
15/Royal Scots 16/Royal Scots 10/Lincolns 11/Suffolks

102nd (Tyneside Scottish) Brigade[6]
20/Northumberland Fusiliers, 21/ Northumberland Fusiliers, 22/Northumberland Fusiliers, 23/ Northumberland Fusiliers

103rd (Tyneside Irish) Brigade[7]
24/ Northumberland Fusiliers, 25/ Northumberland Fusiliers, 26/ Northumberland Fusiliers, 27/ Northumberland Fusiliers

Pioneers
18/ Northumberland Fusiliers[8]

35TH (BANTAM) DIVISION Major General R. J. Pinney

104th Brigade
17/Lancashire Fusiliers, 18/Lancashire Fusiliers, 20/Lancashire Fusiliers, 23/Manchester

105th Brigade
15/Cheshire, 16/Cheshire, 14/Glosters, 15/Sherwood Foresters

106th Brigade
17/Royal Scots, 17/West Yorkshires, 19/Durham Light Infantry, 18/Highland Light Infantry

Pioneers
19/Northumberland Fusiliers

36TH (ULSTER) DIVISION Major General O. S. W. Nugent

107th Brigade
8/Royal Irish Rifles, 9/Royal Irish Rifles, 10/Royal Irish Rifles, 15/Royal Irish Rifles

108th Brigade
11/Royal Irish Rifles, 12/Royal Irish Rifles, 13/Royal Irish Rifles, 9/Royal Irish Fusiliers

109th Brigade
9/Royal Inniskilling Fusiliers, 10/ Royal Inniskilling Fusiliers, 11/ Royal Inniskilling Fusiliers, 14/Royal Irish Rifles

Pioneers
16/Royal Irish Rifles

37TH DIVISON Major General S. W. Scrase-Dickens (sick) then Major General H. B. Williams

110th Brigade[9]
6/Leicesters 7/Leicesters, 8/Leicesters, 9/Leicesters

111th Brigade[10]
10/Royal Fusiliers, 13/Royal Fusiliers, 13/King's Royal Rifle Corps, 13/Rifle Brigade

112th Brigade[11]
11/Royal Warwicks, 6/Bedfords, 8/East Lancashires, 10/Loyal North Lancashires

Pioneers
9/North Staffordshires[12]

38TH (WELSH) DIVISION Major General I. Philipps (relieved) then Major General C. G. Blackader

113th Brigade
13/Royal Welch Fusiliers, 14/Royal Welch Fusiliers, 15/Royal Welch Fusiliers, 16/Royal Welch Fusiliers

114th Brigade
10/Welch, 13/Welch, 14/Welch, 15/Welch

115th Brigade
10/South Wales Borderers, 11/South Wales Borderers, 17/Royal Welch Fusiliers, 16/Welch

Pioneers
19/Welch

39TH DIVISION Major General G. J. Cuthbert

116th Brigade
11/Royal Sussex, 12/Royal Sussex, 13/Royal Sussex, 14/Hampshires

117th Brigade
16/Sherwood Foresters, 17/Sherwood Foresters, 17/King's Royal Rifle Corps, 16/Rifle Brigade

118th Brigade
1/6th Cheshires, 1/1st Cambridgeshires, 1/1st Hertfordshires, 4th/5th Black Watch

Pioneers
13/Glosters

41ST DIVISION   Major General S. T. B. Lawford

112th Brigade
12/East Surreys, 15/Hampshires, 11/Royal West Kents, 18/King's Royal Rifle Corps

123rd Brigade
11/Queen's, 10/Royal West Kents, 23/Middlesex, 20/Durham Light Infantry

124th Brigade
10/Queen's, 26/Royal Fusiliers, 32/Royal Fusiliers, 21/King's Royal Rifle Corps

Pioneers
19/Middlesex

46TH (NORTH MIDLAND) DIVISION (T.F.)   Major General Hon. E.J. Montagu-Stuart-Wortley (relieved) then Major General W. Thwaites

137th Brigade
1/5th South Staffordshires, 1/6th South Staffordshires, 1/5th North Staffordshires, 1/6th North Staffordshires

138th Brigade
1/4th Lincolns, 1/5th Lincolns, 1/4th Leicesters, 1/5th Leicesters

139th Brigade
1/5th Sherwood Foresters, 1/6th Sherwood Foresters, 1/7th Sherwood Foresters, 1/8th Sherwood Foresters

Pioneers
1/Monmouths

47TH (1/2ND LONDON) DIVISION (T.F.)   Major General Sir C. St. L. Barter (relieved) then Major General G. F. Gorringe

140th Brigade
1/6th Londons (City of London), 1/7th Londons (City of London), 1/8th Londons (Post Office Rifles), 1/15th Londons (Civil Service Rifles)

141st Brigade
1/17th Londons (Poplar and Stepney Rifles), 1/18th Londons (London Irish Rifles), 1/19th Londons (St. Pancras), 1/20th Londons (Blackheath and Woolwich)

142nd Brigade
1/21st Londons (1st Surrey Rifles), 1/22nd Londons (The Queen's), 1/23rd Londons, 1/24th Londons (The Queen's)

Pioneers
1/4th Royal Welch Fusiliers

48TH DIVISION (SOUTH MIDLAND) DIVISION (T.F.)   Major General R. Fanshawe

143rd Brigade
1/5th Royal Warwicks, 1/16th Royal Warwicks, 1/7th Royal Warwicks, 1/8th Royal Warwicks

144th Brigade
1/4th Glosters, 1/6th Glosters, 1/7th Worcestershires, 1/8th Worcestershires

145th Brigade
1/5th Glosters, 1/4th Oxfordshire and Buckinghamshire Light Infantry, 1/1st Buckinghamshires, 1/4th Royal Berkshires

Pioneers
1/5th Sussex

49TH (WEST RIDING) DIVISION (T.F.) Major General E. M. Perceval

146th Brigade
1/5th West Yorkshires, 1/6th West Yorkshires, 1/7th West Yorkshires, 1/8th West Yorkshires

147th Brigade
1/4th Duke of Wellington's Regiment, 1/5th Duke of Wellington's Regiment, 1/6th Duke of Wellington's Regiment, 1/7th Duke of Wellington's Regiment

148th Brigade
1/4th King's Own Yorkshire Light Infantry, 1/5th King's Own Yorkshire Light Infantry, 1/4th York and Lancaster, 1/5th York and Lancaster

Pioneers
3/Monmouth (Replaced by 19/Lancashire Fusiliers 6th August)

50TH (NORTHUMBERLAND) DIVISION (T.F.) Major General P. S. Wilkinson

149th Brigade
1/4th Northumberland Fusiliers, 1/5th Northumberland Fusiliers, 1/6th Northumberland Fusiliers, 1/7th Northumberland Fusiliers

150th Brigade
1/4th East Yorkshires, 1/4th Green Howards, 1/5th Green Howards, 1/5th Durham Light Infantry

151st Brigade
1/5th Border Regiment, 1/6th Durham Light Infantry, 1/8th Durham Light Infantry, 1/9th Durham Light Infantry

Pioneers
1/7th Durham Light Infantry

51ST (HIGHLAND) DIVISION (T.F.) Major General G. M. Harper

152nd Brigade
1/5th Seaforths, 1/6th Seaforths, 1/6th Gordons, 1/8th Argyll and Sutherlands

153rd Brigade
1/6th Black Watch, 1/7th Black Watch, 1/5th Gordons, 1/7th Gordons

154th Brigade
1/9th Royal Scots, 1/4th Seaforths, 1/4th Gordons, 1/7th Argyll and Sutherlands

Pioneers
1/8th Royal Scots

55TH (WEST LANCASHIRE) DIVISION (T.F.) Major General H. S. Jeudwine

164th Brigade
1/4th King's Own, 1/8th King's, 2/5th Lancashire Fusiliers, 1/4th Loyal North Lancashires
165th Brigade
1/5th King's, 1/6th King's, 1/7th King's, 1/9th King's
166th Brigade
1/5th King's Own, 1/10th King's, 1/5th South Lancashire, 1/5th Loyal North Lancashires
Pioneers
1/4th South Lancashires

56TH (1ST LONDON) DIVISION (T.F.) Major General C. P. A. Hull

167th Brigade
1/1st London Royal Fusiliers, 1/3rd London Royal Fusiliers, 1/7th Middlesex, 1/8th Middlesex
168th Brigade
1/4th London Royal Fusiliers, 1/12th London Rangers, 1/13th London (Kensington), 1/14th London (London Scottish)
169th Brigade
1/2nd Royal Fusiliers, 1/5th London Rifle Brigade, 1/9th London Queen's Victoria's Rifles, 1/16th London Queen's Westminster Rifles
Pioneers
1/5th Cheshire

63RD (ROYAL NAVAL) DIVISION Major General Sir A. Paris (wounded) then Major General C. D. Shute

188th Brigade
Anson Battalion, Howe Battalion, 1/Royal Marine Battalion, 2/Royal Marine Battalion
189th Brigade
Hood Batttalion, Nelson Battalion, Hawke Battalion, Drake Battalion
190th Brigade
1/Honourable Artillery Company, 7/Royal Fusiliers, 4/Bedfords, 10/Royal Dublin Fusiliers
Pioneers
14/Worcestershire

1ST AUSTRALIAN DIVISION Major General H. B. Walker

1(New South Wales) Brigade
1st Battalion, 2nd Battalion, 3rd Battalion, 4th Battalion
2nd (Victoria) Brigade
5th Battalion, 6th Battalion, 7th Battalion, 8th Battalion
3rd Brigade
9th (Queensland) Battalion, 10th (S. Australia) Battalion, 11th (W. Australia) Battalion, 12th (S. and W. Australia, Tas.) Battalion
Pioneers:
1st Australian Pioneers Battalion

2ND AUSTRALIAN DIVISION Major General J. G. Legge

5th (New South Wales) Brigade
17th Battalion, 18th Battalion, 19th Battalion, 20th Battalion

6th (Victoria) Brigade
21st Battalion, 22nd Battalion, 23rd Battalion, 24th Battalion

7th Brigade
25th (Queensland) Battalion, 26th (Q'land, Tas.) Battalion, 27th (S. Australia) Battalion,
28th (W. Australia) Battalion

Pioneers
2nd Australian Pioneer Battalion

4TH AUSTRALIAN DIVISION Major General Sir H. Cox

4th Brigade
13th (New South Wales) Battalion, 14th (Victoria) Battalion, 15th (Q'land, Tas.) Battalion,
16th (S. and W. Australia) Battalion

12th Brigade
45th (New South Wales) Battalion, 46th (Victoria) Battalion, 47th (Q'land, Tas.) Battalion,
48th (S. and W. Australia) Battalion

13th Brigade
49th (Queensland) Battalion, 50th (S. Australia, Tas.) Battalion, 51st (W. Australia) Battalion,
52nd (S. and W. Australia, Tas.) Battalion

Pioneers
5th Australian Pioneer Battalion

5TH AUSTRALIAN DIVISION Major General the Honourable J. W. McCay

8th Brigade
29th (Victoria) Battalion, 30th (N. S. Wales) Battalion, 31st (Q'land, Vic.) Battalion,
32nd (S. & W. Australian) Battalion

14th (New South Wales) Brigade
53rd Battalion, 54th Battalion, 55th Battalion, 56th Battalion

15th (Victoria) Brigade
57th Battalion, 58th Battalion, 59th Battalion, 60th Battalion

Pioneers
5th Australian Pioneer Battalion

1ST CANADIAN DIVISION Major General A. W. Currie

1st Brigade
1st (Ontario) Battalion, 2nd (East Ontario) Battalion, 3rd (Toronto Regiment) Battalion
4th Battalion

2nd Brigade
5th (Western Cavalry) Battalion, 7th Battalion (1st British Columbia), 8th Battalion (90th Rifles),
10th Battalion

3rd Brigade
13th Battalion (Royal Highlanders), 14th Battalion (R. Montreal Reg.), 15th Battalion
(48th Highlanders), 16th Battalion (Canadian Scottish)

Pioneers
1st Canadian Pioneer Battalion

2ND CANADIAN DIVISION Major General R. E. W. Turner

4th Brigade
18th (W. Ontario) Battalion, 19th (Central Ontario) Battalion, 20th (Central Ontario) Battalion, 21st (Eastern Ontario) Battalion

5th Brigade
22nd (Canadian Français) Battalion, 24th Battalion (Victorian Rifles), 25th Battalion (Nova Scotia Rifles), 26th (New Brunswick) Battalion

6th Brigade
27th (City of Winnipeg) Battalion, 28th (North-West) Battalion, 29th (Vancouver) Battalion, 31st (Alberta) Battalion

Pioneers
2nd Canadian Pioneers Battalion

3RD CANADIAN DIVISION Major General L. J. Lipsett

7th Brigade
Princess Patricia's Canadian Light Infantry, Royal Canadian Regiment, 42 Battalion (Royal Highlanders), 49th (Edmonton) Battalion

8th Brigade
1st Canadian Mounted Regiment, 2nd Canadian Mounted Regiment, 4th Canadian Mounted Regiment, 5th Canadian Mounted Regiment

9th Brigade
43rd Battalion (Cameron Highlanders), 52nd (New Ontario) Battalion, 58th Battalion, 60th Battalion (Victoria Rifles)

Pioneers
3rd Canadian Pioneer Battalion

4TH CANADIAN DIVISION Major General D. Watson

10th Brigade
44th Battalion, 46th (S. Saskatchewan) Battalion, 47th (British Columbia) Battalion, 50th (Calgary) Battalion

11th Brigade
54th (Kootenay) Battalion, 75th (Mississauga) Battalion, 87th Battalion (Canadian Grenadier Gds), 102nd Battalion

12th Brigade
38th (Ottawa) Battalion, 72nd Battalion (Seaforth Highlanders), 73rd Battalion (Royal Highlanders), 78th Battalion (Winnipeg Grenadiers)

Pioneers
67th Canadian Pioneer Battalion

NEW ZEALAND DIVISION Major General Sir A. H. Russell

1st New Zealand Brigade
1/Auckland, 1/Canterbury, 1/Otago, 1/Wellington

2nd New Zealand Brigade
2/Auckland, 2/Canterbury, 2/Otago, 2/Wellington

3rd New Zealand Rifle Brigade
1/New Zealand Rifle Brigade, 2/New Zealand Rifle Brigade, 3/New Zealand Rifle Brigade, 4/New Zealand Rifle Brigade

Pioneers
New Zealand Pioneer Battalion

1. With 23rd Division until 15th July, in exchange for 70th Brigade

2. Exchanged with 110th Brigade of 37th Division, 7 July

3. With 8th Division until 15th July in exchange for 24th Brigade

4. Replaced by 5th/6th Royal Scots, 29 July

5. Replaced by 12/L.N. Lancs., 19 October

6. Attached to 37th Division 7 July–21 August. Replaced by 111th Brigade

7. Attached to 37th Division 7 July–21 August. Replaced by 112th Brigade

8. Attached to 37th Division 7 July–21 August. Replaced by 9/North Staffordshires

9. Exchanged with 63rd Brigade, 21st Division, 7 July

10. Attached 7 July–21 August to 34th Division

11. Attached 7 July–21 August to 34th Division

12. Attached 7 July–21 August to 34th Division

German Order of Battle

2nd Army – General von Below

3rd Guard Division
Guards Fusiliers, Lehr Regiment, Grenadier Regiment No. 9

4th Guard Division
5th Guards Foot, 5th Guards Grenadiers, Reserve Regiment No. 93

5th Division
Grenadier Regiments Nos. 8 and 12, Regiment No. 52

6th Division
Regiments Nos. 20, 24 and 64

7th Division
Regiments Nos. 26, 27[1] and 165

8th Division
Regiments Nos. 72, 93 and 153

12th Division
Regiments Nos. 23, 62 and 63

16th Division
Regiments Nos. 28, 29, 68 and 69

24th Division
Regiments Nos. 133, 139 and 179

26th Division
Grenadier Regiment No. 119, Regiments Nos. 121 and 125

27th Division
Regiments No. 120, Grenadier Regiment No. 123, Regiments Nos. 124 and 127

38th Division
Regiments Nos. 94, 95 and 96

40th Division
Regiments Nos. 104, 134 and 181

52nd Division
Regiments Nos. 66, 161 and 170

56th Division,
Fusilier Regiment No. 35,
Regiments Nos. 88 and 118

58th Division
Regiments Nos. 106 and 107,
Reserve Regiment No. 120

111th Division
Fusilier Regiment No. 73
Regiments Nos. 76 and 164

117th Division
Regiment No. 157,
Reserve Regiments Nos. 11 and 22

183rd Division
Regiments Nos. 183 and 184,
Reserve Regiment No. 122

185th Division[2]
Regiments Nos. 185, 186 and 190

208th Division
Regiments Nos. 25 and 185, Reserve Regiment No. 65

222nd Division
Regiments Nos. 193 and 397, Reserve Regiment No. 81

223rd Division
Regiments Nos. 144 and 173, Ersatz Regiment No. 29

1st Guard Reserve Division
Guards Reserve Regiments Nos. 1 and 2, Reserve Regiment No. 64

2nd Guard Reserve Division
Reserve Regiments Nos. 15, 55, 77 and 91

7th Reserve Division
Reserve Regiments Nos. 36, 66 and 72

12 Reserve Division
Reserve Regiments Nos. 23, 38 and 51

17th Reserve Division
Regiments Nos. 162 and 163, Reserve Regiments Nos. 75[3] and 76

18th Reserve Division
Reserve Regiments Nos. 31, 84 and 86

19th Reserve Division
Reserve Regiments Nos. 73, 78, 79 and 92

23rd Reserve Division
Reserve Grenadier Regiment No. 101, Reserve Regiments Nos. 101 and 102,
Regiment No. 392

24th Reserve Division
Reserve Regiments Nos. 101, 107 and 133

26th Reserve Division
Reserve Regiments Nos. 99, 119, 121, Regiment No. 180

28th Reserve Division
Reserve Regiments Nos. 109, 110 and 111

45th Reserve Division
Reserve Regiments Nos. 210, 211 and 212

50th Reserve Division
Reserve Regiments Nos. 229, 230 and 231

51st Reserve Division
Reserve Regiments Nos. 233, 234, 235 and 236

52nd Reserve Division
Reserve Regiments Nos. 238, 239 and 240

4th Ersatz Division
Regiments Nos. 359, 360, 361 and 362

5th Ersatz Division
Landwehr Regiments Nos. 73, 74, Reserve Ersatz Regiment No. 3

2nd Bavarian Division
Bavarian Regiments Nos. 12, 15 and 20

3rd Bavarian Division
Bavarian Regiments Nos. 17, 18 and 23

4th Bavarian Division
Bavarian Regiments Nos. 5 and 9, Bavarian Reserve Regiment No. 5

5th Bavarian Division
Bavarian Regiments Nos. 7, 14, 19 and 21

6th Bavarian Division
Bavarian Regiments Nos. 6, 10, 11 and 13

10th Bavarian Division
Bavarian Regiment No. 16, Bavarian Reserve Regiments Nos. 6 and 8

6th Bavarian Reserve Division
Bavarian Reserve Regiments Nos. 16, 17, 20 and 21

Bavarian Ersatz Division
Bavarian Reserve Regiments Nos. 14 and 15, Ersatz Regiment No. 28

89th Reserve Brigade
Reserve Regiment Nos. 209 and 213

Marine Brigade
Marine Regiments Nos. 1, 2 and 3

1. Replaced by Regiment No. 393 for second tour
2. Reorganised for second tour, composition being Regiment Nos. 65, 161 and Reserve Regiment No. 28
3. Left division before second tour

Bibliography

Archival Sources

BAYERISCHES HAUPTSTAATSARCHIV, ABTEILUNG IV: KRIEGSARCHIV, MUNICH

The principal holdings relating to the Great War are arranged by division, year and subject matter, making a total of more than eighty files per division for each year. The files on intelligence and prisoner interrogation hold copies of the relevant papers from the other branches of the German Army.

NATIONAL ARCHIVES (THE FORMER PUBLIC RECORD OFFICE), KEW

Series WO 157: Intelligence summaries and extracts

Series WO 339: personal files of officers, including statements of former officer prisoners to investigating committee after return

OFFICIAL PUBLICATIONS OF THE BRITISH GENERAL STAFF (INTELLIGENCE), S.S. SERIES

- 421: *Notes on the German Army Corps. VI. Corps*, May 1916
- 424: *Notes on the German Corps. IX. Corps*, May 1916
- 434: *XIII. (Royal Württemberg) Corps. Fourth Army*, May 1916
- 442: *IV. Corps*, April 1916
- 478. Sixt von Armin, *Experiences of the IV. German Corps in the Battle of the Somme during July*, 1916
- 480: *Lessons Drawn from the Battle of the Somme by Stein's Group* (original document dated 8 September 1916)
- 486: *Extracts from German Documents dealing with 'Lessons drawn from the Battle of the Somme'*, 11 October 1916
- 553: General von Below, *Experience of the German 1st Army in the Somme Battle*, 1917
- 536: *Report on the Defence of Gommecourt on the 1st July 1916*, January 1917

Anonymous and Collective Works

Anon., *Südafrikas Deutsche in englischer Gewalt*, Dresden 1916

Anon., *Unter englischem Feuer. Die Zerstörungen in Flandern und Nordfrankreich*, Berlin 1918

Anon., *List of British Officers taken Prisoner in the Various Theatres of War between August 1914 and November 1918*, London 1921

Anon., *Leib-Grenadier-Regiment Nr. 8*, Oldenburg and Berlin 1924

'Von mehreren Mitkämpfern', *Das K.B. Infanterie-Regiment König*, Munich 1925

Anon., *Das K.B. 9. Feld-Artillerie-Regiment*, Munich 1927

'Verein ehemaliger Offiziere des Regiments', *Das Füsilier-Regiment Prinz Heinrich von Preussen (Brandenburgisches) Nr. 35 im Weltkriege*, Berlin 1929. See also the regimental history by Täglichsbeck (1921), below

Anon., *Das Infanterie-Regiment von Horn (3. Rheinisches) Nr. 29*, Berlin 1929

Anon., 'von Feldzugsteilnehmern bearbeitet', *Geschichte des Infanterie-Regiments Generalfeldmarschall Prinz Friedrich Karl von Preussen (8. Brandenburg.) Nr. 64 während des Krieges 1914/18*, Berlin 1929

'Mitglieder des Vereins der Offiziere', *Das K.B. 12. Infanterie-Regiment Prinz Arnulf*, Munich 1929

'Offiziere des Regiments', *Das K.B. Infanterie-Regiment Hartmann*, Munich 1931

Anon., *Geschichte des ehemaligen Königlichen bayerischen 12. Feldartillerie-Regiments*, Munich 1935

Anon., 'Prince Joachim', *The Irish Sword. Journal of the Military History Society of Ireland*, XII, No. 87, Dublin 2000

Other Works

Ackerley, J. R. (ed.), *Escapers All: Being the Personal Narratives of Fifteen Escapers from War-Time Prison Camps*, London 1932

Adams, Bernard, *Nothing of Importance: A Record of Eight Months at the Front with a Welsh Battalion October 1915, to June, 1916*, London 1988

Allen, Henry T., *My Rhineland Journal*, London 1924

Andrews, E. M., *The ANZAC Illusion: Anglo-Australian Relations during World War I*, Cambridge 1993

Anspach, Siegfried; Flach, Erhard, *Das Kgl. Sächs. Reserve-Infanterie-Regiment Nr. 107*, Dresden 1927

Ashurst, George, ed. Holmes, Richard, *My Bit: A Lancashire Fusilier at War*, Ramsbury 1987

Ashworth, Tony, *Trench Warfare 1914–1918: The Live and Let Live System*, London 1980

Atkinson, C. T., *The Seventh Division*, London 1927

Baring, Maurice, *Flying Corps Headquarters 1914–1918*, London 1930

Bauer, Colonel, *Der Grosse Krieg in Feld und Heimat*, Tübingen 1922

Baumgarten-Crusius, Arthur, *Das Kgl. Sächs. 11. Infanterie-Regiment Nr. 139*, Dresden 1927

Bayerisches Kriegsarchiv, *Die Bayern im Grossen Kriege 1914–1918*, Munich 1923

Bean, C. E. W., *The Official History of Australia in the War of 1914–1918*, 6 vols, Sydney 1921–42

Bechtle, Richard, *Die Ulmer Grenadiere an der Westfront: Geschichte des Grenadier-Regiments König Karl (5. Württ.) Nr. 123 im Weltkrieg 1914–1918*, Stuttgart 1920

Beltz, Oskar, *Das Infanterie-Regiment Herzog von Holstein Nr. 85 im Weltkriege*, Heide in Holstein 1925

Beumelburg, Werner, *Sperrfeuer um Deutschland*, Oldenburg and Berlin 1929

Bewsher, F. W., *The History of the 51st (Highland) Division*, 2 vols, Edinburgh 1921

Beyer, Walter; Scheitzka, Erich, *Königliches Preussisches Feld-Artillerie-Regiment Nr. 221*, Berlin 1933

Bidwell, Shelford; Graham, Dominick, *Fire-Power: The British Army Weapons and Theories of War 1905–1945*, Barnsley 2004

Bilton, David, *The Home Front in the Great War: Aspects of the Conflict 1914–1918*, Barnsley 2003

Binding, Rudolf, *A Fatalist at War*, London 1929

Blacker, Carlos Paton, *Have You Forgotten Yet? The First World War Memoirs of C. P. Blacker*, London 2000

Blair, Dale James, '"Those Miserable Tommies": Anti-British Sentiment in the Australian Imperial Force, 1915–1918', *War and Society*, IXX, No. 1, Canberra 2001

Blankenstein, Lieutenant, *Geschichte des Reserve-Infanterie-Regiments Nr. 92 im Weltkriege 1914–1918*, Osnabrück 1930

Bloem, Walter, *Das Grenadier-Regiment Prinz Carl von Preussen (2. Brandenburg.) Nr. 12*, Berlin 1940

Blunden, Edmund, *Undertones of War*, London 1928

Bölsche, Arnold, *Sturmflut: Das Erleben des 7. Thür. Infanterie-Regiments Nr. 96 im Weltkrieg*, Zeulenroda 1935

Bond, Brian; Cave, Nigel (eds.), *Haig: A Reappraisal 70 Years On*, Barnsley 1999

Boraston, J. H.; Bax, Cyril, *The Eighth Division in War, 1914–1918*, London 1926

Böttger, Karl, et al., *Das Kgl. Sächs. 7. Infanterie-Regiment 'König Georg' Nr. 106*, Dresden 1927

Brandenstein, Colonel, *Das Infanterie-Regiment 'Alt-Württemberg' (3. Württ.) im Weltkrieg 1914–1918*, Stuttgart 1921

Brandis, Cordt, *Die von Douaumont: Das Ruppiner Regiment 24 im Weltkrieg*, Berlin 1930

Brauch, Karl, *Erinnerungsbuch des Ersatz-Infanterie-Regiments Nr. 28. Weltkrieg 1914/18*, Mannheim 1936

Bridges, Tom, *Alarms and Excursions: Reminiscences of a Soldier*, London 1938

Bröcker, Paul; Kayser, Edwin, *Das 5. Loth. Infanterie-Regiment Nr. 144 im Weltkriege*, Oldenburg and Berlin 1928

Brose, Eric, *The Kaiser's Army: The Politics of Military Technology in Germany during the Machine Age, 1870–1918*, Oxford 2001

Brown, Malcolm, *The Imperial War Museum Book of the Somme*, London 1996

Buchan, John, *The History of the South African Force in France*, London 1920

Busemann, Wilhelm, *Reserve-Ersatz-Regiment Nr. 3*, Oldenburg and Berlin 1925

Buttmann, Major, *Kriegsgeschichte des Königlich Preussischen 6. Thüringischen Infanterie-Regiments Nr. 95 1914–1918*, Zeulenroda 1935

Carrington, Charles ('Charles Edmonds'), *A Subaltern's War*, London 1929;
— *Soldier from the Wars Returning*, London 1965

Castle, Harold, *Fire over England: The German Air Raids of World War I*, London 1982

Cave, Nigel, *Battleground Europe: Beaumont Hamel*, Barnsley 1994
— *Battleground Europe: Delville Wood*, Barnsley 1999

Charlton, R., *Australians on the Somme: Pozières 1916*, London 1986

Charteris, John, *At G.H.Q.*, London 1931

Chickering, Roger, *Imperial Germany and the Great War, 1914–1918*, Cambridge 1988

Coop, J. O., *The Story of the 55th (West Lancashire) Division*, Liverpool 1919

Coppard, George, *With a Machine Gun to Cambrai: The Tale of a Young Tommy in Kitchener's Army 1914–1918*, London 1969

Corrigan, Gordon, *Sepoys on the Trenches: The Indian Corps on the Western Front 1914–1915*, Staplehurst 1999
— *Mud, Blood and Poppycock: Britain and the First World War*, London 2003

Croft, W. D., *Three Years with the 9th (Scottish) Division*, London 1919

Cron, Hermann, *Geschichte des deutschen heeres im Weltkriege 1914–1918*, Berlin 1937; trans. Cotton, F. C., *Imperial German Army 1914–1918: Structure, Orders of Battle*, Solihull 2002

Denman, Jerome, *Ireland's Unknown Soldiers: The 16th (Irish) Division in the Great War, 1914–1918*, Dublin 1992

Drexel, R. K.; Gathmann, Theodor, *Einundzwanzig Tage im Trommelfeuer an der Somme August/September 1916: Stimmungsbild auf Befehl des Kommandeurs des K. Bayerisschen 23. Infanterie-Regiments*, Kaiserslautern 1917

Dudley Ward, C. H., *The 56th (1st London Territorial) Division*, London 1921

Dungan, Myles, *They Shall Grow Not Old: Irish Soldiers and the Great War*, Dublin 1997

Dunzinger, Albert, *Das K.B. 11. Infanterie-Regiment von der Tann*, Munich 1921

Dziobek, Otto, *Geschichte des Infanterie-Regiments Lübeck (3. Hanseatisches) Nr. 162,* Oldenburg and Berlin 1922

Ebelshauser, Gustav A., *The Passage: A Tragedy of the First World War,* Huntington (West Virginia) 1984

Eberle, V. F., *My Sapper Venture,* London 1973

Eden, Anthony, *Another World 1897–1917,* London 1976

Edmonds, J. E., *Military Operations, France and Belgium, 1916,* I, London 1932. Continued by Miles, W., *Military Operations, France and Belgium, 1916,* II, London 1938. The British official history

Etzel, Hans, *Das K. B. 9. Infanterie-Regiment,* Munich 1928

Evans, A. J., *The Escaping Club,* London 1921

Ewing, John, *The History of the 9th (Scottish) Division 1914–1919,* London 1921

Eyre, Giles E. M., *Somme Harvest: Memories of a P.B.I. in the Summer of 1916,* London 1938

Falls, Cyril, *History of the 16th (Ulster) Division,* London 1922

Farrar-Hockley, Anthony, *The Somme,* London 1964

Feilding, Rowland, *War Letters to a Wife: France and Flanders, 1915–1919,* London 1929

Ferguson, Niall, *The Pity of War,* London 1999

Fiedel, *Geschichte des Infanterie-Regiments von Winterfeld (2. Oberschlesisches) Nr. 23. Das Regiment im Weltkriege,* Berlin 1929

Fliess, Otto; Dittmar, Kurt, *5. Hannoversches Infanterie-Regiment Nr. 165 im Weltkriege,* Oldenburg and Berlin 1927

Foley, Robert T., *German Strategy and the Path to Verdun: Erich von Falkenhayn and the Development of Attrition, 1870–1916,* Cambridge 2005

Forstner, Kurt, *Das Königlich-Preussische Reserve-Infanterie Regiment Nr. 15,* 2 vols, Oldenburg and Berlin 1929–30

Frerk, Franz Willy, *Die Sommeschlacht,* Siegen and Leipzig 1916

Freund, Franz, *Geschichte des Infanterie-Regiments Prinz Carl (4. Gross. Hess.) Nr. 118 im Weltkrieg,* Gross-Gerau 1930

Frisch, Georg (ed.), *Das Reserve-Infanterie-Regiment Nr. 109 im Weltkrieg 1914–1918,* Karlsruhe 1931

Fromm, Colonel, *Das Württembergische Reserve-Infanterie-Regiment Nr. 120 im Weltkrieg 1914–1918,* Stuttgart 1920

Furhmann, Hans; Pfoertner, Otto; Fries, Nikolaus, *Königlich Preussisches Reserve-Infanterie Regiment Nr. 211 im Weltkriege 1914–1918,* Berlin 1933

Gabriel, Kurt, *Die 4. Garde-Infanterie-Division. Der Rumesweg einer bewährten Kampftruppe durch den Weltkrieg,* Berlin 1921

Gallwitz, Max, *Erleben im Westen 1916–1918,* Berlin 1932

Gemmingen-Guttenberg-Fürfeld, Colonel, *Das Grenadier-Regiment Königin Olga (1. Württ.) Nr. 119 im Weltkrieg 1914–1918*, Stuttgart 1927

Gerster, Matthäus, *Das Württembergische Reserve-Infanterie-Regiment Nr. 119 im Weltkrieg 1914–1918*, Stuttgart 1920
— *Die Schwaben an der Ancre: Aus den Kämpfen der 26. Reserve-Division*, Heilbronn 1920

Gibbs, Philip, *Realities of War*, London 1920

Gieraths, Günther, *Geschichte des Reserve-Infanterie-Regiments Nr. 210 und seine Grenzschütz-Formation (1914–1920)*, Oldenburg and Berlin 1928

Gillon, Stair, *The Story of the 29th Division*, London and Edinburgh 1925

Gladden, Norman, *The Somme 1916: A Personal Account*, London 1924

Gliddon, Gerald, *'When the Barrage Lifts': A Topographical History and Commentary on the Battle of the Somme 1916*, London 1990

Glubb, John, *Into Battle: A Soldier's Diary of the Great War*, London 1978

Goldammer, Arthur, *Das Kgl. Sächs. 14. Infanterie-Regiment 179*, Leipzig 1931

Goodspeed, D. J., *The Road Past Vimy: The Canadian Corps 1914–1918*, Toronto 1969

Gough, Hubert, *The Fifth Army*, London 1931

Graves, Robert, *Goodbye to All That*, London 1981

Greenhalgh, Elizabeth, 'Why the British Were on the Somme in 1916', *War in History*, VI, No. 2, Oxford 1999
— 'The Experience of Fighting with Allies. The Case of the Capture of Falfemont Farm during the Battle of the Somme, 1916', *War in History*, X, No. 2, Oxford 2003

Greenhut, Jeffrey, 'The Imperial Reserve: The Indian Corps on the Western Front, 1914–15', *The Journal of Imperial and Commonwealth History*, XII, No. 1, London 1983

Griffith, Paddy, *Battle Tactics of the Western Front: The British Army's Art of Attack, 1916–18*, New Haven and London 1994
— (ed.), *British Fighting Methods in the Great War*, London 1996

Gropp, Hugo, *Hanseaten im Kampf. Erlebnisse bei dem Res.-Inf.Rgt. 76 im Weltkriege 1914/18*, Hamburg 1932

Grossmann, August; Merkt, Dr, *Das K.B. Reserve-Infanterie-Regiment Nr. 17*, 2 vols, Munich and Augsburg 1923–6

Gruson, Ernst, *Das Königlich Preussische 4. Thür. Infanterie-Regiment Nr 82 im Weltkriege*, Oldenburg and Berlin 1930

Gudmundsson, Bruce, *Stormtroop Tactics: Innovation in the German Army 1914–1918*, New York 1989
— *On Artillery*, Westport and London 1993

Guhr, Major General (ed.), *Das 4. Schlesische Infanterie-Regiment Nr. 157 im Frieden und im Kriege 1897–1919*, Zeulenroda 1934

Haber, L. F., *The Poisonous Cloud: Chemical Warfare in the First World War*, Oxford 1986

BIBLIOGRAPHY

Haig, Douglas, *Douglas Haig: War Letters and Diaries 1914–1918*, ed. Sheffield, Gary; Bourne, John, London 2005

Hancock, Edward, *Battleground Europe: Bazentin Ridge*, Barnsley 2003

Hansch, Johannes; Weidling, Fritz, *Das Colbergische Grenadier-Regiment Graf Gneisenau (2. Pommersches) Nr. 9 im Weltkriege 1914–1918*, Oldenburg and Berlin 1929

Hart, Peter, *Somme Success: The Royal Flying Corps and the Battle of the Somme 1916*, Barnsley 2001
— *The Somme*, London 2005

Hartesveldt, Fred, *The Battle of the Somme, 1916: Historiography and Annotated Bibliography*, Westport (Connecticut) 1996

Hartmann, Alexander, *Das Infanterie-Regiment Grossherzog von Sachsen im Weltkrieg*, Berlin 1921

Harvey, F. W., *Comrades in Captivity: A Record of Life in Seven German Prison Camps*, London 1920

Hase, Armin, *Das Kgl. Sächs. Infanterie-Regiment Nr. 183*, Dresden 1922

Hausmann, Wilhelm (ed.), *Das K.B. 15. Infanterie-Regiment im Weltkrieg 1914–1918*, Munich 1953

Heintz, Hans, *Das Kgl. Sächs. Reserve-Infanterie-Regiment Nr. 133*, Dresden 1930

Henning, Otto, *Das Reserve-Infanterie-Regiment Nr. 235 im Weltkriege*, Oldenburg and Berlin 1931

Herwig, Holger, 'Imperial Germany', in May, Ernest (ed.), *Knowing One's Enemies: Intelligence Assessment before the Two World Wars*, Princeton 1986
— *The First World War: Germany and Austria-Hungary, 1914–1918*, London 1997

Hippe, Konrad (et al.), *Erinngerungsblatt des ehem. Königl. Preuss. Torgauer Feldartillerie-Regiments Nr. 74*, Oldenburg and Berlin 1928

Höfeld, Hugo, *Das K.B. 20. Infanterie-Regiment Prinz Franz*, Munich 1929

Hoffenberg, Peter, 'Landscape, Memory and the Australian War Experience, 1915–1918', *Journal of Contemporary History*, XXXVI, London 2001

Holmes, Richard, *Tommy: The British Soldier on the Western Front 1914–1918*, London 2004

Holt, Toni and Valmai, *Major & Mrs Holt's Battlefield Guide to the Somme*, Barnsley 2003 (repeatedly updated and reissued)

Humphries, Mark Osborne, 'The Myth of the Learning Curve: Tactics and Training in the 12th Canadian Infantry Brigade 1916-1918,' *Canadian Miltiary History*, XIV, no. 4, Waterloo (Ontario), 2005

Hüttmann, Adolf; Krüger, Friedrich, *Das Infanterie-Regiment von Lützow (1. Rhein.) Nr. 25 im Weltkriege 1914–1918*, London 1929

Inglefield, V. E., *The History of the Twentieth (Light) Division*, London 1921

369

Intelligence Section of the General Staff (United States), *Histories of Two Hundred and Fifty-One Divisions of the German Army which Participated in the Great War (1914–1918)*, 1920, reprinted London 1989

Jackson, Robert, *The Prisoners, 1914–1918*, London 1989

Jäger, Lieutenant Colonel, *Das K.B. 19. Infanterie-Regiment König Victor Emanuel III von Italien*, Munich 1930

Jahr, Christoph, *Gewöhnliche Soldaten: Desertion und Deserteure im deutschen und Britischen Heer 1914–1918*, Göttingen 1998

Jancke, Hans, *Flak an der Somme. Eine neue Waffe greift ein*, Berlin 1939

Jünger, Ernst, *Storm of Steel* (trans. Hoffmann, Michael), London 2004

Jürgensen, Wilhelm, *Das Füsilier-Regiment 'Königin' Nr 86 im Weltkriege*, Oldenburg and Berlin 1925

Kabisch, Ernst, *Somme 1916*, Berlin 1937

Kaiser, Franz, *Das Königl. Preuss. Infanterie-Regiment Nr. 63 (4. Oberschlesisches)*, Berlin 1940

Kalbe, Richard, *Das 9. Lothringische Infanterie-Regiment Nr. 173 im Weltkriege*, Zeulenroda 1938

Karitzky, Erich, *Reserve-Jäger-Bataillon Nr. 9*, Oldenburg and Berlin 1925

Keil, Hermann; Littrow, Carl, *Das Kgl. Sächs. Reserve-Jäger-Bataillon Nr. 13 im Weltkriege*, Dresden 1934

Kington, Miles, *Barbed Wire Ballads*, BBC 4 radio broadcast, 11 May 2005. Recordings by the Royal Prussian Phonographic Archive in POW camps, 1915–18

Kitchen, Martin, *The Silent Dictatorship: The Politics of the German High Command under Hindenburg and Ludendorff, 1916–1918*, New York 1976

Klähn, Friedrich, *Geschichte des Reserve-Infanterie-Regiments Nr. 86 im Weltkriege*, Oldenburg and Berlin 1925

Klitzsch, Johannes, *Kriegstagebuch 1914–1918 des Kgl. Sächs. Reserve-Infanterie-Regiment Nr. 101*, Dresden 1934

Kohl, Hermann, *Mit Hurra in den Tod! Kriegserlebnisse eines Frontsoldaten. 17 bayer. Infanterie-Regiment 'Orff'*, Stuttgart 1932

Kuhl, Hermann, *Der deutsche Generalstab in Vorbereitung und Durchführung des Weltkrieges*, Berlin 1920

Kümmel, Adolf, *Res. Inf. Regt. Nr. 91 im Weltkriege 1914–1918*, Oldenburg and Berlin 1926

Lademann, Ulrich, *Das 3. Magdeburgische Infanterie-Regiment Nr. 66*, Oldenburg and Berlin 1922

Lang, Georg, *Das 6. K. Bayerische Infanterie-Regiment im Weltkrieg*, Regensburg 1920

Lawrence, Brian, *Letters from the Front: The Great War Correspondence of Lieutenant Brian Lawrence, 1916–1917*, Tunbridge Wells 1993

Leese, Peter, *Shell Shock: Traumatic Neurosis and the British Soldiers of the First World War*, Basingstoke 2002

Lemisko, L. S., 'A Dubious Reputation? The Performance of the 16th (Irish) Division, 1916 – 20th March 1918', *The Irish Sword*, XII, No. 87, Dublin 2000

Liddle, Peter H., *The 1916 Battle of the Somme: A Reappraisal*, London 1992
— 'The British Soldier on the Somme 1916', *The Strategic and Combat Studies Institute. The Occasional*, No. 23, Camberley 1996

Lossberg, Fritz, *Meine Tätigkeit im Weltkriege 1914–1918*, Berlin 1929

Ludendorff, Erich, *Kriegführung und Politik*, Berlin 1921

Lupfer, Timothy, *The Dynamics of Doctrine: The Changes in German Tactical Doctrine During the First World War* (Leavenworth Paper No. 4), Fort Leavenworth 1981

Makoben, Ernst, *Geschichte des Reserve-Infanterie-Regiments Nr. 212 im Weltkriege 1914–1918*, Oldenburg and Berlin 1933

Mark, Moritz, *Das K.B. 15. Infanterie-Regiment*, Munich 1922

Masefield, John, *The Old Front Line* (1917), Bourne End 1972
— *John Masefield's Letters from the Front 1915–1917*, (ed. Vansittart, Peter), London 1984

Maude, Alan H. (ed.), *The 47th (London) Division: By Some who Served in the Great War*, London 1922

McCarthy, Chris, *The Somme: The Day-by-Day Account*, London 1993

McGibbon, Ian, *The Oxford Companion to New Zealand Military History*, Oxford 2000

Michelin et Cie., *The Somme: Volume I. The First Battle of the Somme (1916–1917)*, Clermont-Ferrand 1919

Middlebrook, Martin, *The First Day on the Somme*, London 1971

Miles, W., *Military Operations, France and Belgium, 1916*, II, London 1938. See Edmonds, J. E. (above)

Möller, Hans, *Königlich Preussisches Reserve-Infanterie-Regiment Nr. 78 im Weltkrieg 1914-1918*, Berlin 1937
— *Fritz von Below: General der Infanterie*, Berlin 1939

Morrow, John H., *The Great War in the Air: Military Aviation from 1901 to 1921*, Shrewsbury 1993

Morton, Desmond, 'Canadian Fannigans in the Kaiser's Clutch: Canadian Prisoners of War, 1914–1918', in Weingartner (ed.), 1994

Moser, Otto, *Feldzugs-Aufzeichnungen als Brigade-Divisionskommandeur und als Kommandierender General 1914–1918*, Stuttgart 1920

Moynihan, Michael (ed.), *Black Bread and Barbed Wire: Prisoners in the First World War*, London 1978

Mücke, Kurt, *Das Grossherzoglich Badische Infanterie-Regiment Nr. 185*, Oldenburg and Berlin 1922

Münstermann, Paul; Begau, Robert, *Geschichte des Infanterie-Regiments von Goeben*, (*2. Rhein.*) *Nr 28 im Weltkriege 1914–1918*, Cologne, undated

Nelson, Robert L., '"Ordinary Men" in the First World War? German Soldiers as Victims and Participants', *Journal of Contemporary History*, XXXIX, No. 2, London 2004

Nichols, G. F. X. ('Quex'), *The 18th Division in the Great War*, Edinburgh 1922

Nicolai, W., *The German Secret Service*, London 1924

Niebelschütz, Günther, *Reserve-Infanterie-Regiment Nr. 30*, Oldenburg 1926

Nobbs, Gilbert, *Englishman Kamerad! Right of the British Line*, London 1918

Pafferath, Fritz, *Die Geschichte des 6. Rheinischen Infanterie-Regiments Nr. 68 im Weltkriege 1914–1918*, Berlin 1930

Palmer, Frederick, *With the New Army on the Somme*, London 1917

Panayi, Panikes, *The Enemy in Our Midst: Germans in Britain during the First World War*, Oxford 1991

Parker, Ernest, *Into Battle 1914–1918*, London 1964

Pedersen, P. A., *Monash as Military Commander*, Melbourne 1985

Pfeffer, Georg; Neubronner, Carl, *Geschichte des Infanterie-Regiments 186*, Oldenburg and Berlin 1926

Pflugbeil, Hanns, *Das Kgl. Sächs. 15. Infanterie-Regiment Nr. 181*, Dresden 1923

Pidgeon, Trevor, *The Tanks at Flers,* 2 vols, Cobham 1995

Pollard, A. O., *Fire-Eater: The Memoirs of a V.C.*, London 1932

Prior, Robin; Wilson, Trevor, T., *Command on the Western Front: The Military Career of Sir Henry Rawlinson, 1914–1918*, Oxford 1992
— *The Somme*, New Haven (Connecticut) and London 2005

Pugsley, Christopher, *On the Fringe of Hell. New Zealanders and Military Discipline in the First World War*, Auckland 1991

— *The ANZAC Experience: New Zealand, Australia and the Empire in the First World War*, Auckland 2004

Purnell's History of the Great War, 8 vols, London 1971

Rawling, Bill, *Surviving Trench Warfare: Technology and the Canadian Corps 1914–1918*, Toronto 1992

Reber, Karl, *Das K.B. 21. Infanterie-Regiment Grossherzog Friedrich Franz IV von Mecklenburg-Schwerin*, Munich 1929

Reed, Paul, *Battleground Europe: Combles*, Barnsley 2002
— *Battleground Europe: Walking the Somme: A Walker's Guide to the 1916 Somme Battlefields*, Barnsley 2003

Reichsarchiv, *Schlachten des Weltkrieges*, 35 vols, Oldenburg and Berlin 1925–30 (see also Stosch, Albrecht, below)
— *Der Weltkrieg 1914–1918: Die militärischen Operationen zu Lande*, 14 vols, Berlin 1925–44

Reimann, Aribert, *Der grosse Krieg der Sprachen: Untersuchungen zur historischen Semantik in Deutschland und England zur Zeit des Ersten Weltkriegs*, Fulda 2000

Reinhardt, Georg (et al.), *Das Kgl. Sächs. 8. Infanterie-Regiment 'Prinz Johann Georg' Nr. 108 während des Weltkrieges 1914–1918*, Dresden 1928

Rettig, G.; Herbert, F., *Kriegs-Kalender I.R. 93 1914–1918*, Dessau 1925

Reymann, H., *Das 3. Oberschlesisches Infanterie-Regiment Nr. 62 im Kriege 1914–1918*, Zeulenroda 1930

Reymann, M., *Das Infanterie-Regiment von Alvensleben (6. Brandbg.) Nr. 52 im Weltkriege 1914–1918*, Oldenburg and Berlin 1923

Riegel, Johann, *Das K.B. 17. Infanterie-Regiment Orff*, Munich 1927

Rintelen, Franz, *The Dark Invader: Wartime Reminiscences of a German Naval Intelligence Officer*, London 1933

Ritter, Albrecht, *Das K.B. 18. Infanterie-Regiment Prinz Ludwig Ferdinand*, Munich 1926

Ritter, Holger, *Geschichte des Schleswig-Holsteinischen Infanterie-Regiments Nr. 163*, Hamburg 1926

Robb, Georg, *British Culture and the First World War*, New Haven and London 2002

Robbins, Simon, *British Generalship on the Western Front 1914–1918: Defeat into Victory*, Abingdon 2005

Rogge, Walter, *Das Königl. Preuss. 2. Nassauische Infanterie-Regiment Nr 88*, Berlin 1936

Rupprecht, Crown Prince of Bavaria, *Mein Kriegstagebuch*, 3 vols, Berlin 1929

Samuels, Martin, *Doctrine and Dogma: German and British Infantry Tactics in the First World War*, London 1992

Sassoon, Siegfried, *Memoirs of a Fox-Hunting Man*, London 1928

Schaidler, Otto, *Das K.B. 7. Infanterie-Regiment Prinz Leopold*, Munich 1922

Schatz, Bruno, *Das Kgl. Sächs. 10. Infanterie-Regiment Nr. 134*, Dresden 1922

Schatz, Josef, *Geschichte des badischen (rheinischen) Reserve-Infanterie-Regiments 239*, Stuttgart 1927

Schindler, D. R., *Eine 42 cm. Mörser-Batterie im Weltkrieg*, Breslau 1934

Schmidt, Walther, *2. Nassauisches Infanterie-Regiment Nr. 88*, Oldenburg and Berlin 1922

Schneider, Eduard, *Reserve-Infanterie-Regiment Nr. 36 – 4 Jahre Westfront*, Eisleben 1930

Schönfeldt, Ernst, *Das Grenadier-Regiment Prinz Karl von Preussen (2. Brandenburgisches) Nr. 12 im Weltkriege*, Oldenburg and Berlin 1924

Schubert, Alfons, *Kriegsgeschichte des 4. Oberschl. Infanterie-Regiments Nr. 63 (1914–1919)*, Oppeln 1926

Schulenburg-Wolfsberg, *Geschichte des Garde-Füsilier-Regiments*, Oldenburg and Berlin 1926

Schultz, Lieutenant Colonel; Kissler, Lieutenant Colonel; Schulze, Lieutenant, *Geschichte des Reserve-Infanterie-Regiments Nr. 209 im Weltkriege, 1914–1919*, Oldenburg and Berlin 1930

Schwab, A.; Schreyer, A, *Das neunte württembergische Infanterie-Regiment Nr. 127 im Weltkrieg 1914–1918*, Stuttgart 1920

Scott, Arthur; Brumwell, P.; Middleton, P., *History of the 12th (Eastern) Division in the Great War, 1914–1918*, London 1923

Selle, Hans; Gründel, Walter, *Das 6. Westpreussisches Infanterie-Regiment Nr 149 im Weltkriege*, Berlin 1929

Seydel, Alfred, *Das Grenadier-Regiment König Friedrich I. (4. Ostpreusssiches) Nr 5 im Weltkriege*, Oldenburg and Berlin 1926

Sheffield, Gary, *Leadership in the Trenches – Officer-Man Relations, Morale and Discipline in the British Army in the Era of the First World War*, London 2000
— *The Somme*, London 2003

Sheffield, Gary; Todman, Dan (eds.), *Command and Control on the Western Front: The British Army's Experience 1914–1918*, Staplehurst 2004
— 'An Army Commander on the Somme: Hubert Gough', in Sheffield and Todman (eds.), 2004

Sheldon, Jack, *The German Army on the Somme 1914-1916*, Barnsley 2005

Showalter, Dennis, 'The German Soldier in the Great War: Myths and Realities', in Weingartner (ed.), 1994

Simkins, Peter, *Kitchener's Army*, Manchester 1988
— '"Building Blocks": Aspects of Command and Control at Brigade Level in the BEF's Officer Corps, 1914–1918', in Sheffield and Todman (eds.), 2004

Simon, Colonel, *Das Infanterie-Regiment 'Kaiser Wilhelm, König von Preussen' (2. Württ.) im Weltkrieg*, Stuttgart 1922

Simpson, Andy, *The Evolution of Victory: British Battles on the Western Front 1914–1918*, London 1995
— 'British Corps Command on the Western Front, 1914–1918', in Sheffield and Todman (eds.), 2004

Smith, Aubrey, *Four Years on the Western Front*, London 1922

Soldan, Georg, *Das Infanterie-Regiment Nr. 184*, Oldenburg and Berlin 1920

Solleder, Fridolin, *Vier Jahr Westfront: Geschichte des Regiments List R.I.R. 16*, Munich 1932

Speck, Wilhelm, *Das Königlich Preussische Reserve-Infanterie-Regiment 84*, Zeulenroda 1937

Spiers, Edward, *Chemical Warfare*, London 1986

Stedman, Michael, *Battleground Europe: Thiepval*, Barnsley 1995
— *Battleground Europe: La Boisselle, Ovillers/Contalmaison*, Barnsley 1997

Stein, Hermann, *Erlebnisse und Betrachtungen*, Leipzig 1919

Stenger, Alfred; Strutz, Georg, *Geschichte des Kgl. Preuss. Trierschen Feldartillerie-Regiments N4. 44 1899–1919*, Freiburg im Breisgau 1935

Stewart, J.; Buchan, J., *The Fifteenth (Scottish) Division 1914–1919*, Edinburgh 1926

Stibbe, Matthew, *German Anglophobia and the Great War, 1914–1918*, Cambridge 2001

Stiehl, Otto, *Unsere Feinde. 96 Charakterköpfe aus deutsche Kriegsgefangenenlagern*, Stuttgart 1916

Stormont Gibbs, C. C., *From the Somme to the Armistice: The Memoirs of Captain Stormont Gibbs, M.C.*, London 1986

Stosch, Albrecht, 'Somme Nord, Die Brennpunkte der Schlacht im Juli 1916', two parts, forming vols XX and XXI, 1927, of Reichsarchiv, *Schlachten des Weltkrieges in Einzeldarstellungen*, 37 vols, Berlin 1921–30
— *Das Königl. Preuss. 5. Garde-Regiment zu Fuss 1897–1918*, Berlin 1930

Strachan, Hugh, 'The Battle of the Somme and British Strategy', *Journal of Strategic Studies*, XXI, London 1998

Strange, L.A., *The Recollections of an Airman*, Bristol undated

Studt, Bernhard, *Infanterie-Regiment Graf Bose (1. Thüringisches) Nr. 31 im Weltkriege 1914–1918*, Oldenburg and Berlin 1926

Stühmke, General, *Das Infanterie-Regiment 'Kaiser Friedrich, König von Preussen' (7. Württ.) Nr. 125 im Weltkrieg 1914–1918*, Stuttgart 1923

Swinton, Ernest, *Eyewitness*, London 1932

Sydow, Gustav, *Das Infanterie-Regiment Hamburg (2. Hanseatisches) Nr. 76 im Weltkriege 1914/18*, Berlin 1922

Täglichsbeck, Hans, *Das Füsilier-Regiment Prinz Heinrich von Preussen (Brandenburgisches) Nr. 35*, Oldenburg and Berlin 1921

Terraine, John, *Douglas Haig: The Educated Soldier*, London 1963

Travers, Tim, *The Killing Ground: The British Army, the Western Front and the Emergence of Modern Warfare, 1900–1918*, London 1990

Trümper-Bödemann, Lieutenant, *Das Königl. Sächs. Reserve-Infanterie-Regiment Nr. 102*, Chemnitz 1929

Tubbs, D. B., 'Aircraft: Higher, Faster, Lighter', in *Purnell's History of the Great War*, 1971, V, No. 3

Tucker, John, *Johnny get your Gun: A Personal Narrative of the Somme, Ypres and Arras*, London 1978

Uys, Ian, *Delville Wood*, Johannesburg 1983

Vischer, Colonel, *Das Württ. Infanterie-Regiment Nr. 180 im Weltkrieg 1914–1918*, Stuttgart 1921

Vogt, Lieutenant Colonel (ed.), *3. Niederschlesisches Infanterie-Regiment Nr. 50. 1914–1920*, Liegnitz 1932

Voigt, Hans, *Geschichte des Füsilier-Regiments Generalfeldmarschall Prinz Albrecht von Preussen (Hann.) Nr. 73*, Berlin 1938 (i.e. Ernst Jünger's regiment)

Vormann, Wolfgang, *Infanterie-Regiment Fürst Leopold von Anhalt-Dessau (I. Magdeburg,) Nr. 26*, 6 vols, Oldenburg no date of publication (late 1920s)

Wallace, Stuart, *War and the Image of Germany: British Academics 1914–1918,* Edinburgh 1988

Watson, Alex, '"For Kaiser and Reich": The Identity and Fate of the German Volunteers, 1914–1918', *War in History,* XII, No. 1, Oxford 2005

Wedersich, Alfons, *Das Reserve-Infanterie-Regiment Nr. 229,* Berlin 1929

Weiland, Ernst, *Hölle Ginchy. Mit dem Königl. Bayr. 7. Infanterie-Regiment Prinz Leopold in der Somme Schlacht. September 1916,* Eisleben 1929

Weingartner, Steven (ed.), *A Weekend with the Great War: Proceedings of the Fourth Annual Great War Interconference Seminar ... September 1994,* Cantigny (Illinois), 1995

Welch, David, *German Propaganda and Total War, 1914–1918: The Sins of Omission,* London 2000

Weniger, Heinrich; Zobel, Artur; Fels, Colonel, *Das K.B. 5 Infanterie-Regiment Grossherzog Ernst Ludwig von Hessen,* Munich 1929

Werner, Bernhard, *Das Königlich Preussische Inf.-Rgt. Prinz Louis Ferdinand von Preussen (2. Magdeb.) Nr. 27 im Weltkriege 1914–1918,* Berlin 1933

Westman, Stephen, *Surgeon in the Kaiser's Army,* London 1968

Williams, John F., *Corporal Hitler and the Great War: The List Regiment,* London and New York 2005

Williams, H. R., *The Gallant Company: An Australian Soldier's Story of 1915–1918,* Sydney 1933

Wilson, Trevor, *The Myriad Faces of War: Britain and the Great War 1914–1919,* Cambridge 1986

Winchester, Barry, *Beyond the Tumult,* London 1971 (on POWs)

Wingfield, Lawrence, 'The Hazards of Escape', in Ackerley (ed.), 1932

Witkop, Philipp, *Kriegsbriefe gefallener Studenten,* Munich 1928

Wohlenberg, Alfried, *Das Res.-Inf.-Regt. Nr. 77 im Weltkriege 1914–1918,* Hildesheim 1931

Wolff, Anne (ed.), *Subalterns of the Foot: Three World War I Diaries of Officers of the Cheshire Regiment,* Worcester 1992

Wolff, Ludwig, *Das Kgl. Sächs. 5. Inf.-Regiment 'Kronprinz' Nr 104,* Dresden 1925

Wolff, W., *Kriegsgeschichte des 2. Thür. Feldart.-Regiments Nr. 55,* Beeskow 1924

Wolters, G., *Das Infanterie-Regiment König Wilhelm I. (6. Württ.) Nr. 124 im Weltkrieg 1914–1918,* Stuttgart 1921

Wrisberg, Ernst, *Wehr und Waffen 1914–1918,* Leipzig 1922

Wynne, G. C., 'The Other Side of the Hill', *The Army Quarterly,* VII, VIII, XI, XIII, XVII, XVIII, London 1923–34

Wyrall, Everard, *The History of the 19th Division,* London undated

Index

Adlam, Second Lieutenant Tom 281

Africa 16

air superiority, battle for 305–13

air support 122, 124, 178, 205, 227, 228, 251, 256, 272, 309–10, 314–5, 323

aircraft: BE2 C 306; De Havilland DH 2 307–8; FE2 B 307; Fokker E I 305–6; Martinsyde Elephant 308; Nieuport scouts 308; Sopwith 1½ Strutter 308; Vickers FE DD 306–7

Allenby, General Sir Edmund 20, 134

Amiens 16

Ancre, the 122, 201, 236, 252, 256, 320

Ancre, battles of the: 13-14 November 256–62; 18-19 November 262–5, 271

Ancre Heights, battle of the 245–6

Anzac Corps 21, 52–60, 188, 202–3: *see also* Australian formations; New Zealand forces

Arnim, General Sixt von 16

Arras 113–4

artillery: 18-pounder 286, 289, 290–1; 60-pounder 286–7; anti-aircraft 310–1, 316–7; anti-tank 304; assessment 325; barrage 26–7, 271; bombardment at Flers-Courcelette 233; British deployment 285–6; British preliminary bombardment 123–5, 125–6, 126–7, 130–1; co-ordination with infantry 292; counter-battery fire 290; creeping barrage 142, 291–2, 322; effect of bombardment 127; French 290; German 167, 243; howitzers 290; observers 286, 288–9, 316; preparatory bombardment 290–1; shells

287–8; targeting 288–90

Artillery Valley 149, 151, 264

Asquith, Herbert Henry 19, 46, 91

assessment 320–8

atrocities 34–5, 35–6, 92–3, 110, 194, 242

Australia: and Gallipoli 55–6; manpower contribution 47, 52, 56; motivation 53; officers 58; opportunities 108; rejects conscription 54–5; threats to 16, 54

Australian Imperial Force 52–3: *see also* Anzac Corps; 1st Australian Division 57, 188, 254; 2nd Australian Division 20, 55, 57, 189; 3rd Australian Division 57, 65; 4th Australian Division 189–90, 202–3; 5th Australian Division 55, 56–7, 65, 183–7; 8th Brigade 55; 14th Brigade 55–6; 15th Brigade 56; 19th (New South Wales) Battalion 55; 53rd (New South Wales) Battalion 56–7; Australian Light Horse 56; casualties 56, 185, 186, 191–2; treatment of prisoners 34

bangalore torpedoes 136, 271

Bapaume 320, 321

Bapaume Road 247–9

barbed wire 17, 120, 166, 268, 271–2

Barter, Major General Sir Charles 220

Battenberg, Louis Alexander, Prince of 31

Battle of the Somme, The (film) 93–4

Bavarians 24–5, 26

Baxter Ellis, Lieutenant W. 77

Bazentin-le-Grand 177

Bazentin-le-Petit 177–8

Bazentin Ridge 176, 232

Bazentin Ridge, battle of (14 July) 60, 173, 176–80, 271

Beaucourt, action at (13 May) 59

Beaucourt Redoubt 260–1

Beaumont Hamel 124, 138, 143, 145, 202, 246, 255, 256, 257–8, 296, 320

Belgium 16

Below, General Fritz von 121, 122, 123, 172, 176, 188, 190, 192, 200, 246, 247

Berthold, Major 140

Beumelburg, Werner 324

Binding, Rudolf 73, 87, 117

Birdwood, Lieutenant General Sir William 21

Black, Lieutenant W. 66, 76, 314

Blowers, Second Lieutenant 225–6

Boelcke, Oswald 307, 308, 309, 311, 312

Boers 47–8

Botha, Louis 48–9

Bouchavesnes 238

Bouleaux Wood 206, 229–30

Braune-Linie, the 206

Bridges, Major General Tom 263

Bridges, Brigadier General William Thorsby 52

British Army: and 1916 15; age groupings 64; armies 20; Army Reserve 68, 69; battalions 22, 67–8; brigades 22, 167; build up 110–2; companies 22; conscripts 72–6; corps 20–1; daily routine 78–9; defensive doctrine 268–9; Derby Men 65, 69, 72–3, 74, 191, 197, 202, 323; digging in 274; discipline 83–5; divisional quality 65; divisions 21, 167; equipment 77–8; establishment 68, 69, 107, 108; executions 84–5; food 79; gains 320; German assessment of 327–8; German names in 32–3;

377